Also by Mary V. Dearborn

Love in the Promised Land:
The Story of Anzia Yezierska and John Dewey

Pocahontas's Daughters:
Gender and Ethnicity in American Culture

THE HAPPIEST MAN ALIVE

a biography of Henry Miller

by Mary V. Dearborn

Simon & Schuster

New York • London • Toronto

Sydney • Tokyo

Singapore

▼

Simon & Schuster
Simon & Schuster Building
Rockefeller Center
1230 Avenue of the Americas
New York, New York 10020

Copyright © 1991 by Mary V. Dearborn

All rights reserved
including the right of reproduction
in whole or in part in any form.

SIMON & SCHUSTER and colophon
are registered trademarks of Simon & Schuster

Designed by Liney Li
Manufactured in the United States of America

1   3   5   7   9   10   8   6   4   2

Library of Congress Cataloging-in-Publication Data
Dearborn, Mary V.
The happiest man alive: a biography of Henry Miller/Mary V. Dearborn.
p.   cm.
Includes bibliographical references and index.
1. Miller, Henry, 1891–1980—Biography.
2. Authors, American—20th century—Biography.
I. Title.
PS3525.I5454Z6595   1991
818'.5209—dc20
[B]   90-19898
CIP
ISBN 0-671-67704-7

Every effort has been made to trace the ownership of
all copyrighted material in the picture sections.
In the event of any questions about the use
of any material, the publisher, while
expressing regret for any inadvertent error,
will be happy to make the necessary correction
in future printings.

For Eric, who saw me through

Contents

"So what, my dear compatriots? How will you label me now? Unamerican? It won't fit, I'm afraid. I'm even more American than you, only against the grain. Which, if you will think a moment, serves to put me into the tradition."

—Henry Miller,
Stand Still Like the Hummingbird (1962)

Preface

"I hate Montparnasse, being referred to as an intellectual, being forty, wearing glasses, and being bald." So Henry Miller, who would become one of the most famous—and infamous—writers of the twentieth century, wrote to a friend in 1932. Every day he trudged to the American Express offices in Paris hoping to find a cable from his wife, June, left behind in the States; it almost never came. Later he would make his way to the *terrasses* of the Dôme or the Coupole, hoping to spot a familiar face who might stand him to a meal.

By all estimates, he was a failure. He had written three decidedly mediocre, unpublished books, and had held numerous jobs, most notably a position of some responsibility with Western Union that he had simply thrown over in disgust. His second marriage was foundering; June, who had earlier taken a Lesbian lover, was a seductive pathological liar whose primary livelihood came from "golddigging," a kind of genteel prostitution. He had come to Paris as a last-ditch effort to make something of himself. But in the first months of 1930 he was more destitute and disheartened than he had ever been in his native Brooklyn.

Yet there, on the very streets of Paris, he began to write the book that would make him famous. "I have no money, no resources, no hopes. I am the happiest man alive," he wrote on *Tropic of Cancer*'s opening page. While he wrote, his circumstances improved considerably: Anaïs Nin provided him with financial support and then took him as her lover. With his friend Alfred Perlès, he moved into a cozy flat in the working-class district of Clichy. By the time *Tropic of Cancer* found a publisher in 1933, he had written the magnificent closing pages of the book, in which the narrator looks at the quietly flowing Seine, "like a great artery running through the human body," and feels a profound peace come over him: "The sun is setting. I feel the river flowing through me—its past, its ancient soil, the changing climate. The hills gently girdle it about: its course is fixed."

With *Tropic of Cancer* Miller felt that his course, like the Seine's, was fixed—at last. The years he would spend in Paris were a period of great fertility. Aside from some minor works, he wrote two more masterpieces: *Tropic of Capricorn* and *Black Spring*. But these books were written in a strange new genre, a peculiar kind of fictional autobiography that had some precedent in Europe—in the works of Proust and Céline, for example—but no distinct counterpart in America. They echoed the works of Whitman and Emerson in their celebration of the self, but they were written in a baroque, surrealistic style that alienated many readers and critics. Moreover, they were saturated with sex and four-letter words, rawer and more explicit than the works of James Joyce or D. H. Lawrence. Published in Paris by a firm that turned out risqué English-language books for tourists, the *Tropics* and *Black Spring* won him acclaim in the European literary avant-garde, but they were banned almost everywhere outside France. When Miller returned to America in 1940, he was unknown to most of the reading public. As a writer of "dirty books," he could not get his major writings published in his own country, and found it equally impossible to get a commercial publishing house to take on anything else he had to offer. For the next twenty years, living in the isolation of California's remote Big Sur region, he turned out what he thought of as his life work, a three-volume epic about his years with June called *The Rosy Crucifixion*. Many times he was forced to barter for food and to circulate "begging letters" asking for supplies. It was not until 1961, when Miller was turning seventy, that the U.S. ban on the Paris books was lifted; this brought him money and belated recognition, but also a host of new problems. He would complain that between reporters, fans, accountants, documentary film makers, and lawyers, he barely had time to write in the genre he liked best: long letters to close friends. The lifting of the ban brought him fame, but it also marked the end of his career as a writer.

Miller's "writing life," then, was an odd, thwarted affair unlike any other in the history of American literature. His personal life was no less complicated. Raised in a rigid first-generation German-American household at the turn of the century, Miller's character was fashioned by an unstable, abusive mother and an ineffectual father with a drinking problem. Yet throughout his "autobiographical romances," Miller intermingled reverent nostalgia with the most harrowing details of his boyhood. From his childhood and adolescence Henry Miller emerged as an enormously complicated sexual being. Deeply distrustful of women, he was sexually conservative, and seldom advocated anything but traditional sex roles—yet in his books he comes across as a veritable Don Juan. At once a misogynist and a romantic, Miller married five times and had at least two significant affairs. Generally speaking, he preferred the company of men, often adopting a kind of sidekick who could play the clown for him and help him seek out women. Friends found him often warm and charming; he was a born conversationalist and unfailingly generous. But he maintained a reticence about his innermost feelings and could drop friends abruptly over imagined slights. His American publisher, Barney Rosset, spoke of Miller as "cool," calling him "the hooded cobra." Miller also tended to seek out strange companions, many of them opportunistic and some of them unbalanced; friends complained he showed a similar lack of critical judgment in publishing virtually everything he wrote, no matter how negligible.

Miller was fond of quoting his hero Walt Whitman: "Do I contradict myself? Why then I contradict myself." A man of rare contradictions, Miller is not easily categorized or, for that matter, understood. Although committed to equality and individual rights, he had a strong streak of anti-Semitism, and, despite his protests to the contrary, he was simply incapable of seeing women as equals. A would-be philosopher and seer, he too often turned to simplistic systems such as astrology and the occult for answers. A dyed-in-the-wool anarchist and pacifist, he romanticized—and claimed to advocate—violence. He spurned the company of more mainstream, serious authors, though he wished desperately to be included in their ranks. A man who professed to write only for himself, he openly craved the Nobel Prize. And, though he wrote time and again of how fans plagued him, he always welcomed them generously, giving over to them many, many days that he could have passed more profitably by writing.

What has Henry Miller to say to us now, in his centennial year? Does he have any message, really, beyond some vague and now quite well-accepted principles of sexual and artistic freedom? Isn't his work sexist and out of date? Because his books were banned for their sexual content, he is thought to have been a freewheeling advocate of sexual expression. But "freedom" is hardly the word to use in conjunction with a world view as sexist as Miller's. In fact, as feminist critics have pointed out, he gave voice to certain male attitudes that reflect the deep sexual neuroses of twentieth-century American culture. Hardly a run-of-the-mill male chauvinist, he shared the conflicts of his generation and class about sex while bringing to them complex responses of his own, and his books can in fact reveal a great deal about sexuality and male-female relationships in our recent history.

Other, less immediately obvious questions are more troublesome. "I've written my own truest biography," Henry Miller told a would-be biographer in 1970. "Whatever isn't said in my books isn't really important." Unlike other writers who looked at societal problems with a detached eye, Miller went at writing as a kind of therapy, reviewing endlessly the problem of Henry Miller and how he got that way—to borrow the title of his 1938 pamphlet about money. He looked forward eagerly to the day when he would have written himself out; when the project was completed, he said that he hoped to go to Tibet and become a holy man.

The result is a body of work that accurately charts the author's inner life but emphasizes his fantasies and obsessions over the factual details of his outer life. "For me the book is the man that I am," Miller wrote in *Black Spring*. "The confused man, the negligent man, the reckless man, the lusty, obscene, boisterous, thoughtful, scrupulous, lying, diabolically truthful man that I am." If his books have value in what they tell us about a fascinating life, it is wrong to treat them as the sole sources for his life. He was both deceptive and diabolically truthful in the writing of what he calls his "autobiographical romances." Often he distorted the truth, leaving out important events and disproportionately playing up others. Almost uniformly, he describes people unkindly, people whom he treated well in all other respects. These lapses from verisimilitude demonstrate that his books cannot be read as biographical documents. He gives events nuances and shadings that are often idiosyncratic, and it is the nuances and shadings that often reveal the truth.

Furthermore, Miller's major work treats only the first forty years of his life. In part because of a promise he made to Anaïs Nin, he wrote only one book, *Tropic of Cancer*, about his decade in France. Although he covered some aspects of his later life in books like *The Colossus of Maroussi* and *Big Sur and the Oranges of Hieronymus Bosch*, for his second great trilogy, *The Rosy Crucifixion*, he returned to earlier ground. To document his years of struggle, the biographer must turn to Miller's massive correspondence—which, for that matter, is not necessarily "truthful." Just as one must make allowances for difference of interpretation and lapses of memory in interviewing friends and acquaintances of Miller, one must consider the documentary evidence with the same care that one must bring to the earlier books.

The other questions that surround Henry Miller and his work are more persistent. Miller's writing is difficult to evaluate; he has, for instance, received almost no serious academic criticism. His works strike a kind of emotional raw nerve: readers tend to be passionate in their responses, either positive or negative. There is even a question of genre—should the *Tropics* be treated as novels? Are his "pieces" essays or stories?

"The difference between me and other writers is that they struggle to get down what they've got up here in the head. I struggle to get what's below, in the solar plexus, in the nether regions." That was how Miller explained his place in literature to *Playboy* in 1970. Miller's explorations of the "nether regions" reflected and shaped sexual mores and social attitudes of Americans, and in the process made literary history. The version of his life that Miller gives in his books shows an American man who constructed a facade of toughness the likes of which America at its most macho had not seen before. His story—from its very beginning, when he saw in Teddy Roosevelt the hero that his father was not—is a story of twentieth-century male identity. It is the story of one man who set himself in opposition to his culture and who, paradoxically, helped to define it.

Part 1

NEW YORK CITY

"From the beginning it was never anything but chaos: it was a fluid which enveloped me, which I breathed in through the gills."

—Henry Miller,
Tropic of Capricorn (1939)

1.

The Skater

1891–1900

Henry Miller, thoroughly German-American, liked to claim that, because of the repeated ravishing of Europe by alien races, he was actually a mixture of Mongol, Chinese, Tibetan, and Jewish blood. For years at a time he was positively in love with the notion that he was Jewish; at other times he preferred the fancy of Chinese ancestry. Neither idea was entirely groundless: he could find no record of his maternal grandparents' baptisms in Germany, which a friend convinced him meant he was undoubtedly Jewish; and his facial structure was indeed a little Mongolian, with prominent cheekbones and eyes slightly Asian-looking. A writer who proclaimed himself, like his literary ancestors Whitman and Emerson, entirely self-made, Miller was at the same time absolutely obsessed with his biological ancestry.

The worst thing about his ancestors, Miller thought, was that they didn't have the sense to come in out of the cold. He opened *Tropic of Capricorn*, that extraordinary autobiographical indictment of his family and the American work ethic, with a diatribe against his people's idiotic preference for the so-called temperate zones. Until he was ten years old, he wrote, "I never realized there were 'warm' countries, places where you didn't have to sweat for a living, nor shiver and pretend that it was tonic and exhilarating. Wherever there is cold there are people who work themselves to the bone and when they produce young they preach to the young the gospel of work, which is nothing, at bottom, but the doctrine of inertia. My people were entirely Nordic, which is to say *idiots*."

What Miller wanted to convey was that his life was botched from the start, that he was born into a family of idiots through no fault of his own, nurtured in a country of idiots, forging a self and learning to write in a society that stacked the odds against him. His life and work would be one long and savage indictment of the forces that made him.

The Miller family album contained "a galaxy of screwballs," he said, and the sentiment, however cynical, was largely on the mark. Nowhere was this more true than in the case of Henry's mother's family, the Nietings.

Valentin Nieting, Henry's grandfather, was a tailor, and proud of his trade. He was born in Stessfield Stessen in Prussia on July 7, 1836. At sixteen, he made the momentous decision to emigrate to America. News of the promised land was in the air. But there was an even more pressing reason than simple economics: an imminent reorganization of the Prussian militia made citizens like Nieting vulnerable to conscription at a time when war with Denmark seemed certain. So Nieting, who would always tell his grandson Henry that he didn't want to be a soldier, crossed the Channel to England. He apprenticed himself on London's Savile Row, where the best gentlemen of England and Europe—and America, if they were wealthy enough—had their wardrobes made. There he acquired his impeccable English—he spoke with a British accent—and became something of a Socialist; he would always be a staunch union man. But his intention was always to emigrate to America, and, ten years later, when his boss announced that he was relocating there and offered him free passage, Nieting left London for New York City.

Nieting, who was a dreamy sort given to spates of distraction that settled over him as he worked, made his home on New York's Lower East Side, among thousands of other immigrants. He soon met a young woman, Emilie Insel, who had been born in Neagleburg, also in Prussia, on January 27, 1842 (her mother was Wilhelmina Schaefer, who married a man named Insel from Bremen). The two were married on April 1, 1866, by a Pastor Pass at the St. Mark's Evangelical Lutheran Church on East 6th Street, and settled down to the business of raising a family. Their first daughter, born in 1867, was called Emilia after her mother; Henry Miller's mother, Louise Marie, was born two years later, on January 13, 1869. The same year, months later, out of loyalty to his new country, Nieting applied for U.S. citizenship. Two more daughters were born, Annie in 1873 and Mary in 1875. Two other baby girls died, and a son, named Valentine Nieting, died before his first birthday in 1878. The family made its home at 153 Avenue A in lower

Manhattan, but these quarters were meant to be temporary; in the 1880s the Nietings moved uptown to the more genteel Yorkville, a German-American stronghold on the Upper East Side.

By the time the hoped-for son appeared, it was clear that all was not well with the Nietings. Henry's grandfather's tendencies to distraction were nothing next to the problems of the rest of his family. Miller's Aunt Mary told him that her mother had been "taken away" when she was young. Henry later remembered being told that his grandmother "went crazy" when his mother was twelve or thirteen, and that, because Emilia was showing signs of instability, most of the responsibility for keeping the household together fell to the young Louise. This, he believed, was why his mother would become such a fierce disciplinarian; "she *had* to be the autocrat to keep her sisters in line."

For a time, Louise had some help. Miller's great-grandmother, Wilhelmina Insel, had been living with her daughter's family off and on since her husband's death. But when Wilhelmina died in 1883, in a home her husband had bought for the family on Driggs Avenue in Brooklyn, the Nieting family was on its own.

Louise became a woman of strict reserve, stolid and disapproving. All his life Miller blamed everything that was wrong with his family— and himself—on his mother's family, which he damned as "sober, industrious, frugal." Like his hero Nietzsche, who sometimes pretended to be Polish to eradicate his Prussian roots, Henry Miller toyed with adopting other nationalities to deny any trace of his mother's Prussian blood.

The truth was that Miller's paternal line was not without fault either, though he didn't hold these relatives up to the same ridicule he did his mother's people. His grandfather, Heinrich Muller, was born in Minden, in Hanover; he married Barbara Kropf, from Bavaria, and emigrated at about the same time as did Valentin Nieting, and for the same reasons. Heinrich changed his name to Miller on his arrival, and, when his son was born in 1865, named him Heinrich Miller. This grandfather was also a tailor, and he set his son up on the same bench he worked at in the family home in Yorkville. Like the Nietings, the Millers prized the eminent respectability of that German-American enclave, though the Millers were lower on the social ladder than the Nietings.

According to Henry, this side of the family, made up as it was of drunkards and musicians (and a fair share of artisans and merchants, though family legend claimed otherwise), was "too kind-hearted, too easy, too indolent, too dreamy." The Muller line was thoroughly German, which popular thought held to be fond of drinking and cavorting, jolly and lazy; Hanoverians and Bavarians were entirely different from the Prussians Heinrich Miller would marry into. Heinrich, who was always impeccably dressed, was primarily a sensualist, his son believed; tailoring appealed to him because he liked the feel of fine woolens and silks.

Heinrich Miller and Louise Nieting met in 1889 and were married in 1890. They were both attractive: Louise was tall, with strong features, and Heinrich was a small but well-made man with warm eyes and a neat mustache. Both were Lutherans—though they didn't attend church—and staunchly aspired to middle-class respectability. But there the resemblances stopped. The Nietings had left money behind in Prussia that they could not get out, while the Millers could make no such claim. Valentin's stint on Savile Row marked him as a gentleman tailor, something Heinrich Miller only aspired to. Temperamentally, too, Louise and Heinrich differed. She believed in strict discipline and hard work; he was easygoing and sunny, inclined to lòaf. While they differed little in ideals and prejudices, they clashed continually over every detail of domestic life. Gradually, too, it emerged that Louise was unstable, given to rages that were protracted over days and could lead to violence. A Prussian woman from a "proper" home, Louise did not take kindly to her new position in what she thought was a "slovenly" Bavarian/Hanoverian household. When her first child was born, she proved to be a good mother of the worst kind; with her second, she became a very bad one.

Henry Valentine Miller was born in his parents' home at 450 East 85th Street on December 26, 1891, a year he found portentous. He noted that Rimbaud, with whom he felt great affinities and whom he likened to Christ himself, died in 1891, a year that ended "a decade in which a number of writers important to the twentieth century [were] born." The date too was significant, one day after Christmas: all his life Miller entertained the idea that he might in fact be another Jesus Christ, a latter-day one, as it were. He had been born as well with a double crown—a rare pattern of hair growth in which there are not one but two "crowns" on the scalp—which superstition held marked him out as special.

It was his mother's fault he was not born on Christmas, Miller thought: she had a "clutching womb." He also believed that he was born hungry, both metaphorically and literally. Describing how he was ruined from earliest childhood, he wrote in *Tropic of Capricorn*, "It's as though my mother fed me a poison, and though I was weaned young the poison never left my system."

Something *was* very wrong with Louise, and the problem wasn't just in Henry's perception of her. Though outwardly she appeared to be a loving mother, she never showed any sign of real affection toward him. The slightest deviation in household routine, the smallest infraction of her rigid, often irrational rules, could send her into one of her rages. To her husband she was brutal and derisive, and she mocked his poor business instincts. She became enraged when Heinrich drank, terrified that drunkenness was the beginning of disgrace; these rages in turn drove him again to drink. From his little bedroom—"just a cell, with one [strangely enough, barred] window giving out on the hallway" —Henry could hear them quarrel while his father dried the dishes his mother had left washed in the sink. One evening, his mother gave his father a "ringing slap" with her wet hands, and his father said quietly, "If you ever do that again I'll leave you." Thereafter Louise confined her physical violence to her children.

Yet Miller also claimed, constantly, that his childhood was the happiest time of his life—and in outward respects it was. He was born with a silver spoon in his mouth, he often said. Family finances were in good shape, and he was given everything he wanted, except a real pony (he had an imaginary one, Dexter). He remembered writing Santa Claus to ask for a drum *and* a magic lantern, fully confident of delivery. He took piano lessons and zither lessons. He was surrounded by relatives, which contributed to his sense of security; only later would he regard the close Miller clan as oppressive.

In 1892 the Miller family moved to the Nieting-owned 662 Driggs Avenue, in the Williamsburg section of Brooklyn, a move that brought them new respectability. Their new home was at one end of a one-block street; since the Millers lived on the top floor of a three-story house, Henry presided over what seemed at first to be a perfect little universe.

Brooklyn was then a thriving autonomous city known, alternatively, as a city of neighborhoods and a city of banks. Both descriptions were apt, for Brooklyn's lifeblood was the middle-class respectability of its citizens. Its first mayor had campaigned in 1833 on a platform of stamping out the spread of saloons and unfenced pigs in the streets, and that kind of bourgeois gentility was still the ideal in the 1890s. Though the city aimed to be independent, Manhattan was essential to Brooklyn's economic survival. In 1893, when Henry was two, *Harper's* Magazine observed that "Every other city earns its own way, while Brooklyn works for New York and is paid off like a shop-girl on Saturday night." The same commentator noted that Brooklyn was a women's town; by day the men were in the shops, or across the river in Manhattan while "the women [had] the city to themselves and rule[d] over children, maids, nurses, shade trees, flowers and pretty dooryards." Around the Fulton Street shipyard area, not far from the Miller home, "carriages [were] few . . . and policemen gain[ed] the appearance of giants among so many women."

As a very young boy, he had only impressions of the outside world: the stink of Haberman's tin factory behind the house, the smell of hot starch from the tailor shop up the street, the sight of Mrs. O'Melio's cats cavorting on the tin roof of the veterinarian's across the way. As he got a little older, he was sent out for pitchers of beer at Pat McCarren's saloon on the corner when the relatives gathered—occasions at once exciting and a little upsetting, given his relatives' various crises. These gatherings of the Millers and Nietings took place in the kitchen of Henry's parents' home. He described them as "frightening, odious sessions from which they always reappeared with long, grave faces, or eyes red with weeping." The Nieting sisters talked endlessly about who would visit their mother in the asylum on Blackwell's (now Roosevelt) Island, about their uncle, George Insel, whose eccentricity was becoming more of a problem as he grew senile, and about Tante Emilia, the eldest of the sisters, who was behaving ever more erratically.

Henry's parents treated him at first as an adorable plaything, dressing him up in elaborate finery. For particularly momentous occasions, like the parade for Teddy Roosevelt and his Rough Riders after their victory at San Juan Hill, he was outfitted in a velvet Eton jacket, complete with knickers, a lacy white blouse, and a creamy-white silk tam o'shanter with a pompom and a snow white feather in its band. He had thought his attire quite grand, and was mortified when the neighborhood children jeered. Only then did he see his getup with their eyes: he was dressed like a girl, and the taunts of "sissy" made him wince.

Much as he came to dislike it, the outfit served as well for the annual Sunday School Parade, an institution in the city since 1829 in which all Brooklyn's churchgoing children marched together through the streets. The parade was a sign of Brooklyn's pride in its stable, devout citizenry and its faith in their offspring. Henry Ward Beecher, who preached in a church in Brooklyn Heights, called the June day on which the parade was held "the most charming day of the year," and the eminent Brooklynite Walt Whitman wrote in his *Brooklyn Eagle* column, "The sight of these pleasant girls and boys, marching athwart the city in every direction, was a sight to make a man's heart grow gentler."

For the Millers, the parade was a solid reassurance of their own respectability. The church and Sunday School were considered stabilizing influences in an era that was experiencing wide-scale urbanization, immigration, and industrialization, and the massive changes in everyday life left in their wake. Urban families like the Millers looked to the church as a bulwark against the threat of the gang and the corner saloon. Henry was duly enrolled first at a Lutheran Sunday School and then at the Presbyterian church on Driggs Avenue at North 5th Street, which his parents liked because the minister, Dr. Wells, was British and therefore cultured; Henry himself remembered Dr. Wells as "a fink." The church elders liked Henry because he was bright, well dressed, and from a "good" family.

Henry was precocious. His parents had great hopes for their offspring, and Henry, because he was so bright, seemed set apart for great things. He learned to walk and talk early and was able to speak both German and English; he could read the newspaper before kindergarten, and once he could read, he asked only for books for Christmas. In fact, Henry read so much that his grandfather Valentin Nieting, who had moved in with the Millers after Henry's birth, feared he would weaken his eyes.

Some of Henry's warmest early memories centered on his grandfather Nieting, whose temperament differed substantially from that of Louise Miller. He was the only one who stood up to her, and Henry loved the old man for it. Nieting passed his Saturday nights at a saloon run by Henry's Uncle Paul, where he and his cronies discussed socialism; the very word, Henry later recalled, inspired an "unholy fear" in his parents. Lying next to Nieting's tailor's bench (Nieting made coats for Heinrich Miller, who worked next to his own father on his bench in Yorkville), listening to the old man whistle "Shoo fly, don't bother me" and *"Ich weiss nicht was soll es bedeuten das Ich so traurig bin . . . ,"* Henry read of the heroic exploits of Teddy Roosevelt and his other Spanish-American war hero, Admiral Dewey, the victor at Manila Bay (who had been born on December 25, the birthday he had been cheated of). A lithograph of the battleship *Maine* hung above his small, curtained-off bed. He would lie in this bed, looking out his little window with the iron bars across it, and dream, first of Dewey, and, later, of his counterpart, "America's sworn enemy," the Filipino rebel Emilio Aguinaldo, whose band of insurgents a Miller uncle in the U.S. Army had pursued and tortured. This uncle's stories of German-made "dum-dum" bullets, which exploded in the enemy's bodies, and of the so-called water torture, convinced Henry that, like his grandfather Valentin, he would become a staunch pacifist. But his earliest heroes were soldiers.

Another companion, Stanley Borowski, whom Henry called Stasiu, lived at the other end of the block in a shabby three-story building. Stanley often joined Henry playing toy soldiers or dominoes alongside his grandfather's bench. Stanley was an orphan, adopted by his aunt and uncle. His uncle, a drunken brute, owned the barber shop on the ground floor of the building the Millers lived in, and Henry was mortally afraid of him. Stanley, on the other hand, shrugged off his beatings—though he too had a terrible temper.

Miller later wrote that he was embarrassed and ashamed that his parents gave him everything he wanted while his best friends sometimes lacked even the barest necessities. In the spirit of spreading the wealth and out of simple generosity (a trait that would never leave him), Henry gave away his best toys, one by one. When he gave away the drum he had received for his fourth birthday, he was severely punished; worse than that, his mother dragged him by the ear to each friend's house in turn, so he could retrieve the gifts. To Henry, material possessions began to seem suspect—useless trappings—and the accumulation of them would remind him of his mother and the rigid, meaningless values she endorsed.

Constantly subjected to his mother's many rages and inconsistencies, the boy looked at first to his father for a sense of safety. Louise's behavior bewildered and often terrified him. Once, when Henry was four, Louise approached her son, sitting in his little chair by the fire, and asked him what she should do about a wart on her finger. Henry, frightened but eager to please, suggested that she cut it off with the scissors. Louise apparently did so, and got blood poisoning as a result. Two days later, she shook her bandaged finger at him, shouting, "And you told me to do this?!" Then she slapped him repeatedly. Miller never forgot this bewildering and nightmarish experience. For him, it would always be the emblem of his mother's continuing emotional abuse.

Louise's conduct grew worse after she bore a daughter on July 11, 1895, whom the Millers named Lauretta Anna. Before very long it was apparent that Lauretta wasn't normal. Her head would not stay up but rolled involuntarily. She would never develop beyond the intelligence of a nine-year-old. After kindergarten, she was deemed too slow to go to school. Her mannerisms also set her apart from the other neighborhood children, who chased her mercilessly in the streets, called her "Crazy Lauretta, crazy Lauretta!", pulled her hair, and otherwise bedeviled her.

It fell to Henry to protect his sister. He defended Lauretta fiercely, though secretly he marveled at the way she just would not develop or grow, even as he grew up beside her. In *Tropic of Capricorn* he would call her "a sort of harmless monster, an angel who had been given the body of an idiot." Because she could never learn, he believed that Lauretta could not truly understand the difference between good and evil, and was therefore, to Miller, the essence of goodness. When she committed what he saw as "some beautiful act of grace" —bringing salt when she was asked to bring sugar, for instance— she was routinely whipped by an exasperated and uncontrite Louise Miller.

Some of the worst of these episodes occurred when Louise tried to teach Lauretta at home. Several times she set up a blackboard in the kitchen and attempted to teach Lauretta the multiplication tables. Predictably, Lauretta could never get the right answer, and instead guessed randomly and desperately. At each wrong answer Louise would slam a ruler across her knuckles, and turn to Henry and ask why God had afflicted her so—again appealing to him as a grown man rather than a boy.

For his part, Henry overcompensated, overachieved. In primary school on North 1st Street he got straight As, and around the neighborhood he was known as something of a sage to the younger boys. When he was five or six, he impressed his friends by strutting about the neighborhood saying "they have found a piece of land sticking out of the edge of the world," which he claimed proved the world was flat. Though his parents read little, they valued learning very highly, and he sought to please them with his success in school. To his doting aunts he recited dizzying lists of facts, dates, conjugations, declensions, and tables; he had a remarkable memory and learned very early how it could impress people. He had become quite proficient at the piano, and he impressed his relatives with exercises from Czerny.

There was something more to Henry's obsessive learning than mere precociousness and a desire to impress, however. He felt a desperate need to compensate for Lauretta's deficiencies and so avoid or divert his mother's incomprehensible rages. In this respect, his verbal performances, which sprang from his need to deflect his mother's randomly violent anger, anticipated his voluminous written achievements. When he saw Lauretta beaten for doing something wrong that she didn't really understand, he was presented with an intellectual riddle compounded by childish loyalties. If Lauretta, who was good, was beaten as if she were bad, what was the use of being good? Following this logic, Henry tried another tack: he decided to be bad—in school. He acted up routinely and was sent home several times for bad behavior, usually for being "incorrigible." His mission, as he saw it, was to make merciless fun of the teachers and the curriculum—of school, for which at this moment he developed a sudden but passionate distaste.

Henry the bad boy was a complicated case, however, for he continued to be, as far as learning went, so very good. Even though he was now a disciplinary problem, he never ceased to get As and to collect every award available. For another conclusion he drew from the riddle of Lauretta's ill treatment was that somehow he must also be very, very good if he wanted to protect himself from his mother's rages. The balance was always tenuous, and it shattered as he reached adulthood. More than thirty years later, in *Tropic of Capricorn*, he would describe a brother-sister relationship in which one side constantly felt compelled to compensate for the other's failings:

> Because [my sister] doesn't grow at all I grow like a mushroom; because she has no personality I become a colossus; because she is free of evil I become a thirty-two-branched candelabra of evil; because she demands nothing of anyone I demand everything; because she inspires ridicule everywhere I inspire fear and respect; because she is humiliated and tortured I wreak vengeance upon everyone, friend and foe alike; because she is helpless I make myself all-powerful.

Often Miller changed places with his sister imaginatively, and suffered her tortures in his own hypersensitive soul. In fact, he developed an ability to hypnotize himself when he saw his mother beat Lauretta. Instead of experiencing the horrible spectacle, he would escape into a dream world. He had witnessed his grandfather's distracted reveries at his tailor bench, and he found autohypnotic trances a convenient and increasingly necessary way to tune out the craziness of his family. Here was born as well Henry's famous hardness, his seeming callousness; in adulthood, when these moods became second nature and thus far less noticeable, he would simply turn a deaf ear when things became unbearable.

One of the more striking passages in Miller's writings describes just such an episode. Henry imagines a bizarre scenario that revolves around a spot of rust on an ice skate, a spot that leads, inevitably, to an escape to his dream world. In this fantasy, his father is rendered as the leaning tower of Pisa (an authority figure about to topple), his grandfather as a snoring machine, his sister a whipping post, and his mother a pterodactyl in human flesh. The whipping post reaches for a kerosene can to wipe the rust off the skate, but accidentally spills a can of prunes meant for dinner. For this she must of course be beaten, which leads to screams. The tower of Pisa, in response, goes out and gets drunk. When he comes home, he chips some paint off the doorway on his tipsy entry. This touches off a battle royal with the pterodactyl, which in turn sends Henry into a trance. For what it all meant, of course, was that the little spot of rust was still on the family skate, and that Henry would have to be the one to get it off, but only by skating so fast and so far as to wipe it out forever. "That little stain of rust under the clamps made me a champion skater. It made me skate so fast and furiously that even when the ice had melted I was still skating, skating through mud, through asphalt, through brooks and rivers and melon patches. . . . I could skate through hell, I was that fast and nimble."

He escaped to the streets, trying to spend as much time as possible out of doors. Williamsburg could not have been a more ordinary urban landscape, but it was intensely captivating to the young boy. Best of all, it was dangerous. He later wrote a friend that he "lived the life of an incipient gangster." An ongoing turf war pitted Henry's end of the neighborhood, the North, against the swanky, snobbish South; the greatest coup was to cross over into the South and beat up some boys, taking captives if possible.

Henry had at least one brush with the law when he was a boy, an incident that went beyond the usual scoldings given to city children by policemen on the beat. He had been out on the streets showing off by reciting big words for some neighborhood children, except that this time the words he reeled off were obscene insults, hurled at the fifteen-year-old Florrie Martin. He so outraged Florrie that she hauled him into the local precinct. There the sergeant said Henry's name aloud and told the boy he knew his father and grandfather and that he should know better. Henry cowered, and later wrote that hearing his name spoken publicly had a "tremendous effect" on him. It was the combination of "Henry" with "Miller" that shocked him so, he believed; he was impressed with the magnitude of a sexually related offense being associated with his family name—and particularly with his father's name, which was the same as his. Miller would in effect repeat this experience endlessly in adulthood, forever being called before the authorities for his so-called dirty words.

But a brush with the police only made Henry's life on the streets seem more exciting. "I am a patriot—of the Fourteenth Ward, Brooklyn, where I was raised," he would declare thirty-five years later in the memorable opening of *Black Spring*. The Fourteenth Ward was his country; he saw it as a microcosm, a world man-sized and suited to his taste. Drunks, beggars, and lunatics roamed the streets, petty bourgeois hopefuls like the Millers picking their way fastidiously through them.

Older boys—boys in their teens when Henry was six, seven, and eight—were gods to him. For Eddie Carney, he would lie, steal, or commit murder; Eddie was a "demigod," Henry said. He and his friends tried very hard to win the favor of these older boys. "Were they to give us a smile or a pat on the back, we were in Seventh Heaven," he remembered.

In these years Henry often journeyed to Yorkville, when he visited his cousin Henry Baumann, the son of his mother's sister Annie and her husband Dave. There Henry was proudly introduced by his younger cousin as "Henry Miller, Henry Miller from Brooklyn," as if he were a visiting dignitary from another planet. From Aunt Annie, he received what he later came to see as a sort of maternal sacrament, a slice of sour rye bread slathered with butter and a little sugar sprinkled on top.

What galled Henry was the contrast between his own family and others. Many of the boys had fearsome fathers, quite unlike Heinrich Miller. Stanley might have a drunken uncle who beat him, but Stanley's aunt, his adoptive mother, gave the boys the same sure sign of maternal love, warm rye bread. And Henry's friend Jack Lawton, who would die tragically at the age of twelve, had a mother whose voice transfixed Henry; she would call out, when Jack came home, "Jackie, oh Jackie," and, hugging him and giving him a kiss, croon "Oh, darling, how are you, how have you been?" Henry had never heard anything like it. He was never kissed or hugged. *His* mother greeted him by warning, "Don't make too much noise and be sure to clean up when you've finished playing." If he wanted some bread he had to get it from the breadbox and slice it himself.

Every household Henry visited seemed preferable to his mother's. In Glendale, Long Island, he visited his friends Joey and Tony Imhof, whom he had met when he was seven, when their parents sang together in the *Saengerbund*, a German singing society. Glendale was in the country, and the Imhofs talked a different language, full of birds, snakes, trees, and pigeon eggs, which made Henry regret being a city boy. He also was deeply impressed by the boys' father, an artist who installed stained-glass windows in churches for a living and made watercolors on the side.

But the chief attraction at the Imhofs was sexual horseplay. Joey and Tony had a sister several years older than the boys who slept in a bed next to the one the brothers shared. Over Tony's protests—Tony was something of a prig—Henry would tiptoe to Minnie's bed and raise her nightgown so the boys could peek at her. She always threatened to tell but never did.

Only toward the end of his life Miller revealed, very casually, that he and Joey "had acquired the habit of buggering one another." They thought nothing of it, but Tony believed they were committing a grievous sin (the Imhofs were Catholic) and threatened to tell the priest. He went on to note that sometimes the two boys tried to bugger Tony, but that "it was useless—he was incorruptible."

Henry's friendship with Joey and Tony lasted for five years, until he was around twelve. While he wrote about the rest of his childhood repeatedly and obsessively, he mentioned this sexual relationship only once. (He would, however, name his son Tony and rename all his best friends Joey.) Henry was vaguely aware that this was the very act enjoyed by the "fairies" and "sissies" he so taunted on the street. The act was not immoral to Henry, who already cared little what his elders thought, but he believed it was unmanly.

Whether or not the sexual activity itself troubled him at the time, all this was terribly confusing for an eight-year-old boy. His own father was ineffectual and avoided being home as often as possible. His frequent absence was the only quality Heinrich shared with the fathers of Henry's friends. Unlike them, he seldom raised his voice or beat his children. But he and Louise fought almost every night at dinner when, as often as not, he came home drunk. Henry, deeply disturbed by these dinner-table scenes, would begin to gag; so traumatized was he by these fights that into adulthood his throat often constricted when he tried to eat. Because Heinrich preferred to stay out with his drinking cronies Louise harangued him for being less than a man, for preferring men to women. Heinrich was an introspective, sensitive man, by his culture's standards somewhat "feminine." And although there is no evidence that Heinrich was actively homosexual in these years, his son must have sensed the confusion in the household. It was his mother who saw to it that the pastor came round for his schnapps, that the life insurance money was paid, and that Heinrich turned over his wages to her every Saturday. By neighborhood standards, the gentle, small-statured Heinrich, with his natty suits and mustaches, commanded little respect.

The elder Millers were absolutely determined to keep up the appearance of a traditional family. But the walls of the apartment on Driggs Avenue could have told a very different story, and Henry came to detest this hypocrisy. Although its nominal leader, Louise, delighted in inventing and imposing rigid codes of behavior to be followed for proper digestion, for the treatment of a retarded daughter, or for being a good son, the household was disorderly to the point of chaos. Louise was so emotionally overwrought that she could keep the household running only through routine physical violence.

Henry looked elsewhere for his heroes, finding them among the older neighborhood boys, in popular culture, and, increasingly, in books. The boys' writer George Alfred Henty enthralled him, as did Rider Haggard, the author of exotic romances like *She* and *King Solomon's Mines*. Both men belonged, Miller wrote later, to the "manly" side of British letters. In fact, Henty was a confirmed invalid who nonetheless developed his physique and insisted that men be tough. Both authors saw the "rough side of life" at an early age and also engaged in pursuits other than writing. They provided Henry with models of male identity that he found sorely lacking in his own family.

Turn-of-the-century American culture preached the gospel of manliness. In 1902 Albert J. Beveridge would advise the young readers of the *Saturday Evening Post:* "Be a man—that is the first and last rule of the greatest success in life." The ideology of the late Victorian age demanded that natural aggressive and sexual urges be repressed; according to this logic, women might dominate men, but they must not unman them. The balance was precarious, and the overwhelming response was the almost absurd romanticization of manhood that was celebrated in every aspect of popular culture. Teddy Roosevelt, who ostensibly proved his manhood in the American West even before his Cuban exploits, was the apotheosis of turn-of-the-century manhood.

Henry idolized any man involved in an activity from which women were excluded. Unfortunately, most of these activities were either illegal or required special talents beyond the reach of a young boy. Henry admired wrestlers and boxers (known as "pugs"), soldiers, adventurers, gamblers, con men, and gangsters. Cops would have made the list, but they were actual everyday authority figures and thus ineligible. All his life he would search out institutions that were exclusively male; he was fascinated by prisons, for example, and the sheer accident that all-male occupations were often criminal ones led him to associate being a man with rebellion, with doing something wrong, or, in his younger years, with being a bad boy.

In the years between 1896 and 1901, when Henry turned ten, American culture was busily putting the ideology of manliness and the virtues of the physically strenuous life into practice. It was the era's perception that the family was in crisis and that the innocence of the nation's children was at great risk. As a result, many looked to the church for guidance. Because of the crisis of faith induced by Darwin's findings, Christianity itself was in the process of transformation to catch up with society's new values. As early as 1880, when Thomas Hughes, author of *Tom Brown's School Days*, published *The Manliness of Christ*, the move was on to inject the church with new virility. Boys were encouraged to see Christ as a he-man. Newly formed boys' clubs, the precursors of the Boy Scouts, infused with Christian principles, organized boys into quasi-military groups where they camped, learned woodcraft, and performed good deeds in a manly sort of way.

In Brooklyn, the Sunday School-sponsored Boys Brigades offered themselves as a solution to the late nineteenth-century "boy problem." The Boys Brigades were paramilitary; their founders stood with Teddy Roosevelt when he wrote in "The American Boy" that "a soldier needs to know how to shoot and take cover for himself—not to box or play football." The boys were trained in military drilling and other soldierly activity.

In 1898, Henry joined Battery A, a Boys Brigade that met in the basement of the Presbyterian church on Driggs and North 5th Street. The boys wore elaborate uniforms with red chevrons—red because the brigade was part of the Coast Guard Artillery, which wore red at the time. Their activities included drilling, physical exercise, and practicing survival techniques under war conditions. On special occasions mock battles were staged. Henry was an enthusiastic member and rose in the ranks to become first lieutenant; he loved the hierarchy as much as the soldiering.

The group was run by an Englishman named Tillotson, whom the boys called Major Tillotson. He loved boys, and their parents thought him a "lovely man." But, wrote Miller at the end of his life, "he loved us a little too much for our own good." Every night that the group met —or "reported for duty," as Miller had it—the Major ushered each boy, one by one, into his little office, where he would make them sit on his lap while he kissed and fondled them.

Henry and his friends dreaded these private sessions, though they were fond of "the Major" and enthralled by the military drilling that followed. They thought about reporting him but decided no one would believe them because the man was so well liked. The fondling continued for several years, and eventually the Major's advances became common knowledge throughout the neighborhood, at which point he was ousted in disgrace. It was a far cry from the glory days of the brigade, when the boys marched smartly with Major Tillotson in the Sunday School Parade under their red escutcheon.

Whatever sexual anxiety these experiences caused Henry, they served to alienate him still further from his parents and from authority. His parents liked Tillotson because he brought them a gift at Christmas, visits that must have been tremendously difficult for Henry, with his secret knowledge. His pain was quickly transformed into rage and then disgust, as it was when he was tormented by his mother. The disgust colors all his autobiographical fiction, from the *Tropics* to *The Rosy Crucifixion*. The rage helped to make the man.

The experience with Tillotson ultimately succeeded in removing soldiers from Henry's panoply of heroes. Shortly after this disillusionment, Henry took up biking, and often passed a military barracks on his long rides; the sight made him experience a feeling "almost of nausea." Although he would never cease to seek the company of men, he could never forget the hypocrisy that undermined an edifice that should have gleamed so brightly and proudly: Battery A, Coast Guard Artillery, Boys Brigade.

The young Henry had loved the pomp of Battery A and just as surely had, for a time, loved the warm old man who led them. But as he grew older, Henry decided that had he taken up "the stupid nonsense [Tillotson] had tried to implant" eagerly as a youth, he would now reject it with equal vigor. Tillotson almost made it into Henry's pantheon of heroes—for Henry was the gentlest of pantheon makers and normally allowed almost any man in—but was denied entry because he had committed what Henry, emerging from the disillusionment of his boyhood, considered the only cardinal sin: hypocrisy. Against the backdrop of his baroque childhood, all other sins counted for nothing, "buggery" as inconsequential as bringing salt when one is asked for sugar. It was in this way that, at a very early age, Henry Miller came to see the world, and his actions, as beyond morality.

2.

The Tailor's Son

1900–1915

In 1900, Heinrich and Louise Miller began househunting. An infusion of new immigrant groups was changing the quality of the old neighborhood, and the Millers felt their bourgeois world threatened. They looked in neighborhoods further inland in Brooklyn that suited their middle-class taste, and found a pleasant rowhouse at 1063 Decatur Street in the Bushwick section of Brooklyn, then a solidly respectable neighborhood.

Henry took the move as a betrayal. Residential Bushwick lacked the excitement of the Williamsburg neighborhood. He felt no sympathy with his parents' bourgeois aspirations, which he wrote off as more hypocrisy. In adulthood, he would remember the new neighborhood as "the street of early sorrows."

Family life continued to be nightmarish. It became clear that Lauretta was not just "slow" but retarded, and that she could never earn her own living or, for that matter, live on her own. Heinrich's drinking grew worse, and Louise became ever more shrewish. Henry began to perceive the magnitude of the family's problems. In the coming years two relatives—his Tante Grussy and his Tante Emilia—joined his maternal grandmother in the asylum. He began to form a deep conviction that the insanity in his family was hereditary, and that he, too, might be touched by it.

Once again, for consolation he looked to the life of the street. At P.S. 85, on Covert Street and Evergreen Avenue, he made friends with another German-American boy, Emil Schnellock, whose chalk drawings on the blackboard filled him with admiration. The neighborhood boys gradually accepted Henry. One of his most cherished memories of the Decatur Street days was of the boys gathering in a vacant lot on the corner of his street, warming themselves over a fire, roasting chestnuts, talking feverishly about everything from cannibalism to the currents off the coast of Japan.

But increasingly, what they wanted to talk about was sex. The boys expatiated on this subject like sages. "The conversation, when it got round to this topic, became rather thick and complicated; it was tinged with a flavor strangely reminiscent of the atmosphere which invested the early Greek schools of philosophy." Miller was drawn to sex, he wrote years later, like a horse into a corral. There would always be something coercive in his approach to sex. The women in his books would often be forced into sex, and in his sexual fantasies he cast himself as a man in an iron mask. Once when Henry was about eight, he and his cousin Henry Baumann took a Yorkville girl named Weesie into a neighboring cellar and made her pull up her dress. The boys were thrilled, but Henry was a little scared; when he remembered the scene he imagined himself wearing an iron mask, forced to look. His early experience was that sex was not a matter of free will, that man was a slave to his body. First as a boy, and then as a man, he was drawn to women almost in fascinated horror.

Given Louise's Puritanical bent and the generally repressive atmosphere of the Miller home, Henry was very conflicted about sexual matters. During his early teens, he suffered from frequent fantasies of being locked up for his deeds, real or imagined. He saw his impulses as totally beyond his control. If he felt sexual urges, what was to prevent him from becoming like the neighborhood's Crazy Willie, who stood on the window ledge of the family home every evening at six o'clock and masturbated for all to see? He felt intolerable excitement climbing lamp posts, or even, to his great dismay, climbing ropes in gym, and took this as a sign that his sexuality was beyond control, almost criminal. But he also felt that there was something exciting in precisely this lack of control, in living dangerously, in living outside the law—a destiny he would later live out when he became known as the "outlaw writer."

His sexual confusion only increased the anxiety he felt about his own manhood. He had, of course, received many mixed messages about what being a man was—from his father, his mother, his culture, and the Boys Brigade. Later, writing about the torments of adolescence, he remembered the existential dilemma he weathered when he realized that *things are the way they are*; the only solution, he saw, was *"Be a man."* But what did that mean?

That injunction—"Be a man"—was his father's favorite piece of advice. Years later Miller wrote, somewhat bitterly, that few deserved the title, very few. As he had done as a boy, and as he would continue to do until the end of his life, he surrounded himself with male companions. To be a man, he concluded, one surrounded oneself with male friends and indulged in male rituals. He lived in what he called "a small Greek world," on the frontier of adult life, and he wished he could make it even smaller, to stay safe in "a world which I can always touch with outstretched arms."

After his graduation from P.S. 85 Henry announced that he would attend not the local high school, but Eastern District High School on Wythe Avenue in the old neighborhood. His parents could not change his mind. In September 1906 he climbed aboard the elevated train that would take him up Broadway to the old neighborhood.

But Williamsburg had undergone a dramatic transformation. With the opening of the Williamsburg and Manhattan bridges, throngs of new immigrants, mostly Jews and Italians, had displaced the older, more middle-class immigrants like Henry's family. The Millers had moved precisely to escape this encroaching immigrant population; Louise Miller was openly distrustful of the Jews, whom she called "sheenies."

In school, Henry found he was one of a handful of students with American-sounding names. He came to feel that his classmates and their families were responsible for the transformation of the neighborhood, and he hated them for it, the Jews, particularly. As the teen-age Miller's nostalgia for the "old" Driggs Avenue grew, he developed the fierce anti-Semitism that would stay with him until World War II. He would form many friendships with Jews, and, as he grew older, aspects of Jewish culture came to seem attractive, even fascinating, to him. But as an adolescent, he focused his hate on the East European Jews who had changed the very character of his old street. "Where they were life was coarsened, cheapened, vulgarized," he later wrote bitterly.

At school, Henry found that his being American-born made him a favorite among his teachers, though he was still given to troublemaking. He had nothing but contempt for his teachers, and idled through his classes, earning As with very little effort. He still read voraciously, but generally things that were not assigned in class, like the set of Harvard classics his parents gave him in his sophomore year. Sir Walter Scott and Tennyson displaced Henty and Haggard as his heroes, and they drew him into chivalric fantasies. He recast his entire boyhood as an adventure out of *Ivanhoe*.

At sixteen, Henry was a striking young man who had no difficulty attracting female attention. His hair was dark blond and parted in the middle. As he grew older, his hair would thin and darken and he would reluctantly begin wearing glasses. He came to look interesting rather than classically handsome. Photographs of him show a young man with the lined face and tired eyes of a much older man; in group photographs he looks older than his friends. Just as the tailor's son had been the best-dressed boy on the block, so he was an impeccably dressed adolescent. Often he sported a Borsalino hat, and with his round spectacles he looked intellectual.

He had had flirtations with a few "nice" girls, such as the fifteen-year-old Miriam Painter, whose greatest charm was her chestnut hair, or Marcella Murphy, who was impressed by his skill at the piano, or Edna Booth of Sparta, whom he had met on a family vacation at Narrowsburg, New York. But Cora Seward, with whom Henry fell in love at sixteen, was his grand passion.

His love for Cora was hardly standard-issue adolescent fare; it had more in common with the world of chivalry he was reading about. He rarely saw her, for example. Only at occasional parties did they meet, and he trembled all over when he danced with her or played a game of "Kiss the Pillow" or "Post Office" in which she participated. He was almost fearful of her presence.

Cora was an embodiment of Woman, hardly a fleshly being at all. He always insisted that she was an angel, not a woman. (To Henry's mind, an angel could not, by definition, be a woman—nor could a woman be an angel.) As he wrote years later: "Strange that I never thought of fucking her. Not that she was too sacred, too holy to be fucked. No, it was Love I felt for Cora, love with a capital L that reached to the skies."

The love affair existed only in his head, and he never sullied it with lustful thoughts. Nightly—for three or four years!—Henry rose from the family dinner table, put on his hat, and walked the long blocks into Greenpoint to Cora's house in Davoe Street, where he walked by hoping to glimpse her through the parlor window. Never did he pause long enough to watch her, never did he muster the courage to ring her doorbell. Only in his dreams could he possess Cora, and there only abstractly. He used to dream that his friend George Wright led him to Cora's house, and he wondered why George, whom he saw as his double, had to appear in these dreams. He simply could not perform—however symbolically—without another man present. This would later be borne out by his distinct fondness for the gangbang over any other form of sexual intercourse. Miller always preferred to have male on-lookers when he had sex with a woman, or, failing that, to find some buddies he could regale with the story afterward. The homoerotic, voyeuristic nature of these episodes escaped him; on the contrary, he would come to consider his behavior the very essence of virility.

Henry's chaste love for Cora would last for three or four years, and he would always speak of her as the great love of his life. Yet something prohibited him from even approaching her, not to mention making love to her.

Not surprisingly, Henry found other outlets for his sexual ener-gies. In his senior year, he visited his first whorehouse, in a red-light district west of Herald Square in Manhattan. He immediately got the clap.

Seeking treatment for gonorrhea was no easy matter. Henry turned to the family doctor, Dr. Rauth. A Dutchman of the old school who moralized to his patients, Dr. Rauth told Henry that he was taking the wrong path and might end up a drunken failure like Heinrich Miller. The whole episode horrified Henry, for he was privately fastid-ious. The fear of venereal disease would continue to haunt him well into his adulthood, and it would surface as a dominant metaphor in *Tropic of Cancer*.

With Cora Seward Henry established a pattern of keeping love and sex rigidly separate. It was critical that sexual maturity be staved off resolutely. A related conclusion that he reached was that sex threat-ened the safe world of male friendships, a world that was crucial in Henry's psychic equilibrium.

In 1908, now seventeen, Henry found great pleasure in the conviv-ial company of a club that was called the Xerxes Society in honor of the boys' predilection for matters Greek and for lofty philosophical debate. The Xerxes Society, a group of twelve boys from the Green-point area of Brooklyn, claimed Henry's undivided loyalty. All were musicians; some played the piano, some the fiddle, and all sang enthu-siastically. Every two weeks they would meet at a member's house and, solicitously fed and tended by the women of the house, sing and play until dawn.

One enterprising Xerxes Society member had pins made up in shop at school with *Fratres semper* ("Brothers always") engraved in gold letters. Members exchanged elaborate secret passwords and a secret handclasp in which one tickled the other's palm with his forefin-ger. Henry later commented on the great bonds of fraternity the boys felt for one another, and that he was probably the most emotionally invested of all. He recalled that when he saw club member Georgie Alford take out his violin and tune up, his eyes welled with tears.

The Xerxes Society members were all from stable middle-class families, and the club served to bring them together and prevent them from forming bonds with less desirable boys. Like Henry, most of the boys could have gone on to college, but for one reason or another, often because family finances prohibited it, college was not an option for them. So the Xerxes Society functioned as a kind of fraternity for non-college men, a way station between adolescence and adult life.

Henry would later look back on the days of the Xerxes Society, which lasted until he was twenty-five, with a great longing and tenderness. Reminiscing in his old age about how the members frequented sports contests, plays, banquets, and lyceums, he often lapsed into the words of the era's popular songs, overcome by emotion. Writing of one evening at Café Bousquet, a French restaurant in Manhattan in the West 40s where the twelve boys were favored patrons, this man who would make his mark as the master of the dirty word described himself and his companions as "we big boobies," and waxed poetic with a call-to-arms to his now scattered comrades:

> Stand up, O ancient members of the Xerxes Society! Stand up, even if your feet are in the grave! I must tell you one and all how much I loved you, how often I have thought of you since. May we all be reunited in the beyond! *We were all such fine musicians.* O fiddledee, O fiddledee, O fiddle-dum-dum-dee

While the Xerxes members claimed to be romantic and chivalrous, much of their talk was sexual. Henry felt a growing apprehension about the group's lofty ideals as contrasted to their earthly, quotidian behavior. He once dreamed that he was sent on an elaborate spy mission to Tokyo by his Xerxes friend Alec Considine. Returning to the White House, he finds that George Wright is President of the United States and that he is engaged in a kind of Cabinet meeting with the rest of the Xerxes Society. On the table is a naked belly dancer. George gives the group permission to leave the room to masturbate, and to a man they do—except for Henry and George. George says to Henry in despair, "You see what we're up against. No matter what we cook up for them it's hopeless. I'm going to make a move to dissolve the club."

He was tremendously bothered by the idea that many of his club-mates were developing sexual attachments with women, but he was equally disturbed by his own insistent sexual impulses and often thought himself to be letting down the group's aspirations. How could he be fit for the high-minded company of "deep thinkers" when he masturbated several times daily and was tortured by lustful thoughts?

When Henry graduated from Eastern District in 1909, his options were seemingly limitless. His cousin Henry Heller was a Cornell undergraduate, and his parents and teachers thought he might attend as well. With little difficulty, he won a scholarship to study German at Cornell. But as the summer of 1909 went by, it became clear that, even with the scholarship, his family could not afford to send him away to school. Henry admitted only at the end of his life that family finances interfered with college, claiming instead that he ran away with a woman on the eve of his departure.

There was an alternative: the tuition-free City College of New York. Henry enrolled in September, but his college career lasted only six weeks. He decided that if reading "Hermann und Dorothea" or "John Gilpin's Ride" constituted an education, he didn't want one. When he had to read *The Faerie Queene* he became convinced that he was in a madhouse. Later he would claim that he felt stifled by what he saw as the college's "intolerably Jewish" atmosphere as well.

Henry quit in disgust, resolving to be a student in what Gorky called the University of Life. He became a confirmed autodidact, indulging his passion for reading; his new literary heroes were Dostoevsky, Nietzsche, and Elie Faure. But anything would do—even the encyclopedia, which he compared to opium. But opium use was preferable, he thought, for encyclopedia reading was too stimulating. He felt the same way about the New York Public Library, which he visited almost daily. It was the only institution he would ever love, and he used the opium comparison again: "I went regularly for my 'dose' and got it." He particularly loved the mythology shelf in the Reading Room, the contents of which, he said, he devoured "like a starved rat." "The tables themselves excited me," he wrote of the library; leaving the building and going out onto Fifth Avenue left him dazed, "with a holy feeling."

Heinrich Miller had never read a book except, curiously enough, one by Ruskin, and Louise told a mystified Henry that she had read one book—about battles—on the toilet. They were puzzled by Henry's reading, fearful that he would hurt his already weak eyesight and uneasy about the potentially explosive new ideas that might be found in those high-minded books he brought home. Nevertheless, they found Henry's failure at college troubling.

The Millers were infected by the turn-of-the-century ideology of success, which held that any boy could be a millionaire—witness Andrew Carnegie and the Horatio Alger heroes. The businessman was the very model of American manhood—not the artisan or tradesman. Work was good, hard work better. Henry Ford spoke for the times when he said, "The natural thing to do is work—to recognize that prosperity and happiness can be obtained only through honest effort." He warned that "nothing is more abhorrent than a life of ease. None of us has the right to ease. There is no place in civilization for the idler."

Henry, of course, didn't agree. He rejected the Protestant work ethic from the start, though he wouldn't make a decisive move to live beyond its reach for another decade. And at this point what society believed continued to trouble him, although he seldom let it show. Instead, he raged internally against its values, imaginatively setting himself in a flat-out oppositional stance to it. It made perfect sense to him, for instance, to scoff at a friend's respectable job in one breath and in the next ask him for a loan. This is the Miller immediately familiar to readers of the *Tropics*. But for all his scathing contempt, he worried that he was a failure in society's eyes; indeed, he often signed his letters "The Failure." Characteristically, he viewed his circumstances in extremes: he was tormented by lustful thoughts, his parents thought him a lost cause, he had no money and no prospects. He knew he was as intelligent as the writers he so admired, but he had no idea what to do with his brains. This Miller was personally (if not morally) fastidious, and his feelings of guilt led him into the practice of concocting rigid codes of behavior for himself. He kept laborious lists of his debts, which he paid off according to a seemingly haphazard but intricately logical system of his own, and he devised complicated schemes of self-improvement that included everything from strengthening his eyesight to reading all he could find about Buddhism.

In desperation, he took a job as a clerk at the Atlas Portland Cement Company on Broad Street in lower Manhattan. Almost immediately he was bored. Filling out inquiries about freight rates to such places as Nagasaki, Pensacola, Singapore, and Oskaloosa prompted reveries about a better life elsewhere. He never saw a sack of cement but had a feeling that the product was pretty bad, though he didn't much care. Too poor to go out to lunch—his pay was a niggardly $25 a month—he whiled away his lunch hour at the Battery, studying marine life at the Aquarium, reluctant to return to the office.

At eighteen, then, Henry began a period of aimless drifting. He would keep the job at Atlas for almost two years, and then held a succession of jobs over the next four years for shorter and shorter periods of time. His parents looked on with increasing chagrin. But Henry affected not to care. He would not conform to their expectations in any sphere; he set out to make sure of this in 1909, when he began an affair with Pauline Chouteau, a thirty-seven-year-old divorcée.

Henry met Pauline at the home of Pauline's friend Louise, when he was giving 35-cents-an-hour piano lessons to Louise's daughter. To Henry, the 35 cents was a pittance—he used to buy two banana splits for 30 cents and throw the remaining nickel in the gutter, disgusted with himself for earning so little—but playing the piano was a pleasure, as much as it had been when as a young boy he rhapsodized over Czerny. After these lessons, Louise would send her daughter off to bed and flirt with him. During one of these flirtations, Louise's boarder and lover, a bicycle repairman named Ed, returned early; she shoved Henry behind a curtain and called out caressingly, "Oh, Ed, is that you?" Henry never forgot the sound of that voice, tantalizingly sexy but emanating from the lips of a woman his mother's age and with his mother's name.

Louise frightened Henry, but his attention was caught by her friend Pauline, who often looked on during the lessons, sitting primly in a chair on the other side of the room. She was neatly groomed, in contrast to the rather sluttish-appearing Louise, her hair attractively arranged and a pleasant smile on her face. She was from Phoebus, Virginia, and her Southern accent captivated Henry. She called him Harry because, she said, she found the name Henry too nondescript.

After the lessons Henry took to escorting Pauline home to her apartment, a neat and cozy place despite her poverty. (She paid reduced rent in exchange for janitorial work.) She lived with her son George, close to Henry in age, who would soon give up his job as a shoe salesman because of his advancing tuberculosis. Pauline spoke bitterly about her ex-husband, whose name she pronounced "Shooter," but otherwise she couldn't be more agreeable, as Miller later wrote:

Pauline was delicate, petite, beautifully proportioned, always of a cheerful nature. Uneducated but not stupid. In fact, her lack of schooling rendered her even more charming to me. She had taste, discretion, and a sound understanding of life.

But it was a difficult relationship from the start. Miller would write about Pauline many times, referring to her always as "the widow"— though in fact, "Shooter" would not die until 1915—and noting that she was old enough to be his mother. That was part of the attraction, of course, but it brought Henry great confusion and torment. He became morbidly preoccupied, for instance, with how Pauline had given birth to George. As she described it, she had locked herself in the outhouse to escape her drunken husband. The vision of her, lying on a dirt floor in the "platinum moonlight" with a bloody bundle between her legs, haunted him. He was constantly reminded, by George's presence, of Pauline's motherhood. She made no end of sacrifices for "her Georgie," who in turn treated her badly. The three of them often sat holding each other, with Georgie and Pauline humming and crooning, and Georgie lamenting that he was no good and then coughing uncontrollably.

Henry had inserted himself in a truly bizarre family drama. He competed with Georgie for Pauline's attention, and this in turn made him feel terribly guilty, for Georgie was after all Pauline's son; moreover, he was ill. Henry's first experience of any note with a woman was with one who had borne a child. He became obsessed with the image of the devouring womb. "The moment I entered her presence a sorrowful quietude would invade me," Miller later wrote about Pauline. "There it was, always open, always in wait for me. Ready, like a flower trap, to swallow me whole."

Drawn inexorably to Pauline, and desperate to escape his parents' disapproval, Henry simply disappeared for two months, moving into Pauline's flat at 366 Decatur Street, just ten blocks from his parents' home. He and Pauline enjoyed a sexual idyll, but Henry was otherwise miserable. Pauline began to seem old to him; he noticed with distaste the red roots of her peroxided hair. Before long he resurfaced at home, resuming his old habit of visiting Pauline after dinner.

To alleviate some of his sexual anxieties, he turned to a contemporary craze that would become a personal passion: physical culture. Physical culture, an intensive program of athletic activity coupled with mental self-improvement, had seemed to Henry, from his late teens, the perfect cure for what ailed him. From 1905 to 1908 he had attended a gym class at the *Turn Verein,* a German social club at the corner of Bushwick and Gates avenues, but when he graduated from high school a year later he was in only mediocre shape. Plagued by failing eyesight (commonly thought at the time to be an effect of excessive masturbation), thinning hair, and a less than robust frame—not to mention his nervous sensibility and sexual doubts—Henry felt drawn to this new "science" of manly vigor. He hoped to learn to control his body and harness its desires.

Physical culturists were given to such habits as thorough chewing of food (advocated in Horace Fletcher's 1895 *Menticulture* and practiced by such figures as Henry and William James), fasting, and the lifting of dumbbells (or "Indian clubs") in the new gymnasiums that were springing up throughout the country. The movement had its predictable share of cranks, the best known of whom was Bernarr Macfadden, whose life would intersect Miller's years later. Macfadden overcame what he saw as his genetic predisposition to weakness by developing a system of "kinesitherapy," which he taught in several "healthatoriums" across the country. Billing himself as "Bernarr le Grand, Le Napoleon de la Force Humaine," he married a woman called "Britain's Strongest Woman" (he had been forced abroad after he was arrested under the Puritanical Comstock laws for posters advertising a physical culture exhibition). Macfadden kept his wife constantly pregnant, and during her first pregnancy he demonstrated to rapt audiences her own particular physical fitness by jumping onto her rounded belly. A great believer in what he called "spermatic economy," he developed the "peniscope," a glass tube with a rubber bulb on one end attached to a vacuum, which he claimed would enlarge the penis.

Sexual activity was inextricably intertwined with the goals of the physical culture movement. On the one hand designed to rein in unwholesome sexual impulses, the movement championed "healthy" sexuality and said sex was necessary for physical and mental health. The inventor of the "peniscope" and the author, as a young man, of novels with titles like *The Athlete's Conquest* and *The Strenuous Lover,* Macfadden told his adherents that sex played a central role in the life of the new man. The physical culture movement glorified "manliness," and defined it as a state of being sexually as well as physically fit. Another fitness promoter, Dudley Sargent, who developed the "Sargent system," a comprehensive diet and exercise program that was taught at Harvard University's recently opened Hemenway Gymnasium, wrote:

The great importance of strong sexual powers cannot be too
strongly emphasized. Their influence on life is marvelous. If
a fine, vigorous man acquires a complaint that weakens his
sexual organs, his powers in every way will begin to decline
—his muscles will grow weaker, his nerves will be affected,
and unless a change is quickly made, he will soon become a
physical wreck.

The message for fitness practitioners like Miller was mixed. Sex
was necessary—without it one could lose one's strength and, by extension, one's manhood—but it was intended solely for the purpose of
procreation. Macfadden avidly supported monogamy and condemned
"trial marriages," a euphemism, he felt, for free love. No doubt his
awareness of the watchfulness of the authorities was in part responsible for this seemingly contradictory priggishness. But the result was
one more confused mandate for American males.

Henry was a vigorous enthusiast, and physical culture became an
important part of the self-discipline program he embarked on during
his affair with Pauline. He even enrolled for six weeks in Sargent's
School of Arms in New York's Columbus Circle. With Sargent, Henry
believed that "Weakness is a crime."

Henry supplemented his physical culture activities with another
contemporary fad that became extremely important to him and at the
same time escalated his sexual anxieties: cycling. Henry's bike, or
"wheel," as it was then called, he would later say was his greatest
friend. He loved cycling with a passion and avidly followed the contemporary sports phenomenon of six-day races, in which cyclists rode
relay-fashion in a banked arena for six days nonstop. He bought his
own favorite bike, a "Presto" made in Chemnitz, Bohemia, from a six-
day rider named Walter Rutt at Madison Square Garden after a race;
he had two other bikes, but this one no one else was allowed to touch.
He oiled it for hours at a time and tuned out his mother's nagging about
the oil he was leaving underfoot. (Years later, when he was living with
his second wife, he had a dream in which his mother "finally allowed"
him to take the bike to bed with him. Afterwards, he woke up and was
disappointed to find his wife and not the bike beside him.)

Henry found in the company of other cyclists the reassurance
about his male identity that he so craved, but the language he used
also suggests the kind of sexual stimulation he found in their company
and on the bike. For several years before and after he turned twenty,
he made a habit of riding daily the route the six-day racers used to

train on, from Brooklyn Heights down through Prospect Park on a gravel bicycle path to Coney Island. Henry fantasized about pacing such cycling greats as Joe Folger and Oscar Egg, stopping to rest with them at a halfway mark, Bedford Rest. In a later dream about bicycling, Joe Folger feels Henry's calf and thigh muscles and his arms and says, "He'll make the grade all right—good stuff"; he then lends his bike to a delighted Henry. The best part of the dream, Miller wrote, was the return to Bedford Rest: "There they were again, the boys all in different accouterment, the wheels bright and gleaming, the saddles just right, all with noses upturned, as if sniffing the breeze. It was good to be with them again, feel their muscles, examine their equipment."

What was for America largely a healthful pastime was for Henry a hypersexual experience, the homoerotic nature of which only exacerbated his fears about his sexuality. He had counted since childhood on the escape provided him by his bike, but by now this too was just another source of anxiety. He would later invent erotic fantasies involving bicycle riding—he maintained his second wife, June, had special leather shorts made so that they could have sex while riding a tandem bike in Paris—and it is not surprising that he falsely claimed in a later biographical sketch to have been a six-day racer himself.

From his stint as a physical culturist and cyclist Henry gained the extraordinarily good physique and constitution that he maintained until his old age. But in his embrace of the physical culture movement and its ideals was also forged the sexually ambivalent Miller of the *Tropics*. Certainly sex was not to be censored—he shared Macfadden's view here—but neither was it beautiful nor, in fact, very nice at all. It was a sign of manhood, of fitness, part of life—but rather more like defecation than eating.

Moreover, sex had severe complications. Sometime in the spring of 1912, Pauline became pregnant. Henry was dismayed, for a pregnancy bound him even more closely to her. They talked about an abortion, but both were in the grip of the torpor that had come to characterize their relationship, and neither was able to act. One day in late summer Henry took an obviously pregnant Pauline to Luna Park to hear a dance band. As they made their way to a dancing pavilion, the couple ran into Cora Seward. Thrown into agonies of embarrassment, Henry bowed mutely; Cora gave no sign. To make it worse, Pauline noticed his shame and demanded fresh proof of his love for her. As it turned out, Pauline lost the baby: in the fall of 1912 Henry came home to find her lying in a pool of blood, the "seven-month toothache," as he called it, dead in a towel in a dresser drawer.

Henry later described the period as characterized by "an apparently insoluble conflict between my spiritual idealism and my voracious sexual appetite." Casting about for an answer, he seized on one of the "manliest" of all possible pursuits: to flee to the West and become a cowboy. In this vision he was influenced by his old hero Teddy Roosevelt, whose face had graced the cover of *Physical Culture* in 1904, and who preached the "strenuous life" as a cure for what ailed America's manhood. Roosevelt repeatedly stressed the association of virility with the West in his speeches and in books like *The Winning of the West*.

The twenty-year-old Henry now regarded the West as the key to recovering his manliness. Pauline still held him firmly in her grasp, and he later wrote that he was running off to cure himself of a "fatal infatuation." "No more books! Done with the intellectual life," he also told himself. It was a rather violent aboutface for such an avid reader and thinker, but he felt an upheaval of some violence was necessary if he was to extricate himself from his intolerable circumstances. He told Pauline that he would send for her when he reached the West, that they could make a new start out there, where nobody knew them—and perhaps he half-believed it.

Henry talked of nothing but the West, and his parents began to see that it might be best to humor him; they hoped the trip would put some backbone in their son. Their financial situation had improved somewhat after the recession of 1910–11, and the Millers were able to scrape together enough money for Henry's train fare. Once he got there, he would have to make it on his own.

To Henry's dismay, when he reached New Mexico in March 1913 he found that the great cowboy days were over. The West was dominated by the great produce farms instead of vast cattle ranches. There was no demand for cattle herders any more—only for low-paid, seasonal agricultural laborers or "pickers." He made his way first to San Pedro and Otay and finally to Chula Vista, California, where he found work as a picker on a lemon ranch, a distinct failure again. The other hands called him "Yorkie," which made him feel like an incompetent city boy. He thrived in the sun, but even the lure of health no longer seemed terribly interesting or important. He described his state of mind in *Tropic of Capricorn:*

> I am alone and working like a slave. . . . Am I coming into my own? I think not. I am a very wretched, forlorn, miserable person. I seem to have lost everything. . . . I am thoroughly healthy and empty. . . . I am so thoroughly alive and healthy

that I am like the luscious deceptive fruit which hangs on the Californian trees. One more ray of sun and I will be rotten.

Like so many other of his enthusiasms, the dream of the strenuous life now proved false and hollow; but Henry had not yet attained the maturity to blame the dream rather than himself. After nine months of wandering and agricultural labor, he missed Pauline and hungered for her sexually; he missed his books. He toyed with the idea of striking out for Alaska but found he lacked the requisite adventurous soul. He felt less a man than ever.

Yet Henry's Western trip was marked by one quite important moment in his life. In California he became friends with Bill Parr, a Montana cowboy temporarily stuck with ranch hand's work, who was a member of the Industrial Workers of the World, or "Wobblies," the labor faction fighting to unite all workers in one big union. To Henry's ruminations about physical culture and "New Thought" movements like it, Parr added political ones. Chula Vista, where Henry had wound up burning brush in orchards, was connected to San Diego by a trolley, and one Saturday the two young men put off a visit to a whorehouse (so Miller said) to attend a talk by the notorious anarchist Emma Goldman.

Goldman, a striking woman in early middle age who was known as a magnetic speaker and a compelling thinker, was in town lecturing on Russian drama with her lover Ben Reitman; rumors of their fiery anarchism and their practice of free love had preceded them, and Reitman would be tarred and feathered by outraged San Diegans. But when Henry met Goldman (she was not allowed to speak when she arrived at the hall, but he buttonholed her on her way out), he was less interested in what she said about drama—though she did steer him to the Russian writers and to Ibsen—than in her advocacy of free love and, by extension, unfettered female sexuality. Writing later about "free love," he said, "it sounded good to me. . . . It was more a question of being able to have sexual relations with the person you were in love with." By openly advocating sexual love, Emma Goldman had blessed his relationship with Pauline, he felt. Moreover, the mere presence of Goldman, a woman so obviously attractive and intelligent and at the same time so obviously a sexual being, was a revelation to Miller, and he was elated. The sexual nature of his relationship with Pauline did not preclude love, he now saw—although the scars of his early, rigid distinction between love and sex would never completely heal.

Henry's encounter with Goldman also led to his discovery of anarchism. He borrowed Bill Parr's copy of Benjamin Tucker's seminal book on the subject, *Instead of a Book by a Man Too Busy to Write One*, and there found a way of thinking entirely suited to his rebellious nature, a kind of anti-philosophy that somewhat formlessly blended cynicism with idealism and a deep suspicion of authority. Given his fiercely individualistic streak, he found anarchism far more attractive, in its rejection of any notion of a collective society, than the socialism old Valentin Nieting had favored. For him, its thoroughly non-judgmental quality was a revelation: in the anarchist's point of view as Henry understood it, an individual's actions were exempt from conventional standards of morality.

On his return, Henry once again took up with Pauline and applied himself even more fervently to self-improvement. His encounter with Goldman left him hungry for new ideas. He consulted an eye doctor—whom he later termed a quack—about his eyesight, as well as a phrenologist, who told him he would make a good corporation lawyer or an architect. And, of course, he continued to read about all kinds of gimmicks in the pages of Macfadden's *Physical Culture*. He was drawn as well to the public speaking halls that dotted Manhattan, where laborers and immigrants, eager for free learning, gathered in the evenings. At the Labor Temple on 14th Street he heard W. E. B. DuBois and, later, John Cowper Powys; he also frequented the Rand School, a Socialist haven in the Village. One speaker who deeply moved him was Benjamin Fay Mills, a popularizer of "New Thought," who threw in a liberal dose of Emerson, the *Bhagavad Gita*, and Freudianism, which was just reaching America's shores. A mesmerizing speaker, Mills preached "fellowship"—a vague concept whose name derived from William Morris and whose import seems to have been the social uplift of humanity. Henry saw something for himself in this new thinking, and he approached Mills after a lecture. He impressed the man enough that he was allowed to serve as an usher at the next few lectures.

Henry's search for answers grew more feverish the more he heard. In 1912, Valentin Nieting had died, leaving enough money for Heinrich to buy a half-interest (with Isaac Walker, the son of the original owner) in a tailor shop at 5 West 31st Street in Manhattan. Almost from the start the business did badly, and Louise had long pleaded with Henry to go to work with his father. Just after his return from the West in late 1913, he grudgingly agreed and began an apprenticeship at the tailor shop.

It was "a joint corporation of father and son, with mother holding the boodle," Henry later wrote. Heinrich's drinking had grown more serious. He downed drinks all day in the hotel bars along Fifth Avenue and Broadway. Once, Henry wrote in his old age, there was a fight in which a Frenchman hurled insults at his father, calling him a drunk and worse. Henry, in good shape from his fitness program, grabbed the man and banged him up against the bar. Eventually the onlookers had to pry him off.

Henry struck up a warm friendship with the Jewish cutters in the back room and enjoyed discussing philosophy and the Russian writers with them. The tailor shop also afforded him a glimpse of the New York City social scene, for Heinrich Miller was a *gentleman* tailor, and his clients ranged from the theater crowd to the city's Four Hundred. Certain customers captivated Henry. The matinée idol and raconteur John Barrymore, for instance, who regaled Heinrich with his famous wit when the tailor slipped out to one of the hotel bars where the actor passed his days. Or Walter Pach, a society photographer who often paid his debts with family photographs of the Millers.

Another customer, Frank Harris, editor of the *Saturday Review* and author of the scandalous *My Life and Loves*, was brought in by Guido Bruno, a Village character who thought Harris's wardrobe was woefully inadequate for a great lover. Heinrich Miller was unimpressed, but his son was entranced, and even more so when Harris engaged the cutters in the back room in talk about Shakespeare, Oscar Wilde, and the Bible. Henry found Harris's habit of not wearing underwear intriguingly defiant. But what impressed him most was delivering a suit to Harris's Washington Square apartment and finding the great man in bed with a woman. Harris further awed him by springing out of bed, naked and unembarrassed, to try the suit on.

A salesman named Paul Dexter, who was a regular customer at the shop, impressed Henry because of the love he bore Henry's father. Dexter saw in the improvident tailor a kindred soul, and the two men gazed at each other with warmth and admiration. The gaze was not lost on the son, who later wrote that the two men often stood there looking adoringly in each other's eyes. After Dexter left, "[Heinrich] would go then into the little cubbyhole of an office and he would sit there quietly all by himself staring ecstatically. . . ." These exchanges unsettled Henry, but he was moved by the depth of his father's affection.

Henry, who had grown up in a loveless household, saw in the tailor shop a world in which love was given freely, a world in which it did not matter if one were a success or failure. "The men who passed through

my father's shop reeked with love," wrote Miller in *Black Spring*.
"They were warm and winey, weak and indolent, fast yachts trimmed
with sex, and when they sailed by me at night they fumigated my
dreams." Perhaps Miller was referring to the tailor shop's suffusion
with the manly odors of tweeds, tobacco smoke, and liquorish breath.
Whatever disgust he felt at his father's failure quickly gave way to pity.
When the old man with his boozy breath sat down at the family table,
Henry would "feel sorry for him and for all merchant tailors who have
to kiss rich people's asses."

Years later Miller would write a piece about the tailor shop that
was an extended meditation on manliness and the bonds between men.
In this world of ultimate manliness, where great lovers were found in
bed with their pants off, men loved each other passionately and devot-
edly. But Henry associated this love between men with failure, and
specifically, his father's failure in business. He was nonetheless moved
by the weakness that accompanied this love:

> The men my father loved were weak and lovable. They went
> out, each and every one of them, like brilliant stars before the
> sun. They went out quietly and catastrophically. No shred of
> them remained—nothing but the memory of their blaze and
> glory. They flow now inside me like a vast river choked with
> falling stars.

The exact nature of this love was not at issue. Although in Miller's
later account of the tailor shop Heinrich does take a friend to bed in a
drunken moment, what interested Henry was not the sexual act—
which he took as a logical extension of the homoerotic, sexually
charged tailor shop—but Louise Miller's lack of sympathy for her husband's bonds with other men. Henry's fundamentally sympathetic nature, and his great love for his father, led him to view relations between
men with intense tenderness and nostalgic longing. Wives and mothers
were incidental to this world, either harpies who threatened it or sexual
beings who were to be enjoyed and then cast aside. Henry came to
value relations between men above all others, thus cementing his lifelong habit of surrounding himself with men—often failures—whom he
loved unreservedly.

While his three-and-a-half-year stint at the tailor shop exacerbated
Henry's obsession with his own manhood, it also raised painful questions about his own place in his extended—and often quite crazy—

family. This period had its climax on a winter morning in 1914, when Henry broached the subject of Pauline to his mother. He wanted to marry her, he said. Louise picked up a kitchen knife and went for him. One more word, she said, and she'd use it. Henry was sure that Louise was murderously enraged by an altogether inappropriate jealousy. He attributed her rage to the Nieting history of insanity, and in particular insanity brought on by incest (a great-aunt was said to have married her brother). His mother, he felt, was motivated by incestuous longings. It is hardly surprising that Henry later said he wrote whole volumes about incest in his head on his walks to and from the tailor shop. He maintained that incest was in the air, always. For him, Louise's act was indicative of incestuous violence and insanity, and Henry would never forget it, writing about it obsessively in his fiction. Often, to underscore the drama, he would have her wielding a cleaver instead of a knife.

3.

"An Obsessional Plant"

1915–1923

Twice in his early years, Miller later said, he wanted to die: once at the age of eight, and once when he was in his early twenties. In 1915, at twenty-three, he believed himself an utter failure. His life was chaos, the most telling symptoms of which were disappointments, failures, and debts. The tailor shop claimed his days, and he was still involved with Pauline; as he saw it, he was attached to her body "like a tick to a cow." He had vague yearnings to be a writer, encouraged by the examples of his father's customers Boardman Robinson and Frank Harris. Robinson was a popular illustrator who also had a newspaper column; Henry visited his studio one day to ask him how one went about writing. Robinson's response was that as far as he knew, you just wrote. Miller went right out and bought a little notebook, writing on the cover: "The Intellectual Tailor's Son."

But not much went into his little notebook. He later wrote his friend Lawrence Durrell that he wanted not so much to write but to "*be* a writer." He toyed with the idea of writing a play. During slack hours at the tailor shop, he wrote a long essay on Nietzsche's *Anti-Christ*. With his friend Stanley Borowski, who had recently returned from a stint in the Army at Fort Oglethorpe, he talked about writers far into the night; Jack London, Dostoevsky, and Herbert Spencer were their favorites. Elie Faure was another idol—Henry felt a link with him because his *History of Art* was translated by Walter Pach, another customer of Heinrich's.

But his idols proved daunting examples. Henry was full of ideas. He still wrote volumes—*tomes*—in his head, but he hadn't the vision or discipline to put pen to paper. When he did produce something it sounded to his ears as if he'd taken a course in a correspondence school, which disgusted him further. In 1916, he was frustrated in one of his earliest attempts to get published, when he sent a manuscript to Guido Bruno, the Greenwich Village character who published a series of chapbooks and short-lived journals with titles like *Bruno's Bohemia*, *Bruno's Weekly*, and *Bruno's Greenwich Village*. Bruno had a knack for wheedling sizable sums of money out of people—especially women— and he somehow got $200 out of Miller, without ever publishing his work. Miller wrote a friend that he had made a "partial recovery," but he was disillusioned nonetheless. In the same letter he complained the only thing worse than having an artistic temperament was thinking you had one. He was pretty sure he did—it explained a lot, at any rate— but he had no idea how to use it.

As Henry struggled with his writing, another woman appeared on the scene who quickly became a formidable rival to Pauline. In October 1915, during the Argonne Drive, Miller wrote not long after, he fell in love with a woman who had the "unpatriotic habit of playing the rhapsodies of Liszt." She was Beatrice Sylvas Wickens, an amateur pianist who was young and pretty, with dark hair and eyes, high cheekbones, a tiny Cupid's mouth, and dainty ways. Brought up by a maiden aunt after her mother's remarriage, Beatrice had been educated in a convent, an upbringing that had left her Puritanical, priggish, and tremendously conflicted about sex.

Beatrice's musical accomplishment was another result of her convent years, and her skill at the piano was what drew Henry. He had always loved music and musical women in particular; music recalled the days of his early childhood and his visits to his Tante Grussy in Glendale, Long Island. He commonly carried around a roll of sheet music; his repertoire, duly trotted out for relatives and Xerxes Society friends, included "The Orange Blossom Waltz," "The Midnight Fire Alarm," "The Chariot Race," and "The Burning of Rome," as well as the Czerny and Liszt his family so loved. His passion grew when Walter Pach gave him some tickets to performances at Carnegie Hall in 1914 and 1915 in exchange for Heinrich Miller's tailoring work; the performances convinced him to study music more seriously.

Miller appeared at Beatrice's house on 9th Street to take piano lessons in October 1915. For a time their relationship was that of teacher and student—she sent Henry home to practice Liszt études on the Millers' newly acquired clavier—but Henry was incapable of sitting next to a pretty woman on a piano bench without making some kind of move. Physical proximity alone called for action.

The battle royal, as Miller put it, was on. Beatrice defended her virtue with ferocity, through a long, drawn-out courtship. Miller found himself spending less and less time with Pauline, and instead passed his evenings shepherding Beatrice to vaudeville shows, concerts at Luna Park, and beer gardens on Long Island, engaging her in long petting sessions in her hallway afterward. For her part, Beatrice was overcome by guilt, though she was attracted to Miller. She behaved accordingly, playing the seductress one minute and the next defending her chastity with genuine outrage. (Henry believed her problems stemmed from incestuous encounters with her stepfather, of whom he was very jealous. But no evidence supports this.)

On one typical night early in their courtship, Beatrice draped herself across a radiator in her 9th Street apartment and let her silk dressing gown fall open to reveal her naked body; Miller made a grab for her, but she changed her mind and abruptly became hysterical, and he took his hat and coat and bolted. Changing her mind yet again, she caught up with him in the hallway, and, under the gas jet, he calmed her and soothed her until she responded again. But when he drew her hand suggestively downward, she became hysterical again, and he made a hasty exit. A few days later a letter arrived saying she never wanted to see him again. Miller grimly wrote to his friend Charles Keeler that "Miss Wickens and I are progressing rapidly toward mutual conquest."

However rapid, progress was difficult. On another night Beatrice showed Miller some acrobatics she had learned in the convent, all designed to circumvent intercourse. It was several weeks before she gave in, and even then she insisted that Miller penetrate her through her nightgown. She wanted to test him, Miller thought, as well as to avert a possible pregnancy.

Gradually Beatrice came to accept his advances more consistently and even made some of her own. Miller frequently visited her in the middle of the day, and she would sit him down and play sonatas for him. Often she would stop playing and go over to fondle him. But these episodes left her despondent; sex in broad daylight made her feel terribly guilty. And the better the sex, the worse she felt.

Things reached an impasse. In 1917 Henry left the tailor shop with no clear idea what he wanted to do next. Though most of his friends at least talked about enlisting, when America entered World War I he showed no interest in joining up. He was getting nowhere with his writing and making only gradual headway with Beatrice. Pauline, who knew she had been replaced, continued to send Henry little notes and to find ways to run into him—occasions that were always painful for both. But for his mother, he might never have got out of his rut. For while Henry might be content to drift, Louise was fed up. One morning in the summer of 1917 she passed her son's bedroom and saw him sleeping in as usual; enraged by his inability to get up morning after morning, she got a bucket of water from the kitchen and poured it over his head. He was to get up and get out, she told him—either enlist or get a job.

Henry recognized that his mother was right: that was partly why he hated her. She spoke for the part of him that knew he was a failure. But she couldn't realize how difficult it was for him to extricate himself from his indolent existence. Neither of the alternatives she suggested suited him. He was frightened of war and admitted it freely; his pacifism, inherited from his grandfather, also made it impossible for him to enlist. (He later wrote that he could kill a man in anger, but never in cold blood or on principle.) A job—at least what Louise Miller meant by the term—was unthinkable as well. The tailor shop had cooled him on any sort of traditional occupation; hereafter, with one significant exception, jobs were to be temporary, stopgap measures only.

Fortunately, in the spring of 1917 one of his father's customers came through again, and told Henry of work with the War Department in Washington, D.C. It was just a clerk's position, sorting mail, but Henry accepted it eagerly and raced down to Washington. During the month he was there, he wrote Beatrice fervent love letters, elaborating his plans for their future—for with absence his ardor returned. He described his success at landing a promise from *The Washington Post* that they would consider any story he submitted, taking the promise as an offer of a free-lance job. But the country was busy preparing for war, and it wasn't long before he received his notice to register for the draft.

Miller made up his mind quickly. He applied for a deferment on the grounds of impending marriage and the hardship of his parents (his father was ill). On the heels of this he returned to New York, putting his Washington ambitions on hold until he solved his draft problem, and moved into the Claridge Hotel in midtown Manhattan with Beatrice. There they devoted a week-long summit meeting to the question of marriage, Beatrice arguing for and Miller against. Though only marriage would guarantee his deferment, he had terrible visions of being locked in a loveless, conventional marriage like his parents'. During their stay at the Claridge, according to a story Miller related years later in his book *Moloch*, a man from Beatrice's past surfaced and proposed to her. When Miller got word of this he went out and found the man and returned with him to the Claridge, from which Beatrice was conveniently absent. An all-night marathon ensued—a "regular Alphonse and Gaston scene," Miller later wrote—in which Miller told the man everything about Beatrice, encouraging him to marry her. His scheme didn't work. The man didn't take the bait, and the next morning Miller married Beatrice at City Hall.

The wedding went forward, although Henry had to borrow the price of a shave and haircut and Beatrice had to pay the court fees. His Xerxes Society friends came through with a wedding banquet at the Café Bousquet, so the occasion was not unrelievedly gloomy. The couple managed a honeymoon at Niagara Falls, presumably with the help of their parents. Immediately afterward Henry resignedly returned to his father's shop, a married man with responsibilities.

The couple moved into a new apartment at 244 Sixth Avenue in the Park Slope section of Brooklyn, surrounded by wedding gifts from Miller's family. Everyone was delighted that he had at last settled down —everyone, that is, but Henry, who dug in his heels and refused to play the part of the hardworking newlywed. Beatrice gave him a meager $5 a week out of his wages, and he never saw any of her piano-teaching money. Newspapers and popular magazines were full of images of bonbon-eating, domineering wives with fat backsides, and Henry loved this slapstick buffoonery. He came to see Beatrice as a cartoon character, a caricature of a housewife. He even came to hate the Liszt music he had once so loved, solely because it was a favorite of his wife's.

Henry fell into the role of the henpecked husband, but he rebelled every chance he got. One night he decided to play what he thought was the conventional husband's part: driven to distraction by her complaints, he hit Beatrice in the face. Horrified, he watched as she dropped to the floor like a sack of sand. Conscience-stricken, he resolved to beg forgiveness. But when Beatrice came to, he was appalled to see nothing but trust in her eyes. She said not a word about it, and Henry concluded that she liked it. But he never did it again.

Conjugal life became even more difficult when Beatrice's mother, complete with poodle, appeared on the scene, announcing that she had come to stay. Miller liked her right away; she was flashy, jovial, and very understanding—which meant she took his side of things. While her mother hummed and whistled her way through the household chores, Beatrice seethed. To get rid of her, the couple had to promise to visit her in Delaware, where she lived with Beatrice's stepfather. Miller feigned indifference about the prospect, just to be difficult, but he was eager for a vacation.

That trip, in the summer of 1918, made everything worse. It began auspiciously. His mother-in-law's home was as cozy as a doll's house and the Millers lay in bed in the mornings with the sun streaming in, waited on like pashas. Beatrice found sex more enjoyable; it was as if she'd received absolution from her mother's presence. But before long it became evident that Beatrice's mother had eyes for her son-in-law. She would call to Henry from the bathtub asking for a towel, for instance. Eventually Henry succumbed—he couldn't resist older women —and the two enjoyed a mild dalliance. Neither seems to have felt they were doing anything wrong.

Seemingly overnight, Miller later wrote, Beatrice became suspicious. She insisted that they leave, but Henry refused. A scene ensued, in which Beatrice said nothing about her suspicions of Henry but confessed her own insecurities and her fears that she would turn out like her easygoing mother. She made him agree that her mother was a bad example, an immoral woman. The scene ended with the two rolling under the table locked in an embrace, Beatrice's eyes swollen and red.

Back at Sixth Avenue, Beatrice learned she was pregnant. The news was unwelcome, both because of the precarious state of their finances and the early tensions of their marriage. At Miller's urging, Beatrice consulted her cousin Alice about ways to abort the pregnancy, and Alice came over one evening with some black pills and advice about mustard baths. It was a sweltering summer night and the three sipped beer to cool off. Before long Alice was drunk and on Henry's lap; by the time she passed out Beatrice was ready to kill her. She didn't take the pills, and made Henry swear never to mention an abortion in front of her again.

After the birth of their daughter—whom they called Barbara Sylvas—on September 30, 1919, the fights only escalated. Beatrice told Miller she knew about his relationship with her mother. "How much do you know?" he asked, forced into a corner, and then, "How much can you stand?" He confessed everything, and they made it up again, but a new dimension of cruelty had entered their marriage. Miller seemed bent on replicating his parents' bad marriage, but with one critical difference: he would stand up to his shrewish wife, where Heinrich Miller did not. He saw Beatrice as another Louise, determined to domesticate him, rein him in. After she bore a child she became even more detestable to him; he had an irrational but passionate dislike for any woman with a young child. He responded to her motherhood by becoming a bullying tyrant, given to black rages like Louise's. He was often overcome by remorse at his behavior, when he remembered the Beatrice he'd pursued so avidly, but these crises of conscience only left him more conflicted.

Something about Beatrice, Miller later wrote, inspired in him the most contemptible conduct. It wasn't long before other women caught his eye. Though he seldom took them to bed, he made up all kinds of excuses to linger away from home. When he did appear at the apartment he usually had a friend like Stanley or Emil Conason in tow; both he and Beatrice made it a point to be alone together as infrequently as possible. The friend inevitably offended Beatrice somehow, and she responded by serving her husband and his guest with clear contempt, which Henry found humiliating. In turn, he made certain that the talk was always sexual in nature, the better to embarrass his wife.

Outwardly, Miller wasn't much of a father either. The atmosphere of silent rage that dominated the household made shows of affection nearly impossible. But privately he adored his daughter: the toddler was bright and pretty and had a loving nature. He often played "horsey" with her, fielding her childish inquiries about why her parents had to fight all the time. Her weekly bath, after which she was dried with great fanfare on the zinc kitchen table, became the subject of a snapshot he carried with him for years. The few moments of happiness he and Beatrice shared were spent when they watched the child together. More and more often, Barbara was the only thing they did share.

Like the fishwife Miller believed her to be, Beatrice nagged her husband almost constantly now. Not only was he unfaithful (so she believed), but he couldn't even support his wife and child. The tailor shop had virtually closed its doors, and Miller had stopped working there for good in 1920. He moved from job to job aimlessly. In between, he set out each day to look for work optimistically but ended up, as often as not, at the public library. He claimed later that he never looked at the want ads once in those years. For a while, he worked at the Bureau of Economic Research, where he learned a Belgian indexing system that he found bizarre. Another stint, assembling a mail-order catalogue for a company called Charles Williams, Inc., ended when the boss caught him reading on the job.

Time and again he was forced to the conclusion that he must be an artist of some sort. But the "running battle" that was his marriage, he later wrote, had soured him on the piano after a year or two. As for the visual arts, he believed himself hopelessly untalented; his friend Emil Schnellock had become an advertising illustrator, and Miller felt he could never draw realistically as Emil did. That left writing. But he still had no vision, no inspiration, nothing to say.

Characteristically, he set out to force the muse. He would simply write, he decided, and inspiration would follow. Or, through sheer perseverance, he would write enough so that something of worth could be fashioned from it. If need be, he would write to order; in a letter to Emil Schnellock in 1923 he reasoned that "all great men write to order," citing as examples Caesar, Balzac, Wells, Shaw, Strindberg, Barrie, "and the one-and-only Dostoevski."

All the prose Miller produced in his earliest years as a writer is baroque, studded with words like "opalescent," "autochthonous," "ichor," "caparisoned," and "lucubrations." He was given to sentences like the following, which appeared in a description of the Bowery Savings Bank in a letter to Schnellock in 1923: "The eye cannot take in all the manifold beauties of ornament that surge in and beat against the retina." Viewing a scene with an eye toward writing about it, he often was overcome by sensation, and he tried to produce the same sensual effect by describing his experience rather than evoking it in the reader. He wallowed in sensation just as he did in words.

For the time being, he concentrated his efforts on commercial outlets, thinking the public would find his a fresh new voice. A five-cent "pulp" magazine called *The Black Cat: Clever Short Stories* attracted his attention in 1919, when the editor announced the revival of the three-year-old Black Cat Club. Subscribers would have the opportunity to critique any story appearing in the magazine, which would enable would-be masters of "the writing game" to hone their technique by studying the technique of others. The Club, wrote the editors, "provides fresh inspiration every month and puts a check upon lagging interest and moral lassitude."

The pragmatism of this plan appealed to Miller, who proudly viewed himself as a self-taught individual, and he duly subscribed. When the February issue arrived (complete with a "Beautiful Rose Gold Good Luck Black Cat Club Emblem"), he studied the lead story, which was Carl Clausen's "The Unbidden Guest." His response was, he hoped, professional. While he could find no philosophical depth in the story, nevertheless "there is a pleasant feeling steals o'er one on reading it which comes with the knowledge that the author really understood the materials and subject matter he used." He mailed off his few hundred words and waited anxiously for a reply.

He learned in May that his "essay" had been accepted, and he received a check for $4.86—a penny a word. He was elated, for the check seemed symbolic: he was a working author. His first impulse was not to cash the talismanic check, but he had too much of his parents in him for that. Instead, he plunged back into what he now saw as his craft, turning out four more critiques in the next five months, for which he received a total of $9.50.

Miller's contributions to *The Black Cat* are, predictably, juvenile and limp. But they reveal aspects of his decidedly quirky personality and literary tastes. One story excited his interest because it was risqué, about a man and a woman forced to share a Pullman bed. The "hook" was the revelation at the end that the pair were husband and wife. The story's cartoonish character appealed to Miller's love of buffoonery, which for him was always related to a certain meanness. In his critique Miller declared that he "fairly held [his] breath" while reading it; he wrote that jealous women, like the heroine, "derive pleasure in a little show of cruelty, especially toward those whom they love." In another critique he wrote that it took only three days of marriage to open a man's eyes, quoting an "old philosopher" to the effect that women always insist on stepping down from the pedestal upon which men have placed them. Generally, he admired whatever seemed to him modern and rejected anything that was not.

Not that he had much use for such contemporary writers as Eliot, Pound, Fitzgerald, or Hemingway, all of whom were in the early stages of their careers. His heroes remained the Europeans, philosophers included. Nietzsche, Tolstoy, Gorky, Darwin, Spencer, Anatole France, Schopenhauer, Mann, and Huxley were the writers Miller praised. He read Freud and Havelock Ellis, as well as Otto Weininger, a psychologist whose systems of gender dualisms greatly interested him. His new favorite was the Norwegian writer Knut Hamsun, the author of *Hunger* and *Victoria*. Hamsun's impressionistic, slightly mystical tales of obsessive grand passions touched a nerve in Miller, recalling his frustrated love for Cora Seward; his heroes are wrongheaded iconoclasts, not unlike Miller himself. He admired Hamsun's language as well, for Hamsun was a precursor of the modernists and was given to adding such surrealistic elements as bleeding pianos to his narratives.

For Miller, at thirty, the world was full of so much absurdity that bleeding pianos seemed to fit easily into his daily experience. The world, with all its hypocrisy, made no sense to him. Innately anarchic, he strived for a kind of literary anarchy. But his models were nineteenth-century Europeans, and the effects he strived for could not be conveyed in nineteenth-century linear narratives. He tried to cram impossible, surrealistic descriptions and chaotic scenes into traditional realistic plots—and the results were disastrous.

Much of this is evident in the letters Miller wrote to his friends in his early thirties; in them he tried out techniques, pastiches, and dramatic scenes. He had begun the voluminous correspondence that he would maintain all his life, writing several twenty- and thirty-page letters in one day. One of his favorite correspondents was Emil Schnellock; he was a frequent visitor to Emil's 55th Street studio in Manhattan, where the two held heated discussions about art and art criticism. Miller's letters to Emil contain his most important literary efforts from these early years, perhaps because he was not "writing to order" as he did in the pieces he hoped to place in magazines and newspapers.

Except for *The Black Cat*—which killed the readers' comment feature at the end of 1919—Miller had little luck getting published in these years. Even when he tried to tailor his writing to a particular audience, he saw his work rejected; he would never be good at taking the public's pulse. He wasn't actually producing very much, for that matter—except for his massive letters. For one thing, he didn't have peace in which to write, with a baby underfoot and Beatrice hounding him to get work. And, for another, it was abundantly clear even to him that he had to get some kind of job. He put aside his scribblings and set out, once again, to knock on doors and stand in lines.

He was willing to take anything. In fact, he reasoned, the lower, the more menial, the better. If Beatrice wanted a wage slave, he would give her the real article. In early 1920, with something approaching defiance, he applied for a humble job indeed: that of a Western Union messenger. His contempt was evident to the employment manager at the company's offices in the Flatiron Building; Miller later wrote that he claimed a Ph.D. from Columbia University on his application. At any rate, he was refused the job.

Beatrice took the news with "the usual leer and sneer," Miller wrote, implying that she knew his application was just a gesture. But, as the day wore on, the rejection festered. He couldn't understand how a seemingly respectable, middle-class man like himself could be

turned down when everyone knew Western Union hired and fired the dregs of humanity daily. *Boys* got jobs at Western Union. He forgot that he had applied, as Beatrice suspected, as a gesture, and became obsessed with his puzzling rejection.

He handled the situation at first as if he were placating his mother, in a spirit of mingled defiance and humility. The next morning he shaved, put on his best clothes—a suit of Bedford whipcord—and presented himself at Western Union's main office on Park Place, demanding to see the president. When he was told the president wasn't available, he meekly accepted the offer of an audience with the secretary to the vice president.

The situation clearly called for Miller's best shot, and he was ready. He pulled off a verbal performance that rivaled those of his boyhood, pointing out the grave injustice of a system that would deny him a job while it rewarded incompetence. Quickly picking up that his listener was less interested in injustice than incompetence, Miller pointed out that the system was inefficient as well, that hiring mere boys when men like him sought work made little sense. This struck a nerve, for the company was, in fact, worried about its work force; the messengers were the "human factor" in this newly technologized organization, and the human factor was breaking down. The messengers were unreliable, and hiring practices *were* at fault. It appeared that Miller had been turned down by a man who didn't even have the authority to hire: Sam Sattenstein, who was only a dispatcher.

The secretary reached for the telephone and asked for the general manager, Mr. Kaplan, who arrived immediately. After much discussion they reached agreement: this articulate (and perceptive) young man had a point. In fact, he was just the person they sought: the employment manager needed to be replaced, and the "college-educated" Miller was the man for the job. They would start him right away, at a salary of $240 a month, though they would first send him on the streets to learn the business. And once in a while, Kaplan added, Miller might visit him in the evenings and let him know what he saw in the different offices, so that he could inform his boss, Mr. Willever.

This was beyond anything Miller had hoped for. The salary was more than respectable, and he immediately interpreted Kaplan's remarks about his apprenticeship to mean he was to be a company spy. Though the ethics initially bothered him—he still had the sense of fair play and loyalty he'd learned from the streets—his cynicism won out. The irony of the situation appealed to him: refused a job as a messen-

ger by a dastardly hiring agent, he'd fast-talked his way into a job spying on the same agent and then, after a few weeks, replacing the employment manager and becoming the agent's boss. (In fact, Miller was one of many employment managers, though he would always present it otherwise.)

Within a few months, as Miller later wrote in *Tropic of Capricorn* about the legendary "Cosmodemonic Telegraph Company," he was ensconced in a new employment office at 33 Park Place, "hiring and firing like a demon." For the first time in his life he was in a position of authority, and he seized the initiative with characteristic energy. He ruled over his empire like an Eastern potentate, assembling a court of faithful hangers-on and old friends. He retained Sam Sattenstein at the switchboard, for Sam—the Hymie of *Tropic of Capricorn*—proved to be doggedly loyal. He hired as his assistant his old friend Joe O'Regan, a cynic given to the raunchy humor Miller was beginning to affect. He decided he needed a secretary as well, and when Joe spotted a young and pretty woman reading a Russian novel in the file room, Miller hired her. Her name was Muriel Maurer, and it wasn't long before Miller developed a crush on her. (She would later, quite coincidentally, marry the critic Malcolm Cowley.)

In reality, Miller's empire was humble to the point of dinginess. On the top floor of the building was the wardrobe storage room, where the messengers' uniforms were kept; on the second floor was a tailor shop where the head tailor, who oversaw the making of uniforms, kept an eye open for any goings-on, which he promptly reported to Willever. The back of the first floor was a dressing room lined with cubicles for the messengers to change in. By the rear door was a zinc-covered table where the messengers packed their civilian clothes before exiting with the bundles under their arms. (Sending the messengers out with their own clothes proved to be a bad idea, for those who tired of their job simply walked off and kept their uniforms.)

The first-floor front was Miller's domain. It was permeated by a smell of camphor and Lysol emanating from the dressing room and the third-floor storehouse. A railing separated the applicants from the office proper, where Henry, Joe, and Muriel had their desks. The entire office was visible from the street; passers-by looking through the plate-glass window saw a cardboard cutout of a messenger in full dress.

From the start, Miller realized that his job was impossible. When he arrived in the morning—he was always late—the office would be jammed with applicants. Before he could take his hat off he had to

make a dozen phone calls, and he was on one of his three desk phones all day. Sam worked the switchboard, shuffling waybills (messengers who had been loaned from one office to another). He and Miller worked fiercely to fill vacancies, but every day they had to begin all over again. Western Union had a monumental turnover problem; the employment office had to hire ten thousand messengers—or "mutts," as management called them—in a year to maintain a working force of a thousand. When Miller first began he managed to reduce turnover to almost 50 percent—a prodigious feat—but then management slashed wages and he could barely find any messengers at all.

The hiring and firing undid him completely. The array of applicants was staggering: men at the end of their rope, some fallen from high stations and others society's rejects. Every one of them had a story to tell, and Miller was a good listener. Letters poured in: fathers writing about wayward sons, people reporting on messengers' behavior, irate ex-employees, and, above all, eager applicants. One typical letter from a Nathan Stillman began: "Being desirous of becoming connected with a firm that directly or indirectly is in some way associated with that great force, electricity, I am taking this opportunity. . . ." Stillman's language struck Miller, and he saved the letter. He also kept one from a William J. Grimmond, who had apparently been fired. Grimmond accused Miller and Joe O'Regan—whom he called Miller's man Friday—of being "pro-German" and employing the same horrible tactics the Germans had used on Belgian children in the war.

Miller quickly learned to be ruthless. The job would have made any man cynical; it made Miller hard-boiled. As he later told Lawrence Durrell, he was an oversensitive young man—and oversensitive people, he thought, grew the toughest hides. Being in authority had something to do with his seeming personality change. Miller had been an autocrat from his earliest days, when he strutted around the neighborhood proclaiming the world was flat. Now, in his little fiefdom, he could exercise that impulse, surrounding himself with friends he controlled —a pattern that would persist in his life. Around this time Miller developed the habit of speaking in a guttural sound that emanated from the back of his throat; he had acquired it after hearing it used in vaudeville skits at the burlesque. It suited his new image. With the Western Union job, he compartmentalized his entire existence: around his buddies and certain women he remained tender-hearted and sentimental, while around the office—and with people in general—he was cold-blooded and uncaring. He was changeable and moody: one morning he would lend a messenger money, and that evening he might fire him. Applicants he might once have found touching he now ridiculed. He opened a folder he called "Humorous File," in which he saved, for example, a letter from a deaf applicant.

The job had great potential for corruption, and Miller took to this avidly; since the Driggs Avenue days, when he had looked on as the older boys ran street gangs, he had longed to rule over his own turf. At Western Union, the rules of the street applied. Favors were bartered, the weak were shaken down, bullies ruled. Every day he was given car fare for the messengers—not a small amount—which he pocketed for his own lunch money, doling some out only to "repeaters," steady workers who knew about the fund's existence. When the company began hiring female messengers, he and Joe—and their other cronies, Sam Ramos and a flunkey named Blackie—attempted to steer them to the zinc table in the back room. Miller continued his active pursuit of Muriel, even though she had taken up with his friend Emil Schnellock; she had a pretty sister, Ethel, who welcomed his advances a little more readily. The pace of his life was dizzying.

Back in Brooklyn, Beatrice watched her husband's transformation with distress. Miller was a man of some stature now, she had to admit. But he was even less attentive to her and their daughter, and he was often bluntly abusive. In response, Beatrice grew even colder. Miller was in the habit of bringing home for dinner various friends or messengers he found interesting, like the Hindu Haridas Mazumdar, with whom he had become close. Describing one such evening with Haridas, Miller later wrote that in the middle of their conversation (which was about sex) he hoped to catch Beatrice in the kitchen and tell her that he knew he was a wretch and that he wanted to stop hurting her, but that it was her coldness that made him behave so badly. He couldn't tell her, though; communications between them had just about broken down.

Matters did not improve when the Millers took in a boarder, Harolde Ross, a musician from Minnesota who had come to study at Juilliard. He immediately made a hit with Beatrice; he was refined, considerate—everything Henry was not. Henry was equally charmed, for Harolde had literary tastes as well; he tried to win Henry over to the poet Carl Sandburg. Harolde's presence at first lessened the tension in the apartment. But gradually Henry came to see that there was a mutual affection between Harolde and Beatrice. According to Miller, another Alphonse and Gaston situation ensued, with Henry hinting that Beatrice could be Harolde's for the asking. Harolde was insulted. Taking another man's wife away was not his idea of gentlemanly behavior. He boarded the train for Minnesota, leaving behind a lovestruck Beatrice.

Miller was at his wit's end. He still cared about Beatrice, after a fashion; the phrase "the mother of his child" could bring him to tears. But her nagging and her reticence about sexuality—she still required lavish displays of affection before sexual surrender and suffered from remorse after the act—compounded the confusion created by his crazy and consuming job. His job, his inability to become a writer—he blamed everything on Beatrice. He came to see her as the embodiment of American womanhood, complaining in a letter to Schnellock about "the whole American tribe of women with their false virginity, their false love, their dirty . . . masturbating tricks." His contempt seemed limitless. He loathed "that foul son-of-a-bitch who bore my child," he claimed—though his real feelings were more complex. He was deeply sentimental about the trappings of marriage and being a father, but the reality of Beatrice and Barbara—who seemed like millstones around his neck, preventing him from plunging full-tilt into the corrupt new world his Western Union job had opened up—made him desperately unhappy.

Beatrice was no less miserable. Miller was impossible, and she missed Harolde, with whom she had begun to correspond. She felt she had to make a move, any move, to get out of the rut her marriage had become. In the fall of 1921 she thought of her old maiden aunt, the one who had raised her, and decided to join her in Rochester, New York, taking Barbara with her. Miller made no protest.

He moved in with Joe O'Regan in Manhattan, determined to live the bachelor life to the fullest. Muriel had moved on to a job buying for a department store, and Miller and Joe had found a replacement for her in a pretty black woman named Camilla Fedrant (the mulatto Valeska of *Tropic of Capricorn*). She liked Miller in turn, and was a frequent visitor to Joe's apartment; she also took the men on exciting trips to Harlem nightclubs like Small's. And there seemed to be an unlimited supply of young women in Western Union's ranks. For a few weeks Miller basked in his new freedom.

But he kept thinking of Beatrice, whom he'd driven away with his callous disregard. Miller's nature, for all its crassness, was strangely but genuinely chivalric in many ways, and if he harmed a woman he felt obligated to her. Indeed, if he treated anyone shabbily he was apt to romanticize his actions and approach the person with new tenderness. Beatrice was no exception. When a letter arrived from her ten days after her departure, Miller fell into a fit of affection and remorse. He telegraphed her money and wrote her a ten-page special delivery letter. There followed a flood of mail back and forth; Miller sent flowers and candy and small gifts for Barbara.

Beatrice softened, and allowed Miller to come to Rochester for a three-day visit. Their reunion was passionate, the sex the best ever. The prospects for the marriage looked good when Miller boarded the train to return to New York. He was delighted to find that Beatrice had tucked a copy of Knut Hamsun's *Victoria* in his bag; the great, impossible love that book described had always moved him.

But by the time he reached the city, he had become more intrigued with Hamsun's portrayal of his hero's need to break from societal restraints than by the hero's love for Victoria. The reconciliation with Beatrice meant that she would no doubt return to Brooklyn and expect him to set up house with her again. That he couldn't bear; like Hamsun's hero, Miller felt he had to break free. He stifled all his new affections and composed a letter to Beatrice, addressing her as Victoria, explaining his plight: "I must run free, mad-hearted, bellowing with pain and ecstasy, charging with lowered horns, ripping up the barricades that hem me in and stifle me. I must have room to expand."

But Miller never mailed the letter—he didn't have the courage for outright rebellion yet—and Beatrice returned after two months, just as he'd feared. Soon she was pregnant again. Horrified at being hemmed in still more tightly, Miller borrowed $100 from Camilla Fedrant so Beatrice could have an abortion; Camilla even nursed her afterward. From then on Miller insisted on using condoms, but even with this precaution Beatrice was quickly pregnant again. This time—in 1923— Miller let Beatrice arrange the abortion herself. He, after all, had far more on his mind—he was now a man of letters, the author of a book.

The book Miller had written was called *Clipped Wings;* he had written it on a three-week vacation from Western Union in March 1922, largely at Schnellock's studio. The title referred to the wings on the Western Union logo, and the book was a portrait of twelve messengers, angels whose wings had been clipped. Miller's inspiration was Dreiser's *Twelve Men;* like Dreiser's, his book would be non-fiction, but with fictional embellishments and an artful arrangement. He began the work in response to a remark of Willever's that enraged him—that it was a shame Horatio Alger never wrote a book about messengers.

Probably no one ever set out to "become" a writer more methodically. Miller resolved to write at least 5,000 words a day and stuck to it, sometimes writing an extra thousand or two, but never less. As he wrote Schnellock on March 20, "The first day of being a writer has nearly broken my back." He began by writing about a "Jew bastard" who used to be a messenger and "practised the gentle art of Non-Resistance." This sent him off in search of some lines of poetry, with the result that eight volumes of poetry, including Lindsay, Masters, Pound, and Maxwell Bodenheim, were stacked on his desk at the end of his first day. (He found his lines in a poem by Irwin Granich called "The East Side.")

If Miller's description of his first day as a writer is any indication, the manuscript he produced must have been fully as dreadful as he later claimed. Only fragments of *Clipped Wings* survive, but these indicate that the book was an extended essay in pure venom, anti-Semitism, racism, and generalized misanthropy. One portrait, of a man Miller calls "The Mental Moron," urges "more children of the better sort and fewer of the worse variety"; it closes with the famous quotation from Nietzsche to the effect that the weak and defective, with our help, must go to the wall.

Miller was aware of the book's defects—the flatness of his characters, the contrived nature of his scenes—but that didn't prevent him from trying to publish it. When Macmillan rejected it, however, he was too disheartened to submit it elsewhere. He must have recognized, too, that the book's anti-Semitism would make it unpalatable. Privately he thought that the world was simply not ready for his revolutionary proposals. He was fond of the book, regardless of its lack of literary quality, and he reworked pieces of it in some of his later work.

For example, Miller took a profile of Tawde, a Hindu messenger, and added to it some ruminations on the Indian author Rabindranath Tagore. He sent this to W. E. B. DuBois, a man he had listened to and admired during his Labor Temple days; it appeared in DuBois's *The Crisis*, the official monthly of the NAACP, in 1924 as "Black and White." He inserted other bits in *Tropic of Capricorn*; still others reappear in his early, unpublished novels. Almost uniformly, these portraits of messengers are vaguely repellent, unpleasant in ways that can't be explained by the subjects' checkered backgrounds or extreme poverty.

The truth was that their creator was filled with bile. He was disgusted by the world, contemptuous of its creatures, and it is evident in every descriptive phrase.

The book was a purging, but it merely washed away one layer of filth. At the very core of his being Miller had discovered a gigantic rage, and the fact that he had willed forth a book did little to still it. To his great frustration he realized that "becoming a writer"—like physical culture, like his Western trip, like marriage—had wrought no great change in his life. At thirty-one he was a Western Union company man, a failure as a husband and father, chronically broke, and now he could describe himself as a bad writer as well. Fifteen years later, in *Tropic of Capricorn*, he wrote that when he took stock of himself this time he found he had never done what he wanted, and that out of this "there grew up inside me this creation which was nothing but an obsessional plant, a sort of coral growth, which was expropriating everything, including life itself." Messengers, women, his wife and child, his friends, his long walks through Brooklyn—all nourished this growth, creating the "obsessional plant" inside Miller, who, obsessed in turn with his own creative growth, found he could barely create at all.

4.

Mona

1923–1924

Miller worked at Western Union for almost five years, from 1920 to the end of 1924. It was, as he saw it, one of the most absurd jobs imaginable. He was trafficking in human flesh, treating human beings like automatons, taking fingerprints, filing applicant data—and all, he later wrote, "so that the American people may enjoy the fastest form of communication known to man, so that they may sell their wares more quickly, so that the moment you drop dead in the street may be apprised immediately . . . unless the messenger to whom the telegram is entrusted decides to throw up the job and throw the whole batch of telegrams in the garbage can." It was a vast technological enterprise entirely dependent on an extraordinarily undependable work force, with men like Miller, as employment managers, at the helm of the operation. What galled him especially was the hypocritical Horatio Alger atmosphere of the company (which shuttled him about, from Park Place to offices on lower Broadway and on Fulton Street in Brooklyn). In every branch office of Western Union hung a prominent photograph of Andrew Carnegie, bearing the ostensibly inspiring inscription: "To our messenger boys of which I was one."

On a typical day the alarm woke him at 7:00 a.m. and he would lie in bed unable to sleep for an hour, the day ahead too awful to contemplate. He dressed himself in a torn shirt—there wasn't time to shave —ate a hasty breakfast, and borrowed a nickel from Beatrice for car fare. If he was in a bad mood he swindled the money from the newsdealer at the subway instead. At the office, where he always arrived out of breath, he found the switchboard lit up, Sam sharpening his pencils between calls, Carey the detective standing at his side to let him know which applicants had applied before under different names. Half of the men swarming in the room would have to be turned away:

some because they were over forty-five (the age limit for messengers), others for physical ailments, and others because Emil Conason, a friend of Miller's studying to be a doctor, judged them too unbalanced to work. After a rushed lunch, Miller returned to step up the pace still faster, for often Willever issued directives to hire more messengers. In anticipation of the never-ending turnover, Miller's men advertised in every paper in New York and for twenty miles outside it and visited schools, charity agencies, and YMCAs, all in search of applicants. (Miller himself had once been billed to speak before a school for "backward" boys to scare up applicants, but he had been too frightened of speaking in public to show up.) Miller described the job as "Chaos! A howling chaos!"

"I was saturated with humanity, with experiences of one kind or another," he wrote later. Ten years of this, he felt, and he would be stark mad. At night he walked the streets with his friend Carey, the Western Union detective, whom he later described as a "bosom friend and incidentally a sort of psychopomp." They traversed the city, with Carey discoursing about all manner of crimes and steering him to the seamiest areas—to the homes of errant messengers, to pool rooms, assorted flops and dives, prisons, asylums, and boys' reformatories. Miller, overwhelmed, imagined himself as Jesus Christ, had Jesus been taken down from the cross and not permitted to die in the flesh. Overcome by the suffering he saw, he suffered himself for the sins committed by others, as he saw it, but he could not transcend this world.

Miller's life had always been touched by violence, but in these years the violence escalated. He became more fascinated than ever by perversion, insanity, crime—or, more precisely, vice. Around 1923 he became friends with a young architect named Sleaco (his first name was Herbert, but Henry never called him that), who was always up to something, full of talk about women and horses. With his fellow architects Blount and Dredge—Miller found the names sinister—Sleaco often showed up at the Sixth Avenue apartment with a bottle of bootleg whiskey. All three drank heavily, and Miller, who previously drank only the sherry Beatrice grudgingly allowed him, joined in.

Prohibition was on, and Miller found the public's routine flouting of the law exciting. Small offenses thrilled him: running out on a restaurant check, avoiding a hotel bill by sneaking out in the middle of the night, arranging abortions for the girlfriends of his Western Union cronies. An abortion, in fact, was the ultimate Henry Miller "crime":

after all, it involved sleazy back rooms, danger, complicated arrangements, and of course sex. Moreover, the law against abortion was flouted as commonly as—if less openly than—Prohibition, and Miller enjoyed widespread defiance of the law with an almost erotic intensity. Just as he had loved the mob spirit and lawlessness that he saw in the Williamsburg streets during the days of the Spanish-American War, he loved the untapped violence of the crowd in New York City. "Running amok" was a favorite phrase of his, and in these years he was doing more than his share of it.

Adultery had become almost routine for him. Camilla Fedrant was a favorite partner, for sleeping with a black woman was doubly taboo. She even inspired Henry to write his first poem, an ode to the Metropolitan Life Insurance Building (he had seen it at dusk, walking with Stanley on the newly named Metropolitan Avenue in the old neighborhood, and was struck, given the coincidence of the name "Metropolitan," by how the imaginary boundaries of his world had changed). A waitress in a Greek restaurant, Gladys Miller, charmed him with her great legs and knowledge of Greek and Latin. In 1923 he almost left Beatrice for her; writing a goodbye note and leaving it on the kitchen table, he quickly lost heart and retrieved it before Beatrice found and read it. He was put off by Gladys's greasy hands and her pitiful boardinghouse existence.

In spite of the big writing desk he had installed in the Sixth Avenue apartment, surrounding it with a semicircle of chairs, Miller was getting less writing done than ever. As he loafed about in the streets of Manhattan—a favorite haunt was the theater district—he told himself that he either had to go home immediately and write his book or else run away and start a new life. Both prospects terrified him; he felt he had too much to say in his book and had no idea how to begin. Even if he could write, he felt, nobody would take his book, and even if he could begin over again it wouldn't be any use, because he was temperamentally unfit for work. He was *different*, he concluded.

Others sensed it too. Miller noted later that it always amazed him how agitated people could become just listening to him. He could hold some men, whatever their background, spellbound with his talk. But in other people he sensed an instinctive distrust, an uneasiness. They were put off by the extravagance of his talk, his allusions to things taboo, the ease with which words came to his lips; as Miller wrote, "I could never get myself quite *au point* with the individual I was talking to."

Not that he lacked for friends. During his Western Union period, he wrote in *Tropic of Capricorn,* "they seemed to spring up around me like mushrooms." Emil Conason met Miller when he approached Western Union hoping to conduct intelligence tests on the messengers; Emil, and later his wife, Cele, became very close to Henry. Bill Dewar was a steady companion as well, whom Miller admired because he hailed from the other side of Williamsburg, where boys talked tough and spat in the streets, and as a man he endeared himself to Miller with his respect for learning, his passion for the burlesque and the dance hall, and his rejection of "feminine" values. Dewar openly derided Beatrice, urging Henry to leave her and the child without looking back.

Dewar and O'Regan got along well enough with Miller's Western Union friends—Steve Ramos and Carey, for example—but at Sam Sattenstein and Emil Conason they drew the line. In fact, few of Miller's friends got along; Stanley Borowski and Emil Schnellock refused to see him in company of any of the others—or with each other. Miller's life was a juggling affair. Sometimes, with the help of liquor, he could bring all his friends together for a rollicking dinner at Childs' or at Joe's Restaurant on 49th Street. More often, though, he had to listen to Schnellock's or Stanley's tirades against new rivals for his attention.

Part of what divided the ranks was anti-Semitism. Miller's thirties were marked by a sustained obsession with Jewishness—a subject that brought him great distress. At one extreme, he idealized Jews, seeing them as exotic and regarding Jewish women as erotic; he also admitted that many great scientists, authors, and leaders had been Jews. However, that was a large part of what galled him. He believed that Jews rightfully thought themselves superior, and that they therefore refused to assimilate, a refusal that was understandable to him but that he still thought reprehensible. In this respect his dislike for Jews was rooted in envy.

This pervasive resentment was ingrained still more deeply when Miller, in his early thirties, revisited his old Williamsburg neighborhood with Stanley Borowski. There he saw Sauer's leather shop and McKinney's veterinary office replaced by kosher delicatessens; black-garbed men and bewigged women hurried along the streets. He found the streets dirty, and concluded that the East European Jews who had transformed his neighborhood liked dirt, just as surely—so he later wrote—as the Germans were tidy, the Irish poor, and the Catholics ignorant. New York belonged to the Jews, he charged.

Miller's romanticism about Williamsburg was so intense that he needed a scapegoat to explain its deterioration. Just as he blamed his parents—and particularly his mother—for taking him away from the old neighborhood, so he now blamed the Jews who had moved in after less recent immigrant groups like his parents' had left. His was a violent distaste that in a milder man might have festered as a largely subterranean prejudice. But the man who saw himself as "Henry Miller to the nth" consciously set out, in his early thirties, to make anti-Semitism an entire system of thought, a virtual philosophy. He built a whole library around it, taking as his bibles Nietzsche, Herbert Spencer, and Spengler (all of whom he distorted) and assiduously devouring works like Hilaire Belloc's *The Jews.* He did "field work" in the cafés on the Lower East Side and held long philosophical discussions on the subject with Dewar, O'Regan, and Emil Schnellock and his brother Ned, as well as with Jewish friends like Conason and Sattenstein.

Miller afterwards claimed that he had more Jewish friends than Gentile, and, though he exaggerated slightly in describing it, his New York *was* largely Jewish. Later, when he put his anti-Semitic thoughts on paper, he wrote to his French publisher that he was simply calling it as he saw it, writing as a man in the street who was part of the melting pot. This, of course, was a specious rationalization, as illogical and dishonest as all racism is.

In another leap of logic, he said that his "honesty" led many to believe him a "renegade Jew." At the height of his anti-Semitism, Miller seized on the notion that he himself was Jewish. Friends like Stanley and Emil Conason thought his high cheekbones and narrowed eyes indicated an Asian—and thus possibly Jewish—background. "How do I know what happened to my ancestors back in the days of the great plagues, in the days of migrations, etc., etc.? One little drop of Jewish blood outweighs a ton of so-called Gentile blood," Miller wrote a friend, quite seriously. He believed he possessed traits he saw as typically Jewish: his bookishness, his love for extended discussion, his very specialness. Just as he once thought he ought to have been born on December 25, and just as he thought he must have an artistic temperament, so too did he decide that he ought to have been Jewish. No matter that he would then be part of a group he affected to despise. In fact, his desire to be Jewish reflected his deep ambivalence about Jews. They, like him, were *different.* If he could not be one of them, their "difference" made them despicable; as a would-be Jew, on the other hand, he saw their "difference" as a source of great romanticism.

All these conflicts would come to a head when Miller met the great obsessional love of his life, a woman who was, inevitably, Jewish.

By the summer of 1923 Henry was spending almost no time at home. Not that Beatrice minded. She just didn't want to know the details, and if Henry told her he was working until the small hours of the morning, she was resigned enough to believe it. She occupied herself with the piano, Barbara, and the succession of boarders the Millers took in to augment Henry's income. When Henry made an appearance, the air was thick with hostility. He commandeered the kitchen, sitting up late with Stanley and talking far into the night. Beatrice was quietly enraged, which Henry had come rather to enjoy. His latent sadism was roused by what he saw as her bovine passivity, and he felt only occasional remorse for his cruelty.

Miller's favorite haunts that summer were the "taxi-dance" halls around Times Square, so named because the women employees took on all comers who could pay the price of 10 cents a dance. The tawdry atmosphere and the suggestion that sex was for sale appealed to him; the signs that prominently warned against "improper dancing" were open invitations, he thought, for the customers to at least try some of the same.

One Thursday night he ambled up Broadway toward the Palace Theatre, his week's pay in his pocket, and stopped at the corner of 46th Street, where there were two dance halls he liked: the Orpheum Dance Palace and Wilson's Dance Hall. He chose Wilson's. After climbing the steep, rickety wooden stairs, he bought a roll of tickets from a Greek cashier and found a good spot to watch the girls.

A few dances later he picked out a woman and took her across the floor a couple of times. He tried to talk to her about Pirandello, but she was uninterested. He went back to the sidelines. Then, moments later, a startling face swam out of the crowd at him, and the young woman asked him to dance. Miller said yes and went off to buy a whole new roll of tickets.

Between dances, they talked about Strindberg—particularly his character Henriette, with whom she said she identified, and Knut Hamsun's *Victoria*, which she claimed she loved as much as Miller did. What was her name? Well, that was complicated, she said. But, for now, why didn't he call her June Mansfield?

Miller wanted to know more; this mysterious woman enthralled him. She looked anywhere between eighteen and thirty. She had blue-black hair and a dramatically white face from which smoldering dark eyes shone forth. Her body was full and lush under her neat blue velvet suit. Miller later wrote in *Tropic of Capricorn* that her whole being was concentrated in her face. He remembered also her smile: "knowing, mysterious, fugitive—a smile that sprang up suddenly, like a puff of wind."

June Mansfield appraised him coolly. She thought he looked like an ordinary businessman, rather sedate, maybe a teacher. She liked his talk about art; she fancied herself, if not an artist, then perhaps an artist's muse. This man was full of promises: he'd said he'd bring her copies of books by Ben Hecht and Sherwood Anderson, and hinted at more substantial rewards.

At Miller's urging, she arranged to meet him at a Chinese restaurant called Chin Lee's after work. There they continued on a literary plane, but when they moved on to spiritualism and Freudian psychology things got more personal. Henry wanted to know more not only about June's literary interests but about her background. She seemed to be concealing something, which drove him to distraction. Her talk was incoherent, maddening; she switched from subject to unrelated subject as if there were connections between them, and Henry raced to keep up. June, in turn, noted his absorption; she had discovered, this early, the way to ensnare him. The deception that so fascinated him was second nature to her, and his paranoia and jealousy constituted her very metier. She was in her element.

Although he took her to her parents' house in the Bensonhurst section of Brooklyn in a taxi at the end of the evening, Miller failed to get a very clear story out of June. She intimated all sorts of things: that she might have Gypsy blood, that her father might have run a race-track, that she was the sole support of her mother and brothers—or she never saw them. She hinted at mysteries even more arcane, including some gibberish about a lost Stradivarius violin. And men? Oh, none at all, she claimed. Except the man who had committed suicide over her, and a rich lawyer who showered her with gifts, and a certain married man. And one man whom she loved without his knowledge. . . .

Only gradually would Miller learn the barest truths about June, and seldom from her lips. She was twenty-one when he met her in 1923, and her very name was invented: she had been born Juliet Edith Smerth. The Gypsy blood was just plausible; she had been born on

January 7, 1902 in Bukovina, in the Carpathian Mountains of Austria-Hungary, the birthplace of her mother, Fanny. Her father was from Galicia, the Polish region of Austria-Hungary, and when he arrived with his wife and five children in 1907 he gave his occupation as "presser." The Smerths fell on hard times in America; as the father was unable to get steady work, the children were sent out to get whatever work they could. At fifteen, Juliet had looked ten years older, and she dropped out of high school to get a job at a dance hall. Like most taxi-dance girls, she affected a stage name, choosing June for its similarity to Juliet and Mansfield because of its elegance. The "Smerth" was changed to "Smith," a surname she used erratically.

Were her stories about men true? It is impossible to be sure. At twenty-one, she was a beautiful young woman, and a beautiful taxi-dancer might indeed have a series of intense, bizarre experiences in a few years. June was what we would call today "streetwise," versed in the wiles of the seamy side of life: confidence schemes and what were then called "sex games," or golddigging. She insisted to Miller that she never gave men sexual favors; at the very most, she said, she accepted $40 or $50 if she had given someone an hour's good conversation.

Miller tried to trust her. On that first night, he believed he had fallen in love, that he had met the one perfect woman for him. His pursuit was avid. June later claimed that he camped outside her parents' house in Bensonhurst for three days straight. In Miller's many versions of the story, he courted her with words, sending avalanches of letters and books. June was seldom at her parents' (which drove him mad with speculation), and the only place he could be sure of finding her was Wilson's Dance Hall. That was where he picked her up for their early dates, when he would take her to Village spots like Jimmy Kelly's speakeasy and The Pagoda Tearoom. Early in their relationship, he brought his friends to Wilson's to show her off; overwhelmed, she made a grand stage play for them with a rose an admirer had given her. Henry's friends were unimpressed, and he suspected they felt a little sorry for him.

If any of his friends did pity him, they certainly didn't pull Miller aside to say so. He was too obviously smitten. In time, June began to take his declarations of grand passion seriously; she had been worried that he had just been "experimenting" with her. But she was not easily won when it came to going to bed with him. One night, encouraged by June's response to a bit of writing he had done, Henry wrestled with her on the sand at Manhattan Beach—he later described it as an "attempted rape." (June said afterwards it was a pity he hadn't forced her.) For all her talk, June drew the line at sexual intercourse, though she made extravagant promises about their sexual future.

In some notes he later made about this period, Miller wrote: "Great despair, jealousy, torment." He realized very quickly that June was severely unbalanced, even psychotic. She hinted that she used drugs, and much of her conversation he described as "coke talk": crazed, almost paranoid rambles of words. But Miller found her hypnotic. Her talk, which was peppered with the colloquialisms used by cops and criminals, was just the kind he tried to emulate, and her psychosis he found entirely consistent with the insanity of New York. No doubt June in her confused thinking reminded him of his sister Lauretta, who called up in him a fierce, devoted protectiveness; like Lauretta, June was oblivious to the distinction between right and wrong. Like Lauretta, she existed in her own small, warped universe and needed protection just as surely as did Henry's retarded sister. Looking for a key to her personality, he remembered that her birthplace had been Bukovina, a mountain pass in the Carpathians from German Austria to Transylvania. Bukovina has a key role in the Dracula myth popularized by Bram Stoker in his famous novel. It is where the hero, Jonathan Harker, waits for the coach to take him to Dracula's castle. It seemed to Henry that June had all the characteristics of a vampire: she changed in shape and demeanor constantly, she preferred the dark, and she rendered her victims powerless. And, like Dracula, she was invincible.

Miller, of course, was sexually fascinated by June; her rambling talk of other men inflamed him. Jealousy was the glue of their relationship, and June made sure to give him ample cause for it. She knew exactly how to captivate him. One night outside her home in Bensonhurst she fell to her knees in the street and called him her god. Over and over she pleaded that he must quit his job to write. She surrounded herself with chaos, and Miller thrived on it. And she kept the relationship, always, at a fevered pitch.

With the enthusiasm of a new lover, Miller woke Beatrice one night to tell her about June. Her reaction was predictable: she shouted, then wept, and finally took him to bed to win him back sexually. On another occasion Miller took Beatrice to the Palace Theatre and then suggested they visit Wilson's afterward, in the hopes that she would see June and thus know how thoroughly she was outclassed. Beatrice, of course, already knew. After his hasty confession, the subject of June was strictly avoided, and when Miller acceded to any of Beatrice's requests he said silently to himself, "Fine, is that all you want of me? I'll do anything you like except give you the illusion that I am going to live the rest of my life with you."

Finally, weeks after their first meeting, June capitulated and let Henry sleep with her. But the setting was not propitious (although it was exactly the kind that titillated Miller): they met at the apartment of one of her castoffs, a man named Marder. According to Henry— who may have invented the occasion, so closely did it follow his homo-erotic and voyeuristic fantasies—the man returned unexpectedly as Henry and June were washing up. Marder, though jealous, had a big feast sent in, and the three got thoroughly drunk. June ended up on Marder's lap singing Viennese songs, giving every indication that she was Marder's mistress still. She confessed to Miller that she stayed with him sometimes, even now—but only to cure him of his drunkenness.

On the heels of this encounter, June disappeared. In the flood of telegrams and letters that followed she revealed that she had skipped town with two taxi-dancer friends—whom Miller thought cheap—to be the guests of a backwoodsman in New England. Understandably, Henry found this implausible, suspecting the backwoodsman was really Marder. But June's letters spoke only of her devotion to Miller: she wrote that she wanted to be his wife. When she returned and met him at the station, she was naked under her raincoat, and Miller was won again. He refused to admit the clear evidence that June, if not precisely a prostitute, did sleep with other men, and that she accepted money in return. With time, he would become in effect her pimp— though June always insisted that intercourse was ruled out in any of her "intrigues" with other men.

Thoroughly immersed in June's world, Henry had come to see his marriage as an obstacle, Beatrice a hopeless encumbrance. He and Stanley devoted hours to the problem, sitting around the kitchen table at Sixth Avenue or walking in Prospect Park. On what he later remembered as a "marvelous night," they lay in the grass in the park discussing "how to get untied." Stanley, ever loyal, promised that he would take care of everything. Henry didn't press for details.

Not long after, in the fall of 1923, Beatrice took Barbara on a vacation. Although he wasn't sure of the exact details, Miller suspected that this trip had been engineered by Stanley, part of the grand plan to free him from his marriage, perhaps by giving Beatrice grounds for divorce. He found he had last-minute misgivings. He went dutifully from the train station to the ear doctor, just as he'd promised Beatrice. But there he found June waiting for him; she always seemed to intuit his movements correctly, making an appearance whenever she sensed Beatrice might be gaining ground.

If Miller wasn't sure of Stanley's plans, June was. Never having been inside the Miller home, she now determined to make the most of Beatrice's absence. She changed into Beatrice's kimono—for she was really Henry's wife now, she explained. She examined Henry's belongings with minute curiosity and wanted to know where he wrote. Upstairs, he explained, on the parlor floor of their duplex brownstone apartment. June was, strangely, reluctant to sleep in the marital bed upstairs, and they slept instead on a couch in the downstairs kitchen.

The next morning, while Henry was fixing a platter of bacon and eggs, the double doors to the kitchen rolled open and there stood Beatrice, with the landlord and his daughter beside her as witnesses. For once unemotional, Beatrice mustered a steely reserve and ordered Henry to get "that woman" out of there at once, turning on her heel and going upstairs. The couple hurriedly cleared out. Miller said later that his only regret was not getting to finish his bacon and eggs, a characteristic remark that surely glossed over some complicated feelings.

Henry and June, for a time, were on the streets. They lived at a succession of addresses, never paying rent or staying very long. First they camped with a friend of Emil Conason's, a Dr. Paul Luttinger in the Bronx, whose house they called Cockroach Hall. Before long they moved on to a five-room apartment on Riverside Drive rented by Miller's friend Harold Hickerson, his wife Ruth, and their small baby. There they occupied a tiny room separated by a connecting hall from another tiny room occupied by Emil and Cele Conason; quarters were very cramped. Aside from their elation at being together, things were tense. June expected Henry to meet her at Wilson's at two o'clock in the morning, when she got off work. After having something to eat, taking the elevated home, and listening to June chatting until she put herself to sleep, it would often be five in the morning—and Miller had to leave for work at seven-thirty. When he found sores on his penis, they abstained from intercourse for a week—which meant June's talk went on all night. While she explained that it was absolutely impossible that he had contracted syphilis from her—Miller's first thought—June was led into still more sexual revelations. Her admirers, she insisted, were all too old for sex—but then she described in detailed fashion how she helped them to orgasm. Miller later wrote that she transformed herself completely on meeting him: transformed her name, her history, her age, her family. Before long she began to call him "Val," shortening his middle name.

The affair continued, but within weeks of leaving Beatrice, Miller, far more affected by the separation than he let on, called her and arranged a meeting. They worked out a weekly schedule for Miller to pay household expenses and visit Barbara. June pretended not to care, but when she first saw the child, whom she always referred to as "the little one," she cried and chastised Miller for abandoning his daughter. Later, Miller remembered June saying, "if that had been my child I would never have left her, not for anyone." Beatrice, for her part, played the wounded wife to the hilt, never calling June by name and acting superior to the whole affair. Before long, however, Beatrice picked up on the fact that the roles had undergone a subtle shift and that now she was, in effect, the other woman. Miller found her newly attractive and sexually receptive, and they discovered all sorts of opportunities for intimacies more unrestrained than Beatrice had ever before allowed.

June, of course, grew suspicious. She telephoned Beatrice and offered, melodramatically, to withdraw from the field. During one of Miller's visits to his wife and child, June attempted suicide—by what means, he never knew—and was saved only by the intervention of his Western Union crony Blackie, who had taken to hanging around Cockroach Hall, mooning over June. Miller raced home to the Bronx, but found his mind was not on June but on Beatrice. In the first months of his marital separation, he felt himself drawn to June but still tied to Beatrice—which of course spurred June to new heights of hysteria.

All these goings-on took place in an atmosphere of constant talk. Henry and June were both great talkers. In June Henry had met his conversational match, and they sought out people who could keep up. At Cockroach Hall, the favorite theme was Jews. At the Hickersons' apartment on Riverside Drive, the endless talk circled around Freud and child psychology before returning to Jews and Nordic supremacy. June, herself Jewish—though Henry only suspected it at this point— felt left out of the discussions, treated like a child. At one point she

made a feeble attempt to leave him, taking a small bundle of possessions under her arm, but she returned almost immediately.

Desperate for attention, June announced her intention to leave the
dance hall and go on the stage, after an evening at the theater with the
Conasons. She began taking classes at the Henry Street Settlement
House, claiming to be related to the actor Richard Mansfield. This
required the invention of an entirely new past, and she duly invented
drama courses at Wellesley, a lifelong obsession with Eleanora Duse,
and the acquaintance of such actors as Jacob Ben Ami and Helen
Westley. To everyone's amazement, she promptly got the lead role in
a production of Shaw's *Joan of Arc*, and plunged into a whirl of rehears-
als and—inevitably—flirtations with the director and the leading man.
Miller, the Hickersons, and the Conasons were dumbfounded by her
ability. June, however, was supremely confident of her powers. As a
budding actress, she became a professional woman to be reckoned with;
Beatrice could no longer dismiss her as a dance-hall girl, and Henry
had to pay her renewed respect as well.

Beatrice had no interest in a legal reconciliation after Henry's
betrayal, and she had begun divorce proceedings. The divorce, which
was granted on December 21, 1923, affected Miller deeply. The judge
was severe in his ruling, chiding him for leaving used condoms lying
out in a household with a child and for bringing another woman into
the marital home. Out of his own brand of chivalric remorse, Miller
gallantly rejected the weekly payment he was ordered by the court to
make to Beatrice as too low, offering instead to pay $30. Immediately
after the trial, in another attempt to switch the focus from his sexual
misconduct to his good intentions, he sat down and fired off a letter of
congratulation to Beatrice's lawyer. On the heels of that gesture, he
visited Ethel Maurer, the sister of his friend Muriel, in her room uptown and offered to marry her. He was drunk on his new freedom, and
his nervous friends urged him to stay single.

June saw the necessity of another bid for Henry's attentions. She
turned her father's sudden death into an occasion of high drama. Henry
bought her a mourning dress; he hoped to meet the family she had
been so secretive about. But June abruptly disappeared for ten days;
he never learned why. When she surfaced at his Western Union office
in the black mourning dress and a black turban, Miller was, as he later
wrote, "stabbed to the heart by her great beauty."

The contest of June's life was on. Henry had touched a nerve in
her turbulent mind, and she was determined to win him. She truly

believed—knew, she said—that he would be a great writer. And he understood her, or at least appreciated the crazy ruses she needed to function. Henry was her one chance, June knew at one level, for a life of Art.

She decided that the best way to secure her prey was to play on Henry's jealousy by describing her sexual exploits. Miller pleaded that she not confess and then, when she began anyway, insisted that he would not allow her to continue. But June could not be stopped. She began with a strange tale of being picked up in a car from the dance hall and raped by three men in a field; the cold grass, she added, in what Henry called a "typical touch of hers," gave her a case of hemorrhoids. From this incident she moved further back in her past, claiming that her mother had sent her out golddigging when she was a young girl. She admitted to numerous affairs. Yes, she had been kept by Marder, and there were other men too: Baker the shoe manufacturer, Jerry the prize fighter, Harris the theater owner, a college boy who had seduced her at Marder's, and countless others. About every one of these affairs June gave the minutest details, torturing Henry with the certain knowledge that she had indeed had sex with many, many men.

June's strategy worked. She had uncovered a deep masochistic streak in Henry, the same impulse that had led him to walk by Cora Seward's house obsessively in adolescence. She played on his voyeurism, recognizing his interest in other men's sexual enjoyment. As early as his third or fourth date with June, she had come up for air during a tussle in a lot next to her family home in Bensonhurst, growling gutturally, "And now for the dirt." Henry was not repulsed but captivated; he gave her the money she needed and resolved to protect her from such self-abasement even at the expense of his own self-respect. In *Sexus*, Miller tried to explain:

> I was quite willing to be made jealous if only I could witness this power she had of making others love her. My ideal . . . was that of a woman who had the world at her feet. If I thought there were men impervious to her charms I would deliberately aid her to ensnare them. The more lovers she garnered the greater my own personal triumph. Because she did love *me*, that there was no doubt about.

With her confessions, June vowed renewed devotion. Henry knew intellectually that she was incapable of remaining faithful to him, but he resolved to believe her. Against the advice of his friends, he reasoned that marriage might settle June down.

Their wedding day—June 1, 1924—should have been triumphant, given the propitious date and the fascination each undeniably felt for the other. Instead it was as disordered as were most of Henry and June's days. They had to borrow money for the marriage license. June had represented herself as being under age, so Henry concluded it would be less risky to get married in New Jersey so she could claim to be of legal age without any records cropping up that would show otherwise. They lined up Emil Conason and his wife, Cele, to serve as witnesses. On the way to the ceremony, June accused Henry of wanting to back out, and they quarreled bitterly. When they arrived in Hoboken, they found that the judge's office would close at noon and there was no sign of the Conasons. Henry was ready to give up, but June suggested they hire witnesses off the street, and the dismal, drab ceremony finally proceeded. Back in town, they got hold of Ned Schnellock and his girlfriend Marcelle to celebrate with, and spent their wedding evening with them at a burlesque house on Houston Street. June threw a hysterical fit, laughing madly, which Henry chalked up to the tension of getting married. It frightened him, however, and he implored Ned to tell her he hoped she would have children, that he and Marcelle would buy her a wedding gift—anything, Miller begged, only don't let her laugh that way again.

The marriage's beginnings were less than auspicious. Both Henry and June were earning steady incomes, but their lives were so unstable that their jobs were in danger. They had no place to live. June was twenty-one to Henry's thirty-two. And her emotional instability encouraged a climate of symbiotic madness. June offered Henry an alternate reality: a lawless realm where talk was valued over truth, where appearance was all, where right was indistinct from wrong. For Henry, believing from early childhood that he existed outside conventional morality, June was the female embodiment of the chaotic intensity he had come to crave. In the seven years of his marriage to her, the *folie à deux* would only escalate.

5.

At June's Side

1924–1926

June Miller had nothing if not energy, and with her marriage she set out to make Henry a writer through sheer force of will. First, like any good actress, she had to set the stage, convinced that Miller had to feel the part before being able to play it correctly. Wearing a new, close-fitting Persian red dress ("at her very best then," Miller recalled), she dragged her husband through the streets of Brooklyn Heights looking for the proper apartment. A new passion had seized them, and they often pressed close in vestibules, oblivious to the buzzers they leaned against.

They found what June wanted on the parlor floor of a brownstone at 91 Remsen Street, once owned by a judge. June insisted that they take it, though the rent was $90 a month, twice what they could afford. The place was sumptuous, with floors of inlaid wood, silk tapestried wallpaper, built-in bookcases, a stained-glass window on the landing, and fifteen-foot-high ceilings. The neighborhood was decidedly aristocratic—Miller later said their mouths watered at the meals their neighbors gave their pets—and theirs was the only house on the street divided into apartments. The landlord, a Virginia man, was impressed by Miller's position at Western Union, and he allowed them to put down only a ten-dollar deposit for the two large front rooms, kitchenette, and bath.

Miller busied himself furnishing the apartment—on credit, of course—while June drummed up the remaining $80 from an admirer who was a room clerk at the Hotel Bossert. (She actually asked for $500, and got $300, but told Henry only much later.) They hung pictures on the walls and selected every object with care. Because they kept the place bare and immaculate, with a low couch in the middle of the polished wood floor, Miller called it their "Japanese love nest." But they were burdened from the start by their impossible rent, especially on top of the alimony and child support Miller had to pay Beatrice weekly.

Not to mention expenses. For June decided they must live like kings, and brought home all manner of gifts for Henry: silk dressing gowns, books, pipes, phonograph records, Moroccan slippers, a chess set. For a time, he basked in this new luxury—he had never known the like—calling in sick to the office with increasing frequency. On nights June spent at the theater, Henry read; he had discovered the Montague Street branch of the public library and made friends with the librarian there. Other times Sleaco and his cronies came by with a bottle. Once, on an occasion when June had not returned all night, he stopped by the Sixth Avenue apartment to pick up a delighted Beatrice and Barbara, taking them for a day-long picnic in the country. When he got home, he found June furious, overwrought with jealousy.

At Western Union, Willever and the forces above were looking askance at Miller's haphazard attendance, his new habit of putting a sign on his desk in the afternoon saying "Closed for the day." Mike Rivise, who as head of a division called the Special Messenger Service acted as a detective who policed the employees, reported that Miller was lazy and shoddy in his hiring practices. Just as he had been turned away for the lowly job of messenger, so too might he now be stripped of a job he hated.

Miller always told people that he quit his job at June's insistence, in order to take up his writing career in earnest. It seems more likely, however, that he simply wanted to avoid the humiliation of being fired, which would bring him ignominy in the eyes of his friends, Beatrice, and his parents. June simply wanted him "by her side"—a phrase both of them used relentlessly in these years. At any rate, on one Monday in September 1924, after not showing up for three days straight and enjoying his leisure fully, Miller forestalled the inevitable punishment by quitting without notice. He had Sam Sattenstein tell his boss and simply walked off, taking the key to his desk with him. He sent June around a week later to pick up his back pay.

Strangely enough, June was deliriously happy with his news—even if it meant the money problem would fall to her. She thrived on such demands, for the larger the sums required, the more elaborate the ruses and deceptions that were needed. Almost immediately, their money problems escalated. June was helping out with her family's mortgage, or so she claimed, and now she had to provide the rent and alimony as well. Miller quickly developed a mortal dread of visiting the apartment on Sixth Avenue emptyhanded. He made protracted excuses to Beatrice—and then often hit her up for a loan or meal. Their sexual intimacies came to a halt as these humiliating visits grew infrequent. Soon Miller abandoned them altogether, living thereafter in constant fear that he would be arrested for non-support, as well as in a state of guilty remorse.

Even though conditions were conducive for him to begin to write, he found it impossible. He later said that he was so in love with the idea of *becoming* a writer that he couldn't write, so full of physical energy that he wore himself out in preparation. Besides, there was no need to hurry, he reasoned. In *Plexus* he described his state of mind at this time: "It was morning now, a long, lazy morning of a holiday that was to last forever. I had elected to occupy a choice seat in Paradise. It was definite and certain. I could therefore afford to take my time, could afford to dawdle away the glorious hours ahead of me. . . ."

"A definite and certain . . . seat in Paradise": these are the words of a man suffering from delusions of grandeur. Miller had always felt himself marked out for a special destiny, of course, and his friends had always been convinced that he had some sort of genius, but his new confidence was probably June-induced. June, who put his genius before her own dramatic gifts—which she held to be considerable—heaped praise on him and fanned his grandiose ambitions into a fair flame of obsession. He decided he needed more experience—the neophyte's favored excuse—which meant that he would remain passive, letting June shape his days.

June took his paralysis for indifference toward her, and she stepped up her golddigging activities, introducing her new suitors to him and trying to seduce him back into infatuation. She took a job as a hostess at Raymo's, a speakeasy in the Village, where she was forced to drink with her customers and frequently came home drunk. When she lost that job, she got another at a tearoom called Perroquet's, where she earned less because they served no liquor. Financially, she and Henry now were in serious trouble. He tried to borrow dresses for her from old girlfriends like Muriel and was angrily rebuffed. He borrowed small sums from old, forgotten friends, assuring his current friends that he was doing fine. He began to develop a whole science of borrowing, governed by strict rules like the following, from *Sexus:* "It is easier . . . to borrow from one who is your inferior than from an equal or one who is above you." His elaborate ethic held that it was necessary to repay only those who had made him loans in the right spirit. He would come to see borrowing as an exalted, even noble act. But all these rationalizations didn't stop him from feeling humiliated about begging, and when his fund-raising attempts were unsuccessful, he became increasingly cynical and crass.

While June was out raising money, Henry raised hell. Sleaco, Blount, and Dredge came around constantly now, Sleaco in the throes of a persecution mania and Dredge given to roaring in at three in the morning. Joe O'Regan was around so often that one day he simply did not go home, installing himself in the household for a few months. Emil Schnellock often showed up, mesmerizing Miller with talk of Europe, which Emil remembered in picturesque detail. Once Angus Bolton, the Montague Street librarian, brought over a bottle of absinthe, and he, Henry, Emil, and Joe sat over it ranting about the Cirque Medrano, the Midi, Renaissance painters—crazed, hallucinatory talkfests.

As the talk and the intensity escalated, Miller was drawn back to an old, obsessive topic: the Jews. In a recent dramatic scene in downtown Brooklyn, while listening to the strains of cantorial music emanating from a synagogue, Henry had asked June if she was Jewish. When she said she was, he was oddly moved and even expressed interest in converting. He began to seek out Jewish outposts on the Lower East Side: a Romanian coffeehouse on Second Avenue, where he engaged a "crazy" Yiddish poet, and Jewish and Polish cafés near the East River, where he played chess. One night with Harold Hickerson and Joe O'Regan at the Café Royal on Second Avenue, Miller created an unpleasant scene. When a bearded old Jewish peddler came to their table offering his wares, Miller insulted him, putting a cigar in the peddler's mouth and asking all manner of offensive questions. Harold and Joe apologized to the old man and scolded Henry for his behavior. *"Acte gratuit,"* Miller wrote in his later notes about the period.

Miller knew his anti-Semitism was offensive, his behavior irrational. Jews roused in him a great anxiety that was strangely connected to his writing. *Clipped Wings* had been in part a eugenicist tract, and his first novel, *Moloch*, would be an exploration of his own prejudice. Anti-Semitism was the only emotion that had sparked his early, flat attempts, and he prized it and nourished it for that.

Just after the experience in the Café Royal, in fact, he mounted a massive, no-holds-barred campaign to write—or, more precisely, to make a living by writing. Earlier he had searched about for a subject so intensely that it had become second nature to look at everything as if he were an enormous eye, as he later wrote in *Plexus*. The result was that he saw subjects everywhere; he believed he could write about anything and make it exciting. He systematically made a list of subjects and sent it around to editors of magazines and newspapers along with a "long, fatuous" letter detailing his objectives. This campaign involved, he said, "altercations and disputes, fruitless errands to editorial offices, vexation, disgruntlement, rage, despair, ennui. *And postage stamps!*" If an editor wrote back with any encouraging word, he took it as a commission, doggedly setting forth to compose his article, which was invariably rejected.

His first manuscript from this period, "Brooklyn's Back Yard," drew on his long fascination with the Brooklyn shoreline: the docks, the Navy Yard, the old ferry houses. In spite of the enormous detail he forced into the piece, he could not evoke the spirit of the place and it remained only a descriptive bit, stashed away in his new filing system as "material." He began a period in which he devoted days to exploring, walking the streets in search of ideas. Chinatown, Harlem, Hoboken, Coney Island in winter: all offered themselves as possibilities. He used his new vocation as an excuse to indulge his passion for nostalgia; he visited his old neighborhood and rediscovered his fondness for the burlesque and wrestling matches. He wrote a short piece about the wrestling hero Jim Londos, "the little Hercules," that he thought quite good. Encouraged, he began a novelette, "Diary of a Futurist," which he read to his harshest critic, Emil Schnellock. Emil was not impressed, and urged Henry to write as he talked.

It proved to be good advice. Henry found that if he came home after an evening's talk and sat down and reviewed what he had said, his monologues had not only continuity and form, but also rhythm and sonority, a mesmerizing quality. He didn't really act on this insight until he wrote *Tropic of Cancer* nearly a decade later. For the time being, he noted his conversational skill only as another indication that he was not like other people, that he was set apart. Instead he resolved that he needed to research his subjects more fully, which led him down impossible bypaths. For an article on how chewing gum was made, for example, he not only visited a gum factory on Long Island, but, when he learned about the Yucatán *chicleros* who harvested the base of the gum, researched the Mayan past of Yucatán. From there he was led to books about the lost continent of Mu, the sea traffic between Easter Island and South America, the Aztec alphabet, Paul Gauguin, and from there to the life and letters of Van Gogh, which he was certain that he had to read immediately.

At first Miller had a little luck in getting his stories placed; in late 1924 he wrote Emil Schnellock that the *Menorah Journal* had given him three assignments, and that they were interested in his piece on the Houston Street burlesque and another piece on the cafés on Second Avenue. But the *Menorah Journal* never found room for his pieces. Nevertheless, the fact that a Jewish publication should be the first organ interested in his work only reinforced his quixotic association of Jewishness with writing, and served further to convince him of his strange and ambivalent affinity for Jews.

Miller was temporarily at a loss. Little money was coming in—at least from his efforts. Masochistically, he approached the one man who was certain not to approve of his efforts: advertising man Bruce Barton, the author of the best seller *The Man Nobody Knows*, a book that portrayed Jesus as the founder of modern advertising. Predictably, Barton told him that writing was clearly not his forte and advised him to get a job. Crestfallen, Henry retaliated by sending Barton a volley of insulting letters.

Another avenue proved more successful. Emil Schnellock's brother Ned worked for a magazine syndicate run by Miller's old hero Bernarr Macfadden, the physical culturist who built an empire around such magazines as *True Story* and *True Confessions*. When Ned was asked to come up with some copy promoting a new Macfadden magazine, he turned to his writing friend Henry and then, pleased with the results, arranged a meeting between the two men. Instead of trying to impress Macfadden with his quick wit, Miller poured forth the story of his quitting Western Union to become a writer. Macfadden, who knew a good story when he heard one, immediately told him to go home and write a serial for one of his magazines, warning Miller not to "get literary" on him.

June and Henry's friends were elated at this promising news, but Henry, though flattered by his idol's response, wasn't sure that he could produce the story Macfadden wanted. He didn't know how to write yet, he told his friends. Success might spoil him. Reluctantly, he let Macfadden's offer go.

A terrible writer's block ensued. Henry would stare at the blank page for hours and then slowly and painfully tap out a sentence or two. When June demanded to see his output he would mumble something about "other pages." His friends were forced into conversational contortions when they discussed his writing projects in June's presence. If they brought up the book he *would* write, her suspicions were aroused, and they had to backtrack and change their verb tenses, describing the book he *was* writing. The discussions ended in nervous laughter; everyone wanted to believe in him but they were finding it increasingly difficult.

Joe O'Regan, looking through Miller's stash of unpublished pieces, came up with an idea that held implicit appeal for the entrepreneurial Millers. Henry would never find an editor to take his work, O'Regan pointed out, so they should publish it themselves. Henry and June worked out a plan to publish a series of prose poems printed on heavy paper that they would sell by subscription to their friends and vast circle of acquaintances. They called these prose poems Mezzotints, after Whistler. The first Mezzotint was a piece extracted from a letter to Emil Schnellock called "The Bowery Savings Bank"; it was the first and only Mezzotint signed Henry V. Miller. They had five hundred copies printed up but were able to sell only a fraction of them; Miller's friends were dubious about his staying power and took out at most a month's subscription. Undaunted, Joe O'Regan took to the streets, selling Mezzotints door to door. The scheme wasn't producing results fast enough for June, who was convinced she could do better herself. She and Henry had had some brief experience selling candy from door to door and had found that their luck improved when Henry waited outside with the stock while June made the sales pitch alone. She proposed to apply the same principle to the Mezzotint campaign, putting her name on the pieces and peddling them in Greenwich Village cafés and speakeasies. A cowed Henry acquiesced.

At first, June's success was spectacular: she sold the Mezzotints for three and four times the prices they hoped to get. Sometimes she sold the whole series. Soon, she narrowed down her clientele, finding it more lucrative to work on her greatest admirers, who would often buy her whole stack for $75 or $80, expecting nothing more, she claimed, than an evening's conversation. Most nights she didn't return until two, waking Miller up to regale him with stories.

It quickly became clear to Miller that the Mezzotint scheme had turned into just another excuse for June to do what she did best: practice a kind of cagey prostitution, in which money was exchanged not for June's sexual favors but, ostensibly, for something else—in this case, Henry's writing. Besides, in signing her own name to the Mezzotints, and in reducing them to a secondary or even tertiary matter in her transactions, June unwittingly indicated to Henry the worthlessness of his efforts. Though she meant well—she was a survivor, and devoted herself fiercely to taking care of Henry and her "Japanese love

nest"—she undermined Henry in the area in which he was most vulnerable. She clung even more tenaciously than her husband to the idea
of art in the abstract, yet she also encouraged his tendency to think of
writing solely in its commercial aspect. With the Mezzotint racket,
Miller foresaw the merchandizing of art, and of the written word, which
would color his entire career.

The stakes were raised when June met the banker Howell French,
an admirer who bought out her entire stock one night and said he
wanted to support *June's* career as a writer. June proposed that she
and Henry encourage him until he promised something concrete. Sure
enough, French soon admitted that he was a good friend of William
Randolph Hearst, and that he could get June a try-out writing a column
a day for two months for the Hearst Syndicate. For the time being, he
would pay June $100 a week out of his own pocket, and then he would
bring her material to Hearst himself.

In his notes about this period, Miller described the scheme and
wrote simply: "Failure." He always maintained that he himself turned
out the column for French for two months, but no trace of this writing
survives, and it is more likely that he quickly saw the plan as just
another of June's ruses, his "columns" simply occasions for June to
see French and extract payment for her favors. Like the leftover Mezzotints, which the Millers and their friends sent off to random names
in the phonebook, whatever columns existed were merely tokens of
exchange, worth nothing if there was no demand for them. Miller
thought it appropriate that throughout the winter of 1924–25 he suffered from a painful case of piles; his humiliation was that intense.

When spring came, Henry and June decided to tackle their money
problem head on. Henry drafted the first of his many "begging letters":
appeals for aid that he would reproduce and send "to all and sundry,"
as he later put it. They addressed the letter to "Friends and Givers of
Alms" and had a friend mimeograph it in a run of fifty copies. Predictably, the response barely covered the costs of the mailing. Few of
Miller's friends were any better off than he, and the "contacts" he sent
it to—customers of his father's, most likely—were not inclined to favor
a married couple who clearly thought the world owed them a living at
the height of the twenties boom, a time when any enterprising young
couple might expect to hit it big. They abandoned this scheme with
reluctance, but Miller would return to it with determination over the
years.

June returned to her old ways, sending desperately worded cables to random acquaintances for large sums when things got really tight; the more imperious and urgent the request, she felt, the surer the result. (In 1925, when the Millers were trying to extricate themselves from the candy-selling business, June wired another room clerk, this one at the Imperial, for $350—"at once." The response was a letter tabulating June's debts to the recipient and threatening suits for extortion and blackmail.)

Meanwhile, their back rent had piled up at an alarming rate at the Remsen Street apartment, and one day the Virginian who managed the brownstone took Miller aside and told him they had to move out. Miller wrote a mournful letter to Emil Schnellock on the eve of their departure, inviting him to bring along a bottle to toast the thirty-five Mezzotints produced to date and the lost glories of Remsen Street. He confided:

> God knows I'd like to keep my wife home at my side, where she belongs; I'd like to pay the alimony and send my kid to a decent school; I'd like to keep on living in nice clean airy rooms in a respectable neighborhood; I'd like to eat regularly three times a day and not have my food go back on me; I'd even join a Church, everything else being equal.

But, he concluded, he supposed that giving all this up was the price of trying to be a writer. On a note of defeat tinged with bravado, he wrote, "I suppose, further, that I am one of those lily-livered pups who hasn't guts enough to go out and get a he-man's job and slave eight hours, maybe ten, for some guy who knows a little less than I do." With some irony, he added a postscript: "Another letter that belongs to you." If he was only a lily-livered pup—the language was Bernarr Macfadden's—he could nonetheless turn out letters and use them as his own tokens of exchange, here offering one to Emil in gratitude and friendship.

Following their eviction from Remsen Street, Henry and June lived at a succession of addresses in Brooklyn, never remaining at any one place for long. At their first address, a furnished room on Garden Place in Brooklyn Heights, the Nova Scotian landlady insulted June by criticizing the couple's way of life. To get even—and also to skip out on the rent—Miller lined up the children of an old friend to vandalize the place, smearing ketchup all over, ripping the sheets, and so forth. Henry and June barricaded the front door and snuck out the back with their suitcases. Miller thought it a great stunt, its showiness disguising any shame he might have felt at his lack of responsibility.

From there the couple went to Stanley's, until he threw them out —handing them car fare condescendingly. Then followed a brief stint as secretaries-cum-handymen with Miller's old friend Karl Karsten, a statistician, at Long Beach. Next they moved to an apartment on Clinton Avenue, but there too found themselves soon in arrears on the rent.

June no longer kept up any pretense of peddling other wares when she made her evening rounds in the Village; she was golddigging "in earnest," as Miller later wrote. Gradually an idea began to germinate: they would open a speakeasy. Miller reasoned that they entertained their friends often enough to begin with—why not make them pay? June's admirers had all kinds of money as well. For her part, June saw a speakeasy as an efficient way to consolidate her business. One room would be set aside for her to entertain her lovers, while Miller served drinks and snacks to the waiting admirers and his friends in the back room.

Funding the venture required a last surge of energy on Miller's part. In mortification and disgust he approached his mother, who turned him down. Eventually, with the help of his uncle, a Broadway speculator who always carried a huge bankroll, they managed to scrape together enough money to rent a small cellar on Perry Street and to stock the kitchen with bootleg gin and a small store of food. Miller pasted up his favorite photograph of Barbara on the wall of the kitchen, and they sent the word out that they were ready for business.

From the start, Miller had to pretend that he was not June's husband; that was essential to the success of the enterprise. He washed dishes, made drinks, and, when things got too crowded, snuck out the back window. He and Ned Schnellock and Joe O'Regan sat around the kitchen playing the ukelele while June met with her admirers in the front room. One Hoboken gangland type often paid $25 for the privilege of staying "after hours," and most likely paid June a larger sum privately. But June's dream of efficient, somehow legitimized, prostitution was threatened by the jealousy her suitors quite naturally felt when confronted with evidence of the existence of other rivals for her favors. Profits trickled in slowly, and the Millers were constantly dodging creditors. The coal man, the ice man, the tradesman from whom they bought Jewish sacramental wine, then the lawyer who had handled

Beatrice's divorce—everyone was on their trail. At night, jealous suspicions often erupted into fistfights among their customers. Miller, pretending to be only a guest, could not escape these late-night scenes. More and more, watching June's Circe-like maneuvers, he felt like Dostoevsky's eternal husband.

Then Joe O'Regan suggested that Miller and Ned Schnellock join him in a scheme to cash in on the Florida land boom. To Henry, anything was better than the dim, smoky, chaotic atmosphere of the Perry Street cellar. June too realized that things had reached an impasse. Though she feared Henry was heading South in order to leave *her,* she saw the financial possibilities in their scheme and set out to raise the money for their venture herself, turning to an old admirer from her theater days. On Thanksgiving Day, 1925, Henry and Joe set off in a snowstorm to join Ned in Washington and make their way to Miami.

The trip was a failure, of course. Success in the Florida land boom required the lightning speed of the expert con man, and Miller was a rank amateur in comparison. What the self-styled "three musketeers" found in the South was a whole tribe of would-be speculators; hearing that it was impossible to find rooms within ten miles of Miami, the three cut their trip short in Jacksonville. They stayed at the YMCA, living off overripe oranges and melons filched from railway sheds. Miller got a job hanging posters for a day, and Schnellock landed one at the local paper by submitting Miller's writing as sample copy. Out of work for a week, Miller and O'Regan appealed to a Catholic priest for help; rebuffed, Henry approached a rabbi, who sent them to the Salvation Army with a chit for a meal.

Ned and Joe were determined to stick with the Florida project, but Henry liked his creature comforts too much to endure more than two weeks. He was crazy to know what June was up to; it was like missing installments in a serial melodrama. To get the return fare, he approached the only person he really felt comfortable about borrowing from: his father. Heinrich was a borrower too, and he understood that an urgent request was not to be denied. He immediately wired his son $100.

Miller, looking out the train window the next morning, mused that he had come perilously close to making a bum out of himself. He had never been so thoroughly down and out; at least in Brooklyn he and June had always had a place to live, however precariously held. The speakeasy, in spite of the demeaning position it put him in, gave him some outward semblance of respectability. With his return from the

South, however, he was flat out. To make matters worse, when he raced down from the railroad station to Perry Street, he found the place deserted and no sign of June. After a frantic search, he finally located her at her mother's in Bensonhurst. In his absence, she explained, her whole elaborate scheme had broken down; her juggling act had required Henry's participation, and it had simply collapsed. After a quick discussion, they concluded it was best to live apart for a while, with their families, in order to try to save up enough to begin again. As Miller wrote in his notes about the period: "No more hopes. . . . Complete failure and submission—absolutely licked." At thirty-five, he had, it seemed, hit bottom. In his attempt to rebel against middle-class respectability he found himself closer to the gutter than to the romantic poverty he had envisioned. He could see no way out.

Louise Miller accepted her son's return to the nest with a grim stoicism. She had expected as much. Henry's marriage had failed to please her, and on first meeting June, she asked if the two were indeed married. When June assured her that they were, Louise retorted, "Too bad, he's no good, he's a murderer." For in her eyes Henry *was* a killer of a sort—a killer of Beatrice's unborn children, and of Louise's unborn dreams. She had tried to adjust herself to the idea of a writing son, but she never could understand why he couldn't write for the *Saturday Evening Post* or the local paper *The Chat*. She urged him to write shorter "stories" (she never could get it straight that his pieces were not stories), reasoning that the sooner he got done with a piece, the sooner his check would come.

For his part, Heinrich was rather glad to have Henry's companionship again, though he was a bit bewildered to have a twice-married son, who was also a father, typing in his dining room. Heinrich had fallen into a deep depression several years before, after first swearing off liquor and then taking up religion. He was happy with the church for a while and seems to have developed a fierce attachment to the minister, but he felt sorely betrayed when the man left for a parish on Long Island. Thereafter he lapsed into a bitter querulousness, taking long walks in the cemetery every day, where he sat for hours on a stone bench. His son's return cheered him a little, and he tried to recall old times with him, but unfortunately, the subject he reverted to, again and again, was the great career of Jimmy Pasta, a neighborhood boy whose success had galled Henry as a child.

In response to these encouragements, Henry began a self-portrait called "The Failure," a title he'd used for himself in his twenties. He sat at the typewriter by the front windows, ready to move himself and his materials into a closet at the sight of a guest. Louise complained about his cigarette smoke, which had to be explained to visitors. When neighbors and relatives came by, Henry hid in the closet, sometimes for hours on end. Overwhelmed there by the scent of camphor balls, he imagined himself the family skeleton; the thirty-two-year-old Lauretta, the real black sheep, now prattled in the open, while he, the son of such promise, lurked behind closed doors.

For Henry, who thrived in adversity, the experience was galvanizing. He set out on another intense effort to get his material published, and perhaps because of his grim determination, he finally met some success. *Pearson's* accepted Miller's Mezzotint about the Bowery Savings Bank, and published it under the name June E. Mansfield. (Whether June submitted the manuscript in her own name or the magazine simply got hold of a Mezzotint is not clear.) Miller submitted a long article on Dreiser to the *New Republic;* the magazine wrote back rejecting the piece, but published a brief excerpt as a letter to the editor in April 1926.

With his much-traveled manuscripts under his arm, Miller now called on Ronald Millar, an editor at *Liberty* magazine; he took Millar's name as a good omen. Henry talked as convincingly to Millar as he had to Bernarr Macfadden, and before long Millar offered him an editorship with the magazine and gave him a $250 check to write an article on words. As usual, the article never made its way into print—Henry always claimed it was rejected as "too good"—but he put away the $250 for the time when he and June would live together again.

Henry learned that June had moved to a furnished room without telling him and was up to her old tricks with other men, making him jealous. Moreover, Beatrice's lawyer had picked up the scent again and was after him with threats of the Raymond Street jail for his failure to pay child support and alimony. Beatrice herself telephoned Louise Miller with all kinds of accusations about June. (To Henry's surprise, Louise sprang to June's defense.) The atmosphere was tense. One evening June telephoned and threatened to run away; Henry searched the streets for her all night. When he found her, he saw she had acquired an alarming tic, which he attributed to drug use.

Henry was nervous about starting in with June all over again. But Decatur Street was too oppressive and June too insistent. In the spring of 1926 they rented a furnished flat on Hancock Street in Brooklyn, in a neighborhood of wooden rowhouses not far from Henry's parents' home. June had a new scheme that did not involve Henry; this time she offered her rich admirers driving lessons. The automobile, of course, provided all sorts of possibilities for sexual intimacy, as Henry grimly realized. To quiet him, June arranged for him to write racy stories for an editor friend of hers, Courtland Young. She brought these to Young herself and signed them with her own name. None of them ever appeared in his magazines (*Young's*, *Breezy Stories*, and *Droll Stories*), but Young paid her anyway, and Henry was kept busy writing more stories. Eventually he simply cannibalized the back issues of the magazines, rehashing old plots. When Young didn't notice, Henry quit writing stories in disgust.

June and Henry appeared to be getting nowhere. When a telegram came from Joe O'Regan announcing that he had finally hit it big in another land boom in North Carolina, they felt they had nothing to lose in joining him. For all their experience in confidence schemes, Henry and June were surprisingly unworldly. They didn't learn from their mistakes, and they were played for suckers as easily as their own marks. Naturally (for Joe was equally hapless), Joe's sudden windfall had vanished by the time they hitchhiked to Asheville. Unable to raise the money for their return fare, they took a furnished room and tried to start up operations in North Carolina, but they found their debts caught up with them more quickly in the South. Finally, as Miller later put it, they were "obliged" to sneak out of their room in the middle of the night with their shoes in their hands. On the way back, in Richmond, Virginia, their stomachs colicky from eating too many green apples, they resolved to get a good meal by an old ruse: eating heartily and then throwing themselves on the restaurateur's mercy. The Greek proprietor was unsympathetic, however, and called the police. Henry and June sent a flurry of faked telegrams indicating funds were forthcoming, and the mollified policeman deposited them at a hotel. They sneaked out in the early morning, and, on a lucky streak at last, finally made it to New York. There, as Miller's notes record, they were met with the "shock of blanched faces, Jewish crowd, smell of city, noise, etc." He continued: "Sleeping at [Conason's] joint in the Bronx. Bedbugs and medical books everywhere. Disgust with N.Y. Trapped again." He and June vowed that it was time to get respectable, and they summoned all their reserves to make yet another new start.

6.

Henry Street and Love Lane

1926–1930

Respectability, for the financially marginal Millers, meant that June would take a job as a waitress and Henry as an encyclopedia salesman. At first, June hoped to carry the burden herself, leaving Henry free to write. But he was "determined to extricate self from life of extortion and golddigging," as he wrote later, and he doubted June's resolve on that score. Besides, he was exhausted by writing to order. All his energies were given over to survival.

The couple took a room, on Remsen Street again but in circumstances far less grand than their earlier establishment. Miller began selling the *Encyclopaedia Britannica* and the *Jewish Encyclopedia* door to door, canvassing in the outlying boroughs and New Jersey from early morning to late at night. June pleaded that he take his meals at the Pepper Pot, the Greenwich Village restaurant where she had found a job, but he refused; he was making a flat-out, last-ditch attempt to overcome his tendency toward idleness and aimless daydreaming. The Remsen Street surroundings reawakened his middle-class, decidedly non-marginal desire to have a nice, clean apartment and a wife who stayed at home.

But the Greenwich Village atmosphere had a strange effect on his wife, Miller observed. Her looks changed entirely: she plucked her full eyebrows into theatrically thin arches and affected heavy dramatic makeup, smearing Vaseline on her eyelids and dusting her face with a greenish powder. She changed her hairstyle and began to dress strangely, cutting the points out of her brassieres so her nipples would show through and going without stockings in all seasons. She wore black and sometimes purple; instead of underwear she wore a strip of black velvet saturated with perfume. Her face hardened, Miller thought, and she seemed to go about all day with a cigarette hanging from her upper lip.

A new set of admirers came on the scene—a man who owned a chain of bookstores, a wrestler, any number of "millionaires"—and presents of books, candy, and money poured in. June called her devotees "dopes" and "saps," claiming, as usual, that they earned only rebuffs for their gifts. Miller felt almost too low to care. He developed a thorough disdain for the Village and its denizens, including men he had once admired like Maxwell Bodenheim and Guido Bruno. "There were nothing but dives and joints, nothing but pederasts, Lesbians, pimps, tarts, fakes and phonies of all description," he later wrote. That June was herself something of a tart and a phony he was not ready to admit.

With the arrival of another newcomer on the scene, Miller was confronted with the possibility that June might love other women. In the fall of 1926, he began to hear about Jean Kronski, a penniless Village artist with a vague past. In late October, after an unexplained three-day absence, June came home with a bizarre puppet named Count Bruga, after a character in a Ben Hecht novel based on Bodenheim. She carried the puppet with her everywhere, back and forth to work, and set it on the headboard of the bed when she was home, insisting that Henry admire it. He found the puppet ghoulish, with its black sombrero and violet hair and eyes—though it was well done, he had to admit. Her friend Jean had made it, June revealed; Jean was an absolute genius. Jean dressed in men's clothes, but only because they were more comfortable, June said. She insisted that whatever Jean did was right and natural—even stealing, or wearing two left shoes, or smoking marijuana.

Miller was immediately suspicious, and June retreated into ever more elaborate subterfuges in order to spend time with Jean. She claimed to be visiting her sick mother, for instance, but when Miller called Mrs. Smerth he found she had not seen June for months. He took to making random visits to the Pepper Pot, invariably finding June absent. In the midst of these goings-on he threw over the encyclopedia job, too dispirited to follow up the meager leads his boss gave him.

"Jean a typical pathologic case—June blind to everything," Miller would observe while working on his notes for *Capricorn* a few years later. In fact, Jean seems to have suffered some intense mental confusion, judging from Miller's accounts of this critical period of his life. Born in the West, she had been orphaned and raised by foster parents and given the name Marion. Because June did not believe "Marion" suited her, and because Jean claimed to be of Russian parentage, June renamed her Jean Kronski, inventing for her a past that included descent from the Romanoffs. When Jean arrived in the Village, she was about twenty-one, "masculine-looking" but beautiful, with a long mane of black hair and violet eyes. She was penniless, and lived in a succession of rented rooms, ostensibly trying to paint and write poems. She had not been in the Village for very long when she was taken into police custody for bizarre behavior of an undetermined nature. The record is sketchy here, but it appears Jean was admitted for observation to Bellevue, and that June designated herself as guardian. Released in just over a week, Jean took up residence on Pierrepont Street in Brooklyn Heights in order to be closer to June.

Miller was deeply distrustful, but he was also curious about the new arrival. June talked about her as if she were a man, a kind of androgyne. He became grimly fascinated by the notion that his wife might be sexually "perverse," as he put it. June's interest in Jean undermined his hard-won sense of manhood entirely. When Jean summoned him to the Pepper Pot for a talk, he told her that he winced when he thought of someone asking what was wrong with him. "Because there must be something wrong with a man," he explained, "so, at least, the world reasons—when his wife is violently attracted to another woman." Other men might have withdrawn from the scene, but Miller was determined to fight this battle to the finish—whatever the cost to his sanity.

He began a desperate second courtship, digging up his old love letters and photos, writing little clownish, self-effacing notes on them, and leaving them out for June to see. One night he propped up the puppet Count Bruga against the headboard, their marriage papers in one hand and his divorce papers in the other. When June returned home with Jean—she had taken to bringing Jean home for the night— she merely asked, "Is this another of your gestures, Val?" There was a subtle agreement between the two women, he believed, that he was a buffoon. His notes for the period indicate "Commence to go really nuts now."

His obsession with sexual perversion intensified. He brought home Krafft-Ebing's works and Forel's *The Sexual Question*, marking appropriate passages for the women to see. He remembered June's (surely invented) description of someone she had seen at the Pepper Pot—a hermaphrodite with the beginnings of a tail. When June insisted that Jean was not abnormal but suffered a case of "arrested development," he called in his physician friend Emil Conason to examine her. Conason pronounced her sexual organs normal, though he had studied enough psychology to recognize that she and June were a treacherous combination. June started in with a lot of gibberish about glands; late in life, discussing her relationship with Jean, she would claim that she was incapable of "Lesbianship." She explained, "I've always had a hyperthyroid condition. I just don't react that way."

Whether gland-induced or not, the relationship was passionate and intense—and, almost from the start, triangular. These two unbalanced, theatrical women needed an audience, a third party whose jealousy would fuel their passion. Alternately, they made each other jealous by encouraging Henry, who had fallen a little in love with Jean himself. With Conason's help, Henry resolved to torture Jean and drive her back to the asylum. In turn, Conason tortured *him* by telling him June had always been a Lesbian.

One alternative was to play the hard line, to be the stern husband he wished his father had been. One night he banished Jean from the house. When she reappeared that very night, he got up and walked the streets, in a snowstorm, until dawn. Returning, he kicked June and Jean out, then lay down and slept for thirty-six hours, exhausted. When he awoke he found that the women had apparently left for good. In desperation, he summoned Conason and told him he wanted to kill himself. They had a long talk about Barbara and how she might be provided for. Then Conason placed some pills on the bedside table and left.

Miller took the pills and lay down, expecting to die. When several minutes passed and nothing happened, he got up and opened all the windows, hoping to die of exposure, figuring (no doubt correctly) that the pills were only mild sedatives. Finally he did fall asleep. Meanwhile, Conason found June, who rushed home with Jean in tow. The drowsy Henry noticed that she hardly read the suicide note he had left her, and that she immediately disappeared with Jean for two hours, ostensibly to get "a bite." Later he wrote, "Now I know I'm licked. Impossible to combat the two of them."

Characteristically, Miller set out to do the impossible. While he was on the morbid edge of complete insanity, he was also energized, alive. His feeble suicide attempt—for surely he knew that Conason would not give him anything lethal—was only a gesture, on the order of one of June's dramatic charades. The disordered life June led, which once seemed so attractive to him, now drove him to distraction. He had gone from the rigid households of his mother and Beatrice to a completely chaotic one. That the chaos was also sexual only increased the threat to his psychic equilibrium. Previous crises had involved his family, love and sex, and his vocation, but this one threatened that very touchy subject, his manhood. When he emerged from it, the stage would be set for his virile masterpiece of chaos, *Tropic of Cancer*.

Remsen Street was too respectable a stage for the Miller menage, and June and Jean found a new apartment for the trio, a cellar on Henry Street in Brooklyn Heights—one door down, aptly enough, from a street called Love Lane. It had once been a laundry. Jean decorated the walls with murals and painted the ceiling violet. They took possession of the apartment in a snowfall, dragging their meager furnishings from Remsen Street in the ghostly silence of the evening. Miller tacked up his photograph of Barbara and a favorite drawing by Emil Schnellock in the bathroom; Jean appropriated the best room for herself, with June's help. In the middle of the kitchen—the one common room—they set up a table they called the "gut table," because they spilled their guts there. Miller later described the apartment for Anaïs Nin:

> Bed unmade all day; climbing into it with shoes on frequently; sheets a mess. Using soiled shirts for towels. . . . Washing dishes in bathtub, which was greasy and black-rimmed. Bathroom always cold as an icebox. . . . Shades always down, windows never washed, atmosphere sepulchral. Floor constantly strewn with plaster of Paris, tools, paints, books, cigarette butts, garbage, soiled dishes, pots. Jean running around all day in overalls. June, always half-naked and complaining of the cold.

Miller hung about the place, he said, "like a stranger."

Some staggering revelations were poured forth over the gut table. Jean confessed to having staged Lesbian performances with another woman in order to get money out of an admirer, which made June frantic with jealousy. Conason increased his efforts to wear down Jean, terrifying her with continuous threats to call Bellevue. June horrified

Henry by saying she loved both him and Jean. In turn, Jean confided to Conason some truths about June's leanings, hoping he'd tell Henry; when he did, Henry confronted June, who said Jean was only playing a game.

The new apartment was like a coke joint, Miller later commented. Round the clock, the women enthusiastically sang "Let Me Call You Sweetheart"; one night Miller got so enraged he ran after them with a stick, trying to beat them. Another time he stuck a knife in Jean's door. Cold and broke, they burned all the chairs in the fireplace and thereafter had to sit on packing cases. At night Miller brushed Jean's long hair and pared her toenails.

He had already given up trying to work—not to speak of trying to write. Now he gave up trying to coax money out of friends and relatives and turned instead to panhandling in the streets. He was getting professional at it, and he spent his days in poolhalls, burlesques, speakeasies, trying desperately to keep busy. His friends, most of whom held respectable jobs and had families, had practically given up on him—except for Sleaco, who was quite mad himself now. When Jean painted on the back of the toilet a line from Virgil, *Et forsan haec olim meminisse iuvabit* ("Perhaps someday it will help to have remembered these things"), Miller was too agitated to see the irony.

Twice he set out for the West. The first time he got as far as Philadelphia, where he dug up his old friend Blount and borrowed some money from him by saying June was ill. The second time he made it to Pittsburgh before he suddenly lost heart and returned. Once Jean tried to leave town, claiming she found June's theatrics tiring. But Miller couldn't get the money together for her trip, and June and Jean recast the whole episode as just another of his tricks. Then June begged Miller to let her go away with Jean, to cure her; he agreed, but they went only as far as Greenwich Village, where Miller exhausted himself trailing them.

If his friends thought Miller unhinged, his parents thought him simply irresponsible. He did his best to hide his domestic troubles from Heinrich and Louise, but the family ethic demanded that he make periodic appearances at Decatur Street. He gave in to June's pleas to bring Jean along to his parents' home on Christmas Day 1926; his only request was that she dress like a woman. But Henry had his hands full getting them dressed and out the door for the occasion, because both women had stumbled in drunk the night before. Jean limped along in her stocking feet, carrying her unaccustomed high heels. At the Miller home, Henry tried to steer the conversation away from any dangerous talk about modern art or radical politics; he was saved when the two women asked to take a nap on the family sofa and slept on through the afternoon. Late in the day the family gathered around the tree to sing *O Tannenbaum*, softly so as not to wake the women. When Jean and June did awake, the family album was brought out and the family eccentrics displayed. To Henry, fearful of his own instability, the scene seemed positively ghoulish.

He had sunk into a deep, murderous depression. Later, in *Nexus*, he would write that he knew he had hit bottom. Most of the time he spoke only in monosyllables, if at all; at other times he would rant for hours. He was capable of staying in one place, in one position, for an indeterminate length of time. June and Jean often returned to find him leaning against a wall like a statue, only his eyes moving; then he might begin to speak tirelessly, like an automaton. Accusations of madness were hurled back and forth. June, who called everyone she liked "mad" and those she didn't "fools," took to saying fondly, "You're such a mad fool, Val," confounding him even further.

His impulse to write had vanished. Instead, he pretended to write. He claimed to be writing a play in three acts with three characters: himself, June, and Jean. He carried around a notebook, writing down any revealing thing the two women said, threatening to expose them through art. He thought of a fresh torture: making Jean take dictation from him. The accounts he reeled off to her of his own suspicions and certainties led to new revelations of even greater betrayal. Miller had ceased to care very much about June's antics with other men, but any indication that she loved Jean more than him, or that she preferred sex with women to sex with him, distracted him for days.

To maintain the charged atmosphere, June conceived a new plan: she and Jean would leave for Paris. It had, of course, been Miller's dream to go to Europe ever since he had listened to Emil Schnellock's raptures about France. But now June appropriated his dream, and in a most maddening way. She was never definite about whether he could join them or not, how long they were going for, or whether they would return. She only knew they had to get there, all three of them, eventually. In their proper setting—for so Paris was perceived by these would-be bohemians—they would thrive. They could create an artistic community more innovative and intense than any Greenwich Village had seen.

"More golddigging on a grand scale—only now it's a burlesque."

So read Miller's notes about this period. New, elaborate plans were mounted. Jean decided to manufacture puppets, and then extended her line to include death masks. Soon the walls of the Henry Street apartment were festooned with death masks of the occupants and their friends. When these failed to catch on, the women set out for the Village in search of golddigging targets, looking, to Henry's eyes, like freaks. Jean tried to hire herself out for medical experiments. Both women eagerly seized on Henry's idea of selling blood, but they were disappointed when they were turned away as anemic. June brought men home now, and Henry sat in the little shed behind the house, freezing, listening to the sounds through the walls. One night, after days of vomiting, June confessed she had been using drugs, but claimed, inexplicably, that she did it as a sacrifice.

This last admission roused Miller from his torpor. He set out to learn more about June, looking up old admirers like Marder and telephoning one of her brothers, who confirmed that she had lied about her past. He followed up with a visit to June's mother, about whom he had been so curious for so long, and found there was no mystery there; June had just left home because she didn't get along with her father. There was also an older sister, Maria, more beautiful than June, of whom June was jealous. Mrs. Smerth even produced June's birth papers, which showed she was born on January 28, 1902, along with a photo of June at eighteen months. The detail that really struck Henry was Mrs. Smerth's comment that June "had always held her head high." It was still true.

Somehow this visit, which at least produced some facts, had a tonic effect on Henry. Shortly after, in April 1927, he ran into his old nemesis Jimmy Pasta on the street. Initially ashamed—his clothes were torn, and he was as usual penniless—Henry found Jimmy very friendly and concerned about his welfare. He had a job with the Parks Department and was sure he could find one for Henry too, if he was interested. Henry conferred with June, who begged him to see them through ("for once," she added) while she and Jean were in Paris. With some misgivings, he accepted the job; he had to work "in the field" for a week first, and then he would be assigned to an office. (He was not, as he later reported, a gravedigger, although he liked the idea.)

The Saturday following his first week of work June woke him with a breakfast of strawberries and cream. Jean sang in the bathroom while he bathed, and June asked him to buy her a brassiere and some stockings with his first week's pay. When he left for work, the two followed him out in the street. He suspected another ruse or intrigue. When he returned that evening, Henry found their trunks gone, the death masks and Count Bruga taken down. He struck a match to read the note lying on the old "gut table," and learned that June and Jean had sailed for Paris.

After Henry's initial shock, he broke every piece of furniture in the house and howled so loudly the landlady came down to comfort him. He then took stock. The Henry Street apartment was filled with memories; the first thing to do was to move. The only place left to go was back to Decatur Street. His respectable job, he hoped, would shield him from his mother's criticism. In less than a week he moved into his old bedroom at his parents' home, giving out bland assurances that June was merely "on vacation" in Europe. Soon cables from her began arriving at the Parks Department office, all demands for money. He sent off whatever he could. However great her betrayal in running away to Paris without notice, June still held him transfixed. Formed in the coils of sexual jealousy and poverty, their code held that any request for money had to be taken seriously. Whatever June wanted, Miller sent, borrowing sums from his Uncle Dave and Jimmy Pasta.

At his typewriter, once again set up on his parents' dining-room table, Miller poured out letters to June filled with questions about Paris. He got almost no response, just more cables. On May 21, 1927, the day of Lindbergh's landing in Paris, he received one of the two letters June sent during her trip. She wrote that Jean had gone off with a crazy Austrian to North Africa and that she was in Vienna with friends. The only way Miller could make sense of her letter was to take the "s" off "friends."

That same day, at his Parks Department office, he began to make some notes. He worked feverishly, and when he was done a stack of thirty-odd closely typed pages sat next to his typewriter. As he wrote, a complete plan for his life's work fell into place. He would write the story of his life with June and Jean: a colossal tale of great love and great betrayal. The notes had no shape, no theme, though they did have motifs: golddigging, battles royal, debauches, lies. He invented fictional names for his friends and catalogued June's lovers; he repeatedly admonished himself not to forget any details. If he remembered an event when it was not chronologically relevant he wrote it out anyway, noting that it should be presented as a "throwback." He made a list of "Bizarre Messengers" and listed "Mss. to be utilized"; the latter included the Mezzotints, some letters to Emil, some of the material for *Snappy Stories*, and his old suicide letter to June. Everything he had ever committed to paper, it seemed, was to go into the work.

The whole thing came to him as a sort of manic vision, hallucinatory in its hyperreality. He was overwhelmed when he realized the magnitude of the task he had set for himself. The story would require a great tome. He must have seen, as well, that he lacked the emotional distance required for an undertaking like this: he hadn't lived the last chapter yet.

In reality, however, the amassing of these notes had set Miller on the road to artistry, if not to health. At last, he had something to say. He had *volumes* to say. He was seized with a determination to communicate the violent upheavals of the soul that he had suffered at June's hands. And, with this new determination, he achieved some peace; no longer racked by emotion, he was strangely calm. His despondency lifted slightly. He had work to do.

Early in July, Miller received a cable at his office saying that June was returning on the *Berengaria* in a few days. With some trepidation, he went to the dock on the specified day and found she wasn't on the boat. When another cable arrived two weeks later, he rented a furnished room and went down to the dock again, this time happily finding June safely arrived, without Jean. In the taxi he stifled his questions about Jean's absence and the delay in sailing. June went on feverishly about Paris: Montparnasse, the open-air markets, the cafés, the public gardens, the grand Parisian avenues. She had met the Russian-born sculptor Ossip Zadkine, who took her on a picnic in the Bois de Boulogne; Cocteau and Picasso both fell in love with her, she reported. She talked of the painters Hans Reichel, Tihanyi, and Michonze; she had met Marcel Duchamp and found him "the most civilized man [she'd] ever met." Now, June said, Miller must join her in returning to Paris immediately: this would become her constant refrain.

Though Miller saw no need for a better place than their furnished room, June quickly found another luxurious apartment at 180 Clinton Avenue near Fulton Street, in a neighborhood of private mansions and elegant brownstones. Miller's parents hoped that June's impending return wouldn't mean that he would quit his new job, but he promptly did.

The expectation, of course, was that now Miller would finally settle down to write. For a time, June tried to maintain a semblance of order in their home, putting on an apron to cook her husband excellent meals, followed by fine liqueurs. From his writing table, Miller looked out on a beautiful garden shaded by two huge trees; the Jewish landlady below often played the synagogue music she knew he liked. They notified none of what Miller called their "pestilential cronies" of their new whereabouts.

But little money was coming in, and Miller began to think of going back to work. June scraped enough together to open a "cellar dive" that she called the Roman Tavern on MacDougal and 3rd Streets in the Village; this time, however, Miller was not allowed on the scene, and, with uncharacteristic docility, he complied. For another admirer had turned up: a man in the fur business who would reveal himself only as "Pop." This man, June claimed, was interested in her as a writer— she had shown him some of the leftover Mezzotints and talked a good game. The upshot was that he was willing to pay her a weekly stipend so that she could write a novel, the only stipulation being that she show him some pages every week.

Miller, of course, would write the pages. The plan had obvious difficulties: a man might write a prose poem and pass it off as a woman's, but to sustain a female voice throughout a complete novel wouldn't be so simple, he feared. Moreover, Pop wanted to hear about the creative process, and June was incapable of simply saying "I don't know" when asked technical questions about such matters as motivation. There were practical difficulties as well—June had told Pop that she was living with her invalid mother. And, of course, there were obvious questions about the real nature of the exchange. As Miller wrote tersely in *Nexus*, "The chances were, of course, that she was giving value for value, and had been from the very beginning."

The writing was fitful. Miller had put aside the notes for his book about June, a subject not likely to work if she was the supposed author. Instead, he began a novel based on his years at Western Union and his marriage to Beatrice. Its real subject was announced on the first page, where it was revealed that the hero, Dion Moloch, "was often said to be anti-Semitic." Anti-Semitism, wrote the narrator, was a prejudice and not a disease. The novel, as it took shape, became an exploration of anti-Semitism, following Dion Moloch's ramblings around New York. Henry tentatively titled it *Moloch*, the name for the Jewish concept of a demonic force yoked under the terrible might of rigid order—

a concept that has been used to describe the rise of Adolf Hitler. Henry's life (and the life of his novel's hero) had been molded by a Moloch-like force, a force Henry both admired and feared.

Writing "to order" was, as always for Miller, difficult. "Every time I sat down to write a page for [Pop]," he wrote later, "I readjusted my skirt, primped my hairdo and powdered my nose." He felt a woman's voice should be literary, dainty, and so far as he had any voice of his own he knew it was neither of these. He looked to other models for inspiration; he had been borrowing from writers like Walter Pater and Henry James for years, and the habit was hard to break. Writing about New York's skyscrapers, he might see an analogy with the congested districts of imperial Rome and dig up a copy of Mommsen, losing his thread for hours. On sunny days he often simply knocked off and took a book to Fort Greene Park—Samuel Ornitz's *Haunch, Paunch and Jowl* or Unamuno's *The Tragic Sense of Life*, for instance.

The weekly quota hung over him. So did June, who hovered over him like an anxious mother. Don't push yourself, she'd say. As Miller wrote in *Nexus*, "But I have pushed. I've pushed and pushed till there's not a drop of caca in me. Often it's just when she says—'Dinner's ready!' that the flow begins." There was no telling what any given day would bring. "Sometimes I sailed into it with huge black wings. Then everything came out pell-mell and arsey-versy. Pages and pages. Reams of it. None of it belonged in the novel." He summed up:

> Such exquisite torture, this writing humbuggery! Bug-house reveries mixed with choking fits. . . . Squat images roped with diamond tiaras. Baroque architecture. Cabalistic logarithms. Mezzuzahs and prayer wheels. Portentous phrases.

The result, in *Moloch*, is a vastly uneven manuscript. The writing is almost uniformly stilted and awkward, but occasional images are striking, bordering on the surreal. The narrator attempts to be tough, slangy (there is much "wiring" to "firms" for money), but to today's ear the language is antique and wooden, and the narrative voice is inconsistent and often obtrusive. The opening is representative: "Dion Moloch walks with the dreamy stride of a noctambulo among the apparitions on the Bowery. I say 'apparitions' because, as every sophisticated New Yorker knows the Bowery is a thoroughfare where blasted souls are repaired for the price of a free lunch." When Miller looked over the manuscript five years later, he wrote his friend Richard Osborn that he almost wept: "I was running around like a dog in the streets, piddling at every corner and sniffing and yelping. I can see now that I was running away from myself."

But the schedule gave him discipline, and he was elated to discover that the finished work was some 100,000 words. Pop liked it—Henry and June celebrated with a bottle of Chartreuse when he approved the first fifty pages—and encouraged June to write another one. June was elated that Henry had proved himself as a writer after all. She ignored the novel's ending, in which the hero returns to the Beatrice figure; she reasoned that Miller no doubt engineered the ending just to annoy her. Miller knew the book was not fully realized and never submitted it for publication, although he did carry it around with him for years, hoping to glean bits from it. It was not the novel he intended to write, anyway; it was mostly a rehash of material he had used in *Clipped Wings*. His major advance had been his creation of an autobiographical hero, his realization that any artistic gift he had was for the artful arrangement of events from his own life.

In May 1928 Henry and June spent a two-week vacation in Quebec, which whetted their desire to go abroad. They ate French food and heard French spoken all around them, but all the same the city seemed decidedly North American. Furthermore, they had plenty of reasons to want to leave New York. By now their old friends had smoked them out at their Clinton Avenue apartment, and June was restless, between schemes. Miller was worried that Beatrice might get wind of their new prosperity—unlike June's other admirers, Pop was reliable—and he was eager to get away. America seemed sterile, New York oppressive. Every writer of any worth was abroad—June had spotted Hemingway at the Deux Magots—and Miller, now a man of letters himself, wanted to be part of the expatriate scene. In the Village, he had rubbed shoulders with Bodenheim, Sadakichi Hartman, and Guido Bruno, but never with Sherwood Anderson, John Dos Passos, or e. e. cummings. Now, he thought, he was ready to mix with his equals.

It was Pop who came up with the passage money, supposedly as a reward for the completed novel. But, as he also supplied money for nine months' expenses, it seems probable that some significant quid pro quo was required from June. Henry didn't ask. In June they began their preparations in earnest, memorizing Métro lines and borrowing the Berlitz book Henry's father had carried about with him for years. In July they sailed.

. . .

The *S.S. Paris* docked in Liverpool in late July 1928, and the Millers went on to London, which they found damp and depressing. In fact, Miller was not at all impressed by Europe—until they arrived in Paris. As night fell, in the cab from the Gare St. Lazare to Saint-Germain, his heart was won.

In America, Miller had marveled over the streets named for writers in Paris; now he walked along them. At the Place St. Sulpice, a favorite haunt, he remembered his friend Stanley's old hero, Anatole France, who he knew had once stood on that very spot. Paris seemed made for the writer, and especially the poor writer; one could linger over coffee for an entire afternoon in the cafés, and Miller often did. June knew Montparnasse like a book, and took Miller around to the Dôme, the Coupole, the Select—all the haunts of the expatriate American.

But Miller took in working Paris as well. He loved the marketplace in the rue Buci on a Sunday morning: it was vibrant, bright—not at all like a lugubrious Sunday in Brooklyn. In tourist fashion, he constantly made comparisons. Some Paris neighborhoods reminded him strongly of the parts of Brooklyn he had loved as a boy, and he haunted the city's fringes. You only had to get on the Métro, he wrote a friend, and everything changed.

The Millers set up headquarters in the Hôtel de Paris in the rue Bonaparte, but both of them were restless. Henry wasn't writing anything except letters, and June had no schemes going. One late summer afternoon, lounging around Montparnasse, they ran into Alfred Perlès in the rue Delambre; June had met this diminutive, charming Austrian writer on her visit with Jean. By her account, Perlès had fallen in love with her—though he had taken off for North Africa with Jean. It was a warm day, and they decided to picnic in the Luxembourg Gardens. Miller was impressed enough by Perlès that, at their parting, he asked if the Austrian needed any money. It wasn't often Miller got a chance to make such an offer, he confided. Perlès declined, though he sensed he had met a kindred soul.

Just after this meeting, the Millers set out, somewhat aimlessly, on a train tour through Belgium, Germany, Czechoslovakia, and Poland. Henry had in mind tracking down their ancestors, although June wanted little to do with that. He also wanted to check the hotel register at the place June said she had stayed in Vienna, not at all convinced her story about her visit there was true. The ghost of Jean haunted them in their travels; since June had left her behind in Paris, there was no telling where she might turn up.

Miller was unimpressed by the Germans, as he expected, and repulsed by the Poles, whom he found boorish and crude. He fretted that they were seeing no real peasant life, only tourist attractions. From Budapest (which they preferred to Vienna), Henry and June took a train toward Romania, heading for June's birthplace in Bukovina. At the border they were detained. When their train didn't arrive in Czernowitz, June's uncle set out in a three-horse carriage to collect them. In the village Miller might not have learned much about June's past, but he saw plenty of peasants, who surrounded her in the Czernowitz cafés.

During a bicycle tour of the Midi following their return to France, the couple realized that their money was running dangerously low. They had their passage back to New York, but no cash. In Nice, they sold their bicycles and hitchhiked to Monte Carlo to see if they could turn up something. But June was less confident in the provinces, and they fell on the largesse of a black American who ran a shoe shine stand on the Boulevard des Anglais. His resources did not extend very far, however, and after three weeks Miller petitioned the American consul to send June to Paris. Once there, she raised Miller's train fare with alacrity.

In Monte Carlo, sitting at a café, Miller had watched June quake with silent tears; her mute misery was new to him. With their European trip, the couple was thrown on their own resources, and they found the balance of power in their marriage had subtly shifted. Without a third party—or a host of admirers—their energy flagged. Miller was finally recovering from the dehumanization he had suffered at the hands of June and Jean; he had written a book in the process, and there was another that demanded to be written. June began to seem very young and a little pitiful now that she was out of her element. In Europe, it was Henry who took the initiative, and the experience changed him. He took in little of what he saw there; in fact, this European trip was one of the rare episodes in his life he found it nearly impossible to write about, perhaps because most of his energy was given over to recovery.

The couple returned to New York in January 1929, staying at Decatur Street only long enough to raise the money to rent another apartment in the Fort Greene area of Brooklyn. June tried for a time to find acting work, but soon she reclaimed her old job at the Pepper Pot and told Pop she was back. Before long, her drug use, until now largely

casual, escalated. Henry watched June's gradual disintegration in silent despair. She was still beautiful and showed flashes of her old
vitality and strong sensuality, but her use of cocaine and alcohol tipped
the fragile balance in her psyche away from romantic mystery and
toward disordered craziness. He remembered her oblique reference to
her drug use as a "sacrifice"; now, she seemed to be living out her own
prophecy. She would do *anything*, she said, to help Henry become a
great writer, her language more desperate than ever.

In the face of such a sacrifice, Henry turned to the great novel he
felt was within him: the story of his love for June. As he plotted it out,
however, he began to alter the facts, caught up in the climate of June's
deceptions. In early drafts he portrayed himself as fighting Jean for his
wife's love, with June herself an unwitting pawn. His hero, whom he
called Tony Bring, would expose all June's lies, which in turn would
justify Tony's jealousy. A long section at the end would present June's
trip to Paris with Jean and her return as a romantic idyll, a peaceful
and happy time for Tony Bring. (For Miller, of course, it had been a
veritable hell.)

Perhaps because the events he was writing about had not yet been
resolved in real life, Miller foundered. He produced version after version of the novel, which he tentatively titled *Lovely Lesbians*. To his
dismay, he found Jean emerging as a central figure: the manuscript
June preferred opened with Jean in the West, a cowgirl apotheosized
into a mythic androgyne. Perhaps in response, Miller had Tony Bring
murder her with a bread knife at the end of one version; in another
version, the Jean figure goes mad. As for his hero, Tony Bring is little
more than a passive object, reduced at the end of one version to barking like a dog. Years later Miller would rescue this ending for *Sexus*,
which closes with the hero wearing a dog collar and barking like a dog.
The image suited the sense of utter dehumanization he wanted to convey.

As his title indicates, Miller was aiming for a bitterly ironic tone,
sophisticated to the point of being jaded. But such a voice was at odds
with the paradoxical mix of innocence and gullibility he brought to
many experiences, particularly his marriage to June. He could not
capture this mix of qualities, and he thought that realistic detail might
compensate. So he included long scenes in which the two women minister to the hero's hemorrhoids, along with lengthy clinical discussions
of various forms of sexual behavior. The existing versions of the novel
have a quality of heightened realism reminiscent of the detail-crammed

novels of Theodore Dreiser, whom Miller very much admired. But Miller wasn't satisfied; he needed to recapture the craziness of those days. So he injected doses of surrealism, but, as in *Moloch*, without any control or mastery.

Later he would blame the novel's failure on June, America, fate. But in 1929 he refused to admit having failed. *Moloch*, written to order for Pop, was one thing, but this novel, born out of agony and love, simply had to be a masterpiece. With *Lovely Lesbians*, which he later retitled *Crazy Cock*, Miller showed the growing critical blindness that would become characteristic of him. Though he sensed that the novel wasn't right—thus all the "versions," each an almost total rewrite— he stubbornly refused to give up. He peddled it for years, and abandoned it only after he reworked many of its scenes into *Tropic of Capricorn*. Even then he kept the manuscript around, cannibalizing other passages for *The Rosy Crucifixion*.

June, too, saw the novel as a success. She viewed it as a celebration of herself, overlooking (or perhaps approving) her character's deceptions and intrigues. Tony Bring was suitably abject, she thought, and the Jean figure suitably larger than life. The pages she read revitalized her memories of the Henry Street period, and she circled around her old lies, reworking and embellishing them, keeping the manuscript in a state of perpetual revision. Under June's influence, it was impossible for Miller to produce a linear narrative—or even a single narrative. There were many stories, each of them as good—and true—as the next. Unwittingly, June did everything to steer Miller away from writing in a conventional manner: first, by encouraging him to view writing as a commodity, producing "bits" to be "reworked," and second, by calling into question the very nature of the reality the artist apprehends. Miller's later work was as retrospectively indebted to June's "coketalk" as it was to his heroes Dostoevsky and Knut Hamsun.

He owed her another debt as well: June brought in the money that enabled him to write. She now had a myriad of new schemes and admirers ("wonderful how she could vary the substantive!" Miller wrote in *Nexus*). Pop was still in the picture, presumably taking a tender interest in her writing career. But there was another, more serious contender, about whom June was uncharacteristically and ominously specific: Stratford Corbett, an insurance man with New York Life. Though she still loved Henry, June's nature was so changeable that she needed fresh intrigue. She may have sensed as well that Henry did, too, that he thrived on fresh wounds and languished when things got too comfortable.

By 1930, June had concocted her last and grandest scheme. She presented it to Miller as a terrific gamble. If he wanted to become a great writer, she decided, then he needed to return to Europe alone. She would support him; alone in New York, she would work some mighty swindles, enough to assure them a life together abroad. But they must sacrifice their present life together for the greater goal: Miller's triumph as a writer and their eventual glory. Of course, Stratford Corbett was in the wings if anything fell through—although she didn't tell Miller that.

June still did have high hopes for Henry's future. But she was also desperate. He seemed unable to function in the world, and he was not happy living on the fringes as she was. Perhaps in Paris, where prices were low and the climate encouraging for artists, Henry might find solace. Failing that, he would at least be less of a drag on her own attempts to make a livelihood. He seemed to thrive on adversity, too, and June suspected he would meet with more than his share of that abroad.

When she laid all this out for him, Miller thought the timing was perfect. It was a year of milestones: he had completed what he considered his first publishable novel. He heard from his old friend Stanley Borowski that Beatrice had remarried. Word reached them too about Jean Kronski, at last; she had returned to New York and killed herself in an insane asylum. That news put the kind of closure on his marriage that Miller had sought in his book. Seven years had passed since he met June, and seven years had been the length of his relationship with Beatrice as well. He was a great believer in fate—a man with so little control over his own life almost had to be—and it looked like fate had something new in store for him. He would go to Europe and see what shook out there.

Part 2

PARIS

". . . it is all Greek to me—the language, the customs, the pissoirs, the labels on the bottles, the sliding scale of tips, the courtesies that are not courtesies, the radiators that give milk instead of steam, the procession des noctambules, the chanteurs ambulants, the calliope that wakes me every morning, wheezing the same tune yesterday as today."

Henry Miller, _Letters to Emil_ (1989)

"When I move I have only to pack a few condoms and I'm off."

Miller to Ned Calmer, July 1932

7.

An American in Paris

1930–1931

Miller sailed for London—aboard the *Bremen*—with $10 in his pocket, loaned him by his old friend Emil Schnellock. He passed the voyage in anguish, reliving his departure. On leaving the Fort Greene apartment he had crossed paths with a man he took to be Pop in his own vestibule. He had not even dared look up to the window where June waved goodbye, afraid that he might spoil whatever intrigue she was operating.

Ten dollars didn't last long in London, where he landed on February 25. There seemed to be absolutely no point to being there; he had grown accustomed to judging places by the plight of the poor, knowing he would likely live among them, and, in the first year of the Depression, London's poor seemed especially miserable. The gloom was so thick, Miller wrote Schnellock, you could cut it with an ax. He killed time, making expeditions to Whitechapel and to see the Turners at the Tate—the only sights that impressed him—until June wired more money, just enough for the train to Paris. Miller realized he was now entirely dependent on his less-than-dependable wife. And if money arrived, that meant she had made a success of her latest adventure, which didn't exactly cheer him. If money didn't arrive, he had no way of knowing whether she had met with bad luck or had forgotten about him.

The American Express office in rue Scribe was one of the first places Miller visited after his arrival in Paris on March 4; it would become a familiar haunt. As often as three times a day he trudged from his shabby hotel room on the Left Bank across the Seine, hoping for a cable or letter from June. More often than not disappointed, he was soon forced into cheaper lodgings, and was frequently without enough money for food.

The first sights that struck Miller were such public notices as the signs on the train from Le Havre reserving seats for *"les mutilés de la guerre,"* and, in Paris, the ubiquitous posters warning against the dangers of venereal disease, picturing the development of the disease from a germ to a leering death's head. He found the posters grimly realistic, haunting reminders that Paris's equally ubiquitous prostitutes carried disease, that sex and death were inevitable partners. Sex, death, decay, violence: these were to be the subjects that characterized Miller's writing in his early Paris years.

To his dismay, Miller found that his rudimentary French had deserted him. Before long, however, he discovered much that he admired in the French people. He learned, for instance, that many of them were easygoing about credit; he was delighted when, after several weeks of meals in the rue des Canettes, the *patronne* said she'd extend him credit "with pleasure." And a waiter in a café at the end of the Boulevard St. Michel lent him not just a few francs but several hundred, whenever he asked, and took him to dinner and the cinema besides.

But Miller was lonely. The Russian-born sculptor Ossip Zadkine, whom Miller had met on his first European trip (and who, Miller suspected, had been among June's lovers), took him to hear an orchestra on the Boulevard Haussmann one evening and tried to introduce him around. Miller was very much a tourist in his first months in Paris, reporting to his New York friends about such matters as the behavior of French dogs (slovenly, lazy), the appearance of the policemen (allowed to smoke on duty, civilized), and the conduct of French children (extraordinarily good). The food drove him to a burst of patriotism; to Schnellock he wrote, "I'm an American, BeJesus! And I'm not used to eating the intestines of dogs, horses, and guinea pigs." Like many of his compatriots, he was soon dismissing the "insufferable [American] idiots" at the Dôme and the Coupole.

But any superiority Miller felt to the expatriate community evaporated as quickly as his funds. He moved from the Hôtel St. Germain-des-Prés to a succession of smaller, cheaper places; he cut back on his meals and tried to subsist on bananas and oranges; he started conversations with strangers, hoping to extract the price of a meal. His friends at home, impressed that he had made it to Paris at all, were usually good for a money order or a shipment of clothing. But these were stopgap measures only. Very few jobs were available for an American without a work permit, and Miller didn't even have a *carte d'identité*, which made finding a job virtually impossible. An American named

Fred Kann suggested they open an academy for American students, but they lacked the capital to follow it through. If he was a woman, Miller thought, he could get by. But he, a man, had nothing to offer. He gave English lessons now and then, but his pupils inevitably drifted away.

While Miller tried to get something going, he composed heroic surrealist letters to Cocteau and Buñuel; deeply impressed by Paul Morand's book on New York, which occupied him for months, he offered himself to the Frenchman as a secretary. But he succeeded in landing only the occasional eccentric little job, like writing to the Pope for a French Catholic acquaintance (why the letter had to be in English he never understood).

For the most part, he was leading a life *en marge*, as he liked to say—it was one of his favorite phrases. Broke, he found a tailor in the rue St. André des Arts who was willing to buy two suits given him by his father, each custom-made and worth at least $100. Miller got only 75 francs—about $3—for both of them, but the tailor took him out for a big lunch, which Miller considered ample compensation. He cared only about his immediate needs: a bed, wine, food—especially food, which became an obsession.

He wrote Schnellock that he was falling into such a "bummy condition" that people nudged each other and pointed at him in the streets. He was acquiring an image. He took to wearing corduroys, which were considered in the thirties to be the uniform of the artist, and often added a gray snap-brimmed hat. With his heavy spectacles and intense pale blue eyes, he was a shabby but arresting presence. Those who met him at the time said he gave the impression of being much taller than his 5 feet 8 inches, for his deep, gravelly voice suggested someone more commanding. His voluminous talk was deceptive as well; more than one friend remembered that he listened more than he talked. Nobody missed his accent, however; it was broad and unmistakably Brooklyn.

Among the crowd on the *terrasses* of Montparnasse cafés, Miller began to make friends. Much of the old expatriate community had left France in the wake of the stock market crash, and those who remained tried rather pathetically to recapture the gaiety of the twenties. The glamor of the "lost generation" days had faded, and the artists who congregated in the cafés now were usually working commercial artists, the writers often journalists with the Paris editions of the *New York Herald Tribune* and the *Chicago Tribune*. Miller's first friends in Paris were American newspapermen: Wambly Bald, the author of the *Tribune*'s widely read gossip column "La Vie de Boheme," and Ned Calmer, a journalist with the *Herald*. This community spoke little French and had only minimal contact with working Paris, and Miller emerged as a popular figure because he claimed an intimate knowledge of the French streets.

This knowledge was largely mythical. As late as 1933, in his fourth year in Paris, Miller wrote to his friend Frank Dobo complaining that he had never known "a French telephone operator, or a dactylo [typist] or a salesgirl in a department store, or a midinette, or a grisette, or a lorette, or a cocotte." Like other expatriates on the fringes of the artistic world, his real aim, he wrote, was to "crash the portals" of French society. "I am going to do it coldbloodedly," he said. "I want to meet these people on their own grounds." He wanted to be entertained in a Parisian townhouse and to drive through the Bois in a sports car with some high society matron who dabbles in the arts, he said, adding disgustedly that he didn't even know the celebrated reigning queen of the demimonde, Kiki of Montparnasse. *Everyone* knew Kiki.

One large part of Paris's working population that Miller did get to know in these early years were the city's foreign-born laborers. These men constituted Paris's cheap labor force—its street cleaners, exterminators, buyers of scrap. His acquaintances among them included the Hindu Haridas Mazumdar, his old crony from Western Union, now a pearl merchant down on his luck, for whom he acted as an unpaid servant in exchange for room and meager board, as well as a Russian named Serge from the Suresnes district. In the neighborhood of the Porte de Vanves he met another Russian named Eugène Pachoutinsky who had a "miserable" job in a cinema; he showed Miller a hotel where he could stay for 125 francs a month—about $5. Even this was too steep, however, and Miller spent a few weeks sleeping on the floor of another transplanted Brooklynite, Albert Kotin, an art student. Among contacts like these, Miller scraped by.

In April 1930, while drinking disconsolately at the Dôme—he had no money, and was gathering up his courage to throw himself on the proprietor's mercy—Miller providentially ran into Alfred Perlès, the Austrian who had gone off with Jean Kronski and whom Miller and June had met in 1928. Perlès was a small, clownish man with a boyish nature. He worked as a proof reader at the *Tribune*, where he also wrote a few features, and was writing a surrealist novel in French. There was an instant rapport between the two expatriates, who shared a strong survivor's instinct and a fondness for clowning. Perlès, in fact, encouraged Miller's tendency toward laziness, as well as his prankishness and his sloppy philosophizing. At the same time, he served as the "second" Miller always needed, the buffoon he required as a foil. Miller immediately proposed they call each other "Joey," taking the name of a childhood friend (Joey Imhof, with whom he had made his boyhood homosexual explorations). Perlès, ever a follower, readily agreed, and soon everyone on the Left Bank was hailed as "Joey," whether he liked it or not.

Perlès also solved Miller's immediate material problems, paying the café bill and paying the rent on a room next to his at the Hôtel Central overlooking the rue de Maine. From his room Miller could see the prostitutes strolling on the Boulevard Edgar Quinet and the workmen eating their bread-and-cheese lunches on the benches below; this was the real Paris, he felt. Though he could not seem to find a job that lasted, he was writing again—and he thought it was some of his best work ever. He carried a notebook about with him, writing short pieces on street scenes and events such as the six-day bicycle races he had seen in March, an Oceanic art exhibit at the Théâtre Pigalle, and the wine merchants at Bercy. His writing began to lose the awkwardness that had plagued his earlier efforts, becoming less wooden and artificial. "Hearing another language daily," he later explained, "sharpens your own language for you, makes you aware of shades and nuances you never suspected. . . . You become more conscious of your own language." He was also enjoying the long letters he was writing, usually to Emil Schnellock: "In a letter I can breeze along and not bother to be too careful about grammar, etc. I can say Jesus when I like and string the adjectives out by the yard." The experience of writing letters gave his prose a conversational quality that it sorely needed, and he worked on developing the anonymous, voyeuristic voice that would characterize *Tropic of Cancer*. In his letters he began to refer to his "Paris book." Many of the pieces he wrote in Paris in 1930 would make their way into his first "real" novel.

For the time being, however, he set his commercial sights on resurrecting *Moloch*; he had managed to interest Henri Müller, an editor at Grasset, in it. Müller had thought it good but not likely to appeal to a French audience. He also showed it to Edward Titus, the editor of *This Quarter* and owner of a rue Delambre bookshop frequented by Americans. When Titus promptly lost the manuscript, Miller took it as an omen and turned instead to *Crazy Cock*, the Tony

Bring manuscript about his life with June. He showed it to Ned Calmer and to Perlès, neither of whom was very encouraging. Its emphasis on sexual perversion, Miller worried, would drive publishers away—and yet "perversion" was central to the story.

None of this, of course, was bringing any much-needed cash. In May he wrote Emil Schnellock that he had been corresponding with his father's old customer, Frank Harris, who was in Nice: "dunning him for the old man," he wrote. Heinrich Miller had fallen on hard times again, and he was reduced to working on commission, which didn't bring in "enough to live or starve." He wrote to his son for spending money, asking for $3 a week for his lunches—to be sent to the tailor shop, not Decatur Street, so Louise wouldn't know. Miller was mortified for his father and sent whatever he could, although he affected to be callous about it in front of his friends. But his father's pleas galvanized him; they brought out his determination.

This, in turn, made its way into Miller's writing. In his earliest draft of *Tropic of Cancer*, which was now starting to take shape from his Paris sketches, he recorded the following admonition: "Hereafter, in referring to myself, nothing but the first person singular, a capital I, and no grimaces behind it. Be a man, as my father always counselled. Out with it!" Writing as a man, to Miller's thinking, required total honesty, honesty to the point of ugliness. Miller began introducing four-letter words in his writing, a new practice for him. He wrote in his notebook that Dreiser had won fame by writing a "dirty" book—*Sister Carrie*—why shouldn't he do the same?

One of the first short pieces Miller produced in this new vein was called "Mlle Claude," written in late 1930 or early 1931. Mlle Claude, the subject of the story, was a well-known Left Bank whore whom Miller admired but seldom patronized. Observing Henry scribbling in cafés, she had asked him what he was writing, and this had given him the idea of writing about her. When he told her this, she became convinced that he was writing something beautiful about her, and to encourage this belief, Miller passed off excerpts from classic British novels as his praises of her. After he finally summoned up the courage to pay Mlle Claude a professional visit, he wrote an American friend that he found her so refined that he had climbed into bed with her and then talked about books, sending her home without having sex.

In the story he was actually writing, Miller cast himself as Mlle Claude's pimp, calling her a veritable angel; the only drawback to life with a whore, he wrote, was the constant problem of venereal disease.

After their son's birth in Manhattan in 1891, the Millers moved to the Williamsburg section of Brooklyn. Henry, at three and a half, in the outfit in which he marched in Brooklyn's Sunday School Parade.

Heinrich and Louise Miller with Henry and his sister Lauretta, born in 1895.
"My family were entirely Nordic—which is to say, idiots," he wrote in Tropic
of Capricorn.

RIGHT: *Heinrich Miller, the son of a German tailor, set up shop as a "gentleman tailor" off lower Fifth Avenue in Manhattan. Even-tempered and easygoing, Heinrich passed many hours in the bars of Broadway hotels, and the business was never a success.*

DEPARTMENT OF SPECIAL COLLECTIONS, UNIVERSITY
RESEARCH LIBRARY, UCLA

BELOW: *In retreat from the new wave of Jewish and Italian immigrants moving into Williamsburg, in 1901 the Millers moved to 1063 Decatur Street in Bushwick, deeper into Brooklyn. Disgusted with the middle-class environs of what he called "the street of early sorrows," Henry insisted on attending high school in the old neighborhood.*

MASTERS AND MASTERWORKS/ROBERT SNYDER

The Xerxes Society, the young men's club to which Henry belonged in his late teens and early twenties. The motto was Fratres semper, *the secret handshake a tickled palm. Henry (second row, far right) took the group's rituals and ideals desperately seriously.*

Henry, the tailor's son, around 1909, when he began a two-year affair with Pauline Chouteau, the woman nearly twice his age whom he always called "the widow." Distraught over her son's unconventional behavior, Louise Miller had pressured Henry to join his father in the tailoring business.

In 1917, Henry married his piano teacher, Beatrice Sylvas Wickens, to avoid the draft. They moved into a brownstone at 244 Sixth Avenue in Brooklyn, where a daughter, Barbara, was born in 1919.

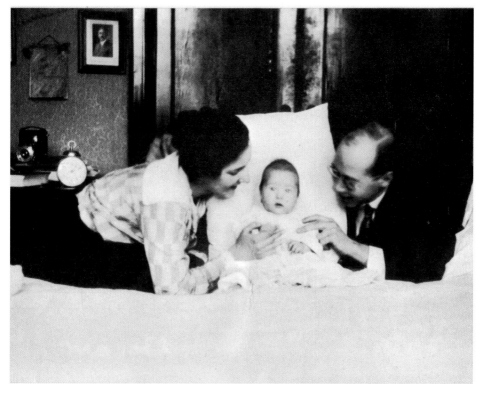

Though Henry doted on his child, he chafed at the bonds of his conventional marriage. He spent most of his time at his office at Western Union (the "Cosmodemonic Telegraph Company" of Tropic of Capricorn*), where he was employment manager, or roaming around the city with his Western Union colleagues and other women.*

"Moloch" — by Henry Miller

Unpublished novel — the first!

Chapter 1.

Dion Moloch walked with the dreamy stride of a noctambulo among the apparitions on the Bowery.   I say "apparitions" because, as every sophisticated New Yorker knows,
the Bowery is a thoroughfare where blasted souls are repaired for the price of a free lunch.

Dion Moloch was a modest, sensitive soul attired in
a suit of Bedford shipcord and pale blue shirt, the collars
and cuffs of which were disgracefully frayed.

Though he was in the service of the Great American
Telegraph Company he did not suffer from megalomania, de-
mentia praecox, or any of the fashionable nervous and
mental disorders of the twentieth century.   It was often
said of him that he was anti-Semitic, but then this is a
prejudice and not a disease.

At any rate, he was not like a certain character out
of Gogol who had to be informed when to blow his nose.   He
was, in short, an American of three generations.   He was
definitely not Russian.

In the summer of 1923, Henry met the twenty-one-year-old June Mansfield Smith, then working as a taxi-dancer in Times Square. An aspiring actress, June was an intense young woman with a flair for the dramatic. Henry fell violently in love, divorced Beatrice that winter, and married June in the spring. June convinced Henry to quit his job at Western Union to write, and they eked out a precarious existence at a succession of Brooklyn addresses.

June would become the "her" to whom Tropic of Capricorn was dedicated, the "Mona" of Cancer and the "Mara" of Capricorn and the autobiographical trilogy The Rosy Crucifixion. Supported by a loyal band of "admirers," June practiced a kind of cagey prostitution that kept Henry hopelessly ensnared. When she installed a Lesbian lover in the household, Henry lost his precarious hold on his sanity —and was galvanized to write about the experience.

OPPOSITE: In the kitchen at Sixth Avenue, Henry made his first sustained attempt at writing, a portrait of Western Union employees called Clipped Wings, which he discarded as a failure. His next effort, the autobiographical novel Moloch, contains chilling fictionalized descriptions of his failing marriage and his, at the time quite marked, anti-Semitism.

ABOVE: *After a trip to Europe with June in 1929, Henry resolved to return to Paris and write. On his arrival in the winter of 1930, he found himself penniless, forced to live on his wits and the kindness of other American expatriates, whom he met on the* terrasses *of expatriate haunts like the Dôme and the Coupole. One such friend was Abraham Rattner, an American painter.*

LEFT: *As seen here in a caricature by a friend, the Hungarian photographer Brassaï. The drawing accompanied a 1931 story about Miller by Wambly Bald in Bald's Paris* Chicago Tribune *column, "La Vie de Bohème." Miller would portray Bald as the "cunt-struck" Van Norden in* Tropic of Cancer.

Miller's fortunes changed in 1932, when he met fellow expatriate Anaïs Nin, a writer whose multi-volume diary and study of D. H. Lawrence earned Miller's respect. The two fell in love, and Nin supported Miller financially for several years. Nin lived with her banker husband Hugo Guiler in a fairytale-like cottage in the Paris suburb of Louveciennes. Anaïs fell under June's spell during one of June's trips to Paris.

Henry on the steps of Nin's house in Louveciennes. Their affair grew more serious, but while Miller thought he and Nin might someday marry, Nin had no intention of leaving her husband.

The Austrian Alfred Perlès, who helped Henry find occasional work proofreading at the Paris edition of the Herald Tribune and often put Miller up in his hotel room. During a period of relative affluence, the two shared a flat in the working-class district of Clichy, where Miller worked on Tropic of Cancer, his blistering account of his early years in Paris. "Alf"—or "Joey," as Miller dubbed him—was Miller's shadow in the thirties and remained a lifelong friend.

Michael Fraenkel, a poet and businessman whose "death philosophy" greatly influenced Miller's thinking in the early Paris years. Fraenkel lived at 18 rue Villa Seurat, where Miller took up residence in 1934. The Villa Borghese, as Miller called it in Tropic of Cancer, was a hive of activity, a home to struggling artists and writers, and a spiritual haven for Miller.

A boyish Lawrence Durrell arrived at the Villa Seurat in 1936, filled with admiration for Miller's work, and with his own Cancer-influenced shocker, The Black Book, under his arm. Miller, Perlès, Durrell, and Nin began a collaboration aimed at founding their own literary movement. Their projects included The Booster, a country club house organ the Villa Seurat group appropriated for their own artistic—and often sophomoric—ends, and several projected series of books and pamphlets.

ABOVE: *Jack Kahane, the British-born owner of the Obelisk Press, which produced the Traveller's Companion series and English-language books, often of a decidedly smutty cast, that could only be published in France. In* Tropic of Cancer, *which Miller brought him in 1933, Kahane found what he felt was a work of genius. Kahane is shown here with his French wife Marcelle and their son Maurice, who, as Maurice Girodias, would become Miller's publisher in the 1940s.*

MAURICE GIRODIAS

RIGHT: *When* Tropic of Cancer *appeared in 1934 and* Tropic of Capricorn *in 1938, both carried a printed slip announcing that the books were not to be taken into Great Britain or the U.S.A. But thousands of copies were smuggled out of France until the bans were lifted in the United States in 1961. Jack Kahane's fourteen-year-old son Maurice designed the cover of* Tropic of Cancer.

RARE BOOKS AND MANUSCRIPTS DIVISION, THE NEW YORK PUBLIC LIBRARY, ASTOR, LENOX, AND TILDEN FOUNDATIONS

Salvador and Gala Dali, Miller, and New York City bookseller Barnet Ruder on the grounds of Caresse Crosby's Bowling Green, Virginia, estate, summer of 1940.

ABOVE: *After a tour of America in 1940 and 1941 gathering material for* The Air-Conditioned Nightmare, *his book about his country, Miller settled for two years in a studio in the Beverly Glen section of Los Angeles. Unable to support himself as an artist, he wrote his well-known "Open Letter" to the* New Republic, *describing what he would later call "the plight of the creative artist" in America. It would be followed by scores more "begging letters," asking for used clothes, painting supplies, and food, offering in exchange his watercolors and his books.*

LEFT: *In the spring of 1944 Miller moved to the remote and rugged Big Sur, a nearly deserted stretch of northern California coastline, where he would live, in spartan fashion, for the next sixteen years. He had long nourished a dream of going to the Far East and becoming a visionary. Instead he established himself as a mystic and guru of sorts at Big Sur, receiving admirers and seekers from all parts of the world.*

LEFT: *On a trip East in late 1944, Miller met and married Janina Martha Lepska, known to all simply as Lepska. A daughter, Valentin, was born in 1945, and a son, Tony, in 1948. Miller continued work on* The Rosy Crucifixion *and also produced several collections for his new American publisher, James Laughlin of New Directions.*

Henry was a devoted father to Tony, left, and Val, above. But Lepska believed in a firm hand with the children, while Henry, remembering his Puritanical upbringing, favored a free rein. The couple divorced in 1951. Henry tried to raise the children himself but eventually shared custody with Lepska.

LEFT: *Henry met his fourth wife, Eve McClure, in March 1952, and a period of domestic tranquility, travel, and creativity followed. Living with Eve, Miller wrote Durrell, was like "living on velour."*

LEFT: *In 1961 Barney Rosset of Grove Press began bringing out Miller's previously banned books, to much public outcry, critical attention, and a flurry of legal action. The attendant celebrity changed Miller's life.*

BELOW: *In 1963 Miller moved to the fashionable Los Angeles neighborhood of Pacific Palisades. Host to starlets, fans, accountants, and lawyers, he transformed the inside of his suburban mansion into a bohemian clubhouse, painting and writing on the walls and encouraging visitors to do the same.*

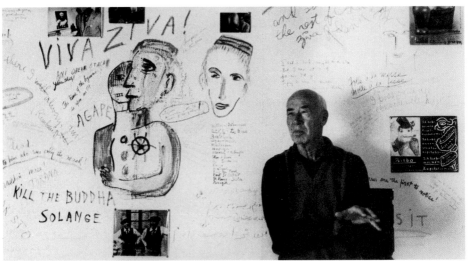

With the publication of the banned books and the completion of The Rosy Crucifixion, *Miller felt his creative mission was fulfilled—though he continued to write. His new fame puzzled him, and the sixties were a restless decade: Eve remained in Big Sur, and Miller traveled through Europe looking for an ideal place to live and a new companion. Despite his new commercial success, financial problems continued to plague him.*

Asserting that Asian women made the best wives, Miller married Hoki Tokuda, a Japanese pop singer, in September 1967. Hoki remained aloof in the face of his passion, and Miller was inspired to write a long meditation on thwarted love, Insomnia Or The Devil at Large. *After much misery, the marriage ended in 1974.*

**COURTESY OF HOKI TOKUDA
MILLER AND JOYCE HOWARD**

At eighty-four, Miller fell in love for the last time, with a Southern beauty named Brenda Venus. Increasingly frail, he spent his last years dependent on caretakers and admirers, shuffling around the Pacific Palisades mansion in an old blue bathrobe. Yet he continued, until his death in 1980, to send Brenda a torrent of passionate love letters.

© *MARTIN*

The story, which hinges on the question of which partner gave the other gonorrhea, brings together all of Miller's anxieties about women, disease, sex, and manliness. Living with this "angel," he wrote, has turned him into a saint; as if he realizes the contradiction, he continues, "When she cuddles up to me—she loves me now more than ever —it seems that I'm just some damned microbe that's wormed its way into her soul. I feel that even if I am living with an angel I ought to try to make a man of myself." In "Mlle Claude," his first significant piece of writing, Miller seems to have been confronting his ambivalent love for his wife, June, whom he viewed as simultaneously a whore and an angel. From *Crazy Cock* to "Mlle Claude": the difference was only in degree. When he recast the story with a working prostitute as the heroine and himself as her pimp (the narrator first uses a French colloquialism, calling himself Mlle Claude's *maquereau* and then substitutes the blunter English term), he found his writing more powerful, his emotions less turbulent and intrusive. With "Mlle Claude," he struck the note he had been looking for; he found his voice, that of the literary *clochard*, the writer as outlaw.

Miller may have been casting about for a new way to deal with June in his fiction because she was now back in his life. She had been threatening to join him in Paris as early as May, when he wrote Schnellock asking him to dissuade her from coming until he had a job. August found him working for Haridas Mazumdar, the news of which so upset June that she scrambled to turn up the money for passage. She arrived in Paris around October 1. There was a mixup at the Gare St. Lazare and Miller finally found her in a café, drinking Pernod, supremely at home. Almost at once the old drama began anew, with June filling him in on all the schemes and suitors of their seven-month separation. When Henry mentioned that he had met the celebrated Germaine Dulac the previous May and that she had made a vague reference to directing an English-language film, June, characteristically, took this as a firm offer of a film role for herself. The fact that Mme Dulac was a well-known Lesbian only made the deal more certain. June pestered Henry endlessly, and he was finally able to secure a promise of a role for June from Mme Dulac.

The film was not set to roll, however, until January, and June's money was running out. After only three weeks she left for New York, intending, she said, to try to get a high-paying job in the theater again before returning at the end of the winter. Her departure left Miller lonelier than ever; putting her on the train, he felt as though it was the end of the world. Temporarily thrown off course, he made up his mind to return as well, writing to his family and Abe Elkus, a friend he'd met through Emil Conason, in mid-November to raise funds for the passage home. He could always finish the "Paris book" in New York, he reasoned. On the edge of a creative breakthrough, he was vacillating; failure had become too familiar.

But June's visit had also caused Henry to wonder if his obsession with her was not easing, if she had not lost her hold on him in some subtle way. Just as he had pulled himself together while she was touring Europe with Jean, amassing the notes for a great book about her, so too did his months alone in Paris toughen Miller, make him more certain that he could survive alone and perhaps write another kind of great book. Less than a month after writing home for passage money, he was full of energy, writing to Emil Schnellock that "The sap is running again, I wake up with semen in my hand, I get ideas in the toilet, on the Metro, in the telephone booths, etc. Good sign. Great tidings. I will write again."

After June's departure he was reluctant to move back in with Perlès, which seemed to be his only option. Fortuitously, Richard Osborn, a banker friend from Bridgeport, Connecticut, offered him a bed for the winter in his apartment on the rue Auguste Bartholdi, not far from the Eiffel Tower. Osborn, a good-natured blueblood with literary aspirations, worked as a lawyer in the Paris office of the National City Bank by day; to Miller's thinking this meant that Osborn was rich, and he had no qualms about taking the ten- or twenty-franc note Osborn left for him in the mornings. Osborn's motivations in this exchange are more obscure. Osborn had already installed his latest girlfriend in the studio, a Russian woman named Irene, who claimed not only royal descent but also a case of gonorrhea. Osborn said that Irene amused him. He kept Miller around, he said, because the place was too big for just him and Irene, and Miller could keep the fire going during the day. It was a raw, cold Paris winter.

Before long, Miller and Irene got on each other's nerves. The Russian chattered tirelessly, and she had a habit of using Miller's towel, which horrified him, as he was terrified of catching gonorrhea from her. After her condition was cured, she wouldn't sleep with either man, claiming that she was a Lesbian. She was unimpressed by Miller's artistic pretensions and Osborn's money. Cooped up in the seventh-floor studio all day, Miller did his best to ignore her, concentrating on his writing.

Despite the obvious difficulties, he was absorbing impressions and turning them into prose at a tremendous rate. The year had begun portentously. On New Year's Eve he had been riding in a taxi that ran into another car and turned it over, but he had escaped without a scratch. As if shedding an old skin, he took a closer look at some of his old artistic heroes and rejected many of them, including Thomas Mann for being too German and romantic in *Death in Venice* (he couldn't bear to reopen *The Magic Mountain* for fear that it might have lost its power for him as well) and James Joyce for being "a broken vomit, a precious sewer, a medieval stew." Proust and Spengler were his new heroes— especially Spengler, whose pessimistic view of history brought some order to the premonitions of corruption and decay Miller had felt since his arrival in France. Another new passion was D. H. Lawrence. In a year he would write to Emil Schnellock that he had lost himself in the universe of Lawrence—and found himself. His favorite Lawrence novel was *Aaron's Rod*. He found fault with the banned *Lady Chatterley's Lover*, in spite of its explicit sexuality; it was too plotted, he thought, too loaded up with ideas.

The same flaws bothered him in his own manuscript, *Crazy Cock*, which thoroughly disgusted him by the winter of 1931. It was overburdened with plot, and his extensive notes for it made him feel cramped and walled in. "I will explode in the Paris book," he wrote Schnellock, explaining his impatience to put *Crazy Cock* aside. "The hell with form, style, expression and all those pseudo-paramount things which beguile the critics. I want to get myself across this time—and direct as a knife thrust." But some unfinished business prevented him from devoting his full attention to what would become *Tropic of Cancer:* he was still gathering material and sorting out literary ideas, as well as recovering from his experience with June.

Miller was just barely surviving on Osborn's handouts. To bring in a little cash he began posing for an American painter named John Nichols, who quickly became an important friend. Nichols came from Woodstock, New York, and looked the part of a bohemian artist, wearing long red underwear under his jeans and sporting a full, thick red beard. In emulation, Miller grew a beard himself—not trimmed, like the Montparnasse beards he scorned, but full and, surprisingly, red.

In a memoir, Osborn wrote that there was "a sort of mutual admiration society" between Miller and Nichols: "they regard[ed] each other as geniuses." Miller had a passion for art, inherited in part from his father, who lined the walls of the tailor shop with reproductions of fine art. Several of his American friends were artists, Schnellock, for instance, a successful illustrator. Miller himself had tried painting with his friend Joe O'Regan about ten years before, rushing out to buy oil paints after seeing some Turner reproductions in the window of a Brooklyn department store. Now Nichols inspired him to try again. He found he had no skill at drawing nor, for that matter, at realistic representation whatsoever, but he had an eye for color and composition. More importantly, he enjoyed painting tremendously, and he found it stimulated his already strong visual sense, which in turn enriched his writing.

With Nichols, he visited the Cirque Medrano, where, as he wrote Schnellock, they had "a fine Seurat night" of it. With the arrival of spring, Miller's days were rich and full. He made new friends through Nichols, among them the painter Frank Mechau and his wife, Paula, and another writer, Joe Schrank, who had had some success writing Broadway plays. Schrank's wife, Bertha, absolutely captivated Henry for a month or two. Her dark good looks reminded him of June, but she was fuller and rounder; Miller flirted with her through the spring and summer of 1931. (The Schranks would appear as Sylvester and Tania in *Tropic of Cancer*.)

By March, Osborn's sublet was up and the inhabitants dispersed, Miller moving in with Fred Kann, who lived near the Montparnasse cemetery. Financially, he was in serious trouble again. He was offered a job washing dishes at the American Restaurant on the Boulevard Montparnasse in exchange for a couple of meals a day, but as he had no working card he couldn't take it. English-language pupils were few and far between. He was plagued once again with the piles—a condition that would trouble him off and on for the rest of his life—and he was constantly hungry. But Paris, he wrote his friend Ned Calmer, was even lovelier when you were hungry: "like being grabbed by a skeleton when you're having an orgasm."

Though his letters home were often buoyant, signed "love and kisses," Miller was once again preoccupied with material concerns in 1931. When Kann could put him up no longer, he returned to Perlès's room at the Hôtel Central. A little money came in when Elliot Paul accepted two articles, at 50 francs apiece, for the Sunday edition of the *Chicago Tribune*, one on the Cirque Medrano and the other on a six-day bike race. Miller and Perlès collaborated on a series of tourism pieces for the edition, often simply rephrasing stories from back numbers. Even if it was dishonest, Miller later wrote, it was better than panhandling.

He seemed to have no direction. But one March evening he ran across Walter Lowenfels, an American poet of some stature, in Montparnasse. Lowenfels had published two books of poetry; with his most recent, he had moved into a new realm, writing a series of "elegies" he intended to assemble as *Some Deaths*. To Miller, he elaborated the "death theme," which he had developed with his friend Michael Fraenkel: with the world in a state of disintegration, the only course was to become aware of death, to *live* death. The "death school" took as its motto Kierkegaard's "What is spirit? Spirit is to live as though dead."

Lowenfels took Miller's characteristic responsiveness for enthusiasm; he was also impressed by Miller's descriptions of his goals in the "Paris book." He reported to Fraenkel that he had found a possible disciple: "Not alive, exactly, but certainly not dead. Alive in a kind of confused, old-fashioned way. An interesting chap." Fraenkel sent Miller a *pneumatique*, summoning him to his studio in the rue Villa Seurat in the 14th arrondissement.

Miller visited Fraenkel in April and didn't leave for four months. He was captivated by Fraenkel, a small, unprepossessing man given to wearing a greasy brown robe, who bore an unmistakable resemblance to Trotsky. Fraenkel was a Lithuanian Jew five years younger than Miller, who had made a small fortune distributing books in America before he became obsessed with death. He came to Paris determined to write, choosing death as his subject, and published *Werther's Younger Brother*, a meditation on death in Goethe, through his own Carrefour Press, which had also brought out Lowenfels's *Apollinaire: An Elegy*.

Like Lowenfels, who worked as a renting agent and whose family owned a large butter concern in America, Fraenkel had considerable income of his own. This alone would have made Miller receptive to his ideas. Fraenkel's studio at 18 rue Villa Seurat suited him too. A dead-end off the somewhat slummy rue de la Tombe-Issoire, the rue Villa Seurat was a bourgeois-looking street lined with gaily colored stucco houses. Miller reported proudly that the street was home to such artists as Foujita, André Derain, Jean Lurcat, and Marcel Gromaire; Dali had a house on the corner. When Fraenkel offered him the floor of his living room, he accepted gladly, ready to be a disciple if that was the price.

Miller's association with Fraenkel was extremely important, especially at this time when *Tropic of Cancer* was in its early stages. Fraenkel took one look at *Crazy Cock* and told him to tear it up. Write as you talk, he told Miller; write as you live. He later claimed that he recognized Miller right off as an anarchic, contradictory person, whose only chance was to sit at the typewriter and let it all go. "A writer's first duty," Fraenkel later wrote, "is to himself—to liberate himself, to come clean of his past, of his death, to come alive. A personal record. No time for anything else. Anything else is literature—with a bad smell!"

Miller would echo Fraenkel on literature in the opening pages of *Tropic of Cancer*, declaring,

> This then? This is not a book. This is libel, slander, defamation of character. This is not a book, in the ordinary sense of the word. No, this is a prolonged insult, a gob of spit in the face of Art, a kick in the pants to God, Man, Destiny, Time, Love, Beauty . . . what you will.

Fraenkel's advice had obvious appeal: Miller *was* anarchic when it came to writing. He hated form, plots, the literary "device." Fraenkel pointed out that what he hated was "literature." Previously, Miller had hated "literature" not on principle but because he was no good at it, and now Fraenkel simply supplied the principle. Fraenkel believed he gave Miller the subject for *Tropic of Cancer*—death—but what he really contributed was an attitude.

"They talked a sort of higher mathematics, those two," Miller later wrote of Lowenfels and Fraenkel. Nothing was ever concrete, all pure idea. Fraenkel was writing something he called "The Weather Paper," Lowenfels his poems. As time went on, Miller was, if not a disciple of the "death school," as Lowenfels and Fraenkel had hoped, at least a communicant, explaining the philosophy in letters to friends. This philosophy was infinitely elastic. As Miller practiced it, it was a vague but strongly felt nihilism, a form of positive existentialism. Above all, it appeared to be profound, and Miller was as attracted to profundity as ever; he began to affect to be profound himself, often with sorry results.

The fact that Fraenkel was Jewish had a good deal to do with his importance for Miller: "being a Gentile, I was naturally interested in what went on in that menagerie of a brainpan," he wrote in *Tropic of Cancer*. In a letter to Fraenkel, he indicated that they often discussed Miller's self-described "incurable anti-Semitism," though, it would seem, not critically. (In the same letter Miller complained that for the Europeans the Jew has been "a terrific and malefic" influence.) Fraenkel's talk reminded Miller of the discussions he had heard in the cafés on Second Avenue in his New York "Jewish period." Now, at the Villa Seurat (as the residents of Number 18 commonly called their building), he fastened on Jews as romantic, exotic beings. Several years later, living again at the Villa Seurat, he would taunt Fraenkel relentlessly; he and Perlès made a sport of stealing from him. But in the spring and early summer of 1931 Miller treated Fraenkel with deference and even an odd kind of reverence.

In July, Fraenkel announced that he was subletting the studio, and Miller was on the street again. Fortunately, Perlès found a job for him on the *Chicago Tribune*, proofreading stock figures. Again, there was some trouble about a worker's card, but Miller at last obtained a *carte d'identité*. (It gave him a secret thrill to give his profession as "writer." It made him feel criminal, he wrote Ned Calmer.) Miller was put on the night shift, working from 7:00 p.m. to 2:30 a.m. After their shift, usually he and Perlès—and sometimes Wambly Bald, if he needed gossip for his column—repaired to Gillotte's, a cheap restaurant favored by journalists, just across the street from the paper's offices in the rue Lamartine. In the *Tribune* production room Miller made the acquaintance of another American, Louis Atlas, who often put him up in his hotel room in the rue Monsieur le Prince, regaling him with stories of Josephine Baker and Oskar Kokoschka. Over the next year or two Atlas also sent some work Miller's way, farming out to him articles to appear under Atlas's name in a Jewish publication in New York.

Miller was beginning to travel in circles of near-notables himself. In early summer he got the news that Samuel Putnam would publish "Mlle Claude" in the fall number of the *New Review*, due out in August. That summer, he and Perlès convinced Putnam to entrust the editing and production of that issue of the *Review* to them while Putnam was in America; they saw it as a great chance to make a statement, to attract the attention of Montparnasse. A series of columns in the *Tribune* appeared announcing the issue, which would contain two stories by Perlès and Miller's "Mlle Claude," as well as a piece described as a manifesto for "the newest and most violent [artistic] movement."

First, the two editors removed from the issue an article by Robert McAlmon, the darling of twenties Paris and thus a representative of everything Miller detested; cutting the article, he wrote a friend, was "a fine sadistic pleasure." Then he and Perlès concocted a thirty-five-page essay called "The New Instinctivism," a self-described "gob of

spit in the cuspidor of post-war conceits, a healthy crap in the cradle
of still-born deities," which Miller was half-convinced would get them
kicked out of France.

A kind of anti-manifesto, "The New Instinctivism" is a sophomoric and anti-intellectual document, perhaps purposely so. The goal
of the moment, according to its two sole members, was simply to be
for or *against*—instinctively. Its "philosophy" was jumbled. The authors argued for the liberation of violence within man, for the necessity
of rebellion, but they also urged the reader who was tired of politics
not to vote. In calling their tract an attack on "postwar conceits," they
revealed the self-interest of their enterprise. The disgust Miller and
Perlès felt for writers like McAlmon was genuine, but their desire to
find similar favor for their own work often prevented them from developing coherent artistic positions. Miller wanted so badly to start a new
"school" that he spent less time thinking through his aesthetic stance
than he did advertising it.

"The New Instinctivism" was more than an artistic statement; it
was also a hodgepodge of short pieces, including a letter (in French) to
Jean Cocteau, a description of Mlle Claude drying herself on the bidet,
a poem called "Hemorroides" (sic), and closing with a piece titled
"Praising the Shit Out of France." Most of the for's and against's were
completely whimsical: "We are against admirals. We like only rear
admirals."

But when the altered *Review* appeared, it was without "The New
Instinctivism." Miller and Perlès had written to Putnam informing him
of their intentions, and Putnam wrote back expressing reservations as
to the "legal liability" he might incur. He was sorry about the McAlmon
story, he wrote, but he supposed it could appear in a later issue. He
congratulated Miller on "Mlle Claude," and wrote that he hoped to find
a way to compensate Perlès and Miller for their efforts. "The New
Instinctivism" had come to nothing. Even so, Miller was gratified by
the attention "Mlle Claude" received. Wambly Bald singled it out in a
September *Tribune* column, and Peter Neagoe asked Miller if he could
include it in his 1932 anthology, *Americans Abroad*, where it would
keep company with work by Hemingway, Gertrude Stein, Dos Passos,
and Pound.

When Putnam accepted an essay from Miller on Luis Buñuel's
surrealist film *L'Age d'Or* (which, along with Buñuel's earlier film with
Salvador Dali, *Un chien andalou*, left a deep impression on him), Miller
felt he was launched at last as a serious writer. In America, he had

only succeeded as a writer for hire—if that; in France, he was immediately classed as he wanted to be—with the avant-garde. Now he took
up the cudgels with enthusiasm, embracing surrealism in its most extreme form. He told Schnellock he wanted to dedicate his next book to
Buñuel, adding, somewhat cryptically, "the orphic myth is being revived." To Ned Calmer, who had shown Miller the draft of a novel, he
said, "fuck the boys. Not only Hergesheimer and Dos Passos, but
Sinclair Lewis and Dreiser." Calmer was in danger of becoming a prig,
Miller advised, and should "chew a little dirt." Miller, on the other
hand, had "the Holy Ghost in [his] entrails." Like a new initiate, he
expounded the mysteries of creativity with the zeal of a man who had
sought conversion for nearly twenty years. In his vocation he had found
his salvation.

Materially, things had changed only a little for him; he most often
slept in Perlès's room, or at Osborn's or Kann's. (Lowenfels and
Calmer had wives and babies, and Fraenkel had disappeared.) To solve
the vexing problem of food, Miller hatched what seemed to his friends
a novel plan: he wrote each in turn, asking if they were willing to serve
him one meal a week—your "homely repast," he wrote to Calmer—
and assigning to each a different day. In return, he reasoned, his
friends would have the benefit of his conversation, not to mention the
accomplishment of having advanced the cause of Art. In this way he
lined up six sets of friends, he wrote proudly to Richard Osborn: Frank
and Paula Mechau, the Schranks, the Lowenfelses, Fred Kann, Zadkine and his wife, and the Calmers.

Most of his friends were sympathetic to his struggle to stay afloat.
He talked often about June, whom no one else was particularly fond of.
During her brief stay in Paris the previous fall she had snubbed Osborn, for example; the Lowenfelses, in turn, hadn't been able to make
sense of anything she said. Now, in her letters to Henry she claimed to
be busy with her stage career; she was acting as New York agent for
Miller's novels as well, cabling him in July that publishers were so
eager for *Crazy Cock* that it was sure of a $500 advance (which Miller
thought strange, since June had previously told him the book had been
accepted by the house of Jonathan Cape and Harrison Smith). In the
same cable she said she must join him by August, which further mystified him.

The summer passed with no sign of her, but in the fall the cables
began again, and by October June was once more at Henry's side. The
balance of their marriage had now shifted. June was thinner, more

desperate, her hold on reality even more tenuous; her drug use had clearly escalated. She found Miller changed, too; she didn't like the pages of the new Paris book, preferring *Crazy Cock*, the novel that celebrated her. "Mlle Claude" she found an embarrassment, an insinuation that she couldn't keep her husband faithful. She even admired the hated McAlmon. Gradually, too, it became clear that she had a formidable rival: Miller had met Anaïs Nin, and was already caught in a much finer and subtler web than June could ever spin.

8.

"The Phallic Significance of Things"

1931–1933

During his first two years in Paris, Miller had led a relatively austere life, in terms of the range of his sexual experience. As his lifelong veneration for Cora Seward bears out, he was greatly given to crushes, and he suffered through his share of these in Paris. Bertha Schrank, with whom he believed himself to be in love, left for Russia with her husband in the fall of 1931; although she had given Miller some encouragement, his interest flagged in her absence. Judging from his letters, he seems to have developed no small passion for Mlle Claude, the subject of his *New Review* story. Like many an American in Paris, he romanticized the city's prostitutes, finding them, in imagined contrast to their American counterparts, delicate and feminine, charmingly coquettish. But his experiences with them were less frequent than his fiction implies. It was not the relatively modest cost, nor any imagined loyalty to June that held him back, but the dread of venereal disease. He was, by his own admission, "mortally afraid" of it. "I am one who takes supreme care in such things," he wrote in 1933. "The one great horror—to me! Unclean!"

With prostitutes thus pretty much off limits, Miller nursed huge lusts in Paris, exacerbated by the news of his less fastidious friends' adventures. Wambly Bald, especially, spoke of nothing but sex; his friends joked that he was "cunt-struck." Osborn and Perlès had regular sorties with French women, not all of them prostitutes. As he did in New York, Miller often played the voyeur, sharing a hotel room with another man and his woman. The ideal sexual arrangement for him was the shared whore, a situation where emotional engagement was impossible. But it remained, for the most part, only a fantasy.

In the past Miller had been capable of extreme callousness toward women, but at great emotional cost. He suffered grievously when he hurt Pauline Chouteau and Beatrice; he almost bled for June when she was hurt by Jean. (One of his favorite fictional images, in fact, would be men menstruating—in sympathy, as it were.) But by October of 1931 he was changing. In Paris, June's various infidelities festered, and his own suffering had worn him down. As he developed a powerful new voice in the "Paris book," he adopted a philosophy to match it, not entirely new, compounded of equal parts negation and affirmation. His new thinking set all convention and tradition aside as false, dangerous—as Fraenkel would have it, dead. Only the immediate, the raw, the vital remained. Both the destruction of the old and the vitality of the new were to be celebrated. By late 1931, when he was hard at work on the "Paris book," these ideas were coming to dominate his thoughts, and he tried them out endlessly, in letters and in conversations in cafés with sympathetic listeners like Perlès and Osborn.

As it applied to women, this attitude meant that social conventions between the sexes—the deceptions of courtship, or of marriage, for instance—were meaningless and destructive. Women, in this view, were too attached to such conventions, and so were worthless as human beings. As Miller wrote Osborn, women are "incapable of friendship—and of loyalty, or gratitude, or reverence, or silence. At bottom, they're angels pissing poison from the sky." But at the same time, he believed that sex, which, in his opinion, lies behind those meaningless social conventions, is the most vital reality. Following through on this thought, he announced to Osborn, "Where [women] meet me, on the hard, fast line of sex, I'm theirs, heart, belly, and cock." He argued for sex devoid of emotional attachments, believing women were emotionally inadequate; yet he felt the only true emotional attachment was achieved through sex. He was driven to such contradictions, perhaps, because of the serious crisis brought on by his passionate involvement with June.

Miller did not see, moreover, that traditional sex roles were as insidious a form of social convention as prudishness. Like Whitman and Lawrence, both of whom he revered, he played with the idea of androgyny but found it too threatening. Instead, he sought to reclaim any desirable "feminine" attributes as male, reorganizing the world in neat dualities, where the positive attributes were male, the negative female. In the same letter to Osborn, he admonished his friend not to be tender with women; men, in their hardness, he wrote, preserve the "tender flame." Tenderness was man's realm—that he had learned from D. H. Lawrence. Real tenderness, Miller wrote, "lies in virility, in manliness, in a stiff penis, in the phallic significance of things."

The book that Miller was tentatively calling *Tropic of Cancer* was emerging as an exercise in "the phallic significance of things." He was including all his Paris friends (and enemies) in it, deploying them as agents of this new philosophy. Thus Perlès appears as Carl, who lives off a "rich cunt" and visits prostitutes with the narrator. Osborn becomes Fillmore, who narrowly escapes the clutches of a French girl who claims he has impregnated her; and Bald appears as Van Norden, who laments the fact that he tends to fall in love with his "cunts," which complicates matters. Miller had his revenge on Bertha Schrank by including her as Tania, whose clitoris the narrator threatens to bite into—and spit out in two-franc pieces. The book was shaping up as a celebration of male identity and male sexuality. Miller had been "unmanned," as he saw it, by June's betrayals and particularly her love for another woman. He had not been a man, as his father had admonished—and as his father had not been. He set out to ensure that this could never be said of him again.

Imagine that her name is Mona Païva, Miller wrote Schnellock in April 1932, choosing the name of a well-known European dancer to describe his new lover. "That her husband is in North Africa and wears the beautiful uniform of the Army of the Crescent . . . that she is Turkish. She comes from Stamboul and only a few years ago she still wore the veil. When I tell you that I want to convey the sacredness that she brings with her sex." Miller met Anaïs Nin in the fall of 1931. What he wanted to convey to Schnellock was Nin's total exoticism, what he saw as her "Oriental" mystery. Anaïs Nin had charms that could displace June's; moreover, she was an artist who could meet Miller on his own ground. Of no less importance was her relative wealth; at forty, after meeting her, he could finally see a way out of the crippling poverty he had known his entire adult life.

Miller was introduced to Nin through Richard Osborn, who worked for her husband, a Scottish-American named Hugh Guiler, in the Paris offices of the New York-based National City Bank. Osborn had been doing some legal work for Nin surrounding the publication of her first book, a study of D. H. Lawrence. He told Guiler about his writing friend, and Guiler may have seen in Miller a cause for his wife to take up: she had an artistic sensibility and felt a little constrained by the conventions of her role as a banker's wife. So it was arranged that Miller would come for a visit to Louveciennes, a village just outside Paris overlooking the Seine, where the Guilers rented a villa on what had once been the estate of Louis XV's mistress, Madame du Barry.

The house at Louveciennes, tucked away behind a green gate at 2 bis rue Monbuisson, was by all accounts a kind of enchanted cottage, filled with color, bright accents, and curiosities from other lands. An Arabian lamp lit the entranceway, filigreed in bronze and casting a rose glow. Inside, the rooms were painted in delicate shades of apricot and peach, and lined with built-in bookcases that were painted a glossy black and filled with books on, for example, William Blake and astrology, as well as sumptuous art books. Charts of the Zodiac hung over the blue mosaic fireplace in the library. The dining room, which was perpetually damp, was customarily warmed by a fragrant fire of apple wood and tree roots. French doors opened out onto a little garden and courtyard. The effect was thoroughly European, artful, and opulent. Miller had never seen anything like it.

He hadn't expected his hostess to be beautiful—and she wasn't, conventionally speaking. She was short and slim, and Miller preferred his women Rubenesque. Her features—huge, almond-shaped dark eyes, a long, thin nose, and a red, Cupid's-bow mouth—were a little too large and irregular for her oval, chalk white face. But with her jet black hair and her elaborate way of dressing—she was given to what she called "costumes," fashioned out of rare materials in rich, deep colors—she was definitely striking. Once people knew her, they would often speak of her as beautiful.

Her background was as exotic as her clothes and her home, if less enchanted. She had been born in 1903, in the Paris suburb of Neuilly, the daughter of a Spanish musician, Joaquin Nin, and a French-Danish singer named Rose Culmell; in her childhood she had often accompanied her adored father on concert tours. Her parents separated when she was nine and her mother took her to New York, raising Anaïs and her two brothers in the distinctly un-European Richmond Hill section of Queens. Like Miller, Nin was an autodidact, quitting high school after a couple of days and, legend has it, setting out to read all the books in the local branch of the New York Public Library alphabetically. She was a shy and introverted child who confided all her thoughts in an intimate and voluminous diary she began at eleven as a dialogue with her father. At twenty, she married Guiler, a businessman with artistic leanings; when he was transferred to National City Bank's Paris office in 1924, the two moved to France. Anaïs remained absorbed in her diaries but was beginning to try her hand at writing for the public when she and Miller met. Her first book, *D. H. Lawrence: An Unprofessional Study*, had just been accepted by Edward Titus, the English-language publisher whose Black Manikin Press was based in Paris.

The Guilers were in many ways a typical expatriate couple of the thirties, but set apart in that they were, if not wealthy, financially secure. Weekend bohemians, they were ideally situated to become patrons of the arts. Miller's championship of spontaneity and his rejection of form appealed to the Guilers' dilettantish instincts. More seriously, Nin longed to preside over a "school" as badly as Miller wanted to be part of one. And, of course, he needed a patron, as well as the artistic encouragement of someone whose mind he respected.

Miller was at his mildest at their first meeting, deferential before this startling woman who had needed just three weeks to produce a book on D. H. Lawrence, one of his idols. Their conversation was constrained by the presence of Osborn and Guiler, but the two writers were immediately curious about each other. Anaïs showed him about the house and grounds, pointing out a studio over the garage that she said might be fixed up so that Henry could live and work there. Before he left, they promised to show each other their work.

But another appearance by June intervened. Miller's dramatic, unpredictable wife had made a considerable impression on the American community during her previous visits, and her return was announced, appropriately enough, in Wambly Bald's column, which commented, "this should interest those who know June and her temperament." Her arrival was triumphant. In an interview she told Bald she had completed a novel called *Happier Days*, and that she was here to reclaim her artist husband, who was on the verge, she thought, of becoming famous. Henry saw at once how much she had deteriorated: her skin was ashy and her thoughts more disordered than ever. (The poignantly titled *Happier Days*, of course, did not exist.) He gradually ascertained that the publishers and advances she had said she had found for his unpublished novels were mythical; there had been a few vague promises about his work, nothing more.

June had a little money, and they moved into the Hôtel Princesse on the rue Princesse ("a fairy address," Miller growled). Almost immediately, Henry stopped work on his book, as he wrote to Anaïs; he also lost his job proofreading at the *Tribune*. June's suspicions were aroused by his descriptions of this new friend, who seemed to have cornered the market on high drama, a market that had always been June's. Henry described Anaïs to her as a potential patron, but this did little to calm June, who knew exactly what having a "patron" involved.

Henry was doing his best to cultivate Anaïs. He changed his mind about allowing her to see *Crazy Cock,* writing her that in its present state he feared it "would only prejudice you against me." Instead, he had asked Osborn to read over *Tropic of Cancer* and to extract a few pages to show her; he was worried about its "coarse language" and did not want to offend her. He would bring her a few more pages, he wrote, when they next met.

It is unclear whether Anaïs asked Henry to bring June to Louveciennes on his next visit or whether June simply insisted on going, uninvited. Either way it would be a momentous event. Anaïs had determined to win Henry, and she wanted to assess her rival. June's motives were similar. She looked the part of the bohemian artist, wearing a velvet dress with torn elbows, a black cape, and a dirty fedora. Henry warned her to watch her language in the Guilers' presence.

But Anaïs was transfixed by June, writing that evening in her diary: "As she came towards me from the darkness of my garden into the light of the doorway I saw for the first time the most beautiful woman on earth." As the evening wore on, Anaïs came to see that June's beauty attracted drama and disorder, and that June herself was a superb actress. Anaïs was falling deeply, immediately in love with June—a feeling that took her by surprise in its sureness and intensity. But she had heard all about Jean Kronski, and she may have sensed as well that the only way to win Henry was to create a triangle and explode it. June seems to have found Anaïs equally fascinating.

Henry had no such scenario in mind, though he was delighted that Anaïs saw June's uniqueness. (So many of his friends saw only the suffering June caused him.) As it turned out, Anaïs's attraction to June drew her even more closely to Henry, as the two discussed her endlessly, trying to unravel her deceptions and remove the magic from her spells. Neither woman acted on her feelings, however, instead talking about them—or in Anaïs's case, writing about them—endlessly. Henry dispatched an unwilling June back to America in mid-November, telling her that he was the one with a "scheme" going this time.

Henry and Anaïs kept things on a cerebral plane for several months, sharing ideas and manuscripts. Anaïs saw the tremendous potential of *Tropic of Cancer*, admiring it for its brutality and strength. She noted in her diary that she could write a book about Miller's genius:

> Almost every word he utters causes an electric charge: on Buñuel's *L'Age d'Or*, on Salavin, on Waldo Frank, on Proust, on the film *Blue Angel*, on people, on animalism, on Paris, on French prostitutes, on American women, on America. He is even walking ahead of Joyce. He repudiates form. He writes as we think, on various levels at once, with seeming irrelevance, seeming chaos.

She recorded with pleasure that Henry observed that she wrote like a man.

Henry was less easily won, partly because of June and partly because he felt the situation required great delicacy and tact. The truth was that while the Guilers led the relatively comfortable life of a middle-level banker and his wife, in those early Depression days an American with a steady income could live like a king in Europe, where currencies were being devalued in a scramble to lessen the shock of the collapsing economy. As a result, a lot of the down-at-heel artists in Paris at the time thought of the Guilers as wealthy. For Miller, it created an impression that Anaïs was far above him in terms of social class, and he was just bourgeois enough that the difference held him back. He was also anxious about Anaïs's husband Hugh—or Hugo, as he was commonly known—whom he did not want to offend. (Later, when their affair was at its height, it was not Anaïs but Henry who would obsess about being discovered by Hugo.) Then, of course, there was the business of money. Very early on, Anaïs began to make small gifts to Henry—such things as railroad tickets and a volume of Proust. She hinted that she might pay for the printing of *Tropic of Cancer* if a publisher could not be found. And, soon, she began slipping him small sums, envelopes with 100 francs, or a check. Miller was encouraged enough to invite Schnellock over to Europe, assuring him Nin would support him as well.

Between Nin's gifts and teaching an occasional English lesson, and with his meals taken care of by the round robin plan, Miller was getting by. Wambly Bald even made him the subject of his column in mid-October, which Miller proudly sent to the boys back home. Bald portrayed him as a carefree freeloader whose only complaint about "being on the bum" was not being able to brush his teeth. Poor as he was, however, Miller's days of living on the street were already largely behind him; for the most part, he stayed at Perlès's or Kann's, or increasingly, in the attic guest room at Louveciennes.

By December, the usual preliminary cables began to pour in from June. She had been away just a month, but the letters she had received from Anaïs and Henry alarmed her. She reappeared in mid-December with no clear object beyond seeing how her presence might affect the situation. She had changed in appearance once again, as Bald noted in another column, this one devoted entirely to June. Her hair had been dyed a dark, almost reddish blond, and she had taken to wearing a single cat's-eye earring and using dark blue mascara and lipstick in startling shades like green and black. She wore "the mask of death," wrote Bald, "and her ghastly beauty ma[de] them stare."

Anaïs, who found June more beautiful than ever, invited the couple to Louveciennes, prepared for high drama. When Hugo politely averted a scene between Henry and June, Anaïs chided him for letting a "living moment" pass them by. Anaïs was overcome by emotion in June's presence, though she noted dispassionately June's inability to tell the truth and the probability that she was insane. On another visit she asked June straight out if she were a Lesbian. June answered evasively. But every signal she sent indicated the sexual nature of her response to Anaïs; she described her friendship with Jean in rhapsodic terms, and commented repeatedly on Anaïs's beauty. A girlish courtship ensued. The two women exchanged clothes and jewelry, discussed their respective husbands, and appraised each other's looks. Henry was all but forgotten. June explained to Anaïs that when discussing both women's relationship with Henry she always tried to be direct and natural, because that was the best way to avert his suspicions about what was going on between them. To Henry June explained, not entirely inaccurately, "Anaïs was just bored with her life, so she took us up."

One of the few matters Miller would leave untouched in his autobiographical writings was his response to the flirtation between his wife and his patron. But it seems safe to assume that he was dismayed and frustrated. For after two productive years on his own in Paris, he found himself relegated once again to a supporting role in one of June's elaborate intrigues. From this point, his references to June in letters become increasingly bitter and contemptuous: she becomes "that Jewish cunt" whom he intends to pay back in his fiction. But he did not actively oppose the relationship between Anaïs and June; indeed, he later wrote to Schnellock that this "affair" was one of the greatest moments of June's life, and one that he had made possible for her. June may have argued that Anaïs was the patron they had always sought. Miller was even more confounded by the fact that he had no real evidence the relationship had gone beyond flirtation. Anaïs would always intimate that she had been willing to take it further than June was.

Old wounds still troubled the marriage as well. Though Henry hounded her for information, June was as vague as ever about her means of support. June in turn accused Henry of infidelity, citing Bertha Schrank and the prostitutes he had written about in his manuscripts. The cross-examinations built up to a violent duel on Christmas Day, and June began to speak of returning to America. The marriage was fueled only by the intensity of the personalities involved, and Henry's energies were now directed elsewhere, in his writing, while June's were consumed in self-destruction.

By the end of January 1932, June had sailed for America. Henry found in the rubble she had left behind a single stocking, which he carried with him to shine his shoes. He could hardly believe it had ever touched her leg—or even that she had once existed. He didn't dare think of her, he wrote Anaïs late in the month, for fear of jumping out the window: "One cold, solid smack and it's all over."

Nin may have been partly responsible for June's departure, perhaps unwittingly. With Guiler's help, she had set up for Miller an interview with a Dr. Krans of the Franco-American Exchange Program, who arranged jobs for Americans as English teachers. Miller disliked Krans on sight as a typical American hypocrite, but he buttered him up thoroughly, sensing Krans liked flattery. Krans offered Miller a job teaching English at the Lycée Carnot in Dijon. The terms were that he would teach ten hours a week, have two days off, and receive free room and board and a small salary. Miller scrambled to raise the money to get down to Dijon, borrowing 100 francs from Walter Lowenfels. (Nin was on a short holiday in Switzerland with Guiler and unable to help.) He had a feeling his friends were relieved to see him go.

Miller knew immediately upon his arrival that Dijon was a "fatal mistake," and his brief stay would form a bleak but often comic episode in *Tropic of Cancer*. The winter there was gloomy and cold, and the food at the Lycée was inedible. The salary never materialized. He searched the town for a typewriter with an English keyboard but couldn't find one. The Lycée itself reminded him of everything he hated about education: one professor told him it was good to give the boys reading assignments that were over their heads, to keep them on their toes—an approach Miller found idiotic. The person he found most sympathetic among the whole staff was the night watchman.

As he did in Paris, Miller rose close to noon and went to bed very late, taking long walks through the snowy, deserted town. He wrote to Nin almost daily, often about June. Until now, he had always sought to understand June and her motivations; now he turned his attention to himself and his own role in the relationship. On February 7 he described to Nin his attraction to a woman he had seen in a café—a woman his companions had identified as a whore:

> I deliberately tortured myself by observing how familiarly the others handled her. I permitted myself to imagine how non-chalantly she gave herself to the first bidder. And I, yes, I would be willing to get down on my knees to her. . . . Only a week here and voilà, une femme! Always seeking for someone to worship. Always choosing those who may be had for the asking. What a spectacle!

All at once, June's departure and his own unfortunate isolation in Dijon brought home to Miller how much material he had to put in order and how large a task he had set for himself in resolving to write about his marriage. Emotionally, he felt less than equal to it. He wrote Nin that he was reading Proust and undergoing "a form of ecstatic suffering." In Albertine he saw another June, though compared to Proust's enigmatic and elusive character June was "more complicated, orchestrated." He measured himself against Proust: "I am where Proust was, only with more complications, more facts, more mysteries, more of everything, except genius." He asked Nin if the rumors about Proust being homosexual were true, admitting that he had once visited the Trois Colonnes in the rue de Lappe looking for Albertine. In the same letter he wrote that the whole issue reminded him of *Crazy Cock*, which Pop, June's old patron, had genuinely believed was written by a woman. June's attraction first to Jean and then to Anaïs was but another "complication" for him.

Miller's confusions about gender and his own manhood surfaced

again, and this time they were closely bound up with new doubts about
his ability to write. It was in the context of these struggles that Nin's
book on Lawrence appeared in early 1932. Miller was genuinely impressed by the work, which he had read in proofs, and he continued to
encourage Nin in her efforts at fiction. But when Waverley Root's
glowing review of *D. H. Lawrence: An Unprofessional Study* appeared
in the *Tribune*, he was horrified by Root's statement that "[Nin] must
have something of the man in her. . . ." He pasted the review in his
scrapbook, along with a note that Root, "the bastard," must have
worked in collusion with another American who "knew that menage on
Henry Street." (This was, of course, quite unlikely; it was probably a
paranoid fantasy.) Any statement regarding sexual identity—especially
in relation to authorship—inevitably called up Miller's associations
with the Henry Street triangle, when he had felt himself not only unable to write but "unmanned." In a letter to Nin, Miller protested
Root's rhetoric, saying, "No, Anaïs is all woman and she has no wings,
thank God." But he continued his comparison of Anaïs to June, whose
identity as a woman was more questionable by his standards, and
lapsed into a surrealist catalogue, the same language he used to describe himself as a boy looking under girls' dresses: "I know one Anaïs.
Let June come. . . . Is that June coming down the street? No, it is a
bottle of absinthe. Is this Anaïs? No, it is a hydrangea. What do I see
beneath their dresses—a dream of Aunt Annie—wooden flowers in a
glass of water, flowers that open only in H_2O." He could resolve his
sexual confusion only linguistically, turning women into objects—bottles of absinthe, hydrangeas.

Miller poured out much of his emotional torment in voluminous
letters to Nin in Switzerland. They corresponded about *Moloch* (which
she thought could be salvaged) and about Guiler (with whom Miller
would later identify, having been in a cuckold's shoes himself). They
exchanged notes for their respective novels about June; Nin was writing a story called "Alraune," which eventually became part of *Winter
of Artifice*. Miller wrote Nin at a furious rate, often twice a day, and
she responded in kind. He repeatedly sounded notes of caution about
her marriage, and Nin questioned why he should be so considerate of
Guiler.

On February 21, Miller received a telegram from Perlès saying
there was a permanent job waiting for him as assistant finance editor
at the *Tribune*, at a salary of 1,200 francs (about $45) a month. Miller
telegraphed Nin for money for a return ticket, taxicabs, and the repay-

ment of several debts, and left for Paris as soon as the money arrived. He moved in with Perlès at the Hôtel Central in the rue de Maine, got the necessary shots for his worker's card, and began his job at the *Tribune*—which consisted of proofreading stock quotations—in the first week of March.

By then he and Nin had become lovers. She wrote in her diary that she had not known how happy she was to have Miller back until she met him in a Montparnasse restaurant at the end of February. During the first days of March he sent her a flurry of love letters, each apologizing for the effrontery of the last. They met at the Rôtonde and the Viking, Miller lingering after Nin left, drinking from her glass and writing her more letters. And Nin took care always to appear at her most exotic and outré, asking him if he liked her ink, which she said was made of "dried Andalusian blood," and sending him a few cryptic lines in purple ink on silver paper. They consummated their affair at around this time, probably in a hotel room or in the studio of Nin's friend Natasha Troubetskoia, which served as Nin's mail drop and occasional pied-à-terre.

For several weeks, they talked of little but the miracle of their coming together. "Here is the first woman with whom I can be sincere," Miller exulted, and Nin recorded that her very being "clamored for Henry." To Schnellock, Miller wrote, "Can't you picture what it is to me to love a woman who is my equal in every way, who nourishes me and sustains me? If we ever tie up there will be a comet let loose in the world." Like so many of his acquaintances in later years, Nin was fascinated by the contrast between the coarseness of Miller's writing and his personal gentleness and romanticism.

Their sexual relationship was passionate in these early weeks, as Miller's letters make clear. Nin claimed in her diary to have been "sexually awakened" by him, though he was by no means her first extramarital lover. If he saw any resemblance between Anaïs and June —both were deceptive by nature, though Anaïs might prefer the term "mysterious"—he didn't comment on it. Whether the two seriously contemplated marriage is unclear. The subject probably came up often in 1932, but Miller was still married and Nin very much dependent, emotionally as much as financially, on Guiler.

But for the first time in his life Miller was happy in a relationship with a woman, and he plunged back into his writing. "Anaïs, you've started the sap flowing," Miller wrote her in the beginning of March. Both were tremendously stimulated by the other's work. Even after a night of proofreading Miller was turning out at least ten pages a day of what would become *Tropic of Cancer*. Nin had started the manuscript of *House of Incest*, loosely based on her experiences with Henry and June. Though she admired Miller's work, Nin preferred abstraction to concrete detail in her own writing and maintained a cool detachment even when writing about the most passionate subjects. At its worst, her prose has a precious, naive quality; at other times it is marred by intense egotism. Often the result is unintentionally comic, as when she wrote in her diary: "Henry, save me from beatification, the horrors of static perfection. Precipitate me into the inferno."

The lyric quality of her writing and the primacy she gave to introspection impressed Miller deeply, however. So did her new interest in psychoanalysis. In April she began analysis with Dr. René Allendy, and she discussed with Miller the insights she was uncovering in her treatment. Henry, in turn, was reading Freud and Jung and discussing them with his old friend Michael Fraenkel, who had returned to Paris. Henry began keeping a record of his dreams, and he discussed with Anaïs his feelings about his childhood. The unconscious, he came to see, was a rich source of creative inspiration; dreams could be used creatively to achieve a surreal effect that heightened the truths contained in them. Little of this made its way into *Tropic of Cancer*—most of what he had written for the book was in a relatively realistic style— but these insights would inform much of the writing that followed.

Nin's patronage made it possible for Miller to give up the life of the street. With Perlès, he moved out of the Hôtel Central and into an apartment on the Avenue Anatole France in Clichy, a working-class district of the city; he later said the neighborhood resembled the upper reaches of New York's Park Avenue in its bland modernity. The kitchen was the central room in the apartment, where the two men cooked and ate their meals. Though Miller commonly represented it otherwise, his life in Clichy was thoroughly bourgeois. He wrote to Nin that he looked forward to his last day at the *Tribune* (he had received notice in late March that his job would end April 15) because then he could "devote [him]self assiduously to the cleaning," staying home "like a well-kept mistress."

In Clichy, Miller developed a daily routine that he would stick to for the rest of his life. He rose late, but was generally at the typewriter by eleven. Mornings were devoted to correspondence and notetaking; at around one he would leave his desk to eat lunch in a café, sometimes with a friend. If alone, he might write another letter, asking the waiter for café stationery. Returning home around two, he put on his pajamas and climbed into bed for a one- or two-hour nap—a practice he would recommend to others for the next forty years. On rising, he sat down before the typewriter again, banging away at a fierce speed. After a late dinner, he returned to the typewriter, often producing his best work at night. Of course, he saw a good deal of his friends and of Nin, but their talk would be given over, by and large, to work. Miller assiduously distributed not only manuscript pages but sheaves of notes to his friends; in these years he was tentative and unsure about his own writing and thinking, although this would change after the publication of *Tropic of Cancer*.

"My life in Paris has become almost a dream," Miller wrote about his Clichy period. He and Perlès were both writing, Perlès turning out two pages a day of the novel that would be published as *Sentiments limitrophes* (roughly, *Borderline Sentiments*). Perlès, who wrote in French, called his work "making flowerpots," and Miller fondly referred to "Joey's flowerpots" in letters to friends. His own efforts were concentrated on *Tropic of Cancer*, into which he was tossing all manner of manuscripts, reviews, lists, and notes. To Schnellock he compared it to a "beautiful big valise . . . of stout leather, that expands or collapses, that you throw things into pell-mell regardless of whether they are starched or pressed or stained or not stained." This practice—of throwing in everything in his notebooks—led Miller to include a 123-word passage from *Finnegans Wake* that he had probably transcribed in his notebook after reading it in *transition* as "Work in Progress" in 1927. This may have been inadvertent on Miller's part; more likely, however, he included the passage as a gesture against Joyce, whose work annoyed him immensely. *Ulysses*, Joyce's epic of the man-on-the-street, could best be understood in terms of elitist literary conventions, he charged; Miller in some ways was writing a proletarian *Ulysses*, and perhaps he used Joyce's words to hint as much to his readers. (The passage is unremarkable, however, and one of the two changes Miller makes is to change the Joycean "mumorise" to the more mundane "memorize.")

The manuscript of *Tropic of Cancer* underwent several metamorphoses. Following a conversation with Fraenkel, Miller decided to use real names—a decision he later reluctantly reversed. A draft from this period contains a long diary section, mostly detailing Miller's inability to finish the book. With characteristic hubris, he wrote that he would not change a single line.

Each of these gestures, of course, only delayed completion. Miller was half-afraid to finish it—and not, strangely enough, because he thought it couldn't be published. Instead, he worried that *Tropic of Cancer* wouldn't create a stir, that it would be considered only risqué or—worse—*entertaining*. He wanted to make Europe and America hate him, he wrote Nin. He wanted the book to be "so disturbing, so volcanic" that the world would never be the same again. He toyed with the title, thinking to change it to the Whitmanesque *I Sing the Equator*. But *Tropic of Cancer*, a geographical and astrological allusion, expressed his sense of the world as diseased. The astrological sign Cancer is symbolized by a crab, which, Miller noted, can move in any direction—a crucial ability in Miller's universe. Opposite Cancer in the Zodiac is Capricorn: the second volume, he wrote Nin, would be called *Tropic of Capricorn*. The last volume, he said, might simply be called *God*.

Tropic of Cancer, as it emerged in manuscript, was a record of Miller's first year in Paris, mostly on the street. It opened with his brief stay with Fraenkel at the Villa Seurat. He set the tone in the novel's first sentences: "I am living at the Villa Borghese. There is not a crumb of dirt anywhere, not a chair misplaced. We are alone here and we are all dead," adding, several lines later, "I have no money, no resources, no hopes. I am the happiest man alive." Miller describes his adventures with Mazumdar (whom he calls Nanantatee), his winter in Osborn's hotel, his passion for Bertha Schrank, and his struggle to write. His stay as a schoolteacher in Dijon went in, as did his friends' experiences with prostitutes. Much was fictionalized. The book closes with the infamous episode involving the efforts of the narrator's friend, Fillmore, to evade a French girl whom he has impregnated. Fillmore gives the narrator a large sum of money for the girl and disappears, and the narrator keeps it for himself. The episode was based on an actual experience of Osborn's: in reality it turned out that the woman in question was only pretending to be pregnant with Osborn's child, though Miller and Perlès had to give her money to mollify her. In *Tropic of Cancer*, the episode is described in a deliberately coarse and brutal tone that suggests a narrator determined to say nothing that would allow his characters to appear anything but completely self-centered and crass. The tone is typical of the entire book, for Miller wanted to banish sentiment completely.

Just as he felt the situation demanded the use of real names, so too did he feel the necessity of using graphic four-letter words. The symbol that dominates the book is the crab, associated both with syphilis and cancer, which the narrator finds pervasive and inescapable in his decaying world: "it is written in the sky; it flames and dances, like an evil portent. It has eaten into our souls and we are nothing but a dead thing like a moon."

In the spring of 1932, certain passages of the manuscript were lyrical, but it remained too bulky and overwritten. Miller would continue revising it for the next two years, adding and cutting episodes, determined to strike the right—that is, the harshest—note.

If the world of *Tropic of Cancer* is decaying and dying and the mood bleak, that is not to say that it is a book of despair. On the contrary, the narrator brings a vitality and exuberance to life lived at the bottom. From this perspective he can exult in the world and even find peace in it. The book closes with the narrator looking at the Seine, which is "always there, quiet and unobtrusive, like a great artery running through the human body." He feels himself part of the landscape; the Seine flows through him. "The hills gently girdle it about: its course is fixed."

Miller may have felt, artistically and emotionally speaking, that his course too was at last fixed. But the novel's publication was by no means assured. In May, Nin discussed the possibility of Fraenkel publishing the book with his Carrefour Press; she was willing to pay for it, she said. But Fraenkel didn't like the latest version of the manuscript, which Miller had shortened severely, because some of Miller's cuts were of material on the "death theme" that Fraenkel especially valued. In June and July, while Nin was in the Tyrol with her husband, Miller had a little luck. He sent a copy to George Buzby, a well-connected friend in America who published the magazine *USA*, and another copy to Samuel Putnam. Neither Buzby nor Putnam nibbled, but Dr. Krans, who had hired Miller to teach in Dijon, put him in touch with William Aspenwall Bradley, an American literary agent. Bradley, who with his French wife, Jenny, ran one of Paris's most celebrated salons in their apartment on the Ile St.-Louis, found *Tropic of Cancer* "magnificent," passing over *Crazy Cock* without a word. He promised Miller he would find a publisher.

Miller should have been elated, but he wasn't. Finishing a complete draft of the book had left him feeling purged but disgusted. As he wrote Schnellock, he felt as though he'd undergone a surgical operation. Like his hero Dostoevsky, he hadn't written the book to cure himself, but rather to get rid of the wounds that festered inside him. (The distinction was subtle but important; Miller did not believe in cures.) To another friend he wrote, "After writing a book like that you get lousy and itchy. You don't want to see crabs, lice, or pubic hairs.

Or even a twat any more." At the height of the summer he shaved his head completely, writing to Nin that he did it out of abasement and humility—so that he could slink around even more inconspicuously. He took up what would become a constant theme: his hope (and fear) that he would be hated, and perhaps punished, for what he did. In his letters to New York friends, he was particularly vituperative about American opinion; what America would do or say in response to his book became a virtual obsession.

But in 1932, America barely noticed Henry Miller. The only publishing house in Paris likely to take on *Tropic of Cancer* was Jack Kahane's Obelisk Press, more widely known for selling English-language books that could not be published in Britain or the States than for launching American bestsellers. Kahane, an unashamed dandy and charmer (he once owned seven bulldogs and fifty pairs of pants,) was an English Jew who had lost his fortune in England and moved to France, taking a French wife. He started the Press in 1931 with his own novel *Daffodil*, under the pseudonym of Basil Carr (he turned out another line of books as Cecil Barr); his specialty was books that were condemned under obscenity laws in England or America. He would buy the rights to these works, repackage them with a new title page and the Obelisk Press cover, and sell them, mainly to tourists. In the thirties, when English-language writers were defying sexual conventions freely, Kahane was able to build up an impressive list, including Radclyffe Hall's *The Well of Loneliness*, Joyce's *Pomes Penyeach*, and Frank Harris's *My Life and Loves*, along with such garden-variety items as *Suzy Falls Off* and *Boy*.

Kahane stayed in business hoping to discover a masterpiece. In his autobiography, *Memoirs of a Booklegger*, Kahane recalled the moment when he was sure he had found one in Miller's book. He had taken the bulky manuscript to his country home, Le Fond des Forêts, for the weekend, and settled in to read it under the shade of a great copper beech. "At last!" he murmured to himself,

> I had read the most terrible, the most sordid, the most magnificent manuscript that had ever fallen into my hands; nothing I had yet received was comparable to it for the splendour of its writing, the fathomless depth of its despair, the savour of its portraiture, the boisterousness of its humour.

Walking back to the house he felt like an explorer who had at last become a discoverer, a discoverer of genius.

Miller, hearing of Kahane's reaction, told Nin that he intended to be a pretty cool customer in his negotiations. He wouldn't have Kahane think he was doing him a favor by publishing him. His years of obscurity apparently at an end, Miller was filled with confidence now, writing to his friend Osborn that he was on the brink of good fortune, possessed of a "splendid chance to reap [his] just reward." He fully expected censure, but he expected fame and fortune too. "They *won't be able* to shut me up!" he wrote Osborn, and the projected *Tropic of Capricorn* would give "them" an "even bigger jolt."

Kahane, however, was having difficulty with his printer and partner at the time, a man known only as Servant, who felt (just as Miller feared) that the book was not sexy enough. Servant argued that the author was a Montparnasse reject who would pester Kahane for his meager royalties. Obelisk's usual clientele were tourists in the market for Parisian "smut," and there were few tourists in Paris in the thirties. It would be an expensive book to produce. Besides, Servant went on, the title might cause the public to mistake it for a medical treatise.

Kahane persevered over Servant's protests. When he sought the advice of his friend Michael Bougalowski, an editor at the mainstream publishing house of Hachette, Bougalowski read the manuscript and told Kahane he would publish it himself if he dared. He confirmed Kahane's opinion: the book was "magnificent, overwhelming," and made *Lady Chatterley's Lover* and *Ulysses* look like "lemonade." He advised Kahane to bring it out in a small edition first, labeled "Privately Printed," with the Obelisk imprint in tiny letters at the back of the book, in the space typically reserved for the printer's name.

Miller wrote Osborn that Bradley and Kahane feared trouble. Kahane was nervous enough about issuing the book that he asked Miller to write a fifty- or sixty-page *plaquette*, or essay, on Lawrence or Joyce —much like Nin's study of Lawrence—which he would publish first, thereby establishing Miller as a serious artist rather than a mere dirty book writer.

Miller bridled at the idea, and at first refused. *Tropic of Cancer* could stand on its own merits. But his vanity eventually caused him to change his mind; however much he professed to hate intellectuals, he secretly envied them. His own discussions of literature invariably centered on content, as opposed to form or style, and he liked to think of himself as a man of ideas.

So he set out to write on both Lawrence and Joyce, but almost immediately what he called "the Brochure" expanded to encompass other authors and thinkers. He wrote Nin that he was determined to unburden himself of all "influences, gods, books, great names, etc. which throttled me before," and in the process produce a critical work that would establish him as an important thinker.

Though Kahane indicated at their next meeting that he now thought the Brochure might not be necessary, Miller overrode him. He was as fired up with plans for the Brochure as he was about the publication of *Tropic of Cancer*, which Kahane was promising for February 1933. In early October, Kahane drew up a contract that Bradley found acceptable; Miller was a bit bewildered by the terms, according to which he would get 10 percent of the selling price in royalties on *Cancer* and larger percentages on his second and third books, which Kahane optioned.

Miller characterized Kahane's terms as "lousy," and he immediately began to lay plans to have a pirated edition appear in America, certain it could never be published there openly. He discussed his plans with Schnellock and Osborn, writing Osborn that he wanted to be pirated by a friend and not "some crummy Jew." (He privately said that American publishers were "a bunch of kikes.") Joe O'Regan or George Buzby might have the resources and initiative to do it, he thought. If pirated by a friend, Miller reasoned, he stood a better chance of receiving some profits. More important to him, however, was getting read in America. To that end, he dusted off *Crazy Cock* and sent it to Pat Covici at Covici-Friede in New York on the advice of Samuel Putnam, who told Miller that Covici had liked "Mlle Claude." (Covici was about the only American editor who did, according to Putnam, who wrote that he heard "Mlle Claude" called "whorehouse stuff" and "plain pornography.") *Crazy Cock* was rejected again, to Miller's dismay, but he continued his efforts to get published in the States, sending various manuscripts to New York literary agent Madeleine Boyd and to George Buzby, who had publishing connections. Writing to Osborn, he struck a note of bravado: "America will call me the lowest of the low when they see *Cancer*. What a laugh I'll have when they begin to spit and fume. I hope they'll learn something about death and futility, about hope, etc. I won't give them a fucking leg to stand on." The book was an attack on art, but it was also a broadside directed at his native land and everything he thought it stood for. America, he claimed, was feminized, sterile, a hell for the artist. "Fuck my god-damned native land," Miller wrote his friend Hilaire Hiler. *"Fuck America!* She's a maniac without balls." *Tropic of Cancer*, set in expatriate Paris, was Miller's indictment of the land that he had left behind—and that had never recognized his talent.

"This time I am not affected by June's mad behavior—I am quite indifferent to anything she does. . . . I know where my real interests lie and am acting accordingly," Miller wrote summarily in October 1932. June arrived in the beginning of that month (preceded by the usual cables), determined to join Henry in his moment of glory—as well as to see what was going on with Anaïs. Perlès suggested that it was Nin herself who arranged for the trip, as a gift for Henry.

Mysteriously, June booked a room in the Hôtel Princesse for ten days before sending Henry a message that she had arrived. She hadn't brought the manuscripts he requested, only an old version of *Crazy Cock*. Almost immediately Henry sensed disaster, writing to Schnellock that "the war is on" and "I expect no mercy, no fair play." He was terrified that June would discover how far things had progressed with Anaïs, fearing that she would be as hurt by Nin's betrayal as his own.

Because of the relationship between Anaïs and June, however, the situation was far more complicated than Miller told Schnellock. Anaïs had upset Henry by telling him on the telephone, upon hearing of June's arrival, that she was happy for him. Henry thought the best course was to be magnanimous, and he wrote Anaïs that she was free to do whatever she liked with June, that he was not jealous. Anaïs revealed in her diary that she and June did spend a night together, in Clichy, with Perlès and Miller in the next room, but that the two women exchanged kisses and little more. June attempted to fuel Henry's jealousies by producing a love letter from Anaïs, but he was unfazed, knowing that Anaïs sometimes made declarations of passion when no physical relationship existed.

June was more restrained on this visit, Henry found; ominously so. He treated her like a small child, praising her whenever possible and never criticizing her, and he thought that the results were gratifying. He wrote Anaïs that June was making "heroic efforts" to please him, and that he was touched. He also thought she seemed healthier and calmer, he said. But he longed to be with Anaïs. June, always so attuned to his loyalties, sensed the battle was lost—and became ugly.

Miller's biographers—as well as Nin herself—have held that the marriage was over when June read the manuscript of *Tropic of Cancer* and became outraged at her portrait there. Even in manuscript form, however, the book does not bear out this interpretation. June appears as Mona, the narrator's wife, who pays one visit to Paris in the course of the narrative. And though the narrator is of course famously unfaithful, he loves no woman but his wife, who is presented as an almost totemic apotheosis of womanhood. June may have been upset by the tone of the book, but she could have had no quarrel with her portrait.

What the manuscript did reveal dramatically was the transformation in her husband. The narrator was a man grown hard, a man who bore little resemblance to the vulnerable and gullible Henry whom June had resolved to keep "at her side." He had left her side for good, in fact. Moreover, he had become an artist—and without her presence. His new self-assurance confused her utterly, and for once her dramatic skills failed her; she couldn't move quickly enough to devise a new way of responding to him. After a bitter quarrel, she left the hotel and moved in with friends from Montparnasse. But even this failed to arouse Miller's jealousy, for he knew the friends to be male homosexuals.

June was not to be shaken off that easily, however. At the grocer's Miller learned that she had been in with a young man and had charged supplies to Miller's account. A *pneumatique* came asking for money. One evening she showed up for dinner at the flat in Clichy, and Miller cheerfully fed her. After dinner she became hysterical, claiming she had suffered from dysentery ever since she'd left Miller, and that Perlès, Miller, and Nin had been slipping poison in her food.

Nin and Perlès, alarmed by the effect June's presence was having on Miller (as usual when June was on the scene, he had nearly stopped writing altogether), arranged for him to pay a visit to London for the Christmas holidays, with Nin furnishing the money. They happened on London because June knew Miller hated it and would never think to look for him there, and Henry himself found he had a desire to hear English voices again. On the eve of his departure, June showed up at the Clichy apartment and found the bags packed and travel folders on the kitchen table. A horrific scene ensued, with June, drunk on Chartreuse, hurling recriminations and accusations at Henry, threatening to expose Nin by telling Guiler. "I listened to the worst vituperation a man can ever listen to from the woman he loves," he wrote Schnellock. "Dirt. Dirt. Vulgar Jewish display. Vulgar histrionics." Henry was speechless; June was beyond reason. Finally, worn down, he laid out the money on the table, telling her to take it all, and even offered to get a refund for his ticket money the next day. Almost immediately June became contrite and offered to return half the money. In the midst of a tearful exit she left the money behind and Miller had to run after her. They said goodbye on the stairs, June giving him a "strange, sorrowful" smile that indicated she would have thrown out the money and rushed back into his arms if he made the slightest gesture. Miller gave her a long look and went back inside, sitting at the kitchen table and sobbing like a baby. He sensed it was their last goodbye.

June sailed home in late December, Perlès seeing her off on the train from Paris. Miller wrote Schnellock that the final item in his scrapbook was a piece of toilet paper on which June had scrawled, "Please get a divorce immediately." The day she sailed Miller went on a drinking spree, ending up in a bar in the rue Pigalle talking to an Englishwoman with bad teeth, and listening to a man at a harp singing "Valparaiso," a song made popular by the French singer Yvonne George. The refrain of the song was "Good-bye, Mexico," and since June would probably be getting a Mexican divorce, the words made him weep. Thereafter, whenever he referred to his divorce, he quoted the refrain.

Miller believed he was free of June at last, that he had seen her for what she was. Indeed, if his letters are any indication, she almost disappeared from his thoughts. If anything, he now felt sorry for her. But five months later, when he received a letter from Osborn, who had returned to America, saying he had seen June in a Greenwich Village café with a younger man, Miller at once composed a nearly twenty-page drunken letter to Schnellock alternately berating June and lamenting his loss. What he couldn't bear, he wrote, was the knowledge that June hated him. He asked Schnellock to tell June that he loved her still, but did not want her. The letter veers hysterically from passion (he would jump in the Seine for her) to vicious hatred. He wrote that he loved June because she was a Jewess but referred to her throughout as "that little Jewish cunt." She had become "June Smith-Smerth-Mansfield-Miller-Cunt-Balls-Whore," and Miller at last admitted that he knew she was unfaithful.

The next morning he appended a postscript, telling Schnellock to read "the enclosed" only for his own amusement. If Emil should see June, he wrote, he should tell her to fuck herself. He added, however, that Emil should tell him what color dress she wore, too, and whether her eyes were painted green or blue—"because I don't give a fuck about her." The young man Osborn had seen her with, Henry concluded, must be Stratford Corbett, the insurance salesman who was courting June when Henry had left for Europe three years before.

June crippled him, he wrote a few weeks after this outburst. He hoped she remembered occasionally all he had given her—what he could never give another woman. He would have done anything for her, he wrote: "Treachery, arson, theft, murder. Anything—just to hold her." In many ways it was June who made his writing possible, for Miller believed that suffering toughened the spirit. She provided him, too, with a lifetime's worth of "material": *Tropic of Capricorn*, which he'd already begun by the end of 1933, would be dedicated "To Her," and his life with June and Jean would later be the subject of his multivolume *The Rosy Crucifixion*. Gradually he conceived the idea of getting revenge on June through his books. If she had found little to hurt her in *Tropic of Cancer*, he would return to the events of *Crazy Cock* and present June in all her treachery and madness. In July 1934, when he was embarked in earnest on *Tropic of Capricorn*, he wrote Osborn that he intended it to be a Proustian epic that would repay June for his years of failure in America. It would be, he promised, "a tomb of June that will live for several centuries to come. That's what comes of injury and insult. The Jewish cunt will twitter!"

9.

Tropical Storms

1933–1935

The scholarly piece Miller had promised Kahane on D. H. Lawrence—
"the Brochure"—nearly proved to be his undoing. "I'm covering a
wide territory," he wrote Osborn in February of 1933. "It will give me
prestige as a thinker." The territory he was covering was wide indeed.
In one letter to Nin, he wrote that the work would have four parts and
an introduction; in his next letter, he wrote that it would have ten major
divisions. "Big Macrocosmic Connections!" he announced.

Everything was going into the Brochure: thoughts on Lawrence
led him to Proust, Spengler, Joyce, the cinema, psychoanalysis, nud-
ism, dreams, Rabelais, Count Keyserling, and Elie Faure. Miller spent
over twenty pages, for example, on notes from entries in the *Encyclopaedia Britannica* on mystery, mysticism, and the Black Death. He
quoted at length, copying out extracts several pages long, until Nin
scolded him, telling him to speak for himself or at least to restate the
passages in his own words. In the same letter she warned in the strongest possible terms that he must not show his work-in-progress to any
outsider, such as Bradley or Kahane. No doubt she knew the enterprise
was doomed.

But Miller persisted, working tirelessly on the Brochure in 1933
and 1934. In early 1933 he developed yet another grand plan. The
Brochure was now to be three volumes: one on Proust, one on Joyce,
and one on Lawrence. A fourth book, he projected, would be "pure
ideas and no names"—presumably a philosophical meditation rather
than literary criticism.

Not that the term "literary criticism" accurately describes those
fragments of the Brochure that survive—most notably a selection published in 1980 as *The World of Lawrence: A Passionate Appreciation*—
or any of his later excursions into other writers' work, for that matter.

Miller rambled through Lawrence's fiction, far more interested in what it told him about the author than he was in the books themselves. He was especially engrossed, for example, by Ursula Brangwen's Lesbian encounter in *The Rainbow* because of the glimpses it offered of Lawrence's feelings about homosexuality. Miller's interest was not exactly biographical, however; it was in the workings of the creative mind, and, most importantly, in his own responses to the artist's work. For now that *Tropic of Cancer* was completed, he was an author with a personality and vision all his own. Instead of simply studying other writers, he had begun to compare himself to them. About Joyce he declared, "I am not ashamed to say that I am too ignorant to appreciate Joyce's writing. . . . The greater he becomes the more I want to shun him." He also expatiated on his own work, often insightfully, as when he admitted his similarities to Voltaire, another blisteringly savage social commentator: "If I am to be a Voltaire to-day I must use other means, other weapons. And I am really much more destructive than a Voltaire precisely because I have left that world of ideas—because I am hitting below the belt."

He wrote Osborn that he was himself against thinking, but that he was "obliged" in the Brochure to be a thinker—and that he had not "left that world of ideas" at all. Nin was becoming increasingly alarmed by the direction Miller's work was taking. In July 1933 she told him that she thought he was unhappy as a philosopher, and that she wished he would return to imaginative writing, to describe his feelings and intoxications. "You do not have *a* philosophy. You have feelings," she wrote. "I say let the intellectual you alone, the savant, the philosopher."

Nin was moved to protest because she had seen several pages of Miller's new book, tentatively called "Self-Portrait," which would eventually appear as *Black Spring*. He had set aside the embryonic *Tropic of Capricorn* because that was to be about June, and he was not ready to face those experiences yet. Instead, he was turning out little vignettes, some autobiographical, some descriptive; the first of these was "Third or Fourth Day of Spring," written in March 1933. The piece was a meditation on Miller's place in the world ("Either the world is too slack or I am not taut enough"), on his view of religion ("our triune god of penis and testicles"), on Rabelais ("For all your ills [I give you] *laughter!*"). Its mood was exultant, although, as in *Cancer*, the narrator saw the world as dead or dying.

Miller followed "Third or Fourth Day of Spring" with more autobiographical pieces, notably "The Tailor Shop," a lyrical evocation of his father and an exploration of his ancestry. "Jabberwhorl Cronstadt," a portrait of his friend Lowenfels—whom he dubbed Cronstadt, after a Paris hotel—is a surrealistic romp; in fact, the manuscript shows his growing indebtedness to the surrealists. To Schnellock, he wrote that his pages contained "hallucinating stuff—streets again—and cracked ideas—the slats of things, the warped, twisted aspect, the universe which has fallen a little to one side, collapsed, gone kerflop." He and Nin had avidly devoured a surrealist number of Edward Titus's *This Quarter*, which contained contributions by René Crevel and Paul Eluard, both followers of André Breton. (He had been disappointed when Titus had not taken a surrealistic piece by Perlès and himself— probably part of "The New Instinctivism"—and suspected Titus was hostile to any contributors to the rival *New Review*.)

Among his other "laboratory experiments," as he called them, were a book on the cinema, a manuscript that documented his dreams, and a film scenario based on Nin's *House of Incest*, which he called "Palace of Entrails." He surrounded his desk with elaborate wall charts, copying his extensive notes onto large sheets of white paper and connecting them together in intricate diagrams. Soon he found that he was not writing books, but books of notes. Sending along one such "book" (his notes on Lawrence) to Nin, he commented, "My head's bursting. Never made so many connections, synapses, syncopes, ellisions and syntheses in my life."

In April 1933, Miller reluctantly granted Kahane a six-month extension on his commitment to publish *Tropic of Cancer*. When Kahane asked for another six months, in October, Miller was tempted to withdraw the manuscript altogether, though he grudgingly agreed again. He was becoming fed up with Kahane and with his agent, Bradley. Kahane's son Maurice Girodias wrote in his memoirs that at this point Nin and Miller mounted a campaign to galvanize Kahane and convince him to go ahead with publication. First, as Girodias wrote, Nin "vamped" Bradley and then Kahane, after which both she and Miller spoke very highly about Bradley in order to impress the snobbish Kahane—although they actually considered Bradley a philistine.

Nin was still trying to devise a plan to underwrite the costs of *Cancer*'s publication herself. At one point, Guiler had been willing to act as a kind of business manager and advance the money to Kahane, but then, to no one's surprise, he balked at the last minute, saying he wouldn't advance a penny for Miller, his "worst enemy." Guiler was the kind of man who tried to look the other way regarding his wife's extramarital activities, but he apparently drew the line at financing her lover's book.

While *Tropic of Cancer* sat on Kahane's shelf, it was Nin who was achieving professional recognition in 1933. Bradley and Kahane both showed interest in publishing her diaries, though Kahane wanted to abridge them, thereby earning himself a scathing letter from Miller, who believed the diaries were one of the age's greatest literary achievements. Nin completed her *House of Incest* and another series of sketches about Henry and June that she called her "Alraune" pages and that would be published as *Winter of Artifice*. She also immediately set to making up a separate copy of *House of Incest* for her father and her husband—one that deleted all the compromising material on Henry and June.

Miller saw himself as Nin's literary mentor, at times acting the part of a Dutch uncle. In October he wrote her a long letter criticizing her work, especially her tendency to tack on artful syntheses at the end of scenes that had no real conclusion, and her overuse of such "slightly ridiculous hyperboles" as "I was stirred in my very womb" and "I am light." She must toughen herself up for criticism, he warned.

Nin did not take well to this. She fired back a long letter accusing him of being "false," and comparing him to Bradley; the implication was that any criticism of her work constituted disloyalty. Nin could be imperious when she wanted, and financially she had the upper hand in the relationship. Miller backed off.

As long as Miller kept his place, the relationship proceeded smoothly. The couple enjoyed idyllic days at Louveciennes during Guiler's frequent business trips, and Nin visited Miller often in his Clichy apartment, though she didn't particularly care for Perlès. She disapproved of Henry's clownish side, which Perlès brought out. But in her diary she describes pleasant evenings in the Clichy kitchen, watching Henry cook, resting her elbows on the oilcloth-covered kitchen table, listening to his powerful voice. She found his ignorance of proper manners exotic and amusing, as when he made the *faux pas* of salting the foie gras, or when, at a Louveciennes meal, he used his finger bowl to hold his dessert.

Both were expanding their horizons and getting to know other artists and writers. Nin took up with the surrealist Antonin Artaud, a fellow patient of her analyst René Allendy; for a time she convinced herself she was in love with him, but Artaud was asserting himself as a homosexual and could not respond in kind. Miller was renewing his interest in painting. Nin had introduced him to Hilaire Hiler, the American painter who was in training to become a psychoanalyst. Hiler was something of a character; born with ears easily twice the normal size, he had undergone cosmetic surgery but was still odd-looking. He also talked with a stutter. Miller began taking painting lessons with him in 1933, reporting proudly to Nin that Hiler thought his work "masculine."

Another new friend was the Hungarian photographer Halasz Brassaï, whom Miller had met casually a year or two before. Brassaï introduced Miller to another Hungarian, a literary agent named Frank Dobo, who would become an important friend. Brassaï was in touch with various segments of Paris's artistic community and acquainted Miller with the French writer Joseph Delteil, the poet Louis Aragon (whose 1931 *The Red Front*, calling for a workers' revolution, had shocked France), and the writer and editor Raymond Queneau. Miller was beginning to enjoy a modest celebrity as the American who had written a book so shocking that even Jack Kahane didn't dare to publish it. He encouraged this image, dubbing himself the "gangster author."

He inserted Brassaï, for instance, in the manuscript of *Tropic of Cancer*, describing him as a photographer who asks the narrator to pose for some nude pictures. Brassaï denied that this incident happened, but other rumors circulated that Miller had made money posing for homoerotic photographs in his early days in Paris. (One story has it that Miller appeared in pornographic films made in Belgium. The closest corroboration for this is the claim of his editor at the *Tribune* that Miller disappeared on a vacation trip to Belgium and thus lost his job. Most likely, the rumors were groundless. Miller, however, did little to dispel them; they suited his image as a literary *clochard* who would do anything for his art.)

Psychologically, Miller felt he was achieving remarkable insights in his analysis of his dreams and in writing about his childhood in "Self-Portrait." He and Nin avidly read the work of Otto Rank, the renegade psychoanalyst and author of *The Trauma of Birth* and *Art and Artist*. In March 1933 Miller met Rank, and after a single analytic session pronounced himself "cured." He had met Rank on his own ground, he bragged in an arrogantly worded letter to Nin, and had impressed the analyst with his grasp of Rank's ideas.

For Miller and Nin, psychoanalysis was less important as therapy than as another quarry from which they could mine ideas to understand their development as artists. What excited Miller about Rank was his analysis of creativity. According to Rank, art grew out of primitive man's inability to make the connection between intercourse and birth; birth shook his belief that his soul could transcend bodily death. Thus man turned to the creation of art, which, during what Rank called the "era of sexuality"—the twentieth century—became eroticized. Thus too was born the cultural view of woman as a sexual being, a symbol of reproduction who disturbs man's conception of the world as a place where there is no real death but only rebirth and regeneration. Any theory that formulated connection between sex, death, and art had implicit appeal for Miller, though he grasped Rank's thesis only partially, and he ignored the analyst's concurrent belief that ultimately the creative impulse should be given over not to art but to "the formation of personality."

Miller's meeting with Rank increased his productivity, already prodigious in 1933. Rank also had a great effect on Nin, who had grown dissatisfied with her own analyst, René Allendy. She entered analysis with Rank in November, and in May 1934 would undertake psychoanalytic training in order to work under Rank.

The summer of 1933 was filled with travel. Nin and Guiler traveled through France, and Miller visited first Luxembourg (with Perlès) and then the provinces, which he found stultifying. Back in Paris, with Nin still away, he was in a particularly cynical mood. When a packet from Schnellock arrived containing Henry's letters to his first wife Beatrice, he decided that they were "tediously stupid and practical" and destroyed them "without a qualm," an uncharacteristic act indeed for a man who saved every imaginable memento for possible material. Around the same time, Osborn, now living in Connecticut and recovering from the breakdown that had sent him back to the States, sent a verbal portrait describing Miller as a good man who was at the same time treacherous by nature, someone who found no one's life important but his own—not even those of his most intimate friends. Miller agreed with Osborn's portrait, he breezily wrote Nin, but found it odd that he should receive it at just the time when he had been plotting a campaign to drive the already unbalanced Osborn totally insane, by writing him letter after letter elaborating on Osborn's paranoias and hallucinations. His fear was not that he would succeed—he was sure of that—but that he would be blamed and punished. His only motive, he wrote, was "vindictiveness born out of sheer indifference."

Antics like these were common enough for Nin and Miller, both at times almost infantile in their behavior. Miller and Perlès were given to gratuitously cruel acts that they wrote off as good times—whether it was picking Fraenkel's pockets or stealing a friend's girlfriend. Nin, too, was capable of wanton cruelty, though she acted with an icy hauteur, disdaining Miller's buffoonery. She could cut a friend over the smallest of gestures, as admirers such as the British poet David Gascoyne found out. Recording in his diary a "ridiculous scene" with Nin the day before, Gascoyne wrote bitterly that she acted pigheadedly out of her taste for the theatrical and the picturesque, "such as is evident in the Moorish decor with which she surrounds herself, the 'barbaric' jewelry, the incense-burning, the glass tree, and other exotic stage-properties that she requires in order to convince herself that she is leading an intensely interesting 'inner life.'" Miller suffered from Nin's whims and sudden chilliness more than once in 1933—over a chance remark or an aesthetic affront. Both artists were seemingly random in their meanness, as Miller's remark about Osborn clearly indicates.

In July 1933 Miller met a down-on-his-luck Jewish tailor he called Max, who would become the subject of one of Miller's most moving short pieces, published in 1938 in the collection *Max and the White Phagocytes*. The story is a masterful and honest evocation of the contradictory emotions aroused by "street people" or bums: the natural impulse to help, of course, but also the frustration and even contempt to which such encounters can give rise. In the story, Miller helps Max, who lacks any resources or friends; he writes to Max's sister in America and lends him clothes and money. He is offended by the callous and condescending way his friend Boris (Michael Fraenkel) treats Max, though he himself believes that the only real solution for a hopeless case like Max is for him to jump in the Seine, and he avoids him whenever possible: "You detest [people like Max] so heartily that your curiosity is aroused: you come back to them again and again to study them, to arouse in yourself a feeling of compassion which is really absent. You do things for them, not because you feel any sympathy for them, but because their suffering is incomprehensible to you." Miller's familiar cynicism is balanced here by a compassion that seems to defy his better judgment.

But in a 1933 letter to Nin Miller described Max in quite a different fashion. According to this version, he actually told Max outright that he might as well jump in the Seine. Five years ago he might have taken Max in, he said, but now no such solution was possible. In the early thirties, with the Fascists taking hold in Europe, the world seemed doomed, and millions would have to suffer. "Millions must go to the wall," he wrote, echoing Nietzsche and his own eugenicist first novel, *Clipped Wings.*

As his response to Max suggests, Miller's preoccupations in 1933 and 1934 had expanded to include politics. Over the next few years, as war approached, he would make all manner of pronouncements about the political scene. The common view of Miller holds that he was apolitical or, at most, a philosophical anarchist. The system that appealed to him most was indeed anarchism—but, like most anarchists, he did not expect civilization to realize anarchy in the near future. In the early thirties, his political vision was apocalyptic, quasi-mystical, greatly influenced by Spengler and Nietzsche. Although he had adopted his grandfather's pacifism, he now advocated violence, and spoke often of the need for strong leaders who would not eschew it. On his stationery he had printed a quote from Balzac: *"L'Europe ne croira plus qu'en celui qui la broiera sous ses pieds"* (Europe only believes in he who crushes her underfoot).

One curious, unpublished piece of Miller's that dates approximately from this period was "The All-Intelligent Explosive Rocket," an essay rejected by John Lehmann at the British magazine *Night and Day*. It begins with the "universal truth" that destruction is not only useful but often "quite agreeable"; the problem, Miller asserts, is its "aimlessness." Therefore he proposes a "cerebrated explosive" that will destroy only what it is directed to destroy. With the premise thus established, he imagines the possibilities of the "All-Intelligent Blith-erington Explosive Rocket." It could help man, for example, to open up the "dark continent" more quickly: "Here the rocket could be instructed to annihilate the women and children of the backward races, as it is the women and children who form the chief obstacle to modern progress in the vast unenlightened wastes of Africa." As his language suggests, Miller clearly intended a satire, but—as would happen with increasing frequency in his essays—his humor is somehow "off," and the political message of the piece is completely unfocused. The reader assumes it to be an attack on war or man's innate aggression, but the tone militates against this reading, suggesting that the author is so cynical about man's aggressive nature that he actually endorses his fantastical creation. The point is lost.

Miller's political vision is also reflected in an item he included in his "Major Program," part of an elaborate "Work Schedule" he drew up in 1932 and 1933 that also contained a "Minor Program," "Daily Program," and "Painting Program." The sixth subject he intended to write about (after "streets," "China," and "artist's patriotism," for example—all topics that would be addressed in *Black Spring*) was "violence." The germ of the idea, he noted, lay in a comment of Brassaï's that one man can destroy an entire city. "The individual as against the collectivity," he wrote—another of his favorite themes. "New type of man," he noted. "Kill history, culture, cyclical development." Sketchy as they are, these notes suggest that he was developing an apocalyptic world view that forecast a world revolution led by an individual with vision; they anticipate the admiration Miller would bear for the energy—if not the ideas—of the Fascist leaders then emerging in Europe.

But violence was just one item on Miller's "Major Program." His energies were enormous when he was working on the Brochure and *Black Spring*, and he worried that he might be moving in too many directions at once. Along with his series of "Programs," he drew up a series of commandments, most of which dictated that he narrow his focus, concentrate on the thing at hand, and forget other books he wanted to write later. He admonished himself to "work with pleasure only" and to "see people, go places, drink if you feel like it." He wrote Hilaire Hiler in the fall of 1933 that he wanted to do a new series of wall charts—one mapping out characters, another chronology, and another topography.

"I am seeing things whole, living whole, fucking whole. A holy man, Emil. A just man, a hero—to myself anyway," Henry wrote Schnellock in December 1933. But he was possessed with a grim sense of his own mortality as well. One night he had a dream about his own grave, and on waking drafted a five-page will. He wrote Nin that he believed he'd had his friend Abe Elkus draw up a will for him in America, in which he had left everything to June. Now he directed that everything be left to Nin, adding a list of debts totaling roughly $3,300. He asked Nin to see that his parents, June, and his daughter Barbara would be taken care of, and left directions that Perlès was to write his biography. This letter is a strange document, written by a man poised on the edge of fame, troubled by his breakneck productivity but absolutely convinced of his own success, and confident that even his letters would have value. Miller repeatedly assured his friends that he would immortalize them in print. At forty-two, he wrote Schnellock, "If any one hereafter says in connection with me [what] Bruce Barton once said, 'it is quite obvious that writing is not your forte'—well, here I am, and I am showing them!'"

By 1934, almost two years after he had finished writing it, Miller was determined to see *Tropic of Cancer* in print. Kahane kept putting him off, citing the precarious economy. In April, Nin would go to London to try to drum up interest in the book on the British literary scene. In the meantime Miller revised the manuscript, shearing out whole sections and polishing the writing. He found it not as good as *Black Spring*, and Nin agreed. But he felt it had to be published.

In February, Miller moved out of the apartment in Clichy. After Nin had begun analysis with Otto Rank in November 1933, she had moved into a residential hotel at 24 rue des Marroniers in Passy in order to be closer to Rank's office. Taking advantage of Guiler's absence—he remained at Louveciennes—she installed Miller in an adjoining room. Passy, "just a stone's throw from the Seine," was a step up for Miller. At night he often sat over a beer in a café across the river at the Pont Mirabeau, listening to jazz on the radio and looking at the reflection of the Eiffel Tower in the Seine. He was still working, intermittently, on *Black Spring*, but he was threatening to chuck the Brochure to write "*the* book of the century," he told Nin, inspired by that favorite topic of Fraenkel's, death. He had returned as well to the manuscript of *Tropic of Capricorn*, but progress on that was slow.

In April, when Nin was in London trying to hunt up a publisher for *Tropic of Cancer*, Miller wrote her that he had been revising the manuscript again and now liked it better. It gave the impression, he wrote, of having been written at twenty-five different addresses— which it had been. When Nin returned with no offers, Miller began to despair. Kahane was claiming to be nearly bankrupt, and Miller had broken with Bradley, denouncing him as an old man who got sadistic pleasure out of critiquing younger men. Then, in June, Kahane agreed to publish the book if Nin would pay printing costs; she agreed to advance him 5,000 francs (about $330).

By July, Miller and Nin were reading proofs. The book needed a preface, Kahane thought, because the material was so inflammatory. He offered to provide one, but Miller declined. Instead, he wrote the essay himself and had Nin sign it (she no doubt had something to do with its composition as well). It was a rare opportunity: he could "explain" the book, praise it, and point out its importance—under someone else's name. Kahane accepted it, and publication was scheduled for September.

These ought to have been happy days for Miller. But troubles had arisen between him and Nin. He had left her quarters in the rue des Marroniers to stay in an apartment belonging to her brother and mother (who were apparently at Louveciennes) in the Avenue de Versailles. Miller suspected, not entirely without grounds, that there was something going on between Rank and his patient. Moreover, Nin announced some time in the spring that she was pregnant. It is not known what passed between them on this subject, and Nin refers to it in her diary only when the baby—a girl—was born dead in August. The identity of the father is unknown: Guiler, Miller, and Rank were obvious candidates, as was Nin's cousin Eduardo Sanchez and even, it was rumored, her own father, who had surfaced the previous year and had been showering his daughter with affection. (Nin appeared to encourage the latter rumor.) No letters between Miller and Nin survive from this period, and while this does not constitute proof, it increases the likelihood that Miller was the father. The matter remains unresolved.

Coincidentally, Miller's daughter Barbara reentered his life at roughly this time. Barbara was fifteen now, and Richard Osborn reported that he had seen her in Brooklyn and that she was pretty; Miller wrote that the news hit him like a thunderbolt. He acknowledged that he would like to see her, and that he might look her up on an upcoming trip to New York with Nin. A week later, however, he wrote that he wouldn't be making the trip after all, because he (inexplicably) feared his father might die and because he didn't want to see Barbara. "From a distance of 3,000 miles I can be hard," he wrote, underlining the words. His fear of Beatrice, based less on his liability for non-support than his horror of her sitting in judgment on him, seems to have triumphed over whatever rudimentary paternal impulses he still felt.

The publication of *Tropic of Cancer* in September 1934 coincided with Miller's move back into the house in the rue Villa Seurat in which he had stayed with Fraenkel in 1931. Walter Lowenfels offered him a studio apartment for 700 francs a month, and Miller was delighted to learn its location. The rent was not cheap, but the studio had the kinds of modern comforts that many Paris homes lacked—steam heat, a private bath, and a two-story window for light. Though he wrote Schnellock that he was afraid of ghosts from his previous stay there, Miller signed the lease and moved in on the very day *Cancer* appeared.

Kahane, in his memoirs, called Miller "the most useful collaborator a publisher ever had." A born self-promoter, Miller launched a major personal publicity campaign for *Tropic of Cancer*, mailing copies of his book to everyone he could think of. He wasn't particularly pleased with the book's appearance. Kahane's fourteen-year-old son Maurice had designed the book jacket, a rather ghastly green, black, and gray composition that featured a crab with a woman's naked body in its claws. Each copy was belted with a paper band that read, *"Ce volume ne doit pas être exposé en vitrine"* (This book must not be displayed in the window), and, indeed, at first few bookstores dared place it in their windows. The price, too, was very high: 50 francs, or about $7.50. Sales were extremely slow. Miller consigned some copies he had bought at the author's rate to Eve Adams, who was well known in Paris as a source for avant-garde books, and she sold several in the Montparnasse cafés, netting him a small profit.

A few copies made their way into England and America, where they were promptly banned. But the action Kahane expected from the French police never materialized. Miller had mailed copies of the book to Aldous Huxley, Ezra Pound, T. S. Eliot, and several other literary figures. The response was encouraging. Blaise Cendrars, the one-armed French writer and adventurer Miller much admired, wrote a glowing review for the magazine *Orbes* titled "Un Ecrivain Américain Nous Est Né" (An American Writer Is Born to Us); he also came to the Villa Seurat expressly to meet Miller, who was tongue-tied in the presence of his idol. Pound wrote a cryptic note recommending that Miller try to publish in *Esquire* and admonishing him to consider "What IS money? who makes it/how does it get that way?///" But he promised to write a review and gave the book to a friend, James Laughlin, a wealthy Harvard student with literary leanings, commenting, "Here's a dirty book that's worth reading." Huxley, Dos Passos, Eliot, and the British critic Herbert Read all responded favorably, though Eliot became a bit guarded when Miller wanted to use his complimentary letter in advertising. Miller even heard from Louis-Ferdinand Céline, a writer whose work he had read in manuscript. Céline offered him a "very slight suggestion"—"Know how to be wrong—the world is full of people who are right. That's why it is so NAUSEATING."

But Miller was frustrated by the lack of American response. His American correspondents wrote that the censors were intercepting his packages, and those old friends who did manage to get copies (Fraenkel had hit upon the scheme of cutting the books up and sending them in batches) didn't like it, Miller complained in a letter to Hilaire Hiler. Responses from the few readers whom it did manage to reach fell into two categories, he soon discovered: huge enjoyment, or utter loathing and contempt. He welcomed *any* response, however; he wrote Schnellock that he'd like to know an "ordinary wench's reaction to [him] writing about cunt." About his family he wasn't so sure. He wrote Hiler's father that he had told Heinrich Miller the book was out, but that he wouldn't be sending him a copy. It would break his father's heart, he said: "You see, much as I like him—and I have a very tender spot for him—he never understood me. And he never will. I have absolutely nothing in common with my folks—never did."

Still, the book's *succès d'estime* with literary celebrities like Eliot and Pound encouraged Miller to pressure Kahane to bring out *Black Spring*, which was just about completed. Kahane pointed out that it was unwise to have two books appear at virtually the same time, but promised to publish it in the spring. Miller sent two pieces from it to Frank Dobo, then in England, but Dobo told him they could never be published there. He also sent carbons of the manuscript to Pound and Kay Boyle. Pound didn't respond, and Miller felt that Kay Boyle, who had included a piece of his in her anthology *1934*, patronized him; he worried that she took him for "a little shit who hangs around the Dôme."

"Now my whole life is opening up," Miller wrote Schnellock in October. "There is some kind of exfoliation going on, and I am happily able to recall the most minute details—where they affected me vitally." Frustrated by the indifference to *Tropic of Cancer*, he had returned to the manuscript of *Tropic of Capricorn*, the book about June. News that she had divorced him by proxy in Mexico City in December fueled his fever to write about her. Anaïs was planning a visit with Hugo to America, ostensibly to visit family, and Miller hoped that once there she would send for him. He was eager to see old haunts like Wilson's Dance Hall, that he was sure would reawaken his memories for the book about June—in which, he told Schnellock, he intended to reveal her as a "pathological liar" and himself as a "creative liar," adding that he considered himself the "most sincere liar" who ever lived. His aim, he said, was to write June's kind of lying out of his system.

Unexpectedly, however, at the end of 1934 he was once again enmeshed in lies—and this time, the lies were Nin's. Her trip to America, he gradually pieced together, was not a family visit at all. Not until a telling mixup in letters brought him a letter addressed to Hugo (and Hugo one to Henry) did he learn that Guiler had not accompanied her to America. Rather, she was there with Rank, who promised her employment at a place called the Psychological Center. And it was Rank, not Guiler, who had given Nin the money for the printing of *Tropic of Cancer. Lies!* The very word, he wrote Nin, threw him back on the "old treadmill" of black jealousy and disillusionment. Her use of the word "we" in talking about her hotel, he observed, might well be one of those "truthful lies" they had reverted to together in their own earlier evasion of Guiler. Now Miller had become one of the evaded, and he was anguished by Nin's enthusiastic embrace of New York City, which he took to be a betrayal; he had made clear to Nin that he hated everything he believed New York stood for, and yet she persisted in describing her delight in the city. He was troubled as well by her accounts of men who had flirted with her and by her silence about when Guiler would be joining her. When she met Schnellock and visited some of Miller's old haunts with him, she reported back that she was moved by the sight of the Henry Street apartment where he had lived with June and Jean—but her description was of lower Manhattan's Henry Street, not the one in Brooklyn, and Miller was dismayed by what he saw as the lack of sympathy in her mistake.

Miller inundated Nin with letters and cables, some bitterly sarcastic, others abject. The separation forced him to one conclusion: they must renounce the pretense of her marriage and live openly together, perhaps marry. He demanded an answer to this proposition—and got none. When he threatened to take the next boat to America, Nin soothed him by saying that he could come over eventually—in March. This delay seemed pointless to Miller, and he resolved to act, cabling Nin that he would arrive on the *Champlain* on January 10. Just before his departure date, he received a letter from her saying that Guiler was on his way as well, and that she would be staying with him in Forest Hills; Miller could use her room at the Barbizon. They would have three weeks together in February, she promised, when Guiler would be traveling. With a sinking heart, Miller realized that his plans for a bold new life with Anaïs were as ephemeral as her whims.

On board the *Champlain* in January 1935, Miller read *Mein Kampf.* He wrote Michael Fraenkel later that year that "there are some profound truths in it!" As usual, the book that had most recently affected him would color Miller's thoughts for the next several months. He had come to associate New York City with everything that was wrong with America: "New York is malign, vulgar, crass, stupid, empty, geometric, Jewish," he wrote to Hilaire Hiler shortly after landing. In his childhood and young adulthood there had been two New Yorks: one the home of his beloved Fourteenth Ward and the magical setting for his discovery of June; the other the hell of Decatur Street, his mother, and the disastrous *ménage à trois* with June and Jean Kronski. On his 1935 visit, the hellish image dominated. Hereafter New York City would become the place to which Miller repaired to do his dirt: to raise cash, procure women, work scams. It brought out the worst in him.

This was true not only of the 1935 trip, but also of a later, brief visit in the winter of 1936. Through the so-called Psychological Center —not, probably, through Rank himself, as she claims in her diary— Nin had lined up some psychoanalytic patients, whom she saw for regular sessions in her room at the Barbizon. When Henry arrived, she sent some his way, and he cheerfully acted the part of a trained psychoanalyst, writing at the end of February that he was seeing four "professional" patients a day. To his friend Hilaire Hiler he wrote, "[It's] not that I give a fuck about [Rank's] work, because I am totally indifferent—but this fifth wheel on a wagon stuff appeals to me more than straight commercial tactics of which I am ignorant and wish to remain ignorant."

Although Nin had undergone analysis twice, once with Allendy and then with Rank, it is difficult to imagine that these treatments could have been successful, especially given her claim that both men were in love with her. Nonetheless, she evidently felt that some of her conflicts had been resolved. She had been in training to become an analyst for seven months in Paris, and by the Psychological Center's standards she may have been technically qualified to treat analytic patients. But Miller—who had considered himself "cured" after a single session with Rank—was in no way qualified as an analyst, even by the casual standards of the 1930s when Freudian methods were not yet widely practiced. Yet, he had no reservations about acting as an analyst, and he appears not to have found his situation the least bit strange.

He fed his patients, he wrote Fraenkel in the winter of 1936, during his second American visit, "a little of the juice of St. Augustine and a little of Emerson." He found himself wise and his patients tedious; many were Communists, and prattled on about the coming Revolution.

Miller was not altogether unsympathetic, writing approvingly in the same letter that "Marx and Lenin have replaced Moses and Christ." But he doubted he was curing anyone, he wrote, especially his Jewish patients, who he remarked would no doubt sink back into their accustomed misery.

New York exacerbated Miller's anti-Semitic tendencies. The city was full of intellectuals—*"Jews mostly,"* he observed to Osborn. He found the Jewish New Yorker a definite type, writing O'Regan that he had turned away a "NY Jewish bugger" who had looked him up in Paris. In a long letter to Hiler from this time, he tried to explain his prejudice, saying that it was "just a pose, and a bad one." But he believed in having prejudices; there was nothing worse or more hypocritical than being "open-minded" or "tolerant." Of course, he continued, there was no legitimate foundation for anti-Semitism; attacks like Hilaire Belloc's in *The Jews* were no more than rationalizations. But, he added, "god-damn it all, this fucking thing exists, persists, endures, and how ever wipe it out?" He went on to draw a distinction between his "emotional prejudice" and "human relations," insisting that anti-Semitism had no bearing on the latter as far as he was concerned: he had Jewish friends, had married a Jewish woman, and ate Jewish bread; perhaps he himself was Jewish. In view of Hitler's ominous ascendancy, however, he asserted that if *Tropic of Cancer* was ever taken up by some ardent Hitlerite and used as anti-Semitic propaganda, he would be among the first to write an attack on the Gentile (rather than a defense of the Jew, he explained, since he was better on the attack).

Unfortunately—especially because it seems that he was Jewish himself—Hiler's response has been lost. The most that can be said on Miller's behalf is that he was outspoken about his feelings in front of his Jewish friends. He discussed the "Jewish problem" with Michael Fraenkel ceaselessly, for example, and Fraenkel took it in good humor, even agreeing with many of Miller's observations. On the other hand, Miller was shrewd enough to edit most of his anti-Semitism out of his writings, indicating that he knew how offensive it was. There were two significant exceptions, both dating from the mid-thirties: the first a volume of correspondence begun in 1935 with Michael Fraenkel, called *Hamlet,* and the other a pamphlet he wrote during his 1935 trip to New York, published in 1936, called *Aller Retour New York.*

Aller Retour New York was written in the form of a letter to Perlès, who, Miller wrote on the title page, "up till now has held the record for letter writing." It is a lively exposition of Miller's quarrels with his native land—from the incurable optimism of most Americans, as exemplified in the ubiquitous popular song "I Believe in Miracles," to the idiocy of American advertising (especially BromoSeltzer injunctions to "alkalize" every morning). He insults not only Jews (who gravitate to the social sciences, he says) but also bridge-playing suburban Gentiles ("dumb"). In the middle of the pamphlet is a three-page letter addressed to "Juliet," who is actually Muriel Cowley, his old girlfriend from the Western Union days. In it he dubs her husband Malcolm Cowley, then the literary editor of the *New Republic*, the editor of a "third-rate swindle sheet," and he blasts them both for not appreciating *Tropic of Cancer*. He tells her to diaper her baby with Kotex and feed it horse piss. (Not long after, Miller would observe that alienating Cowley in this way was probably a mistake—a *"faux pas,"* as he put it.) His prose is often baroque—when he describes the Empire State Building, it sounds like the Bowery Savings Bank of the Mezzotints period—but the writing for the most part has the colloquial force of the best parts of *Tropic of Cancer*.

Miller's other significant literary work while he was in America was, as Nin recorded in her diary, a strange, little-known story called "Murder in the Suburbs." It chronicles the discontent of an assembly-line worker in an automobile factory in the Paris suburbs. Pierre, laid off from his job (a workers' revolution has backfired, resulting in the plant's closing), takes up with a widow named Berthe, whom he marries because she takes care of him; soon enough, however, he becomes jealous and takes to calling her "the old sow." Pierre reads nothing but the newspapers, which he devours, and dreams about the coming revolution, which only serves to make him more violent. One evening, returning home and seeing Berthe with a bucket of beer in front of her, he says, "To-day I am going to chop your head off." Obsessed by the phrase, he goes out to a café, and there, looking in the mirror, he sees his soul leave his body. When he comes to, he is certain that his "double" has chopped off his wife's head. He returns home and finds Berthe decapitated, her head lying some distance from her body. He puts the head back on the body, unsuccessfully, and becomes infuriated that she is in her chemise. "The old bitch!" he mutters, throwing a spread over the body. He falls asleep, reaching for a crucifix and dropping it.

The story is a muddle of contradictory themes and images. Miller seems to be making some point about the alienation of labor, for instance, but it is not coherent. The appearance of the crucifix at the end is at once heavy-handed and obscure. The style is totally alien for him; the piece seems to have begun as an attempt to write "for order" again —perhaps for *Esquire*, as Pound suggested. But what is remarkable is the story's cynicism and violence. "Death in the Suburbs," if read as a kind of embroidery on *Tropic of Cancer*, suggests that behind the misogyny of the longer work lay an unexplored, violent rage against women, that behind *Cancer*'s affirmations lay a monstrous brutality. Significantly, the story was not published until 1946, and even after that Miller lost track of it, complaining in the sixties, when a men's magazine wanted to reprint it, that he was unable to locate it.

Between writing and seeing patients, Miller sought to promote his work. He reported to Emil Conason that Joe Sadow, an editor at Falstaff Press, was interested in bringing out *Cancer* and that both Viking in the United States and Jonathan Cape and Harrison Smith in England wanted to see *Black Spring*. Rumors circulated to the effect that Simon & Schuster had an imprint that published de luxe editions of erotic books, and Miller thought maybe *Tropic of Cancer* could find a place there. He believed the atmosphere was receptive to strong stuff, he added. In the meantime, he hoped to win an underground reputation. He affected to despise his literary countrymen, but he hoped nevertheless to win their approval. He was disappointed to hear, for example, that Sinclair Lewis found his novel "ideologically unvaried," and feared that Lewis's response was representative. Through Hiler, who was now living in New York, he met William Carlos Williams, whose work Miller did not like. (He told a friend, somewhat illogically, that he had admired Williams for a long time without having read him, but now having read him, disliked him.) He also met Nathanael West and James T. Farrell, but the occasion was a drinking spree and he didn't want to tag along. West he liked well enough, but he thought Farrell "a louse, a gutter rat"—an intense reaction, given their similar urban, self-educated backgrounds. He thought he might do better with the "lowbrows" and sent a copy of *Tropic of Cancer* to the humorist S. J. Perelman; he had heard about Perelman's Hollywood connections, and he fantasized about selling his work to the movies. But all American artists, he wrote Hiler, were "mentalizers." For Hemingway, who affected to be "lowbrow," he had the greatest contempt: "I don't like that hard-boiled attitude—it's *inhuman* again. [American artists] don't want to be emotionally susceptible to anything, and that's cockeyed." The only writer from whom he feared any real competition was Thomas

Wolfe since, like Miller, he wrote what could be called "autobiograph-ical romances." But Miller confidently dismissed him after reading *Of Time and the River* in New York: "I am beyond that and beyond all Americans writing here in my native tongue. I have moved out of the realm of fine upholstery. . . ." Correctly perceiving that he could not be categorized with any current literary movement, Miller was trying to create his own—though to date it included only Nin, who would gain recognition even more slowly than he, and Perlès, whose "flowerpots" weren't adding up to very much.

In her diary entry for that March, Nin wrote that Miller "cannot bear rejections, the silence of conventional publishers, formal rejection slips from magazines, obtuse comments of people." He was restless in America, all the more so because Nin had little time for him. Guiler was as well connected in New York's artistic circles as he was in Paris, and through him Nin gained entree to New York's literary scene. She banished Miller to the Roger Williams Apartments on West 31st Street while she was shepherded around town by Theodore Dreiser, Waldo Frank, and Norman Bel Geddes, as well as Rank and his circle. Miller was left to his old friends—Schnellock, O'Regan, and Emil Conason. There is no record that he visited his father and mother and, judging from his behavior on his later visits, it is likely that he tried to keep his whereabouts a secret from them. He did not look up his daughter; nor did he try to locate June.

"When I think of New York I think of a gigantic infant playing with high explosives," Miller wrote Perlès. If he stayed any longer he feared he would go mad. Unsure where he stood with Nin, still up against it financially, he was exasperated with the slow response to *Tropic of Cancer*. In France, he had expected to be arrested immedi-ately when it was published, but the censors looked the other way. On the boat to America, he had been certain that he would be arrested upon landing, and he was a little disappointed that he hadn't been. In New York, he longed to return to Paris and start waging the publicity war with new vigor—or, failing that, to write something that could not be ignored. When Nin and Guiler returned to Paris in May because the bank demanded Hugo's presence, he followed several weeks later on the *Veendam*.

In a letter to Michael Fraenkel written during his second brief American trip, in 1936, Miller remembered something his mother once said to his poor, mad Tante Emilia: "Remember that you are an Amer-ican." This admonition used to drive him crazy, Miller wrote, always making him side with his aunt. Tante Emilia had, of course, wound up in an asylum, where she could contemplate Louise Miller's words at her leisure. But it was from Tante Emilia, Miller wrote, that he had taken up the cudgels against America. He wanted to kill, destroy his entire country; if he could, he would fire a double-barreled shotgun at it. From this point on, he set out to *forget* that he was an American.

10.

The Villa Seurat

1935–1939

"The activity Henry has created is extraordinary," Anaïs Nin wrote in her diary after she and Miller had returned to Paris. "He lives in a whirlpool, drawing everyone to him." From his second-floor studio at 18 rue Villa Seurat, Miller radiated energy. The entire building hummed with activity; one observer likened it to a factory, something like Walt Disney's studio. On the floor beneath Miller's studio was Michael Fraenkel, writing away on a manuscript he called his "Weather Paper," expostulating on his philosophy of death. Richard Thoma, an American writer who with Ezra Pound had been one of Putnam's assistant editors on the *New Review*, lived in another studio in the building. Betty Ryan, an American abstract painter who was considerably better off financially than her neighbors, had the studio across from Fraenkel's. Next to Miller lived a French photographer, Arnaut de Maigret.

Though Miller had allowed Perlès to live in the studio when he was in America, on his return, at Nin's insistence, he kicked him out. Perlès had lost his job when the Paris edition of the *Tribune* folded in the fall of 1934 and could have used a place to stay, but Nin had never liked him and wanted Miller to stop frittering away time with him and settle down to the serious life of a writer. Perlès moved into what he described as a "rathole" in the nearby Impasse de Rouet; his neighbors were a painter named Hans Reichel and a neurotic American dabbler in the occult, David Edgar. Both became closely allied to the Villa Seurat group, which expanded to include the French writers Raymond Queneau and Roger Pelorson, the British poet David Gascoyne, the artist Michonze, the photographer Brassaï, the American painter Abe Rattner, and, in 1937, Lawrence Durrell.

Describing life at the Villa Seurat thirty years later, Miller wrote that days began at five in the morning or two in the afternoon, depending on "astrologic happenings" of the night before. (As expounded by Nin's cousin, Eduardo Sanchez, and Conrad Moricand, a Swiss-born astrologer Miller first met in 1936, astrology was becoming a guiding force in Miller's life.) Miller typically took a walk before breakfast, traveling along the rue de la Tombe-Issoir to the outer boulevards. Coming back, walking along the rue de la Fontaine à Mulard, he would try to fix the images he had seen, fearful of becoming overstimulated before he had even sat down at the typewriter. As Miller described it, his spiritual pulse was quickening in these years. He and his friends lived, wrote, and painted with equal vigor; it was hard to tell which was most important, for they all went together. The creative impulse could express itself in any medium, the denizens of the Villa Seurat believed. The one saving thing in the whole bizarre merry-go-round, wrote Miller, was the knowledge that there were empty wine bottles lying about that could be redeemed for the next day's breakfast. Nobody worried much about the worsening political situation in Europe; as Miller wrote, "The important thing, for us, was not which side of the fence we were going to line up on but who would provide the next crust of bread."

Though he lived elsewhere, Perlès was almost constantly present at the Villa Seurat, the site of what Miller called "our happy life of shame." Their fun mostly consisted in (but was not confined to) baiting their "much-abused friend of the period," as Perlès called Fraenkel. Miller described "some marvelous times" for Emil Schnellock. On one particular evening, he wrote, "We made him blow us—i.e., Fred and I. We plucked him like a chicken." After this Fraenkel slunk off downstairs, worrying about money. On another occasion, when helping a girlfriend of Fraenkel's move in, Perlès carried on with the girl under Fraenkel's nose ("he didn't know whether to laugh or cry," wrote Miller). Then he and Miller swiped some francs from her handbag, and went out and got "potted." Another time Miller flattered Fraenkel upstairs in his studio while Perlès let himself into Fraenkel's studio with a stolen key and rifled through his pockets, taking several hundred francs. Fraenkel didn't even notice, Miller gleefully recounted.

In the same letter Miller described how, while writing the story "Max" just before his trip to America, he tormented Fraenkel by reading him the parts involving Boris, the Fraenkel figure. In "Max," Boris is an overly intellectual Jewish aesthete, too preoccupied with his own bloodless "death" to care that Max lived in the streets without the barest creature comforts. Miller made Fraenkel feel so bad that he vomited. "We treated him abominably," wrote Perlès later. "We exploited him and cheated him, we hurt him and made fun of him, we despised him and made no bones about it."

At the same time that he was participating in these sadistic stunts, Miller liked Fraenkel and was torn between his admiration for Fraenkel and contempt for his vulnerabilities. Fraenkel's idiosyncratic genius appealed to him. In fact, Fraenkel had deeply influenced Miller's work and would continue to do so, long after their association was over. Miller worried that he had "plagiarized" Fraenkel's death philosophy in *Tropic of Cancer* in passages that spoke of death and decay. (In response, after the friends fell out in the late thirties Fraenkel claimed to have inspired the now completed *Black Spring*.) Fraenkel's material contributions to Miller's well-being were also significant. Not only had he put Miller up for several months in 1931, but he and Lowenfels had given him $100 for his trip to New York; Miller believed that the money had come only from Lowenfels, and Fraenkel never disabused him. Fraenkel, absent-minded and preoccupied with intellectual matters, seemed not to notice Miller's mistreatment, or perhaps overlooked it, convinced of Miller's genius.

Under these complicated circumstances the two men embarked on a quintessentially strange literary collaboration. On a fall afternoon at the Café Zeyer, a favorite spot near the Villa Seurat, Fraenkel, Perlès, and Miller were discussing Fraenkel's favorite topic, death, when one of them came up with the idea of corresponding on the subject. They would produce a book of 1,000 pages, no less, decided Fraenkel—"and no more," specified Perlès, who didn't like long books. On reflection, they decided that death was not a sufficiently concrete topic; Perlès proposed "The Merry Widow," but this was rejected as too narrow. Finally they settled on *Hamlet*, which seemed sufficiently capacious and fairly reeked with death potential. Perlès, whose heart was never really in it, soon dropped out of the enterprise. Miller wrote his first letter on November 2; he would write twenty-one more before the correspondence ceased in October 1938. Both writers ranged freely over broad topics: the decline of the West, art and artists, schizophrenia, Jews. Though at times Miller is simply cranky and at others overblown and pretentious, the letters contain passages that are among his best, as when he describes his reactions to his native land on his trips there in 1935 and 1936. But his side of the correspondence was also more and more abusive; he baited Fraenkel about his Jewishness and his death obsession. Miller later called the correspondence "one continual argument."

Nevertheless, the *Hamlet* letters gave him a forum to flex his intellectual muscles. Miller's other writings in 1935 were in an entirely different vein. Over the summer, he composed a breezy pamphlet he called *What Are You Going to Do About Alf?*, which he published with money borrowed from Eduardo Sanchez and Fraenkel, and which he had printed by Servant, who had done *Tropic of Cancer*. Cast as a begging letter (the subtitle was "An Open Letter to All and Sundry"), the piece sought money to help Perlès—Alf—renounce journalism for literature. The first of his many indictments of society's treatment of artists, the "Alf letter" netted little cash (though Miller later noted that the few contributors included André Gide and Aldous Huxley). What money did come in remained in Miller's pockets.

Meanwhile, Miller had convinced Kahane to take *Black Spring*, though it wouldn't appear until June 1936. Kahane was impressed by the book's imaginative unity and the grace of Miller's writing. *Black Spring* would baffle critics, for it is not easily categorized. It is a series of sketches, many, like "The Fourteenth Ward" and "The Tailor Shop," powerful autobiographical evocations of Miller's life in Brooklyn. In "The Fourteenth Ward," Miller explains how he "was born in the street and raised in the street. . . . To be born in the street means to wander all your life, to be free. . . . In the street you learn what human beings really are; otherwise, or afterwards, you invent them. What is not in the open street is false, derived, that is to say, *literature*." In other words, he was consciously inventing his own beginnings, conveniently forgetting his bourgeois background in favor of his Williamsburg neighborhood and life in the streets. In "Third or Fourth Day of Spring" he attempted to clarify his autobiographical intent:

> For me the book is the man and my book is the man I am, the confused man, the negligent man, the lusty, obscene, boisterous, thoughtful, scrupulous, lying, diabolically truthful man that I am. . . . I regard myself not as a book, a record, a document, but as a history of our time—a history of *all* time.

"A Saturday Afternoon" takes the reader on a tour of Parisian *pissoirs;* "The Angel Is My Watermark" describes Miller's clumsy attempts at painting. Some pieces, like "Burlesk," which recounts a scene in an evangelist church, are less than successful; this particular piece recycles material written in the Brooklyn days. "Walking Up and Down in China" draws more successfully on his American background: a meditation beginning with stock market quotations takes him from American Can and American Tel. & Tel. to a wonderful catalogue of American icons, from the Rough Riders, Oscar Hammerstein, the Katzenjammer Kids, and Dorothy Dix to "On the Banks of the Wabash" and beyond. Diverse in subject, the pieces share a creative energy that rivals the force of *Tropic of Cancer*, though *Black Spring* has none of the narrative cohesion of *Cancer*. Even a piece like "Jabberwohl Cronstadt," which is dadaistic to the point of nonsense, is remarkable for the lyricism of the author's voice.

Encouraged by Kahane's enthusiasm, Miller managed to talk the publisher into letting him start a line of books that he would select, to be distributed by Obelisk and named the Siana series—Nin's name spelled backward. Nin agreed to cover the printing costs. Miller initiated the series with a polished version of his long letter to Perlès, published under the title *Aller Retour New York* (1935), or, roughly, *Round Trip New York*. Other Siana books included Richard Thoma's *Tragedy in Blue* and Nin's *House of Incest*. Miller hoped to include works by Fraenkel and Perlès as well.

No doubt Kahane was well disposed to Miller's plans; *Tropic of Cancer* was enjoying a modest success. It is impossible to determine how large the first printing was, but the book went into its second printing in September 1935. The new jacket carried blurbs from Eliot, Pound, William Carlos Williams, and Aldous Huxley. (From Mary Reynolds, the mistress of Marcel Duchamp, Miller received a copy of the book bound in human skin—or so he claimed.) In August he received an admiring letter from Lawrence Durrell, a young British writer then living in Corfu, out of which grew an enthusiastic correspondence. Still, Miller wasn't satisfied with the book's sales and wrote to Durrell in November that he planned to put together a brochure of reviews and complimentary letters like Durrell's own, complete with a picture of himself on his bicycle and a copy of his horoscope.

Miller continued to worry about his American reception. In November he wrote excitedly to Frank Dobo that Walter Lowenfels had interested "*Scribner's* (!!!)" in *Black Spring*; nothing ever came of it. James Laughlin, the American to whom Pound had recommended *Tropic of Cancer*, wrote to Miller asking for permission to reprint a portion of *Aller Retour New York* in the Harvard *Advocate* under the title "Glittering Pie." Miller agreed, but rumors circulated that the "dirty book author" had contributed and the issue was promptly confiscated by the Cambridge police and the editors jailed. Miller was at a loss as to how to get copies of *Tropic of Cancer* to America. Fraenkel was still breaking some books down and shipping them in chunks to contacts in the States; Miller sent others by first-class mail, which was not usually searched. The crucial thing was to get it around over there, Miller wrote Dobo. "God (!) will take care of the rest."

In fact, in the late thirties it looked unlikely that *Tropic of Cancer* would ever circulate freely in the United States or Great Britain. One agency of censorship was the Post Office, whose authority was established when the 1873 Comstock Act forbade the circulation of obscene literature through the mails. Another agency was the Customs Bureau, which could prevent importation of obscene matter from abroad. In 1930, the Tariff Act was amended to allow the Secretary of the Treasury to admit books of "recognized value," or classics, and a court battle in 1933 had exempted James Joyce's *Ulysses* from a Customs ban on the grounds that the book had "recognized value." A wealthy Baltimore lawyer named Huntington Cairns acted as Special Counsel to the Treasury Department and advised them on censorship matters; Miller had heard that Cairns admired his work and so he began a correspondence with him in 1936. He thought his best chance was to have the Customs ban lifted under the "recognized value" clause, but he knew that this depended very much on the climate of the times. He frequently wrote Cairns—whom he always referred to as "the censor" —inquiring whether it was a propitious time to try getting *Tropic of Cancer* in.

He searched out other avenues by which his work might reach American readers. During his 1935 visit to New York, he had made the acquaintance of Frances Steloff, the proprietor of the Gotham Book Mart at 51 West 47th Street. Steloff, three years older than Miller, had opened the Gotham in 1920; her particular interest was in the theater, which became the shop's specialty in its early days. In 1923 she married David Moss, a New York bookseller whose firm of Moss & Cameron dealt in, among other things, erotica. The Gotham's focus gradually widened to include Moss's interests, and it soon developed a reputation for stocking avant-garde works by American and foreign writers.

From the first, Steloff was one of Miller's most ardent champions —although she admitted that she had never read any of his books through to the end. A vigorous opponent of censorship and a sincere supporter of artistic innovation (James Joyce was her favorite cause), Steloff was also a shrewd businesswoman who knew that banned books sold well. By the late thirties she was Miller's most important American contact. She supplied him with the names of other sympathetic American booksellers, drummed up advance orders that enabled him to raise funds to get new works published, and spread the word about where prospective buyers could get his books. Later she would be instrumental in circulating pirated editions of his work.

Meanwhile, Anaïs Nin was distancing herself from the Villa Seurat and from Miller. In July 1935 she had called herself the "young mother" of the group, noting happily that the *femme de ménage* at the building had christened her "Mrs. Henry." But the next month she confided in her diary that she didn't belong at the Villa Seurat. She had never approved of Perlès, and she found Fraenkel's effect on Miller "absolutely sterile, destructive." The climate of the Villa Seurat was misogynistic, to be sure. Even Betty Ryan preferred the company of men to that of women; she often gave dinner parties at which she was the only female present. Still, Nin visited at least twice a week, while Guiler was taking painting lessons from Hans Reichel in the nearby Impasse de Rouet. And she still paid Miller's rent. His writing was bringing in almost no money, though he got 5,000 francs when Perlès sent him an assignment to write a preface for a religious book.

Once Nin had been amused by Miller's lack of manners, but now, despite his efforts not to alienate her, she continually complained about his coarseness. Though she was pleased by the work he was doing on "Palace of Entrails," the scenario based on her *House of Incest,* the pages of *Tropic of Capricorn* she saw in 1935 and 1936 did not please her at all. She found them drenched in sex, far more so than *Cancer.* In April 1936 she made a trip to Morocco; a few months later she moved into a houseboat on the Seine and took up with a Peruvian musician and revolutionary named Gonzalo More. Although she continued her affair with Henry, it was far less impassioned than it had been for the last three years. Her relationship with Miller began to take on an increasingly businesslike tone, especially as his reputation improved. Each had always been aware of what the other could do for him- or herself, but as the romance of their relationship dissipated, this concern began to take precedence.

For his part, Miller was consumed with activity. Along with his *Hamlet* letters, he was carrying on an equally voluminous correspondence with Osborn, Schnellock, Durrell, Hiler—not to mention his appeals to the literati and the monied. He was also planning to contribute to a pamphlet Fraenkel was bringing out with essays by Fraenkel himself and Lowenfels. And he projected ten or twelve stories about his Villa Seurat friends, to be called *Some Pleasant Memories* or *Astrological Effigies*.

Few of these projects got off the ground. But Miller did write a preface for Fraenkel's *Bastard Death*, and he wrote a very enthusiastic portrait of Nin called "Un Etre Etoilique" (or "A Starry Being"), which appeared in England in the *Criterion* and as a separate pamphlet the same year. He finished a film treatment—though there was no film in the works—of Nin's *House of Incest* and gave it to Kahane, who would publish it in 1937 as *Scenario (A Film with Sound)*. He also assembled a number of essays, many previously published, for the volume he thought to call *Max and the White Phagocytes* or *Plasma and Magma*. These included, for the moment, the essay on Nin, the story "Max," a piece on the painter Hans Reichel titled "The Cosmological Eye," and his early article on Buñuel. In 1935 and 1936 he had put "the Brochure" aside temporarily; he was trying to extract articles from it for magazines. In July 1936 he relayed to Schnellock that Kahane had published Nin's *House of Incest* and his own *Black Spring* would be out any day. He was working on "the June book," he wrote, but it had got him off track, and he worried that he wasn't doing her justice. In August he wrote Durrell that he planned three volumes and hoped to have the first done in a year. He intended "the June book" to be a skyscraper, built for a few centuries at least, he told Hiler. It would be colossal, he said, "and mad. This is my last fuck—fuck everybody and everything! Sink or swim, me lads, it's all one. Breaking all connections, all ties. I want to become the monster that I am."

And indeed, he indulged in considerable monstrous behavior during this period. Besides tormenting Fraenkel, he and Perlès were an infamous duo who regularly carried off their friends' women. Maurice Girodias describes a party given by his father in Miller's honor in 1937. When Ginotte, the maid, opened the door, there stood two bald men, nearly identical. The taller one—Miller—reached forward and tweaked Ginotte's nipple; the smaller one handed her his fedora and then did the same. On another evening at the Kahanes', as Miller said goodbye, he reached out and patted the derrière of his hostess, Marcelle Kahane, saying, "Great dinner, Marce." The eight-year-old Eric Kahane set on him, firmly determined to kill him.

Much of this was, of course, a pose: just the behavior expected of a dirty book writer. But Miller and Perlès performed this way at any given opportunity, oblivious to the feelings of their victims or their onlookers. Their contemptuous behavior toward women in particular was a matter of notoriety. One evening at the Villa Seurat they entertained the journalist Roger Pelorson and his wife; Pelorson and Miller had become close friends, seeing each other at least once a week. On this evening both Miller and Perlès had been drinking before the guests arrived—Miller was gay and amusing, while Perlès was boorish and offensive. Miller egged Perlès on, and before long he was on the table, imitating Hitler, strutting about and hurling insults at Pelorson's wife, who was clearly upset. Though Miller wrote his guests the next morning, "conscience-stricken," Perlès's Hitler imitation remained a set piece in the Miller/Perlès act.

Most of Miller's bad behavior, not surprisingly, had to do with money. To a French friend he complained that the more he published the more he was reviewed—and the poorer he became: "The inverse law of compensation—for men of genius!" Nin's contributions never seemed to meet his expenses. In early 1937, when Heinrich Miller wrote with the news of another financial crisis, his son responded in characteristic form. First, he answered the letter and enclosed some money, "promising the moon" in the future, as he later told Durrell. Then he tried to capitalize on the situation, copying out his father's letter, adding embellishments to make it more pathetic than the original, and composing a fake answer pleading his own poverty. He then drew up a mailing list of worthies to solicit with this production, including Somerset Maugham, Rebecca West, and T. S. Eliot. But then he had second thoughts, and sent a sample package to Durrell, requesting his opinion of the "strategic value" of the enterprise. (Presumably Durrell vetoed it, since it was never sent.)

Political matters were also on Miller's mind, and the views he set forth were often willfully offensive. In a letter to Durrell, he said, "I *like* that last speech of Hitler's—makes me sympathize with him and his 'ami' Mussolini." But his instinctive dislike of the Germans made him suspicious of Hitler, whose "cheap, butter-and-egg mysticism" he decried to another friend. He drew the line, too, at Hitler's 1936 speeches attacking the Bolsheviks and the Jews, telling Frank Dobo that even a "Jew-baiter" like himself couldn't "swallow such drivel." What emerges from these half-serious and contradictory asides is a sense of Miller's overwhelming political naivete. He seemed genuinely to think that his genius extended to politics, and he was constantly making pronouncements about the future and the course of the oncoming war that were uniformly as wrong as they could possibly be. He believed, variously, that a world war would cause another war between the United States and Great Britain, that war between the West and the East was imminent, and that Germany would be divided up "like India," thus averting war altogether. Perhaps his most absurdly grandiose observation was that he could solve "the whole damn problem" if he had five minutes alone with Hitler. He would simply get Hitler to laugh, he told Durrell.

Politics also impeded a developing friendship between Miller and George Orwell, the British author of *Down and Out in Paris and London*. Orwell had published a favorable review of *Tropic of Cancer* in the *New English Weekly* in 1935, in which he singled out the book's insistence on the reality of bodily desires, writing: "Man is not a Yahoo, but he is rather like a Yahoo and needs to be reminded of it from time to time." A friendly correspondence between the two men ensued, and when *Black Spring* appeared in June 1936, Orwell wrote Miller about it at length, and reviewed it in a September issue of the *New English Weekly*. He was less enthusiastic than he had been about *Cancer*, complaining that "the written word loses its power if it departs too far . . . from the ordinary world where two and two make four." But he admired Miller's focus on the common man, and thought his prose possessed great vigor. He approved the book's sexual frankness.

When Franco's right-wing revolt broke out in Spain in 1936 and workers' organizations responded by taking over effective control of the Republican resistance, Europe reeled at the spectacle of fascism and communism finally coming to blows. Though Nin and her friend Gonzalo More worked on behalf of the Republican cause, Miller paid almost no notice. Orwell decided to join the Republican forces, and he departed for Barcelona at Christmastime in 1936, stopping off in Paris to collect some travel documents. In passing, he looked up Miller, and the two passed an afternoon together. Miller spoke candidly to Orwell about his own pacifism, saying that he found it idiotic to fight for any cause. Civilization was doomed anyway, he claimed, and it was useless to defend it. Orwell confessed he felt guilty for having served in the police force in Burma, and Miller countered that it was ridiculous for Orwell to want to flagellate himself still further. The two men parted amicably, Miller pressing a corduroy jacket on Orwell as "[his] contribution to the Spanish republican cause." Relations between the two writers remained friendly if somewhat distant, but then Orwell's reviews of Miller's subsequent works began to take an increasingly critical tone. These culminated in Orwell's widely read essay "Inside the Whale," published in a book by the same title. There Orwell praised Miller's work for its portrayal of an attitude of acceptance, even passivity, that Orwell thought rife in contemporary society.

This passivity was the only imaginable response to the imminent collapse of civilization, Orwell observed. But is it right to say "I accept," Orwell asked, in an age of "concentration camps, rubber truncheons, Hitler, Stalin, bombs, aeroplanes, tinned food, machine guns, puttsches [sic], purges, slogans, Bedaux belts, gas masks, submarines, spies, provocateurs, press censorship, secret prisons, aspirings, Hollywood films, and political murders?" Orwell's answer was equivocal: such quietism was not right, abstractly speaking, but it was realistic, and representative of how the common man felt.

Miller dismissed Orwell's essay as a backhanded compliment, and seems to have given little thought to the substance of Orwell's criticism. He considered himself "accepting" only in the sense he felt Whitman was—accepting of the immoral, the wicked, and the cruel, which, as he later observed to Durrell, were often as valuable as the good in the world.

In August 1937, Lawrence Durrell and his young wife, Nancy, arrived at the Villa Seurat, on a pilgrimage to meet Durrell's new hero. Blond, boyish, and sunny in disposition—he laughed so loudly he was often turned out of movie theaters—Durrell had been born in Jullundur, India, in 1912 into a family with a history of colonial service. Although he was schooled in England, he developed a passionate distaste for all things British and had expatriated himself to Corfu in 1935, where he worked for the British consul and as a teacher of English. He had published a small book of poems and, in 1935, a novel, *Pied Piper of Lovers*. In 1937 he had another book coming out, *Panic Spring*, which would be published under the pseudonym Charles Norden. These novels now embarrassed him—"only about heroic Englishmen and dovelike girls etc 7/6d a volume"—but *Tropic of Cancer*, which he read in 1935, inspired him to new efforts. The result was *The Black Book*, which Durrell sent in manuscript to Miller in March 1937. Like *Cancer*, *The Black Book* revels in four-letter words and is peopled by grotesques; its mood is equally apocalyptic. A description of the education of a poet, it is a full-scale attack on what Durrell calls "the English death." Durrell freely admitted Miller's influence on this work, though it also bears marks of the baroque imagination that would later produce the Alexandria Quartet.

Miller found *The Black Book* extraordinarily good, and he was delighted to think he had a disciple. Not surprisingly, Durrell had difficulty getting a publisher for his book. When Faber & Faber proposed bringing out an expurgated edition, he was inclined to accept, but Miller urged him otherwise in the strongest possible terms. He saw in Durrell a younger version of himself, a kindred spirit. Before long he and Durrell and Nin were calling themselves the Three Musketeers.

On their first evening together in the Villa Seurat, over a steak dinner cooked by Nancy Durrell, the two men laid plans. Miller had met Huntington Cairns, the man he called "the censor," the summer before, and had liked him exceedingly; Cairns was encouraging about the eventual U.S. publication of *Tropic of Cancer* and *Black Spring,* and Miller thought he could be helpful about *The Black Book* as well. Plans were laid for a new series of books (the Siana series had failed to bring the group critical attention) to be published by Obelisk that would include *The Black Book,* the collection Miller had been working on, now definitely titled *Max and the White Phagocytes,* and Nin's *Winter of Artifice.* It was to be called the Villa Seurat series, and Nancy Durrell, who had a small independent income, would finance it.

Another plan was considerably more adventurous. The month before, Perlès had been given a literary white elephant: the editorship of *The Booster,* the house magazine of a private organization of expatriates called the American Golf and Country Club. The Country Club president, Elmer Prather, asked that Perlès devote two pages to Club news in each issue, but otherwise gave him full rein. The Villa Seurat group could not resist the opportunity to have a bit of sport at the stuffy expatriates' expense. They also saw a practical goal: gradually to turn it into a literary magazine, a publishing outlet for Miller and his circle. Durrell was enthusiastic. Like Miller, he had always wanted to be part of a school, and *The Booster* had great potential in this respect (though the Villa Seurat series, he thought, was their "Big Bertha").

Durrell, Miller, and Perlès promptly drew up a letter (later used as the first editorial) soliciting subscriptions—particularly life subscriptions at 500 francs each. The letter announced that the editors were planning to "boost, baste and lambaste when and wherever possible. Mostly we shall boost," it continued. "We like to boost, and of course to begin with we are going to boost ourselves." They also sought contributions: "poems, essays, serious articles, witticisms, philosophy or metaphysics, travel and diary notes, fragments, unfinished novels, rejected manuscripts, and . . . the ripe and cheesy things which have been lying in the trunk for years." The letter named the magazine's editors: Perlès was Managing Editor; Literary Editors were Durrell, Miller, and William Saroyan; Sports Editor was Charles Norden (Durrell); and Society Editor was Anaïs Nin. Other editors included Lowenfels ("Butter News," because of his family's butter fortune) and Fraenkel ("Department of Metaphysics and Metempsychosis"). Most of the editors were appointed without first being consulted; Saroyan, for example, claimed never to have met Miller in Paris.

Like "The New Instinctivism" Miller and Perlès had drawn up in 1931, *The Booster* was strongly—and randomly—"for" and "against" a variety of things (for food and against peace, for Shangri-la and against schizophrenia, and so forth). The editors declared the magazine to be "non-successful, non-political, non-cultural." "In general we are *for* things," the letter stated. "But in our own cute way. . . ."

The first number appeared in September 1937. Durrell contributed a poem, Perlès an excerpt from his novel *Le Quatuor en Ré-Majeur*, Nin a fragment from her diary. Miller provided "Letter from the Park Commissioner," a letter he claimed to have rescued from the wastebasket during his job with the New York City Parks Department in 1928. (He liked this letter so much that he later included fragments from it in his last major novel, *Nexus*.) He also contributed an essay on Brassaï, published under his old pseudonym Valentin Nieting, and one on a painter friend known as Benno.

Although their promotional material suggested otherwise, *The Booster* editors were in dead earnest about the fate of their little magazine. For one thing, a certain amount of money was at stake. The magazine inherited the subscription list of the American Golf and Country Club as well as its advertisers, and the new editors had at their disposal 12,500 francs, or $400, when they set up operations. They saw these resources as enabling them to publicize their work—which, for one writer, Miller, already banned and another, Durrell, soon to be, was critical, and almost as vital for Nin and Perlès, who were having difficulty getting their work published anywhere else. All hoped that the magazine's burlesque tone would fit the mood of the time, striking a note somewhere between dadaism and surrealism—even though "isms" were one of the many things the editors declared themselves against.

During a brief trip to London in September, Durrell managed to drum up some subscriptions, and Miller and Perlès had some luck in Paris. But by the second issue their advertisers apparently had begun to disappear. Included in this October issue was Miller's first and last contribution as Fashion Editor, a disquisition on men's fashions under the name of "Earl of Selvage." Though outwardly comical, it displayed Miller's not inconsiderable knowledge about the subject, gleaned from his early life as a tailor's son and his stint in Heinrich's shop. Although he wore used clothes and corduroys in his Paris years, he maintained a keen appreciation for fine fabrics and an eye for a good cut.

The October issue brought the editors considerable trouble, for they had included a slightly risqué translation of an Eskimo legend (lifted from the July number of a rival magazine), and Elmer Prather hit the roof about it. Two more issues appeared, in November and then in April 1938; after that the magazine had changed so much that a new name was needed. Durrell christened it *Delta*. Only three issues of *Delta* appeared, and Miller contributed to only one of them, "The Special Peace and Dismemberment Number with Jitterbug Shag Requiem."

Frances Steloff took several batches of *The Booster* for the Gotham, and Sylvia Beach of Shakespeare & Company always kept the magazine in stock. But the withdrawal of the Country Club's support after the October issue came out removed the core of their subscription and advertising lists, so that the editors were hard-pressed to stay in operation. They found only one advertiser on their own, Madame Baratta Alexander, a black podiatrist from Chicago who plied her trade on the Left Bank; in gratitude, the editors inserted Miller's comic "How to Lead the Podiatric Life" in the next issue.

The October *Booster* had announced a series of *Booster Broadsides*, including titles by Durrell, Lowenfels, Fraenkel, Perlès, and Miller. None of the titles listed ever saw publication—at least as a *Booster Broadside*—except for Miller's *Money and How It Gets That Way*. Written in response to Pound's suggestion that he think about the origins of money, the piece is a mock-scholarly treatment of the history of economics. (Miller would joke that many economists took it seriously.) It was intended to be funny but is virtually unreadable, filled with odds and ends of "data" (most of it apocryphal) about money and trade. Miller dedicated the piece to Pound. He may have been trying to curry favor with Pound, as he had somehow received the mistaken impression through James Laughlin that he would be "taken care of"

—financially, one supposes—if he "swung the bat" for Pound's Social Credit economics. When nothing of the sort came to pass, Miller blasted Laughlin in a letter to Huntington Cairns, saying, "And finally I don't give a fuck about Social Credit, Ezra Pound, Cocteau, or Gertrude Stein!!!"

But money preoccupied him as much now as it had in his poverty-stricken New York days and his first year in Paris. The difference was that at forty-five, as a published author and now a magazine editor, he had begun to see himself as a literary businessman. Subscriptions to *The Booster* could be bartered, for example, and Miller was always looking into schemes to exchange his manuscripts for goods or cash (he was holding out for $1,000 for the *Cancer* manuscript). While he had a regular buyer for copies of books he had annotated, in 1937 and 1938 he was forced to circulate two "begging letters" to friends in Paris and America, asking for clothes and supplies as well as money. He reprinted *What Are You Going to Do About Alf?*, hoping that people would buy it for its literary value this time around, but had little success. With Nin's growing distance from Miller, she had withdrawn her regular financial support. Miller no longer even considered holding a job. He was made European editor of *The Phoenix*, a literary magazine with headquarters in Woodstock, New York, and a contributing editor of *Volontés*, a French revue edited by Roger Pelorson, but neither of these brought in any money. (Each of *Volontés*' seven or eight editors, in fact, contributed 200 francs a month to keep the magazine alive.)

In the midst of these financial setbacks, Miller was receiving encouraging news from America. *Black Spring* had been favorably reviewed by Paul Rosenfeld in the *Saturday Review of Literature*, and H. L. Mencken wrote him an admiring letter. In October 1937 Miller signed a contract for his next three books with Mencken's publisher, Alfred A. Knopf, for which he was given a token payment of $100, but he doubted Knopf would be able to publish him. They mounted an effort to begin with *Black Spring*, but their lawyers advised them that legal costs would be prohibitive. They tried expurgating it, but Miller did not like the result. Blanche Knopf continued to support his cause, showing interest in publishing Miller's collected letters to Emil Schnellock, which contained many bits that had made their way into *Tropic of Cancer*, but Schnellock had stored the letters in a cellar in New York to which he no longer had access. In the same month that he signed his contract with them, Knopf rejected his short story collection *Max and the White Phagocytes*, and Miller soon came to lose faith in them.

He had a feeling, however, that James Laughlin, who had published two excerpts from the early drafts of *Tropic of Capricorn* in his magazine *New Directions*, would take the plunge with American editions of *Tropic of Cancer* and *Black Spring*.

In London, Faber & Faber reluctantly turned down *Max and the White Phagocytes* as well, and Miller brought it out under the Obelisk imprint as the second volume of the Villa Seurat series in September 1938. The final collection included "Max," "Un Etre Etoilique," an excerpt from "the Brochure," his early essay on Buñuel, portraits of the artists Brassaï and Hans Reichel, and "An Open Letter to Surrealists Everywhere," which he had earlier advertised as a *Booster Broadside*. He dedicated it to Betty Ryan, whose largesse had sustained him when his income dwindled to a trickle.

When *Max* appeared, Miller was on what was supposed to be a vacation in the South of France. He believed he had finished *Tropic of Capricorn*, although he felt he had in some ways just begun, now projecting a work of seven or eight volumes. His account in *Capricorn* had brought him just up to his meeting with June ("Mona"), concentrating (in reverse chronological order) on his days at Western Union and his youth and adolescence. The book was dedicated "To Her."

Though the mood reflects the same world view as that of *Tropic of Cancer*, in *Capricorn* Miller turned to his past, and the result was a book more traditionally autobiographical than *Cancer*. But the narration is hardly traditional, as Miller ranges freely over time, creating flashbacks within flashbacks; the result is far more baroque and sometimes incoherent, stylistically a departure from *Tropic of Cancer*. He announces himself at the outset as "the evil product of an evil soil," leading up to a long and often comic account of his career at the "Cosmodemonic Telegraph Company," interspersed with sexual bouts with women like Valeska (modeled on Camilla Fedrant). His subject was his suffering, first in the oppressive Miller home, then in his attempts to conform to society's expectations, and finally in his breakdown during his marriage to June and his eventual rebirth as a writer:

> Until the one to whom this is written came along I imagined that somewhere outside, in life . . . lay the solution to all things. I thought, when I came upon her, that I was seizing hold of life. . . . Instead I lost hold of life completely. I reached out for something to attach myself to—and I found nothing. But in reaching out, in making the effort to grasp, to

attach myself, left high and dry as I was, I nevertheless found something I had not looked for—*myself*. I found that what I had desired all my life was not to live—if what others are doing is called living—but to express myself.

One long section, published in *The Booster* as "I Am a Wild Park," vividly recalls the narrator's childhood and the formation of his own complicated personality; another, "The Land of Fuck," is an hallucinatory discourse ostensibly on sex but really about madness, the life of a "schizerino." His experiences listening to a friend talk about his wife's ovaries—which could send him off into trains of thought ranging over scores of pages—gave the book its subtitle, "On the Ovarian Trolley." The book was far more raw than *Tropic of Cancer*, Miller felt, and indeed, the sex scenes are extended and clinical. With its portraits of New York City, American women, and Western Union, *Tropic of Capricorn* is a scathing attack on the "respectable" urban America that produced the author, and, like *Black Spring*, an unblinkingly clinical self-portrait. It is, moreover, a proclamation that the man described in its pages is an iconoclast, set apart from other artists, from his family, and from his culture—while at the same time he is a product of all that he has met. Though it is dedicated to June, the book is less a portrait of her than, as an epigraph from Abelard concerning his own trial through fire suggests, a "Historia Calamitata," an often comic tale of Miller's misfortunes. As he wrote Frances Steloff, it was the most highly censorable book he had yet written, "and yet the best thing I have done to date. I think they would hang me for it if they could."

Anticipating the possibility that war might break out while he toured the South of France, Miller asked Kahane to keep the manuscript in his safe while he was gone. He then wound up in Bordeaux right in the middle of the Munich crisis: Hitler demanded that Czechoslovakia hand over the Sudetenland, its German-speaking western provinces, and a full-scale European war seemed imminent. Miller's letters from this period are those of a terrified man; he was sure that war was at hand, and he had no intention of fighting. He stayed put in Bordeaux because he could easily slip away by boat, and he urged Nin to leave landlocked Paris immediately. He fantasized a bizarre scheme that he thought of discussing with the American ambassador in Paris: to round up all the amputees and wounded veterans of World War I— the *"Gueules Cassés"*—and send them to Hitler, instructing them not to leave until he made peace. The plan might be even more effective, he thought, if they placed themselves in a large mass at the Czechoslovakian border and challenged the German troops to march over their bodies. Such an idea might be thought crazy, Miller told Nin, but he was frustrated by the fatalistic way in which the French seemed to accept the imminence of war.

Miller was so agitated that he wrote to nearly every one of his friends during his stay in Bordeaux, often several times. He also cabled Kahane for 3,000 francs, the receipt of which made him feel a little easier. If he made it back to Paris, he wrote Nin, he was buying a first-class ticket to America so that he would be able to get out at a moment's notice. He also had Kahane cable six friends to contribute toward the cost of his fare to America: Fraenkel, Durrell, Huntington Cairns, an American editor named Carl Holty, James Laughlin, and T. S. Eliot.

Then, almost overnight, the crisis passed. Neville Chamberlain arranged the soon-to-be-infamous international conference in Munich at which the Czechs were induced to surrender the Sudetenland in exchange for a security guarantee from France, and the British prime minister left for home declaring "peace in our time." As Europeans breathed a sigh of relief, Miller wrote Durrell that he had asked Kahane to cable his friends only because he wanted to see which of them he could count on. (As he had expected, everyone came through except Fraenkel, who had quarreled with him over publication of the *Hamlet* letters, denying him any percentage of the royalties.)

But the crisis genuinely shook him, and for the next year—which would be his last in Paris—he cast about for a new place to live. He continued to write but, as he told a friend at the time, he was "sitting on the edge of a volcano . . . I am working with my bags packed and my hat on my head." He began to develop the idea of an American tour; just as in America he had been transfixed with European place names, so in Paris did he long to visit places with names like Chattanooga and Tuba City. He also began to fantasize about going to Tibet and the Himalayas, where he imagined himself becoming a monk. "China" had described a state of mind in *Black Spring*—the fecund, imaginative zone of the mind—but now Miller began to dream of the real Orient.

"I am struck by the prophetic element that is a part of me," he wrote Durrell in January 1939, when he was reading the proofs of *Tropic of Capricorn*. He had always been interested in the occult, and in Paris he was further encouraged in this direction by his friend David

Edgar and, in particular, the astrologer Conrad Moricand. An occultist and scholar who had recently lost his family fortune, Moricand lived in a shabby hotel room in the rue Notre Dame de Lorette. Miller often visited him there, bringing him assignments to do horoscopes for his friends at 50 or 100 francs each; when his supply of friends was exhausted, he gave Moricand made-up names and birthdates. A dandy who smelled of bay rum and tobacco, Moricand impressed Miller deeply with his extensive descriptions of what he said were traits of the Capricorn, the sign under which Miller was born. Miller was so taken by Moricand's interpretation of his horoscope that he declared his intention to publish it as a brochure, in both French and English.

Miller sent several of Moricand's horoscopes to Count Hermann Keyserling, another occultist whose work he very much admired, and told him that he had painted his own astrological chart on the wall of his studio in the Villa Seurat. And, in the summer of 1938, while walking on the roof of his studio, he fell through the skylight, cutting himself severely in the process—an experience he considered propitious, for Moricand had predicted danger, and had also noted that Jupiter was in the ascendancy on that particular evening. He was saved by his lucky star, Miller concluded.

"I am seeking now with all my heart and soul," Miller wrote to the British writer Frederick Carter in 1938. Taking his cue from Carter's occultist book *The Dragon of Revelation*, he projected a philosophical meditation for his next work, to be called *Draco and the Ecliptic*, after Carter's description of the constellation Draco. "All my titles are symbolical and have a micro-macro-cosmic significance," he told Carter.

Draco and the Ecliptic was never to materialize—not because Miller found what he was seeking, but because other things kept getting in the way. Like "the Brochure," which he eventually abandoned, philosophy was hardly his strong suit. He read the I Ching, Mme Blavatsky, Rudolf Steiner, and books on Zen Buddhism—he was cultivating his "Chinese" side, he liked to say—but the result was that he developed a doctrine of acceptance that was more sentimental and lazy than it was mystical. In the face of the imminent war, Miller dug in, determined to survive, under the guise of a "positive" philosophy of acceptance. "I have ceased warring against the world," he wrote Frances Steloff in 1939. He believed in a greater force than himself, he told her. He was, he said, certain that destiny held something better in store for him, that it was his fate to reap his just reward rather late in life. "For the moment," he wrote, "I am poised, like a bird, not certain in which direction to take off."

. . .

In 1937, a bookshop at the corner of the rue Castiglione and Avenue St. Honoré had been filled with Miller's books and featured a photograph of a bust of him made by a Czech artist, Radmila Djoukic, Miller proudly reported to Frances Steloff in a June 1939 letter. His nine years in Paris—not to mention his emotional apprenticeship in America—had borne fruit, and he was a minor literary celebrity in France. Durrell, who had divided his time in the years following their first meeting in 1937 between Paris and London, wrote encouragingly of his growing reputation in England, and a Christmas visit Miller made there in 1938 brought him the acquaintance of Dylan Thomas, Julian Symons, and T. S. Eliot, whom Miller treated as a mentor even while disparaging his work. Like Durrell, Miller now appeared regularly in the pages of such British journals as the *Criterion, Seven,* and the *New English Weekly,* and Cyril Connolly told them both that they would be welcome as contributors to *Horizon,* the new magazine he was then launching. In America, *The Phoenix* stood by, ready to publish anything Miller sent, and a little journal in Shanghai called *T'ien Hsia Monthly* published contributions by almost everyone in the Villa Seurat group—Miller, Durrell, and Perlès most commonly. Dorothy Norman's new American magazine *Twice a Year* published pieces by Nin and Miller in 1938. These magazine appearances, and the equally frequent reviews of his books, had brought Miller a certain visibility. Literate Europeans now recognized his name. And because his contact with America was limited to personal friends and publishing people, mostly in New York, he allowed himself to assume the same was true there: that he was classed among America's most important living authors. He was convinced that the only obstacle to literary status and financial security was the ban on his works.

Miller's view of his reputation in America was skewed, to say the least. Although the literary world was aware of his name and status as a banned writer, few of his books were being read. They were hard to get and expensive when they could be found. *Tropic of Capricorn,* officially published by Kahane in February 1939 (but not available until several months after that), was priced at $10 at the Gotham Book Mart, an unusually high figure. Still, Steloff had more orders than she had copies in stock. An American Merchant Marine sailor named Morley smuggled in several hundred copies of the *Tropics* and *Black Spring* in early 1939, but this was risky. *Any* scheme to get the banned books in was dangerous, as Miller found out when he tried to send some copies to America through Obelisk Press's jobber. The woman who handled the order made a mistake in addressing the packages, and all the books were seized by Customs; Miller had already spent Steloff's $200 payment for them and apologized profusely for the foul-up. Plans for an underground edition were under way; Steloff and Ben Abramson, a Chicago bookseller, were to back the publication and were looking for a printer.

Miller was better known among collectors and book dealers than he was among readers. There was a lively traffic in his manuscripts, and he upped the asking price for his hand-corrected manuscript of *Cancer* by several thousand dollars. He also began making what are known as "keyed" copies of *Tropic of Cancer*: copies in which all the characters were identified in Miller's hand in the margin. In early 1939 he launched an enterprise that would bring together his skills as a watercolorist and a writer; he would write "original copy" and illustrate it in printers' dummies, which he would then sell as "unique copies" of books by Henry Miller. He was to have absolute liberty, he wrote Dobo—but the buyer could specify the subject. He asked anywhere from $100 to $250 for these, assuring prospective buyers of their eventual worth.

His correspondence was increasingly occupied with such matters. He needed money, his constant refrain. "If I can steal it, I will. I have no scruples," he wrote Dobo. "We are facing the apocalypse. We must work for the fun of it—and die likewise." As the thirties drew to a close, he had found his voice. Now he had to find his public.

Part 3

AMERICA

"One cannot have a definite, positive view concerning the meaning and purpose of life without its affecting one's behavior, which in turn affects those about one. And, sad as the truth may be, it usually affects people unpleasantly. The great majority, that is. As for the few, the disciples so-called, all too often their behavior lends itself to caricature. The innovator is always alone, always subject to ridicule, idolatry, and betrayal."

—Henry Miller,
Big Sur and the Oranges of Hieronymus Bosch (1957)

"I'm what you'd call a dirty saint; I've got a bit of the devil in me."

—Henry Miller,
Reflections (1981)

11.

The Air-Conditioned Nightmare

1939–1944

The impending war made it impossible for Miller to remain in France. By summer 1939, most of his friends had already left: Perlès to England, where he joined the British Army; David Edgar also to England; and Durrell back to Corfu. Lowenfels and Fraenkel had long ago returned to America. Only Anaïs Nin remained, and she was planning to return to the States any day. Early that summer, Miller made plans to vacate the Villa Seurat, arranging to store his belongings with an acquaintance in Louveciennes. He intended to return to America, but only to make a tour of the country and perhaps record his impressions. Then he would continue his world travels; he seriously hoped to join a monastery in Tibet, and he directed Russell & Volkening, the New York literary agents he had acquired at the end of 1938, to find one that would take him. Meanwhile, he arranged for an extended vacation —a month in the South of France at Rocamodour, and then a few months on the Greek island of Corfu with the Durrells.

On July 14 Miller boarded the *Théophile Gautier* in Marseilles, heading for Corfu with stops at Naples and Piraeus. Durrell picked him up at the port in Corfu and brought him back to his house at Kalami. Soon the two writers and Nancy were splashing about nude in the Aegean. At forty-seven, Miller was almost completely bald but for a fringe of white hair; in the village he was known as "the old man."

Resolving not to work while in Greece, he discontinued his habit of writing voluminous letters during his stay there. He read only "spiritual" literature like Madame Blavatsky's *The Secret Doctrine* (which Frances Steloff had been trying to get him to read for years) and Nijinsky's *Diary*. The Greek landscape transfixed him, and he felt it transformed him as well. At Nauplia, Phaistos, and Epidaurus he had what he described as mystical experiences that put him in touch not only with the Homeric heroes but, strangely enough, also with American Indians. He visited an Armenian soothsayer in Athens, who envisioned a great future for him, pronouncing that he would never die and would "bring great joy to the world," a prediction Miller accepted complacently.

On a ten-day visit to Athens with the Durrells, he also met several Greek intellectuals who he liked to think were extremely important to him spiritually and intellectually. The most notable were the poet known as Seferis, George Seferiades, and the critic George Katsimbalis. The latter was a great talker, a monologuist to rival Miller himself (he would become "the colossus" of *The Colossus of Maroussi*, which Miller wrote in New York the following year). Katsimbalis convinced him to write a short piece for a magazine he edited, and Miller dutifully tossed off an essay later collected as "Reflections on Writing."

Very soon after he arrived, Miller wrote to Huntington Cairns that he was "entirely recuperated, lethargic and contented as a lizard." His Greek sojourn was a time of recovery. His ten years in Paris had been filled with activity, and he simply needed a rest. Characteristically, however, he believed it to be an important new phase in his life: here his "spiritual" life would begin. Henceforth he would claim to be a religious man, though not in any traditional sense. He preached acceptance, but, as always, for him acceptance also meant rebellion. He continued to rail against the world, but he claimed to be at peace with it. He seemed not to realize the contradiction—or, if he did, he dismissed it as unimportant. In Greece, Miller began to try out a new role: that of the sage who was also a seeker. His conviction that he had been marked for some special destiny grew stronger. The effect of this new spirituality on his writing would not be a happy one.

The evocative, lyrical prose of the book Miller wrote about Greece, *The Colossus of Maroussi*, sets it entirely apart from his other work. An impressionistic travel narrative, it describes his experience of the country and the people he met there. Its mood is celebratory. The Greek people, he wrote, "brought me face to face with myself, they cleansed me of hatred, jealousy, and envy." Greece, which he thought was the antithesis of his own nation, he found to be "spiritually . . . still the mother of nations, the fountain-head of wisdom and inspiration."

Although certain passages of *The Colossus of Maroussi* are strikingly memorable, in general Miller fails to convince the reader of the wonders he experienced there, and his recounting of one spiritual experience after another tends to bore readers who are not taken up with mysticism. Even his evocation of Katsimbalis, who would become something of a role model for Miller during his Big Sur years, remains flat and unrealized, an unlikely "colossus." Yet Miller—and many of his admirers—thought *The Colossus of Maroussi* to be his finest book. He no doubt found it the most "mystical" of his works; it is a veritable compendium of the Henry Miller "philosophy." Or perhaps he was fond of it because it recalled the extraordinary peace of his months in Greece. That would be the only true vacation he would ever take.

The death of Jack Kahane in September 1939, just after Miller arrived in Greece, came as a terrible blow, he wrote Steloff at the time. As much as he had mocked Kahane, the two men had worked out a truce, and Miller had much to be grateful to him for—not least the 500 francs Kahane had recently begun sending him every month and that now would not be forthcoming. His son Maurice reassured Obelisk writers that he would keep the business going, but Miller worried that his new publisher would be drafted. Kahane's death put him in a morbid frame of mind, and he informed Steloff that in the event of his death, Anaïs Nin, his designated heir, would take care of his debts to the Gotham Book Mart. The belongings he had stored in Kahane's Paris safe would be worth a great deal if he ever achieved some recognition, he thought. At any rate, he told Steloff, he had lived a good, rich life: "It might have been better, larger, fuller—but perhaps that . . . is my own fault. Anyway I blame no one but myself."

Nineteen thirty-nine, however, was not the best year for a spiritual vacation in southern Europe. Durrell was eager to join the Albanian forces fighting Italy (which Miller found incomprehensible), and the Greeks expected their own country to join the war almost daily. By mid-October, Miller was beginning to panic. Due to the war there were restrictions on receiving money from England and France. He had been forced to leave Corfu when the Durrells relocated to Athens, and from there he wrote to Huntington Cairns asking for $250 for the passage to America, appending a list of potential contributors to whom Cairns might appeal. He had abandoned his plans to travel further East, visiting Arabia, Persia, India, China, and Tibet.

Miller bided his time until early December, when all American civilians were ordered out of Greece. He then booked passage for America on the *Exocharda*, sailing December 27. He and the Durrells shared Christmas dinner in a dreary café in Sparta, the rain pouring down outside. When the ship docked for two days at Marseilles, Miller stayed on board, feeling that he had already said goodbye to France.

In spite of his horror of war, he was not eager to return to America. He associated New York with failure and rejection—and not without reason. James Laughlin's new firm, New Directions, brought out in 1939 *The Cosmological Eye*, a collection of short pieces culled from *Max and the White Phagocytes*. His first book-length American publication, *The Cosmological Eye* did little for Miller's reputation. Its contents were uneven; it included the brilliant "tailor shop" excerpt from *Black Spring* and his masterful story "Max," but also two weak essays on film and a fragment from his critical work on Lawrence. There were two mediocre meditations on Nin and her work, and two surrealistic pieces from *Black Spring*. "Via Dieppe Newhaven," a recreation of an abortive 1932 visit to England, was a high point in the collection; it is a hilarious account of Miller's mistreatment at the hands of the British, written in good humor and with a sense of irony. The collection closed with a lengthy "Autobiographical Note," which was a largely fictionalized account of his life. Elements of what would become the standard Henry Miller mythology appeared here: that he had cut short his Western trip (in this version, he was headed for Juneau to be a "placer miner") because he was taken down with a fever; that he had disappeared with his mistress and the tuition money on the evening before his departure for Cornell; that he had worked as a reporter on a Washington paper; and that he had worked as well as a "Dish-washer, bus boy, newsie, messenger boy, grave-digger, bill sticker, book salesman, bell hop, bartender, liquor salesman, typist, adding machine operator, librarian, statistician, charity worker, mechanic, insurance collector, garbage collector, usher, secretary to an evangelist, dock hand, street car conductor, gymnasium instructor, milk driver, ticket chopper, etc."

As a compendium of facts, the "Autobiographical Note" is unreliable, but as an artistic manifesto it is an interesting statement. The real influence on his work, he wrote, was life, and in particular the life of the streets. He owed a lot to the dictionary and the encyclopedia, he said, as well as to Eastern folklore and fairy tales; until he was twenty-five, he continued, he had only read novels by Russian authors. He was interested in religion, philosophy, science, history, art, archeology, primitive culture, and mythology. He barely read the newspaper and had never read a detective story. He catalogued his likes and dislikes: Faure, Dostoevsky, Nietzsche, Proust, and Spengler impressed him. Among American writers he liked Whitman and Emerson and detested Henry James and, for some reason, Edgar Allan Poe. Less insightfully, he wrote that his goal in writing was "to establish a greater REALITY." He closed by saying he hoped civilization would be destroyed in the next hundred years or so. Perhaps the most interesting "essay" in the book, Miller's "Autobiographical Note" is an Emersonian exercise in introspection as well as an egotistical assertion of self-invention, and as such it captures the tone of the collection.

Reviews of *The Cosmological Eye* were generally not favorable. It was a difficult work to characterize: the pieces weren't exactly stories, nor were they essays. Many reviewers disliked the tone of the book. Clifton Fadiman in *The New Yorker* found "his I-am-God attitudes . . . childish." Miller's agent, John Slocum at Russell & Volkening, reported that he could place none of Miller's articles or stories in leading magazines.

When the *Exocharda* docked in mid-January 1940, Miller had no one to meet him. He had hoped to find Nin, who had returned to New York, but she was home with the flu. He checked into the Royalton Hotel in midtown, with no intention of visiting his parents in Brooklyn. Instead, his first stop was the Gotham Book Mart, which would for the next several years be his mailing address and, when he was in New York, his base of operations. He asked Steloff not to give out his real address to his parents should they get wind of his arrival and turn up at the store.

They would barely have had time. Almost immediately, he checked out of the Royalton for a trip to Orange, Virginia, where his old friend Emil Schnellock now lived, teaching art at Mary Washington College. It was a business trip as well, since Miller spent a few days in Washington with the lawyer Huntington Cairns, whom he had met in Paris. Cairns was sympathetic to Miller's plight, although there was little to do regarding the ban on the *Tropics*. Miller contemplated sending for his belongings in New York and recruiting Nin for a tour of the South.

Money problems, as usual, cut short his travels. Caresse Crosby, a friend of Nin's whom Miller had come to know well in Paris, had generously offered him the use of her apartment on East 54th Street;

she was living with her second husband, Selbert Young, at Hampton Manor, her estate in Bowling Green, Virginia. (Her life had been touched by scandal when her first husband, Harry Crosby, shot and killed himself and his mistress a decade earlier.) Miller moved in and started looking for ways to make money. He had learned how to cast horoscopes, after a fashion, from his Parisian friend Moricand; getting hold of a naval *Ephemeris*—the technical manual of the trade—he tried halfheartedly to set up as a professional astrologer. Predictably enough, given his inexperience, he soon found that it was unlikely that he would make his fortune through the stars, and he returned rather listlessly to writing *The Colossus of Maroussi*.

The "Greek book" occupied Miller throughout the spring and summer of 1940. Nin still supported him as best she could, but she had little to spare as she was saving up to buy a small press. She had in fact begun writing pornography, at a dollar a page, for an Oklahoma oil millionaire, Roy Mellisandre Johnson. A New York book dealer whose most lucrative trade was in erotica, had learned that Johnson was looking for original manuscripts; Frances Steloff let the dealer know of her impoverished charges, and he offered Nin and Miller his dollar-a-page deal. A veritable combine of writers existed to meet Johnson's needs; in her *Diary*, Nin writes that she was joined in the business by Caresse Crosby and the poet Robert Duncan, among others. What bothered the writers most was Johnson's insistence that the descriptions be graphic and clinical—anything too poetic he rejected.

Steloff sent Miller to the dealer in February, for which he thanked her dutifully, telling her "something splendid" was happening as the result of the meeting. He immediately set up as a pornography hack, turning out two ribald stories about the imagined erotic adventures of an autobiographical narrator and his friend Carl in a Paris suburb. Titled "Quiet Days in Clichy" and "Mara-Marignan," the stories are loosely based on his life with Perlès in the Clichy apartment nearly seven years before.

The book dealer paid Miller and urged him to write more. At first Miller was amused by the experience, but his enthusiasm for this means of raising cash quickly paled; it was far less work to appeal to a friend or, for that matter, produce a watercolor for a collector. He had no objection in principle to writing pornography, but it bored him to write about sex so mechanically, and he worried about its effect on his other writing. He turned out a few more sketches, which would later be collected in the posthumous *Opus Pistorum*, and then told the dealer he was no longer interested. The dealer kept supplying Johnson with pornography written by the Nin combine, and as a result, to this day a great deal of unpublished pornography circulates among collectors that may or may not have been written by Miller. During his lifetime, Miller publicly denied that he wrote any such commissioned pornography— although this in turn may have been due to his lifelong habit of distancing himself from Nin in deference to her wishes that their relationship remain secret. He did acknowledge his pornography to those he trusted, like his American publisher, James Laughlin.

With the book dealer Ben Abramson in Chicago, Miller dreamed up another pornography-related scheme. There was a great deal of talk about the banned *Tropic of Capricorn* among American collectors of erotica, particularly the section called "Land of Fuck," which was said to be racier than anything in *Cancer*. Abramson proposed that Miller capitalize on the rumor by letting what seemed to be a manuscript of the section surface, which Abramson would then make available to collectors on a limited edition basis. So in June 1940 Miller wrote what would become *The World of Sex*, an essay about his views on sex that contained many details of his sexual past, particularly with respect to his first marriage. He gave it to Abramson with strict instructions to keep the edition truly limited, for he was mortally afraid of what Beatrice might do if she saw it.

On another front, Miller was finally receiving some proceeds from the underground edition of *Tropic of Cancer* that had been underwritten by Steloff and Abramson. Though it was described as a "Mexican edition," the book was actually produced by a printer named Jake Brussels in his Fourth Avenue loft with the help of Gershon Legman, a scholar of erotica. Brussels had given Miller $250 as an advance, and now, with the so-called "Medvsa" edition actually on sale, Miller could expect to receive "royalties" in addition—assuming, of course, the honesty of under-the-counter book dealers.

In short, Miller was dealing with the seamier side of the book industry—hardly the scenario he had envisioned when he planned his return to America. He had a few friends in the legitimate book world —the editor Joe Sadow, now at Viking, for example, and Blanche Knopf, who still hoped to publish him, and John Slocum at Russell & Volkening. But New Directions rejected the manuscript of *Colossus of Maroussi* in July; the book wasn't even censorable, which had been Laughlin's reason for not publishing the Paris books. The manuscript made the rounds of more than ten publishing houses. Publishers were eager to see his work, in hopes of discovering a book on the order of *Tropic of Cancer* that wouldn't land them in court; a reverie about Greece was far from what they had expected. The reception Miller had hoped for in America turned out to be a crushing disappointment.

Miller finally steeled himself to visit Decatur Street. Not surprisingly, he found that his mother could still get under his skin. His parents had aged and shrunk, and Lauretta, too, looked old. The very sight of them made Miller burst into a fit of weeping. But once the initial shock had passed and the family settled into their old configurations again, he sized up the situation quickly. Heinrich, disabled by prostate cancer, had to wear a rubber bag that collected his urine. He was at the mercy of Louise, who controlled their finances. Obsessed as ever with money, his mother skimped on Heinrich's routine medical irrigations to save a few dollars, begrudged the dying man cigarettes, and even had the telephone taken out. They had no income at all, Louise said, and she and Lauretta were exhausted by caring for the invalid. The situation enraged Miller, and he resolved to spend more time with his father. On his next visit he announced that he had received a (nonexistent) big advance and that he could now help the family out regularly. Louise didn't believe him, but she grudgingly accepted his gifts. She still would not pay for Heinrich's cigarettes, so Miller found some means of slipping his father a little extra money. To his surprise, he found himself drifting into a new, comradely relationship with the old man; he drew Heinrich out in long talks about art and literature. He had seen to it that his family had read none of his books, but now he gave his father his little pamphlet on money—the most harmless of his publications and, perhaps more importantly, one that a naive reader might take as the work of a scholar. Heinrich was dimly mystified by his son's career, but he was not derisive like his wife, and, as always, his opinion meant a lot to his son.

Both Heinrich and Louise assiduously avoided the subject of their son's two ex-wives. For his part, Miller thought from time to time of June, but she seemed to have vanished. He could find no trace of her in the Village and assumed she had remarried—perhaps to a more conventional husband, who kept her at home. He was terrified of Beatrice, who had since married a man named Sandford, for he knew she was still in Brooklyn and furious at him for reneging on child support and alimony. He half-imagined that she had a detective on his trail. He also seems to have behaved very curiously toward his daughter, Barbara, whom he had located through his friend O'Regan in 1937. He had written to her in 1938, but she did not reply. In June 1940 he asked Steloff to send the now twenty-two-year-old Barbara a book by Alain Fournier, and almost a year later he asked her to send another book, on Greece. When Steloff congratulated him on having "discovered" his daughter, Miller professed bewilderment: "I don't understand. I haven't heard from her ever, nor seen her?" Fearful to identify himself, he apparently wanted the gifts to be anonymous, very likely expecting Barbara to share her mother's feelings toward him.

At forty-eight, Miller worried that he was as much a failure as a writer as he had been as a father. When Louise nagged him to write a bestseller like *Gone With the Wind,* his failure particularly rankled. The elation he had felt at the reception of *Tropic of Cancer,* his happiness with Anaïs, his serenity in Greece—all had vanished now. *The Colossus of Maroussi* was rejected with stunning swiftness by house after house. Miller's agent reminded him of his plan to travel about America and record his impressions. *That* book could sell, Slocum told Miller: publishers would be eager to have the impressions of a returned expatriate on his native land.

Miller mulled the idea over for some time. It appealed to him; prominent writers like Hemingway had undertaken similar ventures into non-fiction. Perhaps it was the best way to make an impressive entrance on the American literary scene. He was full of original observations about America, he thought, although he conveniently forgot how much he hated his country. Back in Paris, he had begun to refer to America as "an air-conditioned nightmare," and little of what he had seen since his return altered his long-held views.

When Miller mentioned the plan to Abe Rattner, the American artist he had met some years earlier in Paris, Rattner's imagination was sparked, and he proposed to join him, making pen-and-ink sketches to accompany Miller's text. Miller welcomed the idea, seeing in Rattner a potential "buddy" like Perlès who could liven up the trip. With printing costs soaring in the face of imminent war, the two soon learned that publishers were not interested in illustrations, but Rattner hoped to join Miller anyway, at least for part of the trip. Slocum received an offer from John Woodburn, an editor at Doubleday, Doran; Doubleday was willing to advance $500 toward the book. Miller accepted. He applied for a Guggenheim Fellowship but was not at all surprised when he was rejected; he resolved to append to his book the list of successful Guggenheim recipients, all of whom seemed to him to be embarked on obscure or meaningless ventures. He arranged for driving lessons—he had never driven before and the prospect scared him. He made out elaborate itineraries, concentrating on colorful place names and locations where he knew people willing to put him up or whom he wanted to meet. (The list included Zora Neale Hurston, Margaret Mitchell, Walt Disney, and Ernest Hemingway, none of whom he would manage to see.) To his publishers, of course, Miller professed to be open-minded about what he might encounter on his trip, and to bear genuine love for America. Privately, however, he had no intention of writing a conventional travel narrative. His working title, in fact, was *America: The Air-Conditioned Nightmare.*

Miller and Rattner set forth in late October 1940, Miller behind the wheel of a used 1932 Buick, bought with money from his advance; he told a friend it looked like the private car of a funeral director. Both were immediately shaken by a claustrophobic and harrowing trip through the Holland Tunnel. The first leg of the journey took them through New Hope, a Pennsylvania art colony, and Valley Forge, and they wound up in Washington, D.C., where Cairns put them up. Miller reported to Nin that he had let Rattner do most of the driving (although he thought himself the better driver) and that the two men were getting along fine. From Washington they went to Bowling Green, Virginia, where they spent a night at Caresse Crosby's estate. This was bittersweet, as he and Nin had spent a happy month there that summer, marred only by the unpleasantness of Salvador Dali and his wife, also guests of Caresse Crosby, who had snubbed the group of visiting writers and kept to themselves. On this visit, he found Dali more vain than ever; Caresse seemed lonely, complaining of having no one to drink with her. But Miller and Rattner pushed on to Fredericksburg, where they stayed with Schnellock, and from there drove over the Skyline Drive through Virginia. When they reached Asheville, North Carolina, Miller made a hasty trip back to New York in order to be present at his parents' fiftieth wedding anniversary; he found his father even weaker.

Not surprisingly, the expedition was fraught with delays and complications from the start. On the eve of his departure, Steloff and Slocum had telephoned him with suggestions for setting up an emergency fund to help him out financially; Miller agreed to write a circular and urged Nin to help. The fund was never set up formally, but Steloff and Slocum did raise small sums of cash that they sent him on the road. Miller's letters to Nin and other friends are filled with requests for loans of $25 or $50. It turned out that the car needed repairs more often than Miller had expected, and his daily expenses kept mounting up.

"I had to travel about ten thousand miles before receiving the inspiration to write a single line," Miller later wrote. "Everything I could write about the American way of life I could put in thirty pages." From Atlanta he reported that he just got more and more disgusted every day. If he were Czar, he said, he would wipe out the whole population except for Indians and blacks. Charleston, where they spent Christmas and his forty-ninth birthday, he quite liked, and he approved of New Orleans, where they passed a month at New Iberia, the plantation of Rattner's friend Weeks Hall. Rattner then left for New York to oversee an exhibition of his work, and Miller continued on disconsolately; in his friend's absence he found he often talked aloud to himself while driving.

From Natchez, Miller got word that his father was dying. He flew home—it was his first plane trip—but arrived two hours too late. Heinrich had died peacefully in his sleep. Miller was profoundly shocked. He later told a friend that he had never expected to miss his father so much. Everything happened quickly: his father's body was embalmed and laid out in the parlor seemingly within hours. Louise rushed about looking for Heinrich's lower set of false teeth and asked an incredulous Henry to take one of Heinrich's white shirts to the Chinese laundry to be rewashed. After the funeral and the wake that followed, Miller took his notebook out to his father's grave in Evergreen Cemetery and filled two pages with expressions of his grief and thoughts about death. The grave opposite his father's was that of a man named "Authors"—it seemed an odd coincidence. He remembered how his father had written him encouraging letters in Paris, cheering him along, treating his son as if he were a small businessman like himself (which wasn't, actually, too far from the mark). But he also remembered how his father had always held up Jimmy Pasta as an example, how his father had constantly admonished him to *be a man*. A year later Miller would meet the actor John Barrymore, his father's old drinking crony. Barrymore took Miller to task for saying that his father wasn't a man, that he had no culture. "Your father was a man, a real man!" Barrymore assured him. But this was a subject on which Henry was never sure.

Miller resumed his trip at the end of February, traveling through Pittsburgh, Cleveland, and Detroit to Chicago. There he stayed with a couple named the Howards and passed a memorable evening watching erotic films. The experience moved him to write a screen treatment for such a film himself, to be directed, he proposed—with a characteristic mixture of whim and naivete—by Marcel Duchamp and John Ford. There he also met Ben Abramson, the bookseller who had backed the underground edition of *Cancer*. They worked out plans for publishing his 1940 essay *The World of Sex*, and Abramson loaned him $25. Financially, things were a little brighter; New Directions had contracted for another collection of pieces, which Miller tentatively titled *The Enormous Womb*, and Laughlin gave him a $200 advance. By March, when Miller was in Des Moines with his friends Flo and John Dudley, he received word that the *Atlantic Monthly* had advanced him $250 for the magazine rights to his book on America. He told Slocum to give it all to Nin, minus $10 that he owed Cairns. Across the country people were offering him free places to live. Another Midwestern friend, Lafayette Young, offered to set up a press in Mexico to publish all his books, beginning with the *Tropics*.

But his current book was in trouble. He had begun to write in Detroit and was determined to write the whole thing in one great sweep, without an elaborate plot or organization. He swung South, stopping in Jackson, Mississippi, to visit the writer Eudora Welty. There he made a very bad mistake, broaching the subject of writing pornography for a dollar a page. Welty showed him the gate.

From Mississippi he went on to Arkansas and then to Texas. By the time he left Texas he had two hundred pages to show Slocum. He found the Southwest—the Petrified Forest, the Painted Desert, the Grand Canyon—mysterious and appealing, and rested for a few days in April in Albuquerque. There he wrote a long letter to Nin describing his feelings about the trip. He had realized after just ten days on the road that he could never enjoy it, he wrote, and now he simply treated it as something to get over with. It was like living through bad Karma, he said. The book would give his personal reaction to the country, nothing more.

The Air-Conditioned Nightmare, as it was titled when published four years later, reflects this mood. It is a book that might well be best enjoyed on a cross-country road trip, propped up in diners behind bad food, read by the light of a neon sign in a motor court. Disjointed and sprawling, it is also very cranky, for Miller, with a very few exceptions, did not like what he saw. His America was hideous, sterile, and cruel —its poverty oppressive, its values warped. He produced portraits of a few good souls—the photographer Alfred Stieglitz, the painter John Marin, his friend Lafe Young, and the composer Edgard Varèse—but these portraits are neither gripping nor informative. As was often the case when he wrote about men he admired, his prose was uniformly riddled with encomiums, the subject always "a great man," his art—if he were an artist—the best of its kind. Critical writing was never Miller's strong suit.

The book's greatest strength is the author's eye for detail. *The Air-Conditioned Nightmare* is a compendium of vivid images: a cow he saw in Ducktown, Tennessee, chewing a piece of tin foil; an eight-year-old black boy buying comics with a swagger in Charleston; an apartment complex in Chicago with GOOD NEWS! GOD IS LOVE! painted on a wall. Miller's voice is companionable: certain landscapes remind him of his childhood or of Paris and trigger conversational digressions.

But the book's most noteworthy quality was the author's frank anti-Americanism. "Nowhere have I encountered such a dull, monotonous fabric of life as here in America," Miller wrote in the opening pages. He blasted the idea that the country is a society of free peoples, a nation of great promise:

> What have we to offer the world beside the superabundant loot which we recklessly plunder from the earth under the maniacal delusion that this is sane activity? The land of opportunity has become the land of senseless sweat and struggle.

He cursed as well society's treatment of the artist. America seemed not to value its creative citizens, and indeed made life miserable for them. Companionable his voice may be in *The Air-Conditioned Nightmare*, but not happy.

Miller wrote the bulk of the book in Hollywood, where he finished the trip, spending the summer of 1941 at a succession of hotels and then in a garage apartment on Camino Palermo. He intended to stay a while, writing to Steloff for a list of his admirers in the area. There were, actually, several, for erotica had traditionally been popular in the Hollywood community, and many figures in the movie business were avid collectors. The director Josef von Sternberg had a collection worth $100,000, Miller reported to Nin. The Hollywood Book Shop did a thriving trade in pornography, under and over the counter, as did the Satyr Book Shop. Within a week of his arrival on May 12, Miller was offered a job writing film scripts, which he promptly turned down.

. . .

His legitimate writing efforts were now bringing in enough money for him to live on, as long as Nin could come through with a check in emergencies. *Town and Country* editor Harry Bull was publishing a fragment about Weeks Hall from *The Air-Conditioned Nightmare* manuscript in his magazine, Laughlin promised another $100 for the last installment of his collection, and an article Miller wrote on Sherwood Anderson was accepted by *Story* magazine. In early June he learned that *The Colossus of Maroussi* had finally found a publisher: William Roth of the Colt Press in San Francisco. Miller traveled up from Los Angeles to confirm the plans. He hoped to make side trips to see John Steinbeck, Krishnamurti, and a Rosicrucian community, he wrote Anaïs. (The Rosicrucians were especially important to the book he was hoping to write next, *The Rosy Crucifixion*.)

As he drove back down the coast after meeting with Roth, Miller bombarded Steinbeck with phone calls. He didn't particularly admire Steinbeck as a novelist, except perhaps for his commercial success. Rather, he saw the author of *The Grapes of Wrath* as quintessentially American, all the more so, in fact, for being a Westerner and ranchman. Steinbeck had succeeded precisely where Miller had failed; he had a reading public who paid to read his books, and he had a masculine image.

As it turned out, Miller was due to arrive on Steinbeck's birthday. Steinbeck and his friend Ed Ricketts had planned a small party at the novelist's house in Monterey that evening, and as darkness fell, Steinbeck grew increasingly apprehensive at the prospect of Miller's unsolicited presence and wandered off into the pine trees beyond the house. During his absence, the wine and beer flowed. When Miller arrived, he quickly took in Steinbeck's unwillingness to see him, and, unfazed, drew the spotlight to himself. As he saw it, he had an image to live up to. In the house of the masculine Steinbeck, he felt galvanized to perform, to prove his manhood. Grabbing a woman guest, he pulled her outside; the guests peeked out and saw the unprepossessing, nearly bald Miller necking on the lawn. One guest remarked that he thought Miller looked like Alf Landon.

Relinquishing the first woman, Miller grabbed another; he seemed to be enjoying the attention. Suddenly the radio broke off its program of dance tunes and announced that Hitler's forces had invaded the Soviet Union.

Somehow the news reached Steinbeck out in the woods. He came out bellowing, waving his arms about like a wounded beast. He brushed by the now insignificant Miller, went into his room, and locked the door.

The rest of the evening was a distinct anticlimax. Everyone worried about Steinbeck's feelings, and one of the guests offered Miller a place to stay. All could see that Miller hated being upstaged, first by Hitler and then by the distraught Steinbeck. The situation was pathetic; Miller's exaggerated cocksmanship looked immature and petty next to Steinbeck's response to a momentous world event.

During his stay in the West, Miller's relationship with Anaïs Nin grew increasingly strained. She was offended that he seemed content to stay in Hollywood—with her financial help. He still talked about raising money for her to come out and join him, but she wrote back that the real issue was his refusal to see how coldblooded and egotistical he was becoming. She still helped support him from funds she secreted from Hugo, supplemented by her earnings from writing pornography. But Miller's unwillingness to write for the book dealer himself seemed to her a betrayal. She believed his commitment to the book about America—a project that seemed to her a meaningless detour—as well as what she perceived as his intention to live in the West ruled out any commitment to her. Miller, in turn, challenged Anaïs to leave her husband, which she flatly refused to do. They left unspoken their suspicions about each other's fidelity. Anaïs had become infatuated with Luise Rainer, the memorable star of *The Good Earth*, whom Miller had met and admired in Hollywood. Nin spent the summer of 1941 in Provincetown, writing Miller enigmatic letters. He was becoming interested in a young woman named Laure Louie, the ex-wife of an artist named Ferren, who was in Hollywood writing scripts; in a letter to Durrell he referred to her as "the divine Laure." He told nothing of this to Nin, writing her instead that the astrological auspices indicated their "disputations" would abate by August 6, but they apparently did not. By October, when he left Hollywood and started back to New York, their relationship had deteriorated badly. It was now almost completely businesslike, but the two misunderstood each other on this level as well. Nin had looked to Miller to establish an artistic reputation in America, which in turn might pave the way for her creative efforts. But Miller was not practical enough about such matters, in her view, and she took his failure to establish himself as a personal slight.

In New York in the winter of 1941–42, Miller could talk of nothing but the "desert colony" of artists and writers he had discovered in California. The Japanese attack on Pearl Harbor left him unfazed; he only worried about the war's effect on his publisher's decision about the now completed *Air-Conditioned Nightmare*, with its strongly anti-American content. He was sure that Doubleday would reject it, and he schemed to find ways of returning his advance. James Laughlin had given him another $200 for *The Enormous Womb*, now retitled *The Wisdom of the Heart*. *The Colossus of Maroussi* had earned him an $80 advance. But Miller had no regular income. He confided to Abe Rattner that he wanted to find work writing war propaganda, though he didn't make much effort to find it. The year 1941 had brought him little money from his writing efforts, and he had produced a book that he knew was a distinct falling-off from his Paris books. He passed Christmas and his fiftieth birthday alone in Caresse Crosby's West 45th Street apartment. He had told his mother he would be in Washington for the holiday, and sent a letter to her down to Huntington Cairns, asking Cairns to mail it from a Washington mailbox.

Doubleday did indeed turn down *The Air-Conditioned Nightmare*, and Miller shelved it until the war was over. He turned instead to the book he had wanted to write since 1927, *The Rosy Crucifixion*. Miller first referred to a "rosy crucifixion" in *Tropic of Capricorn*, when he differentiates the way he has suffered from the way other people have: "The whole drama which the man of today is acting out through suffering does not exist for me: it never did, actually. All my Cavalries were rosy crucifixions." The title derived partly from the Rosicrucian sect, but it also reflected Miller's belief in the galvanizing effects of suffering and his growing interest in martyrdom. He had always believed that his birthday, coming one day after Christmas, had marked him as special; his sufferings at the hands of June had confirmed this. Now, as a banned writer, he wondered if he might not be suffering for the sins of mankind—for had not *Tropic of Cancer* merely voiced society's desires and regrets? *The Rosy Crucifixion* would chronicle Miller's sufferings with June and Jean and his subsequent resurrection in Paris. He would begin with his first marriage, take the story through June and their trip to Europe in 1928, and close with his own arrival in Paris in 1930. Nin, who well knew how Miller used his writing as a way of striking back emotionally at women who had hurt him, had made him promise never to write about her, thus effectively closing off the years after 1932 as material. He accepted this cheerfully enough, for he had plenty to say about his earlier life. But it was an unfortunate development for his writing, as it encouraged him to traverse and re-traverse the same ground.

The writing of *The Rosy Crucifixion* occupied him through the early months of 1942; what he was writing was raw and graphic, the most censorable writing he had ever done. In the *Tropics* he had used four-letter words and described sexual acts, but seldom at length. In what was to become *Sexus*, volume 1 of *The Rosy Crucifixion*, the pages are filled with descriptions of "juicy cunts," "backscuttling," "shooting a load," and so forth. The female characters use sexually explicit language ("shove it in all the way, harder, harder, break your big prick off and leave it there"). Explicit scenes occur so frequently that the book often assumes the tedium that characterizes pornography.

He spent a lonely spring, ensconced again in Caresse Crosby's Manhattan apartment, making frequent trips to his father's grave. By May he was restless, longing to return again to Hollywood, which he called "Lotos Land." It seemed to be a popular place for writers in wartime, he observed, noting the presence of William Faulkner as well as such European refugees as Thomas and Heinrich Mann and Berthold Brecht. He began to think that he had a future in film, a medium he had always admired. When a writer named Gilbert Nieman, whom Miller had met in Hollywood, offered him a room rent-free, he boarded a train for the Coast almost immediately, hoping to get a job as a screenwriter, make a pile of money, and move eventually to Mexico. He entertained unrealistic hopes that Nin might join him there.

When he arrived in Los Angeles, he learned that the Niemans would actually be putting him up next door to their house on Beverly Glen Boulevard in West Los Angeles in an apartment with the Jordans, a Czechoslovakian detective story writer and his wife. He would take his meals with Gilbert and Margaret in what he called "the green house." The Niemans' home was located in a canyon within walking distance of UCLA and Westwood and nearby Hollywood. Miller would have to get along without a car. One of the things he would remember most vividly about his time in Beverly Glen was trudging along the hot and dusty boulevards of the city, day and night, without being offered a ride.

Miller traveled light, arriving in the West with little to tie him down. He had appointed Emil Schnellock his literary "executor" in the thirties; now he set up some other repositories. Herbert West, a Dartmouth professor, had written a positive review of *Aller Retour New York* in the *Dartmouth Alumni Magazine*; he was an avid book collector and had corresponded with Miller for some time. Just before he left New York, Miller sent on a number of his old manuscripts and letters to West. Soon after his return to Los Angeles, however, he made the acquaintance of Lawrence Clark Powell, a librarian at UCLA; Powell convinced Miller to establish an archive there. In 1943 Miller would attempt to place the entire archive with an Oakland editor and friend, George Leite. Miller shifted his manuscripts from person to person, bringing some back into active circulation when a publisher or collector expressed interest. In 1942, for example, he heard that the British publishing house Secker & Warburg was interested in his *Air-Conditioned Nightmare* manuscript; finding he had no copy, he retrieved one from West's collection.

Film work was harder to find than he expected, and soon he was hard up against "the money question," as he wrote to his friend Cyril Connolly. The way movies were made disillusioned him; it was all too technical. Moreover, he had no idea of how to go about getting a job. He had a number of connections—Julian Josephson, an executive at Fox, was a fan; Donald Friede, formerly of Covici Friede, was working as a Hollywood agent; and Russell & Volkening steered him to the Myron Selznick Agency. But he had a reputation for being "pure," he complained to Nin, and he wasn't sure he could do the work in the first place. When the Selznick agents told him that what they needed was "just plain shit wrapped in cellophane," he wrote that he was ready to give up. But in the same letter he boasted of contacts with Budd Schulberg and Stanley Ross, who was Saroyan's agent.

He had a bit more success when he focused his efforts. In mid-July, poking around in a second-hand bookstore, he found a used copy of Jakob Wassermann's *Dr. Kerkhoven*. The novel, part of a metaphysical trilogy known as *The Maurizius Case*, about a man unjustly accused and the guilt of the real criminal, transfixed him. He set about writing a screen treatment of it; at about the same time, Marcel Friedman, whom Miller had met in New York, fortuitously acquired the movie rights to Wassermann's story. Miller hoped he might be given the job of adaptation, but the studios showed no interest, and Friedman paid Miller only a $100 flat fee for his work. Miller's treatment just gathered dust.

By the end of the year Miller was desperate. Gilbert Nieman had gone North to oversee Mexican immigrant laborers, and he thought he could find a similar job for Miller, especially given his "personnel experience." This led nowhere. In December Miller appealed to the Office of War Information, asking for a job writing propaganda, but this too came to nothing. He was subsisting on the occasional check from

Nin and proceeds from the occasional sale of his original manuscripts to collectors.

In November and December he launched a no-holds-barred campaign of begging, writing letters spelling out his desperate plight to every name in his address book. To editors, he requested assignments for book reviews. To collectors, he offered manuscripts. To art colonies and foundations, he asked for applications. To all others, he asked for old clothes, food, postage stamps, a loan. He literally wore out his fountain pen and typewriter—the machine had to go into the shop.

With the new year, he began to see results. He got numerous promises of review assignments, offers of free housing, and small five-dollar commissions for painting watercolors. A New York bookseller, Terence Holliday, promised to ask the writer Stephen Vincent Benét if anything could be done for Miller through the National Institute of Arts and Letters, and the Institute ultimately came through with a $200 loan, with no stipulation that it be repaid by any specific time. This was just the sort of fund Steloff and Slocum had been trying to set up when Miller's American tour had begun, and Miller saw some justice in taking the money.

What he sought was the time to finish *The Rosy Crucifixion* without worrying about money. Instead, he found himself deluged with correspondence and appointments. He had always devoted two or three hours a day to writing letters, but now he found the job had swollen so that it ate up nearly the entire day. Moreover, there were always people underfoot in "the green house," which he continued to occupy after the Niemans' departure. He led a communal sort of existence, he wrote Nin. He was having such a manic time that he wrote volubly to his friend John Dudley, urging the Midwesterner to join him; Dudley was recovering from a divorce and took him up on it immediately.

Miller later called the Beverly Glen period a time of Rimbaud, astrology, and watercolors. Sometimes he and Dudley painted watercolors all night. On his walks to Westwood Village Miller met an art store owner named Attilio Bowinkel, and Bowinkel encouraged him, saying he had definite potential as a painter. Miller and Dudley drew up a circular to send to friends announcing a permanent exhibition of "aquarelles" at "The Green House Thatched with Women's Hair," advising that "ladies will be treated with respect" and that the gallery's hours were the same as the hours of the inhabitants. "It goes without saying," the circular read, "that the masterpieces on exhibition are for sale."

Visitors marched through the green house. The artist Man Ray and his wife, Julie, friends of the Niemans who knew Miller by reputation from their Paris years and who now lived on nearby Vine Street, were regular guests. Man Ray and Miller had a lot in common: their fathers had been tailors, neither artist had attended college, and each had made extended trips to Paris. Man Ray photographed Miller, fully clothed, with a naked woman wearing a mask. Other visitors included the writers Charles Henri Ford and Parker Tyler; Miller wrote a preface for Tyler's book on the cinema and often contributed to *View*, a magazine published by Ford. Dane Rudhyard, a Hollywood astrologer, was a frequent guest. He introduced Miller to a young musician and astrologer named Pierce Harwell, who astounded Miller with the accuracy of his predictions. Miller wrote to Nin that Harwell reminded him of the Armenian in Greece, the one who had said he would never die. (Unfortunately, Harwell was also given to telling people about their deaths, in elaborate and chilling detail, as Nin noted in her *Diary*.)

Miller was moving more certainly than ever in the direction of the mystical and the occult. He sought out mystical works like Algernon Blackwood's novels and self-improvement books like Aldous Huxley's *The Art of Seeing*. He began a correspondence with the writer Claude Houghton, author of *A Kingdom of the Spirit*. He particularly admired Houghton's idea of an occult brotherhood; he had been developing a similar idea in the last few years, Miller told Houghton. Polygamy had worked among the Mormons, for example, and in the South, Miller went on blithely, white men had mated with black women freely and with no objections from the women until white women had put a stop to it. "A high degree of spirituality," he observed, "goes hand in hand with the stud farm." For that matter, he continued, women didn't like to be romanticized, and only kept themselves distant because they thought men liked it. Miller believed that promiscuity was not natural for men; he complained that with each sexual conquest he was obliged to pledge eternal love, and the romance was exhausting him.

This "philosophy" was entirely antithetical to Miller's actual experience in 1942 and 1943. He had, by and large, remained faithful to Anaïs Nin, although their affair had cooled considerably. His relationship with Laure Louie had amounted to little, and his sexual conquests were few and far between. But his statements to Houghton indicate that his misogyny was escalating to a veritable sexual panic. At a time when he was writing about his humbling experiences with June, he wanted fewer women, not more. His was a vision of polyandry: many men would share one woman, united this way in a kind of "brotherhood." The need for "romance" would be obviated, as women would be reduced to sexual beings alone.

Interestingly, the women Miller was involved with in this period were sexually unavailable to him. The first, a Greek woman named Melpomene Niarchos, was a Pasadena matron, the wife of the prominent Greek shipowner, who admired *The Colossus of Maroussi*. She offered him a cabin on her Long Island estate that he was sorely tempted to take; to him she was the "apotheosis of all Greek womanhood." But Melpo (as Miller called her) had a jealous husband who spirited his wife back to New York before Miller could make any advances. Miller kept track of her there, sending messages through Frances Steloff and Pierce Harwell, his astrologer friend, but after a while he lost interest in pressing his suit long distance.

Melpo was quickly replaced by another Greek woman, Sevasty Koutsaftis, whom the UCLA librarian Lawrence Clark Powell introduced to Miller as a potential translator of *The Colossus of Maroussi*. Miller wrote Herbert West in July 1943 that he was totally in love with Sevasty. But Sevasty was as unattainable as Melpo; her mother, who lived with her, watched her closely and did not approve of Miller. A poet herself, Sevasty inspired Miller to write a poem, the second he had ever written. (Entitled "O Lake of Light," it appeared in *Harper's* in 1944.) So infatuated was Miller that he obtained a graphologist's report on Sevasty's handwriting, but it failed to explain her refusal to commit herself to Miller. When Sevasty sent him a letter saying she wanted to be friends, he tore it in two, announcing to Herb West that his love affair was definitely dead.

Recovering from these romantic setbacks, Miller lost himself in work, painting watercolors by the dozens. Attilio Bowinkel was paying him the honor of putting his framed watercolors in the window of his store, and in December 1943 he was given a show at the American Gallery of Contemporary Art on Hollywood Boulevard. To fill out the exhibit, Miller called in watercolors from his friends across the country, eventually rounding up some sixty paintings. A little publicity helped; before the show even opened Miller had sold six watercolors at $50 each, which struck him as an incredible figure. Watercolors seemed to make money more easily and reliably than writing.

In fact, the bulk of Miller's income in 1942 and 1943 came from another activity: begging. When he saw the results of his fund-raising campaign in December 1942, he sat down and wrote another "Open Letter to All and Sundry" on March 14, 1943. Through Ben Abramson, he mimeographed it and sent out over a hundred copies. For good measure, he sent off copies to various periodicals, with little hope that it might be published.

But the editors of the *New Republic*—where Miller had a Greek friend on the staff—were enough impressed by the letter to publish a fragment of it in their November 8 issue. The fragment contained the essential information: that Henry Miller was offering his watercolors in exchange for a sum to be named by the buyer, and that anyone wishing to encourage "the water-color mania" might send him paper, brushes, and paints, as well as old clothes. He provided his measurements: he was 5 feet 8 inches tall, weighed 150 pounds, wore a $15\frac{1}{2}$ neck, 38 chest, 32 waist, hat and shoes both 7 to $7\frac{1}{2}$. "Love corduroys," he added.

The results were gratifying. Donations poured in. A few respondents were unsympathetic—one man suggested he might think about working for a living, and others found his specification about corduroys pretentious. But many readers were touched by what they saw as the modesty of his request. Miller followed it up with yet another "Open Letter," which appeared in the *New Republic*'s December 6 issue. *Time* magazine picked up the story and ran an article on December 13, which brought Miller even more attention. He had so many requests for watercolors that he had little time to write. He wrote a New York friend that he greatly preferred making watercolors—or "w.c.'s," as he took to calling them—to writing reviews; it was much more stimulating for his real writing.

Little enough real writing was getting done, however. Miller was more than content to sit around the green house with Dudley, surrounded by his photos of Krishnamurti, Keyserling, the Duse, Nin, and Rimbaud. Over the kitchen door Dudley had written, in colorful chalk, "when I hear the word Culture, I reach for my revolver," Goebbels's sentiment, which Miller often quoted approvingly. What he missed most, he wrote Abe Rattner, was a woman. He wanted a "female thing" around, he said—perhaps a "peasant." Someone to cook, to talk to, to look at. Maybe he was paying for some past crimes, he speculated, or maybe, at fifty-three, he was just too old. But it was a lack nonetheless.

12.

"Little Henry, Big Sur"

1944–1949

In 1944 Miller was working feverishly—but not on his writing. Two California friends, George Barrows and Norman Holve, had committed themselves to produce a substantial work by Miller, a limited-edition, oversized book called *The Angel Is My Watermark*. The book—which cost $30 per copy for materials alone—included a brief holographic essay about painting, Miller's "Open Letter," photographs of "the artist at work," and an original watercolor by Miller. Barrows and Holve sent out a circular in Miller's hand advertising the book for $50. The copies were to be made up individually only as orders came in; Miller expected that they would receive more than a hundred.

James Laughlin bought the first copy and Dartmouth professor Herbert West the second. But then orders slowed to a trickle, and only fifteen or sixteen books were eventually produced. (In recent years, *The Angel Is My Watermark* has become the rarest of Miller's works.) Miller and his two young publishers had little to lose, of course, since each copy was, loosely speaking, produced on commission. *The Angel Is My Watermark*, for that matter, was only loosely speaking a book. It was a typical Henry Miller product, a ready-made collector's item that would not exist at all unless paid for in advance. It was the kind of venture that would draw Miller again and again in the years to come. The limited edition, the recycled text, the obscure publishing imprint: these devices are characteristic of Miller's later writing. They assured his collectibility at the same time as they limited his readership.

Miller didn't see it that way, of course. He was genuinely interested in the idea of combining art and writing. His painting had improved, and he had developed a characteristic style. His primitive, gaily colored watercolors were appealing and instantly recognizable. While he never really learned how to draw, he often achieved good effects with black ink and a watercolor wash. Favorite subjects were sailboats, the sun and moon, animals, and clowns; he produced some fine self-portraits. He also loved beautiful books, and commonly gave his publishers lectures on jacket and cover art. *The Angel Is My Watermark* was the first of many such limited editions featuring Miller's watercolors.

In 1944 Miller was also finding a variety of opportunities to publish. He had been corresponding with George Leite, a Berkeley writer who drove a taxi and was just beginning publication of *Circle*, a literary magazine that was, for the time being, run off on a mimeograph machine. When he received a letter from Leite soliciting a manuscript, Miller answered with a long diatribe about the injustice of publishing writers without paying them fairly; Leite published the letter in his first issue as "An Open Letter to Small Magazines."

Another person eager to publish Miller was a young nuclear physicist named Bern Porter, who was then in Berkeley doing some government work related to the Manhattan Project. (He would quit his job as a personal protest after the dropping of the atomic bomb.) Porter had learned about Miller's work while visiting Paris in the late thirties and had obtained copies of the Paris books from Ben Abramson in Chicago. An avid amateur publisher who himself produced highly original art books composed of found materials like magazine ads and instruction manuals, Porter was captivated by the fragmented, surrealistic quality of the *Tropics*—not to mention their sexual frankness. He had sought Miller out in Beverly Glen when he had first come out to California, intending to assemble a complete Henry Miller bibliography. He also said he would publish anything Miller would give him. Laughlin, of course, had first option legally on Miller's books, but Miller had a backlog of shorter works that Laughlin had shied away from and that Miller was eager to see in print.

Both Leite and Porter lived in the San Francisco Bay area, and Miller began to think of relocating further up the California coast. Other friends in that area included Jean Varda and his wife, Virginia; Varda was a versatile sculptor who worked in many mediums, including what are today called "found objects," or junk. In February 1944 Miller traveled up the Coast to visit Varda at his red barn on Hawthorne Street in New Monterey, a celebrated gathering spot for area bohemians. He stayed for several weeks, making frequent trips to the Bay Area to see Leite, who showed him around Berkeley.

One rainy day Varda brought Miller to meet Lynda Sargent, a

young woman who lived in Big Sur, a tiny community perched among the ridges south of Monterey. Miller had been bowled over by the Big Sur country on his last visit in 1941: it was remote, forbidding terrain, with the Santa Lucia Mountains sheering steeply down to the rocky coastline. Route 1, carved into the mountainside partway up, was the only access; the fifty-odd Big Sur residents were dependent on Jake Hodges, the mailman, for delivering food, medicine, and other supplies three times a week. Few homes had plumbing, electricity, or telephones, and most were simply shacks. Sargent's log cabin was set on a cliff just off Route 1. If it was more accessible than most Big Sur homes, it was no less dramatic: the ocean broke fiercely on the cliffs far below.

Sargent was a transplanted New Englander who was writing a novel and contributed columns to a newspaper in nearby Carmel. Her cabin had a small room used by a servant, but she had no servant at the time, so she offered the room to Miller for as long as he liked. He decided to stay. "I have much work to finish and am seeking peace and isolation," he wrote Nin in March. The situation looked good: he liked Lynda well enough, although she was in her forties and not his physical type, he said. He even liked his address, as he told a Hollywood friend—"little Henry, Big Sur."

Miller's decision was a revealing one. He could have picked any place in the country to settle—for a man his age, he was remarkably unencumbered—and yet he picked one of the most isolated spots possible, an unlikely choice indeed for a man who liked to think of himself as affable and gregarious. In fact, it seems to have been a choice born of Miller's growing inability to function in "regular" society, the culmination of his despair of finding a place for himself in wartime America. For if he was without encumbrances, he was also without resources. His struggle to make a living in the years since his return to America had exhausted him, and he welcomed the opportunity to heal in the near-complete isolation of Big Sur. Moreover, the choice represented his rejection of traditional American society; his decision to live there was the closest he would come to making a political statement.

He stayed in Sargent's log house and then in an outbuilding on the grounds in March and April; in May he rented a cabin from Keith Evans, an ex-mayor of Carmel who was then in the armed services. The rent was $10 a month, but Evans was so grateful to have the cabin occupied that he made the rent optional. Soon Miller found that simply performing general chores in such a rugged spot consumed almost five hours a day; he had to chop wood, clear brush, and lug his groceries and mail up the long road from Route 1. But he felt healthier than ever, he wrote friends. He described for Durrell how he opened the door in the morning, looked out over the Pacific, and turned to the East to watch the sun rising over the mountains with a glad heart. The mountainsides were covered with purple lupine and were often shrouded in great fogs.

Slowly, Miller was accepted by the Big Sur residents. Above him, higher up in the mountains, lived the eccentric Jaime d'Angulo, a long-time resident and amateur anthropologist who often ran through the canyons naked. The writer Lillian Bos Ross, whose book *The Stranger* was about Big Sur, lived nearby with her husband; they called themselves Shanagolden and Harrydick. Jean Wharton, a former Christian Scientist and distant relative of James Laughlin, was also a neighbor; she reminded him of Frances Steloff because of her penchant for New Thought. Another neighbor was Ephraim Doner in Carmel Highlands, an artist and, like Miller, a great conversationalist.

At first, Big Sur seemed a perfect refuge from the world. With time, however, it came to seem like the promised land. Miller wrote to Emil White, an Austrian-born book dealer whom he had met in Chicago two years before, asking him to join him. White had been in the Yukon, where he had gone to evade the draft; he had then gone down to Los Angeles to join Miller, unaware that Miller had moved, and now answered Miller's summons without hesitation. A painter and writer who had admired Miller's work before they had met, White was a true disciple. He settled into a cabin near Miller's and proceeded to make himself indispensable in his life, answering his mail, helping with the chores, cooking meals, and generally providing companionship. It was Emil, for example, who dealt with any banking; Miller had an irrational hatred of banks and would enter them only when absolutely necessary. He preferred to keep his money in cash, and tended to cash checks at a liquor store in Monterey.

Shortly after settling in, Miller wrote Durrell: "Yes, there we are, Larry me lad. A long way from the Villa Seurat days." But he had in fact created another congenial community in Big Sur. He was surrounded by the kind of companions he liked best: people who cared little for convention and loved to talk far into the night; in Emil White, he even had a sidekick comparable to Perlès. He discovered that California wine was good (and cheap) and that California women were easygoing. On many evenings he and Emil and a visitor such as Bern Porter, the Berkeley physicist, summoned Lynda Sargent and a female friend of hers to the cabin to dance for them in their underwear, while Porter stripped down to a University of California jockstrap. Often after dinner, over the sound of Louis Armstrong on the phonograph, Miller would hold forth in his characteristically low, resonant, very Brooklyn voice, punctuating his words with long "hmm's" and "don't cha know's." He had mellowed in his new surroundings.

But as he had said himself, what Miller lacked most keenly was a woman. Now over fifty, and on distant terms with Nin, he felt the lack of female companionship even more insistently in his new isolation. Because of the elemental nature of life in Big Sur and the survivalist imagination it demanded, male area residents saw women as another vital commodity, like food or shelter. In April, Miller wrote to the *Saturday Review of Literature* asking if he could place a personal ad for a female secretary, offering bed and board as pay and specifying that Chinese, Mexican, Greek, or French applicants were preferred. Then he had some second thoughts, worrying that the magazine would find his ad too explicit. (No such ad appears in the 1944 issues, though Ben Abramson, Miller's Chicago bookseller friend, advertised in the May 20 issue for stenographers.) By May he abandoned the idea of advertising, for he had begun a torrid romance-by-mail with June Lancaster, an attractive dancer in her early thirties.

Miller had found this second June with the help of Harry Hershkowitz, a merchant marine seaman with aspirations to write, whom he had met in Beverly Glen in 1943. Hershkowitz had moved to New York, where he eventually spent much of the winter and spring of 1944 recruiting women to join Miller in Big Sur and, along the way, making some conquests himself. He and Miller exchanged lengthy letters evaluating female qualities, with Miller suggesting possible "lays" for Harry. They discussed strategies to bring Miller money as well. Miller dissuaded Hershkowitz from hitting up Charlie Chaplin for funds (although he listed other movie stars who were fans of his in the same letter) and urged Hershkowitz to visit the writer Kenneth Patchen, who was financially strapped, and initiate him into the subtleties of begging. Following an earlier pattern, Miller also dispatched Hershkowitz to find his daughter Barbara, but urged him to avoid her mother, Beatrice, to whom he still owed back alimony. And, as long as Hershkowitz was looking, Miller suggested, he might as well look up June Mansfield. But Hershkowitz passed on the news that Janice Pelham, a mutual friend, had already encountered June and found her pathetic—old-looking, ugly, and horribly dressed.

There were certainly enough drawbacks to Big Sur to deter any woman from joining Miller there. His cabin had no plumbing, electricity, heat, or hot water, and for the time being he had no car. Though Big Sur was an extraordinarily beautiful spot, it was not everyone's idea of paradise. Winters were especially difficult, when fogs and rains shrouded the mountains. Emil White foresaw the same difficulty; he too was engaged in the pursuit of a mail-order bride, Marjorie Lehman.

Miller now became preoccupied with how he could decide on any of the women proposed to him without photos of them. It was also difficult to tell through correspondence, he worried, whether they would get along. He hounded Hershkowitz for more details.

Hershkowitz concentrated his efforts on getting June Lancaster to join Miller in Big Sur. In her first letter to Miller, written February 15, 1944, June agreed to call him Val as his second wife June had done. But despite her seeming receptiveness, both he and Hershkowitz had doubts about her. She confided to Hershkowitz that she had been married, news that he passed on dutifully to Miller; he also said that he feared June was not domestic. Then Miller worried that at thirty-three, she was too old. June had her share of doubts as well. She told Hershkowitz she feared Miller was some kind of Svengali of sex who would make her give up her plans for a dancing career.

Despite his doubts, Miller was persistent. He saw June Lancaster as a sort of double for the other June, and he begged Hershkowitz to plead his case, asserting that he was totally in love. Instead Hershkowitz bedded June himself, and then reported to Miller that she had smallish breasts but a firm, attractive body; to soften the blow, he wrote that throughout the act he had urged her to go out to Miller in California. But Miller wrote Harry that he didn't care if Harry seduced his daughter Barbara if he found her. Hershkowitz must have garbled this remark, because he soon after reported that June was upset to learn that Miller wanted to seduce his own daughter.

Before long, though, June had nicknamed Miller "Bliss" and was drawing snails, flowers, and clouds around his name in her letters to him. She sent him a nude photo of herself, which he propped on the ledge of his fireplace next to other photos his female correspondents sent him. By May 8, June had made up her mind to join him.

In a flourish of ceremony, Jean Varda picked up June in San Francisco and brought her back to the Vardas' barn, where he and Virginia dressed her in a dramatic circus costume and decorated the barn with flowers. When Miller, Lynda Sargent, and Emil White arrived, they met June, standing on a barrel, posed with her arms above her head, ready to serve. Miller stared—she was beautiful, with long black hair—and then fell at her feet. She came down from the barrel and the two embraced.

A party followed, after which the couple returned to Miller's shack on Partington Ridge. There the mail-order romance quickly fizzled out. June was beautiful, and she shared his second wife's name, but she had none of June Mansfield's ability to captivate him. While she seemed to be the purely sexual being that Miller had thought he wanted, she bored him otherwise. Moreover, she couldn't cook or help with the housework; she simply didn't know how. During the day, when Henry wanted to write, she was underfoot. She often slipped away into the woods to practice dance steps at a barre Emil White set up for her. Finally, one day she simply disappeared.

Though he lamented the loss in several letters to friends, Miller seemed barely to notice. He had surrounded himself with activity, just as he had in the Villa Seurat. Bern Porter supplied him with new stationery, which featured Bern's drawing of a nude alongside a list of Miller's book titles. Miller began to work on new schemes. What he needed was a patron to support him while he wrote, he decided. He had discovered that he couldn't do without money even in a place as spartan as Big Sur, and few neighbors could afford a handout.

In March, Miller composed another Open Letter, this one addressed to about twenty well-placed friends. He was looking for someone, he said, who would give him $50 a week for fifty weeks, and was contemplating placing an ad in literary magazines to that effect. Since he had returned to America, he wrote, he had made a yearly income of only $300 to $400—with the exception of 1943, when watercolors had brought him $1,400. He owed nearly $24,000, he estimated (the bulk of it presumably in back alimony and child support). He had seventeen books or pamphlets—mostly of work he had done in France—coming out in 1944, which made him a good risk, he added. He was proposing that his agents, Russell & Volkening, would turn over his royalties as repayment; for good measure, he offered to repay $5,000 for the $2,500 he hoped to borrow. All he wanted, he said, was the time to finish *The Rosy Crucifixion* and a manuscript that he considered to be the second volume of *The Air-Conditioned Nightmare.*

Copies of the letter went out to Ben Abramson, Caresse Crosby, Huntington Cairns, James Laughlin, Melpo Niarchos, and Frances Steloff, among others. None of them stepped forward to be his patron, though a few sent money; Cairns wrote that he knew of several people who might be interested. Then Russell & Volkening reported that someone had appeared at their offices volunteering to meet Miller's terms. The man gave his name as Harry Kogh Vare—obviously a joke, a pun on *haricots verts*, the French term for green beans—and had said only that he was a painter living in California, that he was himself poor, and that he would be obliged to borrow the money to lend Miller. All the same, "Vare" came up with an initial monthly payment of $200, and said that Miller could pay it back whenever and however he liked.

When he did have money, Miller often gave it all away. Characteristically, he arranged to give half of his anticipated monthly stipends of $200 to Anaïs Nin, and to split the remaining $100 with Harry Hershkowitz, who, Miller now claimed, had been sending him $3 a week for months. Nin was angry at him for throwing away his windfall; she had seen him do the same too often. She also felt he equated Hershkowitz's writing with hers, and the insult stung. She misunderstood Miller's generosity, which was based on far more unconventional views of charity than her own. He believed that if a person had money he or she should help a friend, expecting nothing in return; she could not comprehend the idea of giving financial aid with no strings attached.

It hardly mattered, however, for Harry Kogh Vare disappeared after three months, perhaps because he learned how Miller was using his monthly stipends. Miller had foreseen that his good fortune would not last, and he had written to Huntington Cairns on May 5 seeking another patron. Even $50 a week was not sufficient for him to live on, he explained. The letter was a bitter one. He complained about the stinginess of his friends, citing as exceptions his new ones, Bern Porter, Emil White, and George Leite: White even gave readings of Miller's works and then passed the hat for the author, Miller wrote reproachfully. If Cairns should find a patron, he continued, then he must instruct the person that any money must be given without conditions—*as a gift*. The man who had always given away whatever money he had with so little thought could not understand why his readers should be so reluctant to give to him.

No patron materialized, however, and 1944 proved to be a very lean year for Miller financially. This in spite of the fact that many of his books were now in print: New Directions brought out the collection *Sunday After the War*, which included outtakes from *The Air-Conditioned Nightmare* and fragments from *The Rosy Crucifixion* as well as essays on Nin and Lawrence. It also contains a fine account of his reunion with his family in Brooklyn in 1940 that reveals the compassion he felt for his father and his disgust with himself for his inability to help materially in some way. Bern Porter brought out a collection of the "open letters" under the title *The Plight of the Creative Artist in the United States of America*. Porter also published *Murder the Murderer*, an anti-war polemic that originated as a letter to Perlès, who had enlisted in the British Army. It was published at considerable risk to Porter, whose government job made it highly embarrassing for him to be associated with a pacifist tract in wartime. Porter was also preparing *Semblance of a Devoted Past*, a collection of Miller's letters to Emil Schnellock about watercolors, and *Echolalia*, a volume of Miller's watercolors.

Porter supported his publishing venture by means of a kind of pyramid scheme, in which authors agreed to plow any profit back into financing other Bern Porter books. Miller quickly grew impatient with that arrangement, and turned increasingly to other small publishers like George Leite and Judson Crews of Waco, Texas. To the latter, he wrote a long letter on May 19 (carbons of which he sent to his "short list" of friends and potential patrons) outlining the titles he wished to have printed, most of which had already been printed in one form or another. He acknowledged that Laughlin had the legal option on his writings, and that he considered Porter to hold a "moral and ethical" right to his work, but he offered the titles nevertheless.

Porter was also assembling a collection of essays written about Miller by friends and critics that he would title *The Happy Rock*, after a phrase Miller used in *Tropic of Capricorn* to describe himself (he often told friends it was Durrell's nickname for him). Porter convinced Durrell to contribute an essay; others, like George Leite and Richard Osborn, his friend from Paris, needed no convincing, and the result was a collection of adoring essays and memoirs. Durrell was absolutely dismayed by the book. He felt that between the isolation of Big Sur and the nickel-and-dime moneymaking schemes, Miller was losing his drive to write, and that he deserved stiff criticism rather than encomiums. Durrell wasn't the only one who thought so. Kenneth Patchen, when asked to contribute to *The Happy Rock*, wrote Miller a postcard calling the other contributors "so many sloppy-eyed nobodies" and exclaiming, "For God's sake, Miller, the important thing is not to be liked by these people!"

But Patchen's admonition and Durrell's disapproval had no effect. And both overlooked the possibility that Miller simply had no choice. He was constitutionally unable to cultivate important literary figures,

as his experience with Steinbeck had proven. As a writer whose important works were all banned in his own country, he found himself so
thoroughly excluded from the publishing world and the literary scene
that he took his admirers wherever he could get them. And in the mid-
forties he gradually collected about him what may have been the
strangest group of patrons, admirers, and occasional publishers ever
to be associated with a major American author. What they had in
common was that they were people he believed could do something for
him. If they had no money—like Walker Winslow, a young writer he
made friends with in these years—they could type manuscripts, orga-
nize letter campaigns on his behalf, or look for potential patrons.
Friends came into his circle and fell from favor with astonishing rapid-
ity. Harry Hershkowitz, for instance, Miller would simply drop cold
after he outlived his usefulness, and Miller and Bern Porter would part
in 1945 over disagreements about finances, with Miller complaining of
Porter's "betrayal." There was, however, a core of friends to whom
Miller was unswervingly loyal, Emil White among them. Outwardly
they were his protectors, but often they basked in the glow of his
growing celebrity, enjoying his cast-off women, cadging financial gifts,
and prompting Miller to make appeals on their behalf. Many collected
his works assiduously, but they also sold them for the first good offer.
Ironically, the man who valued male friendship almost above all else
found himself increasingly surrounded by men whose motivations were
self-serving.

In September 1944, Miller received dismaying news: his mother had
cancer. She was scheduled for an operation in October, and on the 6th
he left for New York City. When he arrived, he found that her condition was less serious than he had thought, and he wrote friends that it
looked as if she would live for decades. Since his father's death he had
maintained an uneasy truce with Louise. He sent her fruit from California and had asked her for linens when he moved into his cabin in
Big Sur. But he was still deeply conflicted about her. Louise's illness
revived those mixed feelings and also reawakened his sense of responsibility for his sister Lauretta, who would be his charge after his mother's death.

Miller took Louise's improved condition as an opportunity to tour
the East, visiting friends. But he was afraid to visit Nin, as her recent
letters had been chillingly distant; instead, he wrote her a note. He

looked up some of the women Hershkowitz had picked out for him and tried to set something up with Marjorie Lehman for Emil White. He was determined, he wrote Emil, to find two or three women he could "corral" into returning to Big Sur for the winter.

In New York, Hershkowitz, who had not yet fallen from grace, introduced Miller to a young Polish-American woman and her sister. Janina Martha Lepska was twenty and had graduated from Bryn Mawr; now she had enrolled at Yale to study philosophy. They talked about Bryn Mawr philosophy professor Paul Weiss, who was a mutual friend, and Miller told her about his books and his life in Big Sur. (Hershkowitz, of course, had already filled her in on Miller's background.) She thought him too old, Miller feared, and he saw little hope of anything sparking between them.

On November 7 Miller traveled to New Haven, where Wallace Fowlie, a Yale professor whose specialty was French literature, had arranged a watercolor show for him. There he saw Lepska again—for so she liked to be called—and this time he believed that she was interested in him. Certainly he found her attractive. Lepska was blond and delicate, with nearly perfect features. She looked girlish, but her nature was resilient—Miller believed she was just the sort to take to life in Big Sur. Moreover, she had a quickness of mind that appealed to Miller; after his experience with June Lancaster, he was interested in women who had good minds as well as good bodies. She was something like Anaïs Nin, he thought, but without Nin's changefulness. Before long, he invited her to go to California with him and she promised to think about it. At fifty-three, Miller was still, in his idiosyncratic way, a handsome man; he came across in conversation as warm, gentle, and good-humored. His reputation as the author of banned books made him seem sexy—at least to some women—and the picture he painted of life at Big Sur was a romantic one.

From New Haven, Miller left for Dartmouth, where his collector-friend Herbert West had arranged a lecture for him. He hated to lecture, but he agreed to speak to a small group of students, many of them returned soldiers and sailors. The result was a brief but disturbing brush with the ideological paranoia of wartime. One man, for example, repeatedly asked Miller obnoxious questions about his patriotism and his military background. The whole experience was ominous, and Miller was not surprised when a friend passed on to him an attack called "Odyssey of a Stool Pigeon"; it appeared in *New Currents: A Jewish Monthly*, as the journal's monthly column on "The Enemy

Within." The author, Albert E. Kahn, was the heckler at Dartmouth, and in the article he claimed that Miller had collaborated with Fascists in his Paris days. Noting Miller's stint as an employment manager, Kahn also branded him as a "labor spy." The charges were groundless, of course, but the article shook Miller. After it appeared, West was visited by the FBI. While Miller's less-than-patriotic attitude toward the United States was well known, the experience unnerved him. It was an indication of the level of feeling he evoked: people either loved or hated him, and when they hated him, they could be vicious.

While he was at Dartmouth he received a barrage of notes from Lepska, all declaring her love. He stopped in New Haven to pick her up and took her with him on a trip to Washington, where he visited his old friends Caresse Crosby and Huntington Cairns. There he went daily to the Library of Congress, where Cairns had arranged for him to record readings from *Black Spring* and *Tropic of Capricorn*—unobjectionable passages only, of course, the irony of which was not lost on Miller. From there he and Lepska traveled to Fredericksburg, where they visited Emil Schnellock. While there, Lepska agreed to marry Miller. Various obstacles prevented them from legalizing their union, however, until December 18 in Boulder, Colorado, where they stayed with Miller's old Hollywood friends, Gilbert and Margaret Nieman.

In Miller's letters to Durrell, Emil White, Herbert West, and others, he referred to Lepska as "the little Polish girl." Indeed, she was much younger than his own daughter, and on the train ride West the bride—with her unlikely-looking husband—was ogled by scores of leering servicemen. But she was tough and had considerable inner resources. And, somewhat to Miller's surprise, she loved Big Sur. Before long she had befriended all the locals and brought order to the Partington Ridge cabin. They began to speak of having a baby. By May 1945 Lepska was pregnant, and the couple was elated.

The marriage stabilized Miller, directing his attention away from raising funds and back to his work. *The Rosy Crucifixion* still gathered dust, but he had begun a new project: a study of Rimbaud. The French poet had fascinated him ever since the days of the Henry Street menage, when Jean Kronski had quoted him constantly. During his stay at the green house in Beverly Glen, Miller read Enid Starkie's account of Rimbaud's life and was struck by the numerous parallels with his own. Like Rimbaud, he had lived through his "season in hell" in his years with June; like Rimbaud, he felt he belonged nowhere. Even their mothers were alike: critical, Puritanical, unloving.

The study of Rimbaud that occupied him in 1945 threatened to become another autobiographical exercise. But delineating features of Rimbaud's personality and comparing each to his own, Miller gained some insights into his own psyche. Looking back at his past, he decided that his "golden period" had been during the writing of *Black Spring*, when he found some peace in accepting the idea that all men wanted to climb back in the womb. Nevertheless, he understood that his revolt against his mother, no matter how fruitless, had been essential, just as it had been for Rimbaud.

Other conclusions he drew were far more suspect. He believed that he and Rimbaud were powerfully connected because he had been born in the year Rimbaud died, and that he was Rimbaud's natural successor, his spiritual brother. Miller also hints portentously at his own martyrdom and his possible sanctity. The Rimbaud study—which New Directions would publish in 1946 as *The Time of the Assassins*—was an attempt to draw up a mystical aesthetic, to invent a spiritual blueprint by which connections between art and life can be understood. It represented Miller's increasing attraction to mysticism and his growing sense of himself as a kind of literary savior. His books had been banned, he felt, because of their frank expression of human functions and needs; so, he reasoned—with rather difficult logic—that in the punishment inflicted on him by the banning of his books, he was suffering for the sins of humanity.

He was at work that year on *Remember to Remember*, a less ambitious book that he always insisted was a second volume of *The Air-Conditioned Nightmare*. Actually it is a hodgepodge of fugitive pieces dating back five years and more. Into it he tossed some essays that he had written for George Leite's magazine *Circle*, including one on Jean Varda; he also included an expanded but less effective version of his anti-war essay, *Murder the Murderer*, and an article on Beauford Delaney, a black artist and friend, which had appeared in London's *Now*, New York's *Tricolor*, and as an Outcast Chapbook put out by Oscar Baradinsky's Alicat Press. Almost everything in the book was similarly recycled. One exception, "The Staff of Life," stands out among his short pieces. It is a brilliant extended meditation on the quality of American bread. He provides a recipe for the American staff of life:

> To begin with, accept any loaf that is offered you without question, even if it is not wrapped in cellophane, even if it contains no kelp. Throw it in the back of the car with the oil

can and the grease rags; if possible, bury it under a sack of coal, *bituminous* coal. . . . When you get to the house . . . take a huge carving knife and rip the loaf from stem to stern. Then take one whole onion, peeled or unpeeled, one carrot, one stalk of celery, a huge piece of garlic, one sliced apple, a herring, a handful of anchovies, a sprig of parsley, and an old toothbrush and shove them in the disemboweled guts of the bread. . . . Put the loaf in the oven for ten minutes and serve.

But the piece is not only about American bread. It is an attack on American eating habits and, by extension, the American way of life. Because the focus is kept rather narrowly on food, "The Staff of Life" is one of Miller's finest social commentaries.

In the summer of 1945, Miller asked Emil White to handle his correspondence for $5 a week; this request merely formalized their existing arrangement. White's first duty was to mail out a form letter stating that he now handled all Miller correspondence. Each day, he was to open every envelope on the offchance there was cash or a check inside. Routine matters like bills and editors' queries were to be dispatched straightforwardly. But soon it developed that there was no such thing as a routine matter—Miller wanted to be informed about every transaction, every request, every fan letter. Moreover, because of the unorthodox way he did business, there was no distinction between Miller's personal and business correspondence.

Just as he had carried a notebook with lists of creditors in his Brooklyn days, so now did he tack above his worktable a chart listing debts owed. The only difference was that now, as often as not, he repaid debts with what he called "scripts," with books, with holograph letters or inscriptions. Often the results of his begging were comical: one "open letter" that he asked Frances Steloff to post on the bulletin board at the Gotham Book Mart requesting a thermos bottle that could keep his coffee warm while he wrote brought in an ocean of thermos bottles that cluttered up the cabin for years.

His financial plight was now as dire as it had ever been, so severe that when Lepska announced her pregnancy in the spring, he doubted that he could support the child. The only certain income was $50 a month from James Laughlin at New Directions; Laughlin had hit upon the payment system as a way to check any improvidence on Miller's part, which Miller greatly resented. In truth, his books were barely earning even that amount, although most of his books had gone into second printings. Royalties from his other publishers were practically nil.

There was one important exception: his Paris publisher. After the liberation of Paris the previous year, Maurice Girodias, Jack Kahane's son, had resumed publication of the old Obelisk titles with his own new publishing firm, Les Editions du Chêne. *Tropic of Cancer* sold steadily during the war, when American GIs bought copies and smuggled them home in huge numbers. In the fall of 1945 Girodias wrote Miller that he intended to bring out reprints of the Paris books and pay him royalties of 410,000 francs. Miller quickly converted francs to dollars and realized that over $8,000 would be due him. But when he reread the letter he found that postwar regulations made it almost impossible to take large amounts of money out of France. Only if he moved to France or found some means of converting his francs to dollars could he collect any of the income.

Durrell and Perlès urged Miller to invest these proceeds in property in France, and for a time he considered it. He hesitated too long, however, for the franc was being devalued at an alarming rate. In January 1946 its value dropped a third, and, with intervening devaluations, the royalties owed him were suddenly worth closer to $3,500. He thought he might solve the problem by getting a French agent, so he dropped Russell & Volkening and his British agent, Patience Ross, and signed up with Agence Hoffman in Paris. What kept the French nest egg from disappearing altogether, however, was the reappearance of a large French reading public for the Paris books. Girodias had reprinted the *Tropics*, *Black Spring*, and *Max and the White Phagocytes*, and editions were selling out quickly.

Sales received a further boost in March 1946, when a minor scandal—*l'affaire Miller*—engaged the attention of the French literary community. Daniel Parker, a French citizen, registered a complaint against Editions du Chêne and Editions Donoël (the latter had acquired the rights to *Tropic of Cancer* from the struggling Maurice Girodias) for pornography, citing a 1939 anti-pornography law and claiming that Miller was a psychopath in need of medical treatment. The committee that decided the case ruled against Miller, and moved to suppress the *Tropics* and *Black Spring*. Almost immediately French writers mobilized, forming a committee in defense of Miller that included André Breton, Albert Camus, André Gide, and Jean-Paul Sartre, among others. The issue outraged and electrified the French intellectual community. Their response so encouraged Maurice Girodias that, with the

Société des Gens de Lettres, he brought suit against Parker for libel. Parker backed off and the furor abated, but *l'affaire Miller* had made Henry Miller a household name in France. Sales of his books soared. By the summer of 1947, he had 4,470,000 francs in his French account; even with devaluation, this amounted to almost $37,000.

Miller devised all sorts of stratagems to get his money out of France. He wrote Durrell that he thought of commissioning Man Ray to buy up Picassos and Braques with the funds and bring them over to be sold. He even enlisted Nin's husband, Hugo Guiler, who he hoped could transfer money through the National City Bank. Around the same time, he wrote a letter to Osbert Sitwell, asking him if he could bring his case before British royalty, though he did not say what good he thought that might do. Another idea that didn't quite work was for friends who were traveling to France to pay him dollars and then collect francs from Girodias. Michel Hoffman, Miller's new Paris agent, actually succeeded in getting a little more than $7,500 out in 1946, and Miller's old Paris friend Frank Dobo pulled some strings from New York that brought over further substantial sums; but three years were to pass before a workable means of moving the money appeared. Finally, in the summer of 1948, Girodias was authorized to pay $500 to Miller every month.

This outcome was still unforeseeable on October 19, 1945, when Lepska delivered a daughter, a 6 lb. 4 oz. girl whom she and Miller christened Valentin Lepska, after Miller's grandfather and Lepska's father, who shared a first name. Miller announced the baby with beaming pride in his letters to friends; he was smitten with her, just as he had been with Barbara twenty-seven years before. Valentin—soon nicknamed Val—gave absolutely no trouble, Miller told several friends. She's "a real back-to-the-womber," Miller wrote Durrell, meaning that she seemed blissfully contented. He admitted that he spoiled her completely.

Henry remembered with horror his mother's Puritanical strictness, which had left him with the conviction that children should be allowed to develop at their own pace. Now disciplining the child became a sore spot between him and Lepska. He thought discipline was so pernicious that he would have let the child run wild, had Lepska allowed it. But she most emphatically did not, and some of their worst quarrels flared up around the issue. Beneath Lepska's sturdy good humor was a firm sense of discipline; she believed in order, schedules, and rules. Miller was orderly in his own habits, but he disliked this quality in others and hated it in the abstract. While Henry and Lepska both tried to make the marriage work, the arrival of Valentin threatened to tear apart the entire fabric of their relationship.

This shaky domestic equilibrium was further threatened by an influx of well-meaning visitors, for by the mid-forties Miller was beginning to attract a cult following. These fans were further titillated by talk about the bohemian lives of the Big Sur colonists—whose aspirations to sexual liberation, as propounded by the then-notorious Wilhelm Reich in *The Function of the Orgasm*, seemed deeply exotic. Miller's Partington Ridge cabin was just a couple of miles away from the sulfur springs that would later become the home of the Esalen Institute; already a group of freethinking young pioneers had set up a colony there, reading the works of Reich, Miller, and other proponents of sexual freedom. Some of Miller's new admirers associated him only with his banned books without having read any of the many books of his that were in print. When George Leite or Bern Porter came down from Berkeley, for example, they often brought along a horde of curious Berkeley students, eager to meet the controversial "sex writer." Matters only got worse when an article by Millicent Edie Brady appeared in *Harper's Bazaar* titled "The New Cult of Sex and Anarchy," a sensationalized account of the goings-on in the colony of artists and writers at Big Sur. She confided archly that Miller's admirers read *Murder the Murderer* and *The Air-Conditioned Nightmare* for their "mysticism, egoism, sexualism, and surrealism."

In truth, *The Cosmological Eye, Wisdom of the Heart,* and other Miller titles available in the forties had more to say about spirituality and astrology, and despite their low sales figures these books were also finding an audience of their own. The people who did read Miller seriously found him deeply religious—though hardly in a conventional sense—and few of those who sought him out were disappointed when they met the author. He kept an audience of visitors rapt while he held forth on such subjects as modern art, world peace, or relations between the sexes. His visitors might examine his paintings or stay for dinner— usually a casserole served by Lepska with the help of female visitors, who otherwise stood in the sidelines. (Meat was seldom served, although when a deer was killed on Route 1, the colonists would stage a feast.)

Much later, Miller's old Paris friend Walter Lowenfels commented on the unique quality of his fans. He wrote Miller that he inspired a reverence in his readers in a way no other author did—not Hemingway, not Fitzgerald, and not T. S. Eliot. The only comparable figure, he noted, had been Walt Whitman. Women crossed the ocean to marry Whitman, and he attracted male followers from the ranks of soldiers, farmers, carpenters, and the like. Miller's devoted admirers saw in him a man who had dropped out of society, taken a young wife, and lived on a mountaintop preaching the virtues of sexual liberation and spiritual fulfillment. Details like his trekking to Slade's Hot Springs to wash the baby's diapers confirmed their sense of his humility, a quality they elevated to the level of saintliness. Many were encouraged by his example to cast off conventional jobs and to take up writing, a course their exemplar explicitly recommended. Even when Miller was curt or dismissive with them—as he often was—their loyalty was astounding.

Many of his fans were also extremely generous, keeping Miller in used clothes, painting supplies, and food. He devised a system to record their gifts: he wrote the name of each one on a 3 x 5 note card, together with notations indicating loans or gifts of money, other gifts, and books they purchased from him. Many ended abruptly, with scrawled notes by Miller reading "Drop him!" or "What a bore!"

However generous they were, the fans also made extraordinary demands on Miller's time. Women sought him out, asking to learn sexual secrets. Young men brought him their manuscripts to read and books of his to autograph. Several wrote asking for money, explaining that they were simply following his own example. Others asked to visit, usually for an indefinite period. The Millers were besieged with such requests.

Then, in the fall of 1947, Miller received an appeal for help from an unlikely source. June Mansfield wrote that Stratford Corbett had deserted her and that she was ill and destitute. She had ulcerated colitis, she explained, and her weight had dropped to 75 pounds. She was living in a rooming house on Clinton Avenue in Brooklyn. From her letters, Miller gathered that she had degenerated mentally; she seemed paranoid and incoherent. June wrote that he would be shocked if he knew her story, the "great injustices and criminal mistakes and cover-ups involved in the past." This at least sounded familiar. Miller dispatched a money order and got in touch with Irving Stettner, a friend in the East, who delivered $30 to June. But now that she had found him, June didn't intend to lose track of Henry again; she would write him off and on for the next decade, as she continued to deteriorate, winding up in a welfare hotel on New York's Upper West Side. Miller sent her small checks whenever she requested money and often arranged for medical care, but he usually left any communication to his wife. He told Frances Steloff and others about June's disintegration, but in truth he found it all hard to believe: June, who had always held her head high, was actually begging from him.

Another ghost surfaced in 1947—the astrologer Conrad Moricand, who wrote Miller that he was wiped out, absolutely penniless. As a displaced aristocrat and supporter of the Vichy government, Moricand had fled to Switzerland for safety after the war. Miller had corresponded faithfully with him in the years since he had left Paris, and he could not bear to hear of his old friend's suffering. He saw the astrologer as a kind of kindred soul; like himself, Moricand was an outcast, left behind by the modern world and without the means to maintain some shred of his old distinction. Miller associated Moricand with his own last magical months in Paris, with the mood of exultation amidst decay that colors *Tropic of Capricorn*. And Moricand's occultism and vaguely reactionary world view appealed to Miller as well. Before long he extended an extraordinary offer to Moricand, asking him to come to Big Sur and live there, to be taken care of by the Millers for the rest of his life. It was some months before this could be arranged. Miller had first to guarantee to the immigration authorities that Moricand would not become a ward of the state, and his Swiss landlady had to be paid the astrologer's back rent. But by Christmas of 1947 he had arrived at the Millers' house on Partington Ridge in Big Sur.

Almost at once it was clear that the arrangement was doomed. Miller had warned Moricand about the rugged life of Big Sur, but his old friend was unprepared for the total isolation of the area. He craved delicacies, asking for Yardley talcum powder and fancy writing paper; he wanted peanut oil substituted for the olive oil the Millers used. And he complained ceaselessly about the weather, the food, and his poor health. Because Moricand spoke only French, mealtimes were particularly uncomfortable. But the last straw was his attitude toward little Val. He was supposed to teach her French, but he loathed children and treated her accordingly. He shocked Miller with a story about having sex with an eight-year-old girl. When he casually said, *"Je l'ai eue"* ("I had her"), Miller was horrified.

In the meantime, Moricand had developed festering sores on his legs and begged Miller to find him some codeine. This was impossible, so Moricand wrote to Paris. When an envelope containing the illegal drug was delivered, Miller exploded. Moricand coolly responded that he was in such pain that he would gladly return to France, but he would first need a hotel room so that he could be treated by a doctor in Monterey. Miller installed him in a hotel and spoke with the French consul general in San Francisco, who arranged free passage to Europe for Moricand on a freighter. But Moricand declined to return by sea, and when the consul arranged an airplane flight, he failed to show up at the airport. After the consul had arranged yet another flight, Moricand demanded that Miller deposit $1,000 for him in a French bank. Miller flatly refused. Moricand then called the *San Francisco Chronicle* and described his dire mistreatment at the hands of the famous "dirty book author." Then he began a letter campaign, alternately insulting and beseeching Miller, who simply did not answer. By summer the stream of letters stopped, and Miller assumed that Moricand had somehow made his way back to Europe.

Miller began writing an account of this fantastic episode, which would appear as the "Paradise Lost" section of his 1955 book *Big Sur and the Oranges of Hieronymus Bosch*. He exploited the rather grim humor of the situation, portraying himself as a puzzled, good-hearted soul who was exasperated by a changeable and fiendish intruder, with whom he still felt a regretful affinity. The result is a rather charming cautionary tale, one of Miller's most successful short narratives.

Spurred on, perhaps, by the reappearance of June and this other troubling figure from his past, in 1947 Miller took up his manuscript of *The Rosy Crucifixion*, which he had begun in 1942 in New York. It was over a thousand pages long, and he had only covered his life through 1923, the year in which he met June. He decided that the project would have to run to three volumes, which he would title *Sexus*, *Plexus*, and *Nexus*. He worked swiftly, completing the manuscript of the first volume by fall. Appropriately titled, the book was saturated with sex. The story of his first marriage, to Beatrice ("Maude"), it recounts the narrator's guilt at leaving her and his subsequent sexual attraction to her. In October Miller wrote Durrell that he was making final revisions on the manuscript before sending it off to Girodias, who was going to publish it first in English, then in French. He had no hope of interesting any of his American publishers in *Sexus;* it was even more censorable than the *Tropics*.

When Girodias brought out an English edition of *Sexus* in France in the summer of 1949, it created a huge stir. This time no defense committees were formed, and the book was banned in 1950. Girodias was fined and given a prison sentence. Miller was philosophical about the banning—such things had happened to him often enough—although he could not help feeling that the French had let him down this time. He was far more ruffled by an attack from an unexpected quarter: Lawrence Durrell.

Durrell had been Miller's ardent champion throughout the forties, promoting him whenever he could. Now in Alexandria with a new wife, Gipsy Cohen, Durrell had found in the Egyptian city the setting and themes of the Alexandria Quartet, the first volume of which, however, would not appear until 1953. Miller was still very much his mentor; still, Durrell had access to publishing outlets that Miller did not, and he sought to bring Miller's work to a larger audience. On the eve of the publication of *Sexus* he had written an insightful essay for Cyril Connolly's influential magazine *Horizon*, assessing the strengths and weaknesses of Miller's work. Miller had not taken the criticisms from his old friend well, writing to Durrell to correct him on several minor points. He was nervous about Durrell's reading *Sexus*, which was in many ways, he said, "a reversion to pre-*Tropic* writing." Durrell had preferred the *Tropics* to *The Air-Conditioned Nightmare* and Miller's recent New Directions collections, and Miller was correct in his assessment of *Sexus*—it had more in common with *Crazy Cock* than *Tropic of Cancer*. Still, he could not have anticipated the tenor of Durrell's response. Durrell wrote Miller a stinging letter when he was three quarters of the way through *Sexus*, taking him to task for the "moral vulgarity" of the book, for what he saw as its gratuitous obscenity, and for its stretches of bad writing. Ten minutes of thought, he wrote, would have saved the book, but now Miller had failed himself and violated the laws of artistic taste. For good measure, Durrell telegraphed from Corfu five days later: SEXUS DISGRACEFULLY BAD WILL COMPLETELY RUIN REPUTATION UNLESS WITHDRAWN REVISED LARRY.

Given his tireless promotion of Miller's Paris books, Durrell's response was understandable. In his view, all that ground was lost with the publication of *Sexus*. But Durrell's promotion of Miller's works had never been devoid of self-interest. Ten years would pass before he would win fame and acclaim for the Alexandria Quartet. For the present his reputation was confined to *The Black Book* and a few volumes of poetry. His biggest literary asset, in one respect, was his well-publicized connection in the minds of many critics with the more famous— or notorious—Miller. It was understandable, then, that Durrell felt an almost proprietary interest in Miller's reputation. But his response to Miller's latest work was no less significant for all that. In their subsequent letters, both writers tried to smooth the incident over, agreeing to disagree. Miller gracefully conceded that he might be written out, but he defended *Sexus* with extraordinary cogency. Whether the trilogy was a monster or not, he wrote, he had to unburden himself of it. He had been sincere in the book. In fact, sincerity had been the whole point: "If it was not good, it was true; if it was not artistic, it was sincere; if it was in bad taste, it was on the side of life." He urged Durrell to attack him in print, but Durrell had already retreated, asking forgiveness from *"cher maître."*

Miller's writing of the forties had been a series of fits and starts, travel books, astrological and spiritual ramblings, none of it very rewarding. Now, however, he was again tapping a vein of memory that was as urgent to him as ever. And he was writing with spirit and intensity. By the time he had patched up the *Sexus* flap with Durrell, he had already completed volume two of the trilogy, *Plexus*. The book was ostensibly about his marriage to June, but the great bulk of it is devoted to reminiscences of his boyhood and adolescence. The tone was not unlike that of "the Brochure." Miller includes long ruminations on Spengler and Freud, on public libraries, on science. It ends with a discussion of suffering, in which Miller explains that he vowed to write the account of the wound his soul received in his experience with June, but adds that since taking the vow the "wound" has healed. His motive was now somewhat different, as he explains:

> Suffering *is* unnecessary. But one has to suffer before he is able to realize that this is so. It is only then, moreover, that the true significance of suffering becomes clear. At the last desperate moment—when one can suffer no more!—something happens which is in the nature of a miracle. The great open wound which was draining the blood of life closes up, the organism blossoms like a rose.

His misery, his rebirth: that was once more his subject.

Perhaps as a respite to such high seriousness, he tossed off a sentimental little tale about a clown called Auguste; it was published as *The Smile at the Foot of the Ladder* by Duell, Sloan, & Pearce in 1948 and would be reprinted several times by other publishers. The misunderstood Auguste is a mouthpiece for the misunderstood Henry when he says, "To be yourself, just yourself, is a great thing. And how does one do it, how does one bring it out? Ah, that's the most difficult trick of all. It's just difficult because it involves no effort. . . . You do whatever comes to hand." Again, Miller tried to explain the peace he had won in Paris, when he gave up the ghost—to use his phrasing—and found his self. Perhaps inevitably—given the simplicity of his message—*The Smile at the Foot of the Ladder* was a slight effort, though well received at the time. It would become one of Miller's own favorites among his books.

At about the same time Miller embarked on one of the most ambitious of his self-publishing efforts, in the same vein as *The Angel Is My Watermark*. With a friend, the Israeli artist Bezalel Schatz, he put together *Into the Night Life*, a special edition of a dream sequence fragment from *Black Spring*. Miller wrote out the text and Schatz illustrated it in silkscreen, using an elaborate system of stencils. Each numbered copy cost them $73 to make, they estimated, so they had to charge $100 per book. What they produced is a remarkable work of art, a truly beautiful book, but at that price they could find few buyers. They were forced to offer individual pages for sale, and they also sold "trial runs," or botched copies. For $1,500, the entire record of the book's creation was available: preliminary sketches, the prints made at different stages of the stenciling, and, of course, the finished pages, all classified and indexed and bound in linen portfolios. Miller would peddle this book—and its various "products"—for years, never very successfully.

All this activity, of course, merely distracted him from the real task at hand—finishing *The Rosy Crucifixion*. He had only to write the third volume and he would be through, at last, with the project he had been planning since 1927. But the distractions he took up along the way were no accident. *Nexus* was to pick up with the appearance of Jean Kronski, and that meant reliving some of his most painful memories. So now, once again, he put aside *The Rosy Crucifixion*. Nearly ten years were to pass before he took it up again.

13.

The Family Man

1949–1959

For years Miller had been in the habit of answering chain letters—the kind that ask the recipient to send a dollar to the first name on the enclosed list and to send copies of the letter to six friends, promising that the recipient will receive a small fortune when his name heads up the list (and often threatening dire consequences if the recipient "breaks the chain"). He put a great deal of hope in them, as he wrote to a Los Angeles friend in March 1949. Good luck often came in the mails, he found.

In February he had felt compelled to issue another "open letter" about his financial plight. As before, he offered a firm proposal: an exchange for his work and his services. He appended to the letter a list of things he needed (canned baby food, evaporated milk, olive oil, tea and coffee, nuts and cheeses, smoked ham or tongue, good watercolor paper, stamps, postcards, air letters, and cigarettes) and a list of what he had to offer in exchange (watercolors, manuscripts, and editions of his books). The giver was to estimate the value of his gift and expect an appropriate response. Or, he continued, "perhaps you would like some special services which it is in my power to perform." The letter worked so well that Miller kept it in circulation for almost four months.

Its success may have been due to the news it announced: that there were now four in the family. Lepska had given birth to a son on August 8, 1948, whom they christened Henry Tony and called Tony. They had moved to new quarters on Partington Ridge in Jean Wharton's house, which they bought from her for $7,000, together with two and one-half acres of land. Their neighbors were Nicholas and Tirzah Roosevelt, he a cousin of Miller's childhood hero Teddy Roosevelt and a retired *New York Times* editor. But Nicholas Roosevelt was no fan of Miller's, and relations between the two families were sometimes strained.

Still, the family was, by and large, accepted by the Big Sur community, and Henry was very much a part of it. The area attracted a disproportionate number of would-be writers, some of whom eventually became successful. Among them Miller counted as his friends Norman Mini and Walker Winslow; the Niemans, his friends from Beverly Glen days, had moved to Big Sur, and Gilbert Nieman was writing a novel. The sculptor Beniamino Bufano lived close by, at Free Camp; Bezalel Schatz, Miller's collaborator on the silkscreened *Into the Night Life*, lived near Bufano. Bill and Lolly Fassett had bought the old "log house" property where Miller had stayed with Lynda Sargent, and had built a restaurant around the cabin, which they called "Nepenthe." The restaurant quickly became a tourist attraction and, especially when the weather was bad, a gathering place for the locals.

A new mailman, Ed Culver, had replaced Jake Hodges, and Miller quickly ran up sizable debts to him for postage stamps and small loans, as he had with Jake. His daily correspondence was burgeoning. Kathryn Winslow, a young admirer and, coincidentally, an ex-wife of Walker Winslow, opened a gallery in Chicago called "M: The Studio for Henry Miller," which featured Miller's watercolors and books. It brought Miller a whole new set of correspondents, and it also brought him much-needed money, for Winslow turned over all of her not inconsiderable profits to him. When she displayed his February "open letter" at the gallery, the response was such that she was able to ship him several cartons of supplies.

But Henry did not welcome publicity efforts like Winslow's with the enthusiasm he once had. He was now thinking a little more carefully about his reputation. He sent a steady stream of books her way, yet he seemed to take no interest in details about the gallery or in the news about sales of his books. Winslow had a copy of *Into the Night Life* at the gallery (which she hadn't been able to sell), and she was deeply hurt when Miller put out a circular listing the places the book had been exhibited without mentioning Chicago. In response, Miller admitted that he was a bit embarrassed to have a gallery devoted to him. He needed the support of admirers like Winslow, but he also resented his dependence on them. He wanted, it seems, to achieve success in mainstream—i.e., "literary"—circles, and to be the kind of writer who didn't need galleries—or cults, for that matter—devoted to his work in order to survive.

Kathryn Winslow was also instrumental in helping Anaïs Nin, with whom Miller was still on chilly terms. On the West Coast, Nin had become involved with Rupert Pole, a man much younger than she.

Hugo Guiler, her husband—who was soon to renounce his banking job for a career as an engraver and film maker under the name Ian Hugo —knew nothing of Pole, for Nin simply shuttled back and forth between Guiler in New York and Pole in Sierra Madre, California. But she needed money to keep this arrangement going, and she appealed to Winslow for help in selling her manuscripts. Winslow found willing buyers at Northwestern University, who purchased Nin's collection of manuscripts for $500. Nin also wanted to sell her collection of Milleriana, including several first editions and a manuscript, and Winslow helped her find a collector to buy these as well.

That success prompted Nin to write Miller. She believed he was being taken advantage of by Lawrence Clark Powell, the librarian at UCLA. She told him that Powell was providing only storage space for materials that could otherwise be sold for the cash that Miller needed. She chalked it up to Henry's masochism: "On the one hand you know the world should support you, on the other you allow exploitation." Powell had thought he could get her own diary manuscripts simply by taking her out for lunch, she added.

Miller was well aware of the value of his manuscripts, but he had a difficult time saying no to Powell. The librarian represented himself as another Miller promoter; he maintained lists of the manuscripts in the library's collection, to which Miller could refer buyers. And he had done a real service in taking the correspondence off his hands; few collectors, after all, would buy fan letters, which Miller thought were important enough to preserve.

In early 1950 Powell presented Miller with an idea. He suggested that Miller put together a list of the books in his life that were important to him, which Powell would then publish as a brochure and circulate to friends of the library. The original plan appears to have been to raise money for Miller, either by enabling the library to buy more of his manuscripts or simply by having the library pay for manuscripts already in its possession.

It was an idea certain to grip the imagination of any self-educated man, and Miller readily agreed. Almost immediately, however, the project expanded. Surely a straightforward list was inadequate to convey the great importance of books in his life. Couldn't the story of his life almost be told through the succession of the books he had read? And, of course, as soon as he began thinking about making such a list, each book that was to go in suddenly had to be reread, re-experienced.

For an enterprise of this scale he needed help from his friends. In

February 1950 another "open letter" went out, this one asking for lists of the books important to them, or for the books themselves. Then Miller wrote to all of his contacts at university libraries (there were now quite a few such friends). He needed not only books, but bibliographical help, he announced. He knew, for example, that the books of George Henty—history books for boys—had been very important to him, yet he couldn't remember a single title.

Miller let Powell know that the pamphlet idea would have to be abandoned. He was working on a book-length project that would consume him for more than a year. Initially, his goal was to show how unnecessary reading was—how many worthless books the average person read. But as the project began turning into a book it carried a contradictory message, for when he reread old favorites like Rider Haggard's *She*, he found them still wonderful. The project brought his childhood back to him, and he digressed freely. At the end of the book he intended to append a list of more than two thousand books that he had read. As the manuscript pages mounted, he wondered whether he would need to write another volume to do the subject justice.

By February 1951 he mailed the manuscript to Laughlin, who would publish it in 1952 as *Books in My Life*. (The title was not Miller's choice; this was the single time in his life when he was at a loss to come up with a felicitous title). As autobiography, the book is engrossing, for Miller recalls vividly his school days, boyhood reading, and adolescent preoccupations. He discusses individuals he regards as "living books," among them John Cowper Powys, an old favorite. Much of the book is given over to long praises of old heroes like Blaise Cendrars; like so much of his work, it required—and did not receive—a sharp critical eye and expert editing. His passion for reading is apparent, however, and the work is successful in conveying how much books meant in Miller's life.

That same year he received a long letter from Lawrence Durrell, warning him that his literary reputation was at a critical point. A British writer named Graham Ackroyd had proposed to bring out a selection from Miller's letters, and Durrell feared it would be another negligible collection of trivia like Bern Porter's *The Happy Rock*. Durrell made several recommendations. Miller should find someone to write a *serious* study of his work; he should stop writing for free for little magazines and only allow his work to appear in dependable quarterlies; and he should find a publisher to issue an anthology of his best work.

However elitist they may appear, Durrell's recommendations were essentially sound. By associating primarily with small magazines and small presses, Miller had almost guaranteed his own marginality—his work simply did not reach enough readers. Durrell knew how easily Miller was exploited by editors who pretended to be doing him a favor. What he overlooked was his friend's stunning inability to distinguish between the good and the bad in his own work. Miller simply could not see that the collections Laughlin published were dangerously uneven, that *Black Spring* was superior to *Money and How It Gets That Way*, or even that a letter to Emil Schnellock, however long, was not necessarily literature.

This fuzzy thinking was not confined to his own writing. Indeed, it characterized most of his enthusiasms in the forties and fifties. Miller was always taking up a cause—usually that of an obscure writer. In 1949 and 1950 it was George Dibbern, the author of *Quest*, which told how Dibbern had renounced his German citizenship to become the first "citizen of the world," traversing the oceans in a sailboat. Miller urged everyone he knew to send clothes and money to Dibbern's wife, who was stuck in Germany. He agitated for a reprint of *Quest*, which had come out in 1941. Another "cause" was an Egyptian writer, Albert Cossery; Miller urged his *Men God Forgot* on Laughlin for years. Still another was Haniel Long, the author of *The Powers within Us*, an inspirational book about the explorer Cabeza de Vaca. He was also devoted to the plight of the poet Kenneth Patchen, author of *The Journal of Albion Moonlight*. The only thing these writers had in common was their relative obscurity. Miller pushed these causes in letters to friends, but few could see what he saw in them (with the exception of Patchen). Sometimes he wrote testimonials about his pet writers for the little magazines, which Laughlin would later collect and publish. But Miller was particularly inept at portraits; too often they lacked any critical perspective. His "causes" came to be regarded as eccentricities. Friends' eyes would glaze over when he brought up yet again the neglected works of a Haniel Long or a Dibbern.

To Durrell, Miller answered that he supposed he *was* irresponsible, but that he couldn't very well preserve his reputation all by himself; "I leave it to the gods," he wrote. Durrell dropped the matter for the time being, but he fully intended to do something to enhance his friend's reputation. In fact, Durrell's values were very different from Miller's, and Durrell also seems not to have understood that his comments might have offended Henry; Henry was, in reality, quite bitter about his critical status, even while he affected to reject the literary world. He understood that his Paris books were the products of genius, but those books were literally against the law; thus on one level he saw the whole notion of literary acceptability and acceptance as hypocritically farcical, while on another he craved serious literary attention. It was infuriating to him that Durrell—his disciple, after all—did not understand that of course he had considered his reputation—that indeed, he was obsessed with it—but that he saw no alternative way to write and publish.

Miller often observed that his liaisons with women tended to last seven years, a rule that certainly applied to his time with Beatrice, June, and even Anaïs. Now it looked to be true in the case of Lepska as well. Miller wrote a friend on July 4, 1951, that he expected a visit from his father-in-law on the 16th, and that Lepska planned to travel East with him to visit family, perhaps taking the children with her. That was not quite how it turned out, however. The sequence is not entirely clear, but at some point Lepska announced that she had fallen in love with a biophysicist named Vergeano. On her trip to visit her family in New Jersey, she took Tony and Val, a move that seemed ominous. But after the summer she returned the children and decamped for Long Beach near Los Angeles, where Vergeano lived.

Though it happened with stunning swiftness, Miller was not surprised by Lepska's move—their quarrels had increased and intensified as the children grew. Lepska was frustrated by Henry's casual ways and what she saw as his irresponsibility, his tendency to chuck his work to spend the day with the children or a visiting admirer. The couple bickered almost constantly and, since neither was the bickering sort, they had become desperately unhappy. Once the marital bond had been severed, however, Miller hoped he and Lepska could remain friends. They had survived some difficult times together, and Miller was very attached to the children, whose custody he hoped to gain. With Lepska gone, he immediately began looking for a woman to care for them. While Lepska had initially been inclined to let Henry raise Val and Tony, she soon changed her mind, proposing that they spend six months with him and six months with her and Vergeano, whom she would marry as soon as the divorce was granted.

At first, Miller enlisted the aid of his friend Walker Winslow, who was then living on the grounds of the Miller home, to help take care of both children. Then, convinced that Tony, not yet in school, would be too difficult, he reluctantly sent him down to Long Beach to be with Lepska. Shortly thereafter, a woman named Ivy appeared on Miller's doorstep, announcing that she had heard he needed a caretaker for his children. When Lepska brought Tony to Partington Ridge to celebrate Val's birthday, she agreed to leave the boy with his father. Soon, however, Ivy decamped, and he and Winslow found themselves overwhelmed with the rigors of watching over two high-spirited, constantly quarreling children. Henry had always been a loving father, but he found their day-to-day care exhausting. Writing was impossible, and he even neglected his correspondence.

Winslow pointed out that Miller could not continue this arrangement; it was ruining him, and doing the children no good. Miller agreed. He was sixty and felt too old to be running after children, and the "new mother" he was seeking had not materialized. He dispatched a telegram to Lepska asking her to take the children.

Almost immediately he regretted it, for without them the place seemed empty. He missed telling them stories and teasing them, and he even missed their fights. "Wherever I strayed," he wrote later, "I stumbled over something they had dropped and forgotten. There were toys everywhere. . . . And tops and marbles. And spoons and dishes. Each little object brought tears to my eyes. With each passing hour I wondered aloud how they were doing." He telephoned the children frequently, and was dismayed to hear Tony answer his questions in monosyllables; his son seemed the most affected by the separation. The winter rains had come, and Miller passed a subdued Christmas alone.

But he found another companion very quickly—a woman several years his junior, who seemed to be as accommodating as Lepska had been difficult. Eve McClure, twenty-five, was the sister-in-law of his friend Bezalel Schatz. Of Scots, Irish, French, and Jewish background, Eve had been married briefly to an actor named Lyle Talbot, who had been almost sixty when they met, and she was now divorced. McClure lived in Beverly Hills, where she painted and made etchings.

The two met through correspondence, probably at Louise Schatz's suggestion. Eve admired Henry's work, especially the *Tropics*, and told him so in her letters. He hung the letters and photos she sent him on the walls of his cabin, just as he had done with those of his earlier "bride," June Lancaster.

Late in March 1952 the two arranged a meeting. On the pretext of Val's case of the measles and his own bad cold, Miller prolonged a weekend visit to the children in Long Beach, and drove to visit Eve in nearby Beverly Hills. Henry was struck by her beauty: she had dark brown hair, green eyes, somewhat heavy, sensual features and perfect skin, and her body was supple but full. Henry was himself still a good-looking man, wiry but solidly built, his fringe of white hair clipped short around his tanned bald head. He had not expected such a striking woman, and doubted that she—or any woman in her right mind, for that matter—would come to desolate Big Sur to live with a sixty-year-old man and care for two active children. But Eve McClure was a warm-hearted woman with great reserves of strength. And she had fallen in love with Henry, she said, almost immediately. When he returned to Big Sur on April 1 she went with him; they planned to marry as soon as Henry's divorce came through. (They would not marry, in fact, until almost two years later, on December 31, 1953, when Miller needed the deduction for tax reasons.)

Henry thought at once that Eve was everything Lepska was not. He approved of the description a German friend provided: she was like a squaw, for she was regal and "knew how to be silent." She brought grace into his life, and a new serenity. Living with Eve, Miller wrote Durrell, was like "living on velour." Like Anaïs Nin, he said, "she brings with her the feeling of ease and abundance." She saw her husband's faults, but she bore them stoically; she did not try to reform him as Lepska had. She was, he said, the first real mate he had ever found. Like June Mansfield, Eve was sensuous and down to earth, qualities Henry prized. But where June had left Henry, as he saw it, unmanned, Eve catered to his whims, which suited him perfectly. Moreover, she truly did become the "new mother" he had sought for Tony and Val; she was maternal by nature and soon won their respect and affection. A kind of camaraderie sprang up between her and Val, who called her young stepmother "Darling Evie-O" and generally treated her as an adored big sister. A new arrangement was worked out with Lepska: Henry and Eve were to have the children for summers and alternate years.

By the end of the summer of 1952 Miller was working on *Nexus* again. His life was full, rich, and happy, he told friends; it made him recall his days at Villa Seurat. In fact, he was consumed by a desire to see Europe again with Eve at his side. Money was coming from Girodias with enough regularity now that they could realistically contemplate such a trip. Miller felt he needed a vacation, and he was eager to visit old haunts in Paris—and, perhaps, to show off his young and beautiful companion to his old cronies there. On December 27 they began the first leg of their trip, staying with their friends Robert and Edie Fink in Los Angeles. In New York, they had planned to stay with Frank Dobo, but Miller begged off, giving the excuse that he had to see his mother and that they were spending the night with a friend of Eve's out near the airport; he hoped they could get together in Paris.

Miller had not taken a real break from writing since his visit to Greece in 1939, and as a rule he was unable to work when he was traveling. But he had many people to look up in the city he had not seen in a dozen years, and almost immediately after they arrived in Paris—on the 31st, in a snowstorm—Henry and Eve were besieged by visitors, including such friends from the past as the journalist and translator Georges Belmont (as Roger Pelorson was now known), the painter Hans Reichel, and the surrealist writer Joseph Delteil and his wife, Caroline. In France, Miller was famous and his books were big sellers; here he found himself accorded the respect and honor that eluded him in America. By now, with the help of his agent Michel Hoffman, he had been taken on by several European publishers: Ledig Rowohlt in Germany, Arnoldo Mondadori in Italy, and Edmond Buchet in France. Buchet's books were distributed by the large French firm Corrêa, and shortly after Miller's arrival Corrêa arranged a reception for him in honor of the appearance of the French edition of *Plexus* on January 15, 1953.

Henry and Eve stayed at the apartment of Maurice Nadeau, a French critic who had helped to form the committee in Miller's defense during *l'affaire Miller* of 1946. After a few weeks the Millers decamped for Le Vesinet, where they passed two weeks with Buchet, and then headed for Monte Carlo for a rest. There they received an offer to stay at La Ciôtat, at the country house of the French actor Michel Simon. (It was Simon, said to be a well-known collector of erotica, who had rented Anaïs Nin her houseboat back in the thirties.) La Ciôtat was an eighteen-room unheated castle, and Miller complained frequently about the cold. They were visited by Girodias, who at the time was experiencing serious financial problems. Hachette, the large French publishing house, had taken over Les Editions du Chêne when he had been near bankruptcy, and now he was struggling to start a new imprint, the Olympia Press. But with characteristic haplessness, Girodias had actually failed to issue *Plexus* in English before Corrêa had it translated and on the shelves in French. Miller still regarded Jack Kahane's son as a sincere, good-hearted friend, he wrote Belmont, and he sympathized—perhaps empathized—with him over his business troubles.

From La Ciôtat Henry and Eve returned to Le Vesinet where, to Miller's delight, the writer Blaise Cendrars, whom he had long venerated, gave a reception in his honor. Before long they were back in Paris, where they were joined by Bezalel and Louise Schatz. Together they traveled down to Montpellier, where they had arranged to meet Joseph and Caroline Delteil for a trip through Spain—a special pleasure, for Delteil was a surrealist writer whose work Miller had long admired; Carl Dreyer's film *La Passion de Jeanne d'Arc* had been made from Delteil's screenplay and was a Miller favorite. He was currently celebrating the publication of his completed works. Caroline Delteil, *née* Dudley, was an American woman who had come to Paris in 1925 to manage Josephine Baker, the black jazz sensation. The time Miller spent with the Delteils cemented an important friendship. Delteil shared Henry's enthusiasm for astrology and the occult, and in Montpellier the two men sought out a Dr. de Fontbrune, a well-known Nostradamus scholar. De Fontbrune predicted a third world war as well as a French civil war, and Miller took these predictions very seriously, writing Durrell that he was prepared to flee to America at any moment.

The Delteil/Miller contingent left for Spain on May 10. In Barcelona Miller was reunited with Alfred Perlès, who, with his wife, Anne, had traveled down from England to visit his old friend. Relations between the two men had been somewhat strained in the forties, for Miller had found Perlès's decision to become a British citizen and fight in World War II incomprehensible. He thought England sterile and repressive, and he could not reconcile Perlès's new patriotism with the detachment Alf had affected during the thirties. But at their reunion he found that Alf had changed very little, and they spent two days together, reminiscing and laughing about the Paris years. He still couldn't understand why Perlès would want to live in England; nor, he noted, did he find Perlès's literary efforts as interesting as he once had. But the two old friends fell easily into their respective roles, clowning outrageously and leering at their laughing women.

Henry and Eve had plans to visit Durrell in Cyprus, but the trip never materialized. Instead they traveled further in France, then to Brussels, and finally to Wales where, in Corwen, Miller visited his old idol John Cowper Powys. His admiration dated back to Powys's lecture tour in America, when he had heard "Prester John" speak in the Labor Temples in New York. Moreover, the two autobiographical writers had much in common; both had a great interest in sexuality as a literary subject, and both were uncommonly prolific. Miller also admired Powys's extraordinary energy—at the age of eighty he still radiated warmth and vitality. After Wales, Henry and Eve stopped off for another visit with Perlès at his home in Wells.

Miller's audience with Dr. de Fontbrune, the Nostradamus scholar, may have left a residue, for he was troubled throughout the trip by the sense of impending doom. Nostradamus's prophecy was coming true, he wrote Emil White: there would be a revolution followed by the rise of an evil dictator. The hot summer, followed by floods, was a sure sign.

Such apocalyptic pronouncements were not unusual for Miller. In fact, he made them regularly, often based on misinformation. In the forties, he had written to the poet Kenneth Rexroth at length about Sir Francis Bacon, who he had heard was actually reborn as Christian Rosenkreuz, a key figure in Rosicrucian history. Miller vaguely suspected an epochal occult conspiracy that had something to do with world rule. Rexroth, astonished at Miller's lack of critical sense, wrote back telling him that he was virtually certain about Sir Francis Bacon's mortality. "Don't make yourself ridiculous," he added.

Miller was also a passionate believer in UFOs, and during the 1950s he would come to believe that an invasion by aliens was imminent. For a time he promoted a book called *Flying Saucers Are Real*, by Donald Kehoe; friends like Durrell were merely amused. He also believed, but less passionately, in the principles set forth in L. Ron Hubbard's *Dianetics*, the bible of the Church of Scientology. While such interests were not uncommon in California at the time, Miller's lack of discrimination was striking; he seemed unable to distinguish the crackpot from the visionary. Throughout his life he carried his openness to new ideas to extremes, and listened uncritically to every passing stranger.

Miller still held no great love for his native country. When the couple returned to the United States in late July, Henry found America even more disgusting, and complained to Durrell that it was "even emptier and more poisonous than ever." He told Georges Belmont that if it were not for Big Sur, he would commit suicide. He began to entertain the idea of living abroad, if not in France, then perhaps in another European country. (Though he had always hoped, since the days in Villa Seurat when he had discovered Buddhism, to visit Japan or China, he had finally abandoned his long dream of moving to Tibet.)

Eve loved France and hoped to influence Henry to think about moving there; she believed that his self-image had been damaged by his critical neglect in America and that he should make his home among those who appreciated him.

Back in Big Sur, however, Miller returned to his old life of "circularizing and begging and wheedling." The children were with him for the year, aggravating his money problems. But the presence of Tony and Val also brightened his life, for he was a doting father and immensely interested in their development. He had fought bitterly with Lepska over the issue of their education, arguing that they should be taught at home, and that they should determine their own developmental pace. He had at last given in, however, and allowed Val to be sent to school. In the fall of 1953 Tony was not yet ready to go to school, so he remained at home, attending the painting classes Eve had begun to give to the neighborhood children.

Miller started to notice distinct personalities in his children. Val, at eight, was shy and introspective and inclined to bookishness; she had no interest in art, an attitude Miller found deplorable. She was, however, good at sports, and soon she began agitating for a horse, which her father eventually gave in and got for her. With Tony, Miller was beginning to develop a special relationship. He played games with the boy for hours; he described to Belmont how he pretended with his son to be first a physician, then a mechanic, then a drill master, then a plumber, then an architect, then a gardener, and finally a clown. He insisted that the children be allowed to interrupt him when he was hard at work in his shack.

In February 1954 Miller heard from his daughter Barbara. Now thirty-five and living with her mother in Pasadena, she had seen a magazine article about Miller and wrote him to ask if she could visit. Miller had heard no news of her since 1944, when a woman who had been sent to do a feature on him for *Collier's* mentioned that she knew Barbara; he had done nothing with that piece of information. Their meeting was awkward, he told friends, but Miller liked his daughter and noted with pleasure that she resembled him. She needed to lose a little weight, he thought, and she was somewhat directionless for a woman of her age. But Miller was glad to be reunited with her; he had always felt guilty about leaving her, and still cherished the snapshots he had kept with him of her after her bath. Thereafter Barbara visited periodically, and Miller encouraged her in her efforts to become a real estate salesperson. Strangely enough, he heard not a word from Beatrice; he had expected her to sue him for back alimony now that she knew his whereabouts, but perhaps she had softened with time, he hoped—although reports from Barbara indicated otherwise.

In November, Alfred Perlès made his long-promised trip to Big Sur; he had with him the manuscript of a book he had written about Miller, which would appear in England in 1955 and America in 1956 as *My Friend Henry Miller*. Perlès's account was meant to be a biography, but it was more accurately a memoir of his years with Miller. The touchiest matter in his account was Miller's relationship with Anaïs Nin, who insisted to Perlès that he not use her real name. Perlès refused to compromise on this matter until Nin threatened to sue, when he finally backed down and compromised: Nin appears in the memoir, but is described only as a friend. Perlès inserted a fictitious second woman as Miller's lover and patroness, naming her Liane de Champseur.

The incident served to increase the distance between Miller and Nin. She had not seen him since a brief, chilly visit to Big Sur in 1947 and would not see him again for several years. Emil White had tried briefly to patch things up between them, but Nin felt that Miller's beliefs and behavior were too far from her own to allow for friendship. Despite her unique marital situation, Nin wished to put her bohemian days behind her, and she was irritated by Henry's casual ways, while at the same time she affected contempt for his role as a family man. She approved of little of his writing, believing it, on the whole, inferior to what he had produced in Paris. For his part, Miller had become impatient with her imperiousness. As he later wrote bitterly, "She was like a *duchesse* dispensing her favors or withholding them at will. Often one fell out of favor with her over a trifle. To regain her good graces was like climbing Mount Fuji." As literary success continued to elude her, she became even more testy with her old friends.

During his visit, Perlès tried to get Miller to return to Europe. He was too loyal to say so outright, but he felt California had had a baleful influence on his friend. Like Nin, he believed the writing Miller had produced in Clichy and at the Villa Seurat was much better than what he was turning out now. Eve seemed to make him happy, but Perlès also worried about the toll his demanding Big Sur fans were taking on him. Like Eve, he wondered why Miller chose to live in a country where the critics failed to appreciate him. Miller made light of Alf's exhortations. The house in Big Sur had become his base of operations; with the help of Emil White and other devoted friends he had forged a system there that allowed him to deal with the outside world, and he was reluctant to abandon it. As he had learned on his tour of America —not to mention in his years at Western Union—he did not function well when he tried to live as others did. Nor did he have the reserves to be able to live as he had once lived in Paris, without a job or a home or regular meals. Most of all, he didn't share Perlès's view of his recent work. He was confident about his writing, if not about his status.

In fact, Miller was just beginning a new book about his life in Big Sur. It would evolve into a rambling, discursive account of his neighbors, his conversations with his children, his writing habits, and his response to the wilderness in which he had now lived for ten years. A long section toward the end, appropriately titled "Paradise Lost," is based on his disastrous attempt to make a home for his astrologer friend Moricand. (The piece was published separately, as a Signet paperback, in 1956.) The book's title, *Big Sur and the Oranges of Hieronymus Bosch,* is derived from Bosch's triptych "The Millennium," in which oranges are the fruits of Paradise—much to be preferred, Miller wrote, to those harvested by Sunkist. The narrative is the work of a happy man, and it contains some of Miller's finest, most relaxed writing, including wryly amusing passages that detail how he was taken over by "The Voice" when writing the *Tropics.* One superb passage describes the almost hallucinatory peace the Big Sur landscape evoked in him. He appended to the manuscript a long Epilogue, which he had intended to publish separately, titled "This Is My Answer!" It notes in detail the volumes of correspondence he had already received, and then asks his readers *not* to write to him.

The publication of the Big Sur book did more to draw fans than to repel them, of course. They descended in droves. Some bore manuscripts, others books to be signed. Still others wanted their idol's advice, and many wanted simply to sit at his feet and absorb his wisdom. Some asked for money, which was, of course, laughable. Young women appeared on Miller's steps, offering themselves sexually (one of the "perks" of Emil White's job as gatekeeper, of which he took full advantage). As always, Miller found it difficult to turn anyone away. Nor could he leave fan letters unanswered; almost every one struck some sort of chord in him, and he would write back to recommend books or give advice on how to write. Emil White tried to act as a kind of guard, for his shack was hard by Route 1 and visitors often stopped there to ask directions. But he was no more successful in fending off visitors than in screening Miller's mail.

In the prologue to *Big Sur*, Miller tallied up his publications. His only work-in-progress was *Nexus*. *The World of Lawrence*, "the Brochure" begun more than twenty years before, had been abandoned, he finally announced. He listed those of his titles still banned in the United States: *Aller Retour New York*, *Tropic of Cancer*, *Tropic of Capricorn*, *Black Spring*, *The World of Sex*, *Sexus*, and *Plexus*. *Quiet Days in Clichy*, which combined the two "commissioned" works of pornography he had written in the early forties, had just been published in Paris by the Olympia Press, and he was sure it would be banned too. For some reason he did not mention his available New Directions books, nor *Nights of Love and Laughter*, the 1955 Signet paperback selection from his works with an admiring Introduction by Kenneth Rexroth. (Another Signet collection, *The Intimate Henry Miller*, would appear in 1959, as would a New Directions *Reader* edited by Durrell.)

Miller's financial outlook was improving. His foreign sales, particularly in Japan, Germany, and France, were high, and the Signet paperbacks sold well in the United States. He had even received important critical attention: an essay by Edmund Wilson in the *New Republic* in 1952 praised *Tropic of Cancer* as a representative document of "the twilight of the expatriates," and Philip Rahv wrote a thoughtful piece published in his 1957 *Image and Idea*. But Miller had no standing whatsoever in academic circles—this in spite of the fact that many, if not most, of his American readers were college students. Too many of his readers knew only his New Directions titles or *The Colossus of Maroussi*. Some twenty years had passed since the writing of the *Tropics* and *Black Spring*, and he still had little hope that they would appear in the United States. From time to time he or a friend would think of a scheme to bring them out. Harry Hershkowitz, for example, had suggested that Miller pretend he was dead and then, once the books were published and acclaimed, reappear. Miller toyed with the idea of publishing the books with the four-letter words blanked out and including a note saying that readers could write the author for the missing words. More practically, Frank Dobo suggested in 1955 that Miller allow his books to be published in expurgated form and make a fuss after they were out, claiming he had not authorized any cuts.

None of these plans materialized, however, and Miller bemoaned Laughlin's cowardice and the hypocrisy of American publishers, even as he recognized that any attempt to challenge the current U.S. obscenity laws and publish the banned books openly would be punished by immediate government action, involving a costly legal defense, and even imprisonment. Jake Brussel, the printer of the pirated "Medvsa" edition of *Cancer*, had reportedly been arrested and jailed for his actions. Miller himself was extremely careful in mailing copies of the banned books, and showed great discretion in helping his readers locate copies without giving them explicit advice. On some level, he may even have come to feel that the Paris books were ancient history— though surely he was eager for the U.S. publication of the three-volume *Rosy Crucifixion*.

The domestic tranquility of the mid-fifties was upset in the early months of 1956, when Miller again received word that his mother was ill. The last news he had had of Louise and his sister had been from Perlès, who had stopped in New York to see them on his way home after his 1954 visit. Perlès had reported that both were well, and that Louise had told him "Henry was always a good boy." Miller had affected, of course, to be unimpressed by Perlès's report, though in fact he was oddly moved. He had felt a similar response in December 1954 when, nostalgic about his boyhood chums, he placed a query in the Brooklyn *Citizen*. Several of his old friends replied, including Stanley Borowski and Johnny Paul. He was also touched by a letter from the sister of Eddie Carney, who wrote that Eddie had been gassed in World War I; the phrase that moved him was "Eddie was always a good boy." As he later wrote, "With it a great wave of emotion swept over me. I wondered, deeply wondered, if *I* had always been a 'good boy,' as my mother was fond of telling people." So Perlès's message was one he badly needed, although his deep distrust of his mother led him to repress that part of himself that depended on Louise's approval.

When they heard the news of Louise's illness in the winter of 1956, Miller and Eve journeyed East, where they checked into the Hotel van Rensselaer on East 11th Street in Manhattan. He found the house on Decatur Street in Brooklyn in total disrepair. Lauretta, now an elderly woman of sixty-seven, was eerily thin; he understood only later that both she and Louise had become severely malnourished as a result of their efforts to economize. (Their total income from insurance and from renting the second floor of the house was a very meager $350 a year.) Lauretta slept on a broken-down box spring and mattress that, as Miller told his friend Robert Fink, a bum would refuse, and the house was lit only by twenty-watt bulbs. Louise was in the hospital when they arrived, but soon she recovered enough to go home, and Henry and Eve took over her care.

While they were in New York, Miller confided to Fink that he and Eve were pretending not to be married; under this ruse, Eve, using the name McClure, came separately to the Decatur Street house every day. Presumably he did not want to upset Louise with the news of his divorce from Lepska—a strange thing indeed for a man of sixty-five to be concealing from his mother. It is difficult to imagine what Louise— or Lauretta—made of the presence of the beautiful young woman who was constantly at Henry's side.

Perhaps Louise was too ill to notice. She and Lauretta were so undernourished that Miller had to give them Sustagen, a liquid protein mixture. He had to feed Louise every twenty minutes, and it was hard to find food she would accept. Before long it became clear that she needed a professional nurse, an idea she resisted, so much so that Henry almost had to restrain her physically when the issue came up. By mid-March she relented, however, and a nurse was installed on the parlor floor, leaving Miller free to turn his attention to the neglected house. He installed a new boiler, paid overlooked bills, and stocked the pantry. He was able to report that Lauretta had improved, at least in physical appearance. His mother, however, was fading. There was nothing organically wrong with her, he wrote Fink, but she had a weak heart and no real interest in living, Miller said. By the end of March 1956 she was dead.

Miller struggled with her to the last. He described a typical scene with her for a friend: he would stand over her and say, "Look, you're in bed. You can't get up. For the first time in my life I'm going to tell you what to do. I'm giving the orders now." But Louise would tell him he couldn't order her around like that, and struggle to get out of bed; Miller would push her back down, and then he would go out into the hall to cry. When she was laid out in the funeral parlor, he imagined that one of her eyes opened every time he bent over her. And at the gravesite in Evergreen Cemetery, the pallbearers had trouble angling her coffin into the grave. "It was as if she was still resisting us," Miller later wrote.

Louise's death created a number of material difficulties. Miller turned over the chore of selling the house to his cousin Henry Heller, who still lived in the old family home at 662 Driggs Avenue. The sixty-seven-year-old Lauretta, however, could not be foisted off on a relative; she was clearly her brother's responsibility. Though she still drove him crazy with incessant prattling, she plainly adored her brother, and after Louise's death she looked to him with confidence. She obviously could not live alone, nor could Henry and Eve afford to set her up in the Decatur Street house with a caretaker, so after the funeral they brought her back to California to live with them and the children in the Partington Ridge cabin. After a few painful days, Miller realized that Lauretta needed more care than they could possibly give her. He and Eve looked frantically for some facility that would care for her, finally settling her at the Del Monte Rest Home in nearby Pacific Grove, where she could stay for $200 a month. Henry promised to visit his sister weekly, a promise he kept for many years.

Other ghosts from the past had resurfaced during Miller's stay in New York, along with some further responsibilities. Emil Conason, one of the few friends he looked up, told him that June Mansfield was now in Pilgrim State Hospital, committed by a brother for reasons that sounded murky. Conason visited her there from time to time and reported that she was much improved and could be released if someone sponsored her. Miller did not step forward, though he passed on $25 for Conason to give her. She was released in May. Miller realized that he had some responsibility for June, and arranged for Annette Baxter, a Barnard professor and Miller scholar, to visit her regularly to see that she was taking care of herself. Baxter and her husband James reported that June was living in a furnished room in a welfare hotel on the Upper West Side. She was still severely underweight and her teeth were very bad, but because of a heart condition she could not undergo the anesthesia that would be required to fix them. As for her emotional state, she could not be made fully well, they wrote regretfully.

All these developments were painful for Miller; they also created considerable financial burdens. He was in the process of building a new studio for himself, and that, together with Lauretta's care, was crippling him financially. Lepska still owned half of the house on Partington Ridge, and she was dickering with him to buy her share—though he couldn't possibly afford it. On his sixty-fifth birthday, he told his friend Bob Fink that he had never been poorer.

In fact, however, Miller had achieved a rare contentment by the late fifties. He took to wearing a Yemenite silver talisman inscribed in Hebrew, a gift from his brother-in-law Bezalel Schatz; he felt it brought him luck. Life was rustic, but it was far from spartan. The new studio was completed in 1956, and it was comfortable and attractive, decorated with tile mosaics made by his friend Ephraim Doner. Big Sur had finally been wired for electricity in 1954, and Bob Fink had provided Miller with a stereo system to replace his old hand-cranked Victrola. It was designed to be controlled by a single knob, since Miller couldn't handle anything technologically more complex; even dial telephones confused him. Thanks to gifts from fans, he had plenty of records and books. The Millers' wine was provided by a friend with a liquor company. They grew fruit and vegetables for their table and chopped their own wood for the stove. Although Eve confided to a friend that she suspected Henry had a secret yearning to live high on the hog—he admitted to a desire for a fancy car—he seemed content with the second-hand Cadillac he bought in 1955.

Work on *Nexus* was going slowly, however, and Miller would not be able to finish it until the end of 1959. Other, lesser projects still occupied him, such as a three-way correspondence between Durrell, Perlès, and himself, which would be published in 1959 as *Art and Outrage*. He also wrote a long letter about the distinction he drew between obscenity and pornography, addressed to a Norwegian lawyer who was defending *Sexus* before Norway's Supreme Court. Miller argued that his use of obscene words was necessary to awaken the reader; pornography, which was designed only to titillate, he observed, was objectionable. Despite his adamant views, the distinction he made remained unclear. He had been over this ground some years before in an essay collected in the 1947 *Remember to Remember*, but he had refined his views somewhat in the intervening years. The letter was published as "Defense of the Freedom to Read" in the November 1959 *Evergreen Review*.

The *Evergreen Review* was a periodical issued by Grove Press, the New York publishing house run by Barney Rosset. Grove had recently published D. H. Lawrence's sexually explicit *Lady Chatterley's Lover*. The novel was highly censorable: four-letter words were used and entire pages were devoted to descriptions of sex acts. As expected, the Postmaster of New York intercepted twenty-four cartons of the book in the mails in April 1959. But Charles Rembar, Grove Press's lawyer, mounted an impressive defense, and in July judgment was rendered in favor of Grove.

Miller followed the case with absorption but without much hope. In early April he had received a telegram from Barney Rosset making an offer for the U.S. rights to *Tropic of Cancer*. Miller declined the offer, saying that his book offered many more challenges than Lawrence's. *Cancer* would be twenty-five years old in September, he wrote, and he predicted that it would be fifty or one hundred years before his banned books would be available in America. He also urged Rosset to publish the works of his latest causes: Blaise Cendrars, Albert Cossery, and Jean Giono. After so long an interval, he was naturally apprehensive about any American publishing offer, and he didn't quite believe that Rosset would go through with publication even if Miller agreed to it.

But in Barney Rosset, Miller had at last encountered an American publisher willing to take a chance on the banned books. Born in 1922 to a wealthy Chicago family, Rosset was known to be an iconoclast—so much so that when the Freedom of Information Act was passed in the early 1970s, Rosset found that his FBI and CIA files filled three cabinet drawers. The first entry was a notation to the effect that twelve-year-old Rosset had chosen Mussolini when asked to name his favorite living person. Naturally rebellious, Rosset discovered Miller while attending Swarthmore College in 1941, where he wrote a term paper on "Henry Miller v. 'Our Way of Life.'" (He got a B−.) In 1951, Rosset bought a small publishing house named Grove Press, located on Grove Street in Greenwich Village. When his father died the following year, leaving Rosset a substantial inheritance, he decided the money could best be spent acquiring good books for publication. In 1955, he bought Samuel Beckett's *Waiting for Godot*, and building on that, recruited more talent from abroad, including Eugène Ionesco, Jean Genet, Marguerite Duras, and Harold Pinter. By the time of the *Lady Chatterley* case Grove had acquired a reputation for introducing American audiences to cutting-edge European and American writers. With the publication of *Lady Chatterley*, Rosset came to be known for his willingness to take risks.

Rosset pursued Miller avidly, determined to get him to accept the offer. He flew to San Francisco and drove down to Big Sur, where he found Eve Miller alone in the log cabin. Miller was out, visiting Lauretta, but he was expected back shortly. Eve knew Rosset's reason for coming and suggested a plan to him: when Henry came back she would pretend to disagree with Rosset and urge Henry to reject his offer, knowing that when she pushed something with him he tended to turn contrary and disagree with her.

The strategy, however, didn't work. Miller was firm. He also believed he owed a debt to James Laughlin, because when Miller had been stranded in Bordeaux during the Munich crisis nearly twenty years before, Laughlin had cabled him money after extracting a promise that Laughlin would have all rights to American sales of his books. Evidently Miller believed this amounted to a contract, or at the least a gentleman's obligation, and he was strict about such matters, in spite of his distrust of publishers. Rosset assured him that he had spoken with Laughlin and had been told to go ahead. But Miller still hesitated.

By the publishing standards of 1959, Rosset was offering Miller substantial sums: first he offered a $10,000 advance for *Tropic of Cancer,* and a promise that he would pay all legal fees to defend the book in court. When Miller declined, Rosset offered him a $2,500 option that stipulated Miller would not place the *Tropics* or *Black Spring* with any other American publisher in the next four years. But Miller declined even this, which would have given him a nice sum for, in effect, not publishing the *Tropics*—a refusal that suggested he was perhaps more ready to have the books published than he said he was. Perhaps he did this because by January 1960 the proposed advance looked better to him. There were major upheavals in his personal life, he wrote Rosset, and he might need "whacking" amounts of money. He seemed to have no idea of the major upheavals that signing a contract with Rosset would precipitate.

14.

Fame

1959–1965

With the first volume of *Nexus* finished (he projected a second volume), Henry and Eve traveled together to Europe in April 1959, buying a second-hand Fiat that they intended to leave there for future trips. As Eve's mother was in a San Francisco hospital with liver cancer, they couldn't stay long this time, but they were hoping to return there to live.

Miller complained in a letter to Emil White that this vacation, one of only six he claimed to have taken since the age of twenty-one, was the worst he had ever experienced. He was plunged into the grim state of mind that characterized his previous breaks from work, and was given to dark rumblings about space travel and astrology and the dire fate of the universe. A visit with his German publisher, Ledig Rowohlt —and his wife, Jane—lifted his gloom somewhat, but more and more he was coming to question whether he wanted to go on with *The Rosy Crucifixion*. Visiting Albert Maillet, a schoolteacher he had met on his last European visit, Miller conceived a book called *Lime Twigs and Treachery*, after a Brahms lied, attacking the American educational system. The American school typified everything that was wrong with the country, he always complained. But for better or for worse, it was a project that he would never get around to. After a stay in the South of France near Durrell, where they were joined briefly by Perlès, the Millers returned to America in August 1959.

Miller's letters toward the end of the year reveal a man in crisis. He reverted to language he had not used since his years with June, referring to men menstruating and the many charged nuances of a phrase like "Darling, where are you?" "In this house," he wrote Durrell, making the Partington Ridge cabin sound like the Henry Street apartment in 1927, "truth is served up at all hours." He suspected Eve of seeing another man—their neighbor, Harrydick Ross—and his jealousy was intense. In a long letter to Durrell outlining his plans for the second volume of *Nexus*, which was to cover his trip to Europe with June, he fell into a meditation about a young woman he had seen on the street in Paris nearly thirty years before. Revealingly, he compared her to Guinevere in the Arthurian legend, confiding that Guinevere's infidelity had always deeply affected him: "It makes her a woman," he wrote. "She had to step down or be lost in legend. And as she sinks Arthur rises." For that was how he saw his experience with June: through her abasement—as well as his own—he was born anew, made a new man. That Guinevere—or June, or Lepska, or Eve—had, simultaneously, to sink was not his concern.

Once he suspected that his marriage to Eve was foundering, he characteristically hastened its inevitable end. In September Eve wrote the Durrells that a young woman was in love with Henry, and that he had sneaked off to San Francisco with her while Eve was visiting her sick mother. He looked like the proverbial cat who swallowed the canary, she related. The young woman was Caryl Hill, a waitress at Nepenthe; she had been married and divorced and had a young child.

Eve took action. She confronted Caryl when she dropped in one afternoon, and told her, "Love is great and so is Henry—so go on upstairs to bed." Caryl and Henry did, but Caryl was unable to face Eve afterward, as Eve wrote Durrell, so Eve at least succeeded in removing some of the romance from the situation. For his part, Henry was confused, telling a friend that he seemed to be faced with a new drama every day. Just as it had during his period of suffering in the twenties, everything seemed charged with significance for him now. He knew that Caryl was incidental, but he could not seem to direct his energy toward trying to salvage his dissolving marriage; on the contrary, he seemed compelled to make it fail.

When Miller was invited to be a judge at the International Film Festival in Cannes in early 1960, he readily accepted, making plans to leave early and travel throughout Europe first; then he would move on to Cannes, where he had arranged for Caryl to meet him. After that, he hoped to continue his travels, perhaps to Japan. His spirits lifted a little at these prospects, and he wrote Durrell that, while his marital situation was in flux, he didn't "give a fuck any more" about it. Even as the marriage deteriorated, Eve kept up her usual role of caregiver; by all accounts, she took Henry's defection stoically, trying to maintain her dignity in an ignoble situation. During his absence she made a brief trip to the Squaw Valley ski resort, but she needed to be in Big Sur to make weekly visits to Lauretta, a task that had fallen to her during the past few years. She also made vacation plans for Tony and Val, who were spending this year with Lepska. And she stopped seeing Harrydick Ross in the interim, sensing that involvement with him at this stage would only hasten the marriage's end.

Trouble had been brewing for some time before either Caryl Hill or Harrydick Ross arrived on the scene, however. One evening in Paris during their 1959 trip, for example, Henry and Eve were having dinner with Miller's old friend Georges Belmont and his wife. Belmont sensed a distinct strain in the marriage. Eve had been drinking heavily—she had a problem with alcohol—and after dinner she burst out, "Georges, do you know what it means to be Henry Miller's wife, mistress, and servant, plus the mother to two children who aren't yours?" There followed a litany of the burdens of a young wife trying to care for an older man who had already lived several lifetimes over. Miller simply listened in silence, occasionally nodding and "hmmming," apparently in agreement.

In April 1960 a new threat to the marriage arose. On his way to Cannes, Miller met Renate Gerhardt, a far more formidable rival to Eve than Caryl Hill, in whom Henry was quickly losing interest. Like Eve, Renate was nearly thirty years younger than he; she also had two young boys. She reminded him of Falconetti, the thin, intense, large-eyed actress whom he had admired in the silent film *La Passion de Jeanne d'Arc*. A translator for his German publisher, Ledig Rowohlt, Renate spoke English and French fluently, and was at work on the German translation of *Nexus*.

In May, when Miller was in Cannes, Eve wrote him that she wanted a divorce. It wasn't because of Caryl, she wrote—though the Big Sur community looked askance at that business—but because she felt it was useless to keep up the sham of their marriage. She had seen their lawyer, and he had advised her to file on grounds of desertion. She wrote that she had consulted with Lepska, and that they both agreed that Big Sur—and the whole Nepenthe scene, which was getting pretty wild—was not a good place for Tony and Val to grow up.

Instead of pleading with Eve to stay with him, Miller agreed to the divorce. What he worried about most, he said, was the children's disappointment over their summer plans. The situation at home seemed hopeless. The children claimed not to like Lepska, although when they weren't with her they missed her. And Lauretta was a continuing problem, since she expected weekly visits.

Meanwhile, from Cannes Miller wrote love letters to Renate. He wanted badly to stay in Europe to be with Renate, he said, but his travel plans had already been set, and, with the separation from Eve impending, he wanted to see the children again. He and Caryl returned home on separate flights.

When he reached Big Sur, Eve told Henry that she needed to be alone for a while, so he drove his old Cadillac down to Pacific Palisades, the Los Angeles neighborhood where Lepska, whose second marriage had just ended in divorce, lived with the children. He thought about writing—there was another volume of *Nexus* to be written, and *Lime Twigs and Treachery* was still on his agenda—but for the most part he watched television and played Ping-Pong with Tony and Val. He had become a crack Ping-Pong player and was passionately competitive about it, bragging to Durrell that his son couldn't beat him in a single game.

In September, Miller announced his plans to return to Europe and make a home for himself there. He would bring along Vincent Birge, a Texan friend, to serve as chauffeur, companion, and sidekick; Emil White would join them for a brief time. Eve would stay in Big Sur. Plans for a divorce were still not final. He was encouraged by a couple of love letters from Renate, whom he went to see immediately after his arrival in Hamburg late in the month.

He began to talk of a future with her, though Durrell and others warned him not to marry again. The couple had developed a daily routine, drinking gin and tonics and making plans far into the night at Renate's apartment in Reinbek, just outside Hamburg. From there, Miller began his search for the "ideal place," a home where Renate and he could raise her two boys and where Val and Tony could spend their summers. Renate refused to raise her boys in America, so Europe it had to be. Visions of living in the Orient had completely vanished; Miller would never visit Japan, Tibet, or China. Somewhat reluctantly, he acknowledged that his years in Big Sur were over. He didn't want to give it up altogether, but the situation with Eve had wrought a major change in his attachment to the area he had so often referred to as "paradise." He couldn't imagine being happy anywhere else in America, and he hadn't forgotten the ambitions to live abroad that he had put on hold twenty years earlier. Now he felt it was time to take them up again. Besides, if publication of the *Tropics* in America was indeed inevitable, as Rosset claimed, he envisioned being forced to remain abroad to avoid arrest.

Making Reinbek and the Rowohlt Verlag offices their headquarters, Miller and Birge set out in Miller's 1953 Fiat to find the right place to settle; they would search for almost a year. Rowohlt, whom Miller called the "Prince of Publishers," had set up a Ping-Pong table in the office and directed his staff to give Miller a game whenever he wanted one. He also put at Miller's disposal a Mercedes-Benz that Miller liked to claim never ran at less than 140 miles an hour. Even more generously, he let Renate take time off from work to show Miller around Hamburg.

In late 1960 Miller and Birge toured the German countryside, including the birthplaces of Miller's grandparents in Darmstadt and Minden. "Can't understand how my grandfathers abandoned this landscape for that horrible New York City," Miller wrote Perlès. But he was as put off as ever by the German character, and absolutely ruled out West Germany as a place to live. With Emil White, Miller and Birge then visited Switzerland, where Miller spent four days at the Lausanne home of the novelist Georges Simenon, whom he had met at Cannes; Charlie and Oona Chaplin were also house guests. (Simenon was relieved when Miller left White and Birge at a Lausanne hotel, observing in his journal that they seemed "parasitical.") Henry and Chaplin laughed themselves into tears several times, Miller reported to Eve.

Christmas found him back in Reinbek, hoping to spend the holidays with Renate. But she had taken her children to see her parents in Baden-Baden, so he passed Christmas and his sixty-ninth birthday alone, eating spaghetti and painting watercolors—he made eighteen over the holidays. He also started writing a play, something he had never tried before. It emerged as a bizarre farce that he described, without further explanation, as a "melo-melo," titling it *Just Wild About Harry*. It was set in Brooklyn, and the situation recapitulated his years with June, with Henry cast as the swaggering Harry, a womanizer and near-gangster. He had terrible trouble with the logistics of stage directions, wondering, for example, when a character should sit down, stand up, or eat. And he was preoccupied with assembling the accompanying music; eventually he incorporated many of his old favorites dating back to the turn of the century, such as "My Wild Irish Rose" and "Comin' Through the Rye." By January 13, 1961, he had finished a draft. Rowohlt promptly turned it down, and questioned Renate's objectivity when she tried to change his mind.

While Miller's books were enjoying tremendous sales in Europe, he still had money troubles, severe enough that he considered auctioning off some of the manuscripts that were in UCLA's Special Collections. Ledig Rowohlt urged him to take Barney Rosset's latest offer to publish the *Tropics*, but Miller still balked. He now said that he thought the real test of the U.S. obscenity laws would be William S. Burroughs's *Naked Lunch*, published abroad in 1959 but not yet in the United States; it was a book far more raw, he thought, than the *Tropics* or the novels of Lawrence and Joyce. Still, he held out hope for American publication and even dissuaded Heinemann from bringing out the *Tropics* in Britain because such a move might delay American publishing plans. Some of the books Rosset wanted to bring out (the closely autobiographical *The World of Sex* and *Sexus*, for example) might be libelous, he feared, and he was convinced that his first wife would surely sue him if they came out in the United States. He also had a deep distrust of all publishers and Rosset, at this point, was no exception. Unaware that their temperaments were strikingly similar, the two men circled each other warily; Rosset nicknamed Miller "the hidden cobra" because of his reserve. He weakened his case with Miller when he accepted a fragment from *Nexus* for Grove's magazine, the *Evergreen Review*, and then cut it. Miller had never been edited—not by Kahane, or Laughlin, or Bern Porter—and he didn't take to it well.

Miller was convinced that the American legal system was innately intolerant, and he felt the same was true of the American public. At sixty-nine he was, understandably, worried about going to jail. While a permanent move to Europe would require a large infusion of cash and a reliable source of income, he simply could not believe Rosset's financial promises.

By the end of January, nevertheless, Miller weakly promised that he would discuss publication of the *Tropics* and *Black Spring* with his agent, Michel Hoffman. The stalling might have continued had not Rosset learned that there was a pirated edition of *Tropic of Cancer* in the works. The book had never been copyrighted properly, because of complications arising from the ban; nor had *Tropic of Capricorn*, *Black Spring*, or *The Rosy Crucifixion*. Pirating was a real threat, and Rosset urged fast action to ensure that the Grove Press edition would appear first. He was now offering a $50,000 guarantee to be paid in five installments, with $10,000 to be paid on signing, $15,000 on the anniversaries of the signing of the contract in 1962 and 1963, and the $10,000 balance on the same date in 1964. But Rosset agreed to pay any legal fees and guaranteed that in the case of litigation Miller would not have to appear in court. Miller could hardly refuse the terms under these conditions.

Astrologically speaking, it looked like a good year for publishing and finances, he told Eve. On February 18—Eve's birthday, coincidentally —Hoffman and Rosset flew into Hamburg. They met Miller at the Atlantic Hotel, where, with some drama, Miller signed the contract.

When Rosset arrived back in New York, however, the Obelisk Press copies of the *Tropics* and *Black Spring* that he was carrying were seized by U.S. Customs. It seemed a bad sign. And Miller was having second thoughts. He worried, for instance, about a passage in *Tropic of Capricorn* in which he reported killing a boy in a rock fight; a malicious reviewer could make much of that, he feared. He was most worried, however, over the obscenity issue, and his doubts were reinforced when the Post Office officially seized *Tropic of Cancer* in June.

By now, *Tropic of Cancer* had a long history in America. The Customs ban on the book had kept it out of the United States for twenty-six years. A painter named Dorothy Upham, as a personal protest against censorship, had challenged the ban by importing *Cancer* in October 1960; Rosset now engaged the civil liberties lawyer Ephraim London to work on her case at Grove's expense. The summer of 1961 brought nothing but good news: on June 13 the Post Office lifted its ban, after being advised by the Justice Department that it would lose in a court battle. On August 10 Customs followed suit, at the same time lifting the ban on *Tropic of Capricorn* and *Plexus*. While this would seem propitious, there were other problems. By making peace out of court with the federal authorities, Grove lost the opportunity to obtain a federal court judgment allowing publication, and so was still open to prosecution in the courts of any state where the book was sold.

While local authorities were left to debate what action to take, Grove published *Cancer* on June 24, 1961. Sales were phenomenal: 68,000 copies sold in the first week, and Grove soon had 130,000 copies in print. *Cancer* climbed the best-seller list. The reviews were also generally positive, treating the book as a serious work of literature rather than a court case or a piece of sensationalism. Karl Shapiro, Maxwell Geismar, George Wickes, Terry Southern, and Kenneth Rexroth all spoke out in the book's favor. But some critics took a dim view of the publicity and the huge sales figures, as did the reviewer for *Life*:

> *Tropic* will be defended by critics as an explosive corrective
> Whitmanesque masterpiece (which it is) and attacked as an

unbridled obscenity (which it is). It will probably sell a million. On *Tropic*'s literary merit? Guess again.

Some critics had reservations about the book itself. Stanley Kauffmann in the *New Republic* found it dated and its reputation inflated. The *San Francisco Chronicle* thought that the writing was "on a level reached by hundreds of English majors in California colleges." Such judgments, of course, had little effect on the book's sales; nor did they particularly trouble Miller, who had long ago learned to ignore reviews.

Very soon local prosecution of the book began: it was banned in Massachusetts in July 1961 and in the city of Dallas in August. Grove published a paperback edition in October, much sooner than they would have otherwise, but a pirated paperback was rumored to be in the works. Rosset was sure the local actions would escalate in number and intensity when the book appeared in paperback. To that end Grove prepared a legal packet, which included statements about *Cancer* from John Ciardi, Norman Cousins, T. S. Eliot, and William Carlos Williams, among others, as well as reviews, affidavits, editorials, and a copy of the court order dismissing the Customs ban in the Upham case. All these distinguished testimonials barely had any effect, however, as community after community banned *Cancer* as obscene.

Only rumblings of this reached Miller in Europe. He was once again traveling, still ostensibly looking for a place to live. He considered Lausanne but rejected it because of the strict Swiss school system; in Ticino, the climate was wrong. He foresaw numerous other problems—he didn't want Renate's boys to have language difficulties, for instance. He worried about his own children flying over alone, but boat travel was just as big a problem, for his daughter Val, who had just discovered boys, would be unchaperoned. His astrologer predicted that Portugal would be his best bet, but he ruled it out because of the extreme poverty he saw there. This left France, where he still hoped to find something, perhaps in the South near Durrell.

He was looking forward to the summer when the children were to join him. Renate's boys had only a five-week vacation, but he hoped they all could be a family for that short time. When summer came, however, his life still seemed too disordered for Tony and Val to be with him. Lepska wanted to take them to Oregon, and Henry reluctantly agreed, but after the decision was made he was disconsolate. A deep depression had been building for some time. Miller blamed it on his Saturn, but it was more likely due to his anxiety about the

American success of *Tropic of Cancer*. Miller was learning the hard way about becoming a celebrity. He was no longer a cult hero but an internationally famous author; he would quickly become a popular icon. In 1959 his first "fan club" had been formed—the Henry Miller Literary Society, convened by Eddie Schwartz and Tom Moore in Minneapolis. The club's newsletter charted his every move, along with essential information for collectors and others who sought his books. Now, in Europe, reporters from the world press followed him everywhere.

Miller found it all bewildering. Even when he received word that the first edition of *Cancer*—30,000 copies—had sold out, he was dejected. He remembered a poster in the Big Sur Post Office that proclaimed the mails free of dirty literature, and he wondered what Mrs. Ewaldsen, the Big Sur postmistress, would think now. In the thirties he had delighted in the image of himself as an "outlaw writer," but he was over seventy now and found the image less appealing. He was uncomfortable being known as a writer of dirty books, and at first he tried to distance himself from the man who had produced *Tropic of Cancer*, the book now so famous. After all, it had been written nearly thirty years ago and he had produced a great deal since then, little of it censorable. The literary recognition he had so long sought had been achieved, but it was compromised by what he felt was a less-than-dignified public image. In a long letter to Barney Rosset, he had predicted that he would be known as "the King of Smut," known for writing to amuse and to titillate. His primary goal had been to teach, to inspire, and to awaken, he said, and he cited *The Colossus of Maroussi*, *The Books in My Life*, and *Hamlet* as proof—books that interested his public very little now. In interview after interview he tried to steer the conversation away from sex, but almost always in vain. The public and press persisted in seeing him as the grand old man of sex, and eventually Miller gave up fighting the popular image.

Meanwhile, personal matters plagued him again in the summer of 1961, on the first wave of his fame. Renate had turned frosty, and he thought she probably blamed him—rightly—for not having found a place for them to live. Once again, he had put off the children's scheduled visit, and he was tremendously depressed because of it. He described his condition as being close to a breakdown, worrying that he might have to go to a sanitarium to recover. It seemed an absurd irony that he should be so miserable at the height of his success, but he was thoroughly unprepared to function on his own. He had been a needy, dependent iconoclast for the last twenty-five years, but that era was coming to an end. He wondered as well whether he had made a mistake in leaving Big Sur; he had lost the equilibrium he had discovered so gratefully there, especially with Eve.

Still hoping to make a go of it with Renate, Miller visited his Danish publisher Hans Reitzel in Copenhagen. There he met the Italian composer Antonio Bibalo, who had written an opera based on Miller's clown story, *The Smile at the Foot of the Ladder*. From Copenhagen he went to Milan, where he stayed with his Italian publisher, Mondadori; the sculptor Mario Marini made a bronze bust of his head there. Then he joined Alfred and Anne Perlès for a tour of England and Ireland.

Along the way he was constantly thrown together with new people, many of them celebrities. At Abe Rattner's studio in Paris he met James Jones, William Styron, and Eugène Ionesco; he felt a particular affinity with Ionesco, although he had read none of his work. He struck up a friendship with the German actress Hildegarde Neff and her husband, David. But none of these activities lifted his gloom. He complained about his lumbago and his creaking joints, and he hinted in letters that he was ready to die. Renate remained stony. Though Miller held out hope for several months that they would marry, he sensed the relationship was doomed. He returned to America in September, hoping to rest for a while in Pacific Palisades.

First, however, he stopped in New York, where he had arranged a reunion with June Mansfield, who was now living in Forest Hills, Queens. He described the meeting in a letter to Eve: June looked terrible. She had never really recovered from her hospitalization five years earlier at Pilgrim State, where she had suffered a crippling fall while undergoing shock treatments. His old friend Emil Conason was looking after her physical ills, but June was well aware that most of her troubles originated in her head. Henry was impressed by her courage. She seemed possessed of a greater inner strength than he had seen in her before. Nor had she lost her striking voice. As an actress she could have been overwhelming, he told Eve. The whole experience was another ordeal for him, but an eye-opening one. That chapter in his life seemed finally played out. It was a great shock to see June so reduced; and it was indeed as if he had triumphed in her decline, winning his reputation by writing about June.

Miller made two more trips to Europe in 1962, one in the spring and one in the summer. The first was paid for by Grove Press, which had asked him to be a judge in the international Prix Formentor competition for recent fiction. Significantly, besides "causes" like George Dibbern and Haniel Long, the only contemporary writers Miller liked were John Cowper Powys and Céline, though he would later speak highly of Saul Bellow, Isaac Bashevis Singer, and Jack Kerouac. He didn't even read many of the entries. The jury awarded the prize to the young German writer Ewe Johnson but also, at Miller's instigation, sent a cable of homage to Powys.

In Mallorca, Miller came down with the flu, along with a bad case of hemorrhoids—his old complaint. During a physical exam he learned that his heartbeat was irregular; he was troubled too by a prostate condition and an arthritic hip, which made it impossible for him to ride his bike any longer, an activity he still treasured. At seventy-one, age was finally catching up with him. But his physical appearance had changed very little, and he was still a vigorous and compelling presence. June had once called him "handsomely homely," and the description fit.

That summer Miller also had a reunion with Anaïs Nin. She had become anxious about her letters to him, which he had deposited at UCLA, because they were frank and compromising. She asked the librarian, Lawrence Clark Powell, to let her exchange them for Miller's letters to her, most of which she had kept. Powell agreed. Then Nin thought of publishing the letters—severely edited, of course—in a volume that might lead to the publication of her diaries. When she contacted Miller about this, he not only agreed but insisted that she take any royalties due him, since the letters were really hers. (*Selected Letters to Anaïs Nin* was published in 1965. *The New Yorker*, which was seldom kind to Miller, called it "one of the silliest books of the year.")

It had been sixteen years since Henry and Anaïs had last seen each other. Anaïs was friendly when they met in Pacific Palisades; she made no allusions to their past differences, and Henry was relieved to patch things up. She would become a frequent visitor of Henry's, although tensions often sprang up between them. Anaïs never quite forgave him his earlier dependence on her or his cowardice in not running off to Mexico with her in 1940; she conveniently forgot her own refusal to leave Hugo. Henry could not forgive her ridicule of Perlès and the other friends who were important to him, and he was uneasy about all the money he'd accepted from her over the years. But now that Miller had realized celebrity, he was useful to Nin once again, and she resolved to capitalize on the situation. Plans were made to bring her diaries into print, in particular those volumes from the thirties in which Miller figured prominently. Miller was willing enough to agree to this, and was in fact relieved that he could at last repay his former patron in some material way.

Meanwhile, Renate Gerhardt was writing Miller again from Berlin, asking to see him. She understood that it was wisest to be direct with him, she told him, to force him to confront emotional truths he would rather evade. Renate objected to the strange closeness that seemed to spring up between Miller's wives, for example, which he did much to encourage. (Eve was friendly with ex-wives June and Lepska.) She thought this phenomenon was connected to his feelings about his mother, which Miller had never fully resolved. Until he sorted out his ambivalent feelings about women, she wrote, a relationship between them was impossible.

Renate's letter revived Miller's interest in her. When he flew to Europe in 1962 to attend the first Edinburgh Writers' Conference, he stopped in Reinbek to urge her to change her mind. But Renate stood firm, and Miller went on to Edinburgh without her.

The affair with Renate Gerhardt had an unfortunate coda, one that was all too typical of Miller's later years. In 1962 she opened her own publishing house in Hamburg, but soon ran into financial difficulties. She turned to Henry. In December she asked him for $6,000, which he promptly sent. The following March she wrote for $2,000 more; in May and again in June she requested the same amount. Miller never denied her requests for money, which persisted for more than three years; all told, he gave her nearly $30,000. But there is little trace of friendship in Renate's letters to Miller over the entire period; they were simply appeals for cash. He responded to her out of his instinctive generosity and, perhaps, in tribute to their past relationship. Her appeals were duplicated by many others during the sixties and seventies, and Miller would learn to be a bit more cynical about such requests—though never cynical enough.

The furor surrounding *Tropic of Cancer* reached a peak in the summer of 1962 when a Brooklyn court issued a warrant for Miller's arrest, citing a conspiracy between him and his publisher to "prepare and author" a work of pornography. Most of those concerned found the charge laughable, since it implied that an impoverished American living in Paris and a twelve-year-old Barney Rosset had formed a pornography ring in the 1930s, but Miller was frightened. When news of the warrant reached him at Lepska's Pacific Palisades home, where he was visiting the children, he took refuge with his friend Robert Fink at Fink's house in the San Fernando Valley, staying there for a week. On the eve of his next trip to Europe he told a French friend that he feared passing through New York. "Even on the tarmac of Idlewild, I could be arrested and clapped into jail," he said. But the charge in Brooklyn was eventually dropped.

For the time being, and for the first time in Miller's life, money was abundant. In 1962 he sold the film rights to *Tropic of Cancer* to the independent producer Joseph E. Levine, who announced he planned to make a two-million-dollar film, which was, for the time, a major production. In September of the same year Rosset brought out *Tropic of Capricorn*, which also climbed the best-seller lists. New Directions had published a collection of recycled essays called *Stand Still Like the Hummingbird* in June, and this too brought in significant royalties. Grove published *Black Spring* in 1963, and sales were brisk.

Miller's audience had grown with his notoriety, but with no help from the critics. When a copy of *Black Spring* was sent to the literary critic Lionel Trilling, he declined to make a comment, saying, "This is a book which I will be glad to defend but not to praise." Book reviewers were more negative. Leon Edel complained that the author of *Black Spring* was "not yet capable of thought, and maturity of feeling." *Time* rightly thought *Stand Still Like the Hummingbird* was full of "gamy generalities (art is good, materialism is bad)." *The New Yorker* found that Miller's work generally was "marred by [his] philosophical jargon, political ranting, and self-conscious reflection of literary 'influences.' " Things were better at the *New York Times*, where Miller's books were often reviewed by Miller champions Annette Baxter and Harry T. Moore.

Most commonly, the complaint against Miller was that his personality as it emerged in his books was not very likable; critics often reviewed the man rather than his books. There were those who sympathized with Miller's plight in his books and those who did not. Artistic considerations were usually not at issue, which seems odd in light of the innovative techniques of his early work. Critical battle lines were quickly drawn, lines that would remain in place for decades.

In the meantime, Miller was at loose ends, beginning to feel harassed by the financial complications of his new good fortune. His tax situation had become byzantine; in the fall of 1962 he formed a corporation to reduce the burden. So that he might be able to deduct mortgage payments, he also decided to buy a house. Returning to Big Sur was out of the question; Eve had moved in with Harrydick Ross, and, now that their father was famous, it wasn't a good place for the children. Tourists had discovered the area in earnest, many through Miller's work. At the Nepenthe restaurant, the owner, Bill Fassett, set up a telescope that he charged a quarter to look through; it was trained on the Miller home on Partington Ridge.

In January 1963 Miller made still another appeal for funds, cabling Durrell and several other friends that he urgently needed $5,000. He had found the place he wanted to buy, and he had no ready cash. It was a two-story white house with a swimming pool on Ocampo Drive in Pacific Palisades, which he intended to share with Lepska and the children. He could get along fine with Lepska now, he told Eve. (Lepska soon remarried, however, and she and her husband would move out in 1964.) The Ocampo Drive house was an imposing structure, a veritable mansion, worlds apart from his cabin in Big Sur. It was oversized and suburban, and Miller would never be entirely comfortable there. But Los Angeles had always appealed to him, and he had several good friends in the area, most notably the cameraman Leon Shamroy and his doctor friend Robert Fink. Soon he was writing enthusiastically to Durrell about meeting such luminaries as Aldous Huxley and Christopher Isherwood—although he confided that he found Harpo Marx and Jerry Lewis more to his taste.

Surrounded by celebrities, Miller also found himself dependent on accountants and lawyers, all with a host of recommendations for maximizing his profits and reducing his tax bill. The only solution to his immediate tax problem—and to the problem of financing the Ocampo Drive house—his advisors told him, was to make significant charitable donations that could be deducted from his gross income. The easiest way to do this was to give his watercolors to university libraries and museums. He had already given many away, of course, but he had never assigned them a dollar value. Now he asked Elmer Gertz, a Chicago lawyer and friend who was defending *Tropic of Cancer* in court there, to obtain a price quotation for a Miller watercolor from the Art Institute of Chicago. Eventually Miller set the value at $200 apiece, and grimly set to turning out watercolors—scores of them—to reduce his tax liability. His technique had improved, he thought, but some of the joy—and, of course, the spontaneity—had gone out of his painting. Making watercolors as a recourse to a complicated financial situation was entirely characteristic. His years of poverty had made it impossible to deal with money in any kind of sophisticated way, and he was completely mystified by the concept of long-term financial planning.

Miller set his priorities in a revealing fashion in a 1963 letter to Elmer Gertz: "I am not only trying to finish Nexus (and make paintings to help reduce my taxes) but more important, I am helping the script writer on the *Cancer* project." Once again, as he had contrived to do so often in the past, during the first half of the 1960s he was simply too busy to write. The projected second volume of *Nexus* had been shelved after a last burst of writing in 1959. His reunion with June had perhaps put some kind of closure on his real-life "rosy crucifixion," and he no longer felt the need to write about it. *Just Wild About Harry,* the play he had tossed off at Christmastime in 1961, had been done with his left hand. A number of collections of his work appeared, such as his letters to Nin in 1965 and his correspondence with Durrell in 1963. In fact, Miller produced no significant literary work in the sixties.

Instead, he had become what he had most feared: the King of Smut. His name was all over the papers again in 1964, when the legal furor over his work heated up once more. The lawyers Ephraim London and Charles Rembar, on behalf of Grove, brought a writ of *certiorari* in the U.S. Supreme Court asking for a review of a Florida court ruling that had established certain obscenity standards applicable to *Tropic of Cancer.* To their great relief, the Court granted *certiorari* and reversed the Florida decision, effectively declaring that *Tropic of Cancer* was not obscene, and thus putting an end to litigation in state and local courts. The victory was hailed as a landmark advance for the cause of free speech.

But the ban on his books had taken its toll on Miller's spirit. The decades of poverty and obscurity had confirmed his sense that the plight of the creative artist in America—the title of one of his pamphlets from the forties—was dire indeed. The ban shaped his character, and it shaped his work in complex ways. Because of it, he became a cult hero, attracting hangers-on who distracted him from his purpose. He wrote for little magazines and for those who were already fans, unable to reach a larger audience and more tough-minded critics. In the enforced isolation of Big Sur, his eccentric habits of mind were given full rein and made their way into his writing. Finances dictated that he spend good parts of every day devising publishing schemes and drafting appeals for aid. He worked almost in a critical vacuum, and his work might have benefited greatly from intelligent responses. Perhaps most damaging was the effect on his world view. At his best when most jaded, Miller became increasingly and often unpleasantly bitter with the passage of time, so that his work was characterized less by the lusty protest that fuels the *Tropics* and increasingly by the lazy crankiness that characterizes collections like *Remember to Remember*.

Moreover, the damage had been done: Miller was internationally known as a dirty book writer. Time and again, the literary value of his writings was overlooked in favor of their explicitly sexual content. The letters columns of newspapers across the country were devoted to passionate denunciations and defenses of him and his work. He was depicted in several editorial cartoons as a leering bedroom voyeur scribbling in a notebook. When he began appearing as a guest on television talk shows—his earliest appearance was on the Steve Allen Show in 1964—he was more often asked about his sex life than his writing. Although he contributed an article about love to *Mademoiselle*, he more commonly was featured in magazines like *Rogue, Modern Man*, and *Playboy* (the last adopted him as a kind of patron saint).

On the other hand, he gained a new audience for his work, for the lifting of the ban on his books coincided with the beginning of the sexual revolution of the 1960s; the publication of these books in America could not have been timed more shrewdly. Had the *Tropics* appeared a decade later, they might have met with less excitement—mainly because of Miller's treatment of women—but in the early 1960s they seemed revelatory. A new generation of readers discovered him—a younger and extremely enthusiastic group who saw him as a champion of the new sexual freedom. As many of America's young struggled to free themselves from bourgeois conventions, Miller's epics of sexual emancipation spoke directly to them. He became *the* expatriate hero, for his characters, with their stunning ability to stay serene, even happy, in the most horrible circumstances, seemed to have far greater appeal than the suffering, romantic heroes of Hemingway or Fitzgerald.

Miller was also warmly endorsed by the new literary heroes of the period: Allen Ginsberg, William S. Burroughs, Lawrence Ferlinghetti, and Jack Kerouac. For his part, however, Miller didn't care much for the Beats, with the exception of Kerouac. He found Allen Ginsberg's Buddhism insincere, and he championed Burroughs but confessed he was unable to read him. He was impatient with Ferlinghetti, who pestered him for manuscripts to print in his City Lights series. Kerouac he rather liked, and he wrote an Introduction to Kerouac's *The Subterraneans*. For his part, Kerouac was rather in awe of Miller, possibly because his own sexual insecurities led him to admire the grand old man of sex. The one time Kerouac set out to meet Miller, in 1961, he got too drunk to complete the journey.

Miller was gratified, of course, to have a new audience, but he was often mystified by it: he thought many readers were missing his point when they took his books as bibles of the sexual revolution. And although he welcomed publicity—having sought it for so long—it dismayed him to be taken for a "character" rather than a distinguished artist. Of course, his public image was partly due to his own temperament, which at least on the surface was decidedly not serious. But underneath he cherished his old adolescent dream of becoming known as a great thinker and writer, on the order of his idol Dostoevsky.

There were other disappointments. Even with large checks arriving regularly from Grove, money problems continued. Late in 1963 he surveyed his earnings and found that, after taxes, he had only $1,500 in his bank account, despite the fact that he had earned $140,000 in the last two years. Quarterly tax payments were overwhelming him. Because he was a consultant on the film of *Tropic of Cancer*, he had become enmeshed in its legal difficulties. He reported to Gertz that Bernard Wolfe, a writer who had been working on the script but had been recently replaced, was suing his corporation. His hip bothered him; he was in nearly "perpetual pain." In a letter to Eve he quoted Picasso as saying, "One starts to get young at the age of 60—and then it's too late." He grieved for the failure of his marriages, and began what would be a common refrain in letters to friends: artists were impossible to live with, and he was no exception. Although he began dating again—primarily starlets who were attracted to him because of his celebrity—he missed being in love. He had always found it nearly impossible to live without a woman because, although he could cook and clean adequately, he hated these chores, believing they were women's work. He craved being taken care of, and when he found a spare minute to take stock, he discovered that, for all the activity around him, he was lonely.

In 1964, when Barney Rosset began to press for publication of Miller's other censorable works, Miller was not inclined to listen. He resisted Rosset's pleas for over a year, still claiming that *Sexus* and *The World of Sex* would bring lawsuits from Beatrice (although, as he admitted in a letter to Rosset, anyone portrayed as she was might not want to identify herself publicly by starting litigation). But in June 1965 H. L. Hamling, who was associated with *Rogue* magazine, announced his intention of bringing out a "pirated" edition of all five unpublished books—*The Rosy Crucifixion* trilogy, *The World of Sex*, and *Quiet Days in Clichy*. This was not wholly unexpected, because these books had never been properly copyrighted either. In any case, Hamling's announcement forced Miller's hand, and Grove swung into action, producing 250,000 copies of each book in eight days, at a price significantly lower than that announced by Hamling's Greenleaf Publishing.

The appearance of *The World of Sex* and *Quiet Days in Clichy* in the summer of 1965 only reinforced Miller's popular reputation. These sexually frank books—*Clichy*, of course, had been written as dollar-a-page pornography—cemented the image of Miller as the grand old man of dirty book writing. The publication of *The Rosy Crucifixion*—the trilogy of *Sexus*, *Plexus*, and *Nexus*—in the same summer did nothing to improve his standing either; many readers got no further in the trilogy than *Sexus*, the most explicitly sexual of all Miller's works.

But the books were no less popular for that. Over the summer they held the top five spots on *Publishers' Weekly*'s best-seller list. Now that Miller was a familiar literary name, sales outstripped even those of *Tropic of Cancer*.

Surprisingly, the critics held *The Rosy Crucifixion* superior to the *Tropics* and *Black Spring*. Relentlessly autobiographical, the trilogy adheres closely to the notes Miller had mapped out so assiduously in 1928. *Sexus* details the narrator's meeting with the figure based on June (whom he first calls Mara, then Mona) and his sexual experiences with his now discarded first wife, here called Blanche; it closes with the narrator utterly dehumanized by his experience with the two women, literally reduced to barking like a dog. *Plexus* shifts to Miller's early married life with June, including his early attempts to write, but it ranges freely over his life, with many scenes from his boyhood thrown in. *Nexus* is a short, swift account of Jean Kronski's entry into the Miller household. The intended second volume of *Nexus*, which Miller planned would cover his trip with June to Europe, was never written. No doubt he was simply tired; the trilogy was over 1,600 pages long.

Even without Volume 2 of *Nexus*, there is a completeness to the trilogy, which is impressionistically suggested by the titles of the individual works: *Sexus*, *Plexus*, and *Nexus*. Moreover, as the use of the word "Crucifixion" in the trilogy's title suggests, it is the narrative of a hero who undergoes great suffering and is reborn. Miller intuitively knew that June was not part of his rebirth; *that* began when he left her to go to Paris alone. So the trilogy closes with the narrator embarking for Europe with his wife, addressing a catalogue of American icons, from Hiawatha to P. T. Barnum. *The Rosy Crucifixion* is a picaresque tour de force, a cynical, scathing indictment of American life as Miller experienced it. It chronicles the narrator's life in the minutest detail, often painfully so. Unlike so much of Miller's writing, it is not surrealistic, but rather hyperrealistic: the reader is not spared, for example, the sordid particulars of the Henry Street menage. The result is a strangely powerful picaresque masterpiece, a kind of sexual Bildungsroman; Miller meant it to be his life work, an outsized and not entirely comprehensible statement.

With the completion of *Nexus* in 1959 and the American publication of the trilogy in 1965, Miller was at last finished writing about his life with June. He continued to plan the second volume of *Nexus* and a supplementary short work called *Draco and the Ecliptic* for several years, but he sensed he had made his last significant artistic statement. He was tired, and tending to his non-literary affairs took up most of his energies. Any future writing, he hoped, would be light and undemanding. With *The Rosy Crucifixion*, he had had his say.

15.

Pacific Palisades

1965–1980

Miller's colonial-style house at 444 Ocampo Drive in Pacific Palisades looked, with its columns and portico, like the home of a movie star. It had a heated swimming pool in which Miller swam daily. The occupants of the house varied; sometimes Tony and Valentin were there, although Valentin had married a man named Ralph Day on Valentine's Day in 1964. She and her husband moved back into Ocampo Drive in September of that year, joined by Tony, who had grown tired of the military academy he had persuaded his father to allow him to attend. Often the children's friends stayed overnight, and many stayed on for months. During the day Miller himself had a steady stream of callers. Sava Nepus, a Beverly Hills importer, was a frequent visitor and companion. And usually Joe Gray was on the premises; an ex-pugilist, Gray was a movie stuntman and stand-in (very often for Dean Martin, to whom he bore a striking resemblance). Like Miller, he was self-taught. Gray adored Miller and protected him fiercely from fans and others out to exploit him. He also talked a big game as far as women were concerned, although he had very few relationships with them; in this respect he became another Perlès figure in Miller's life.

Lepska had taken almost everything when she moved out, and the house was scantily furnished. The dining-room table, for example, was a picnic table covered by a tablecloth. Several rooms upstairs were empty and looked vandalized, for over the years guests drew and wrote all over the walls. Downstairs, the most used room contained the Ping-Pong table, a piano, and, in a corner, a TV set with a comfortable chair in front of it. The walls were decorated with Miller's watercolors and graffiti written by Miller and his friends, and the ceiling was covered with psychedelic posters. On the same floor was Miller's small bedroom, originally a maid's room. A photograph of a Chinese sage was tacked up next to his bed. But the most striking room was the bathroom: it was plastered with a collage of drawings and photographs, many of them of nudes, as well as suggestive or humorous slogans and titles cut from magazines. The collage grew gradually and was constantly changing.

Miller usually stayed up until two or three in the morning, and didn't rise until noon (he had finally given up his custom of disrobing for an afternoon nap). Upon rising, he ate a meal prepared by a guest or a secretary/companion—many of the latter were recruited from among the children's friends—and turned to his voluminous correspondence. He sometimes received letters that had been addressed simply "Henry Miller, California." In an average week, he estimated, the mail would bring twelve books to write blurbs about, several requests to read from his work or give a lecture, and at least one request to photograph him or paint his portrait. People wanted to collaborate with him on everything from theater pieces to juvenile delinquency programs. The telephone rang all day, but he ignored it; he detested the telephone and, if somebody else picked it up, he generally asked that the caller be told he was away on a trip. After business was taken care of—although new business kept cropping up all day—he would try to find time to swim in the heated pool, which helped his arthritis.

At six he generally had one gin and tonic, fixed without ice in the European fashion, although later he replaced this with a single glass of Dubonnet. Usually there were guests for dinner, and always there was a good French table wine. After dinner the talk might continue for hours, with Miller holding forth, lighting cigarette after cigarette. Or he might paint, or play the piano. He had rediscovered his passion for music—the pianist Jakob Gimpel gave him lessons—but had not rediscovered his technique. He merely "pretended" to play, imitating a histrionic pianist, lifting his hands melodramatically from the keyboard, playing random notes.

More and more he was surrounded by movie people. He liked celebrities, and many of them were fans of his. Ava Gardner was a devoted fan. He also met and admired Kim Novak, Gloria Swanson, and Elke Sommer. Joe Gray, who occasionally got Valentin work as an extra, introduced him to Dean Martin. One of the starlets Joe Gray brought around was Ziva Rodann, an Israeli actress with whom Miller was half in love in 1963 and 1964. She was replaced in his affections by a Polish actress he said he discovered in *Playboy*, Zofia Slaboszowska, with whom he corresponded.

The ex-wives had dispersed. Beatrice lived nearby in Pasadena, and he often received reports of her from Barbara. She still had the capacity to get under his skin; when Barbara reported that her aging mother had renewed her driver's license, Miller, who had been forced to give up driving, was incredulous—envious and a little bit angry. June Mansfield had moved out to Arizona to stay with her older brother and had fallen silent. Lepska would soon move to Santa Barbara; the strain of their life together on Ocampo Drive had made a close relationship impossible. Then, in the summer of 1966, he received word that Eve had died—rumor around Big Sur was that she drank herself to death. Miller had not realized how seriously her death would affect him. He had written her steadily, even after their divorce in 1962, and he had visited her and Harrydick frequently. Eve was young and vital, the most loving of his wives, and he found that he truly missed her.

Anaïs Nin, recently reconciled with Henry, still remained somewhat guarded around him—and he with her. In 1966 Harcourt Brace & World had published the first volume of Nin's *Diary*, covering the years 1931–34. While the volume detailed her own artistic growth, it was devoured by many as a wonderful compendium of writerly gossip. There Anaïs reported at length on the drama between Henry and June, and on her own romance with Henry. Miller was a bit perplexed by the critical and popular success of the *Diary*. He had always believed it one of the twentieth century's greatest literary achievements. Nin of course showed him only the briefest of extracts, and it is likely what he admired most was not the actual work but the *idea* of it. He assumed it to be an Emersonian exercise in introspection, of the sort for which he had the highest regard. He had given no thought to its gossip value, and was a little disappointed that Nin was not taken more seriously as an innovator. He seemed to see no irony in the fact that Nin, who had always insisted on the utmost secrecy, was now airing the frankest details of her past.

In 1966 another woman appeared on the scene to distract him. She was Hiroko Tokuda, nicknamed Hoki—a twenty-eight-year-old Japanese pop singer and actress. Miller saw her singing in a piano bar at the Imperial Gardens, a Los Angeles restaurant, and was immediately captivated. For years he had been singing the praises of Asian women; he thought they embodied the very essence of femininity. They could be submissive but strongly sexual, he pronounced, and would make ideal wives. He finally met Hoki at a party given by one of his doctors, Lee Siegel, in February 1967.

At seventy-six, Miller saw no problem in the age difference between Hoki and himself. He often invoked the love affairs of Pablo Casals and Goethe, both of whom had fallen in love with younger women. He felt young, and he still believed in romance. While he was no longer very active sexually, he maintained a considerable interest in sexual matters; he was carrying on a number of erotic correspondences with women who sent him photographs of themselves naked and even clippings from their pubic hair.

Hoki was not like Miller's fans, however. She was the first of quite another kind of woman who was to play a substantial part in Miller's last years. For one thing, she kept her distance. Just as June had, Hoki inflamed Henry with jealousy: he was driven to near-distraction watching her sing love songs to leering male customers. She showed little interest in him at first, which tantalized him even more. In December he wrote Emil White that he understood Japanese women felt honored and safe to be involved with older men, but that he was having his troubles winning Hoki's affection.

He began to suffer from terrible insomnia—a new complaint. Often he was up as late as 4:00 or 5:00 a.m., agonizing over Hoki's changefulness. In this mood he began to write again, scribbling passages about his hopeless love. "First it was a broken toe, then a broken brow, and finally a broken heart," he began. The manuscript that emerged contained his only truly distinguished writing of the 1960s and 1970s, his only significant writing after *The Rosy Crucifixion*. He called the book *Insomnia Or The Devil at Large*. A handsomely illustrated volume, it was published by the Loujon Press in 1970 and later reissued by Doubleday.

However distant, Hoki gradually became a fixture in the Ocampo Drive house. Tony and Val didn't approve of her, nor did most of Miller's friends, especially Joe Gray; she had all the makings of a golddigger, friends warned, and would make him unhappy. But he began to speak of marrying her, and they realized he might be serious.

In the summer of 1967 Hoki's visa expired and she was told she had to leave the country. This turn of events apparently made her far more receptive to Miller's suit for her affections. To his delight, she agreed to marry him, and on September 10 they were wed in a ceremony at Lee Siegel's. The whole business was very rushed because Miller was scheduled to be present at the opening of a show of his watercolors in Paris on the 20th. He planned to bring Hoki with him, he wrote Durrell. They would go on to Sweden for another show, and from there—at last!—to Japan, where Miller's writing was hugely popular.

The wedding was captured on film by Robert Snyder, a documentary film maker who, after being refused many times, had convinced Miller to be the subject of a short film. His crew had virtually moved into the Ocampo Drive house, replacing all the light bulbs with very high temperature bulbs suitable for color filming. After shooting the wedding, Snyder ran out of funds, and Miller loaned him money to bring the crew to France in order to complete the project. But Snyder was not prepared for the intensity of Miller's French reception. Reporters met Henry and Hoki at Orly and pursued them relentlessly for the next few days. At the reception following the opening of his show the police had to be called to escort Miller, Hoki, and the crew safely out of the gallery.

The Miller entourage also included a young Canadian, Gerald Robitaille, and his wife, Diane. Robitaille was acting as Miller's secretary, companion, and chauffeur. An ardent admirer of his employer, Robitaille saw himself as a sort of son. According to Robitaille, Miller wanted him to write his biography. For the time being, however, Robitaille acted primarily as a buffer, keeping unwanted intruders at bay.

Miller and Hoki spent just two months in France. They visited Durrell in Sommières, a village in the South of France, and Durrell traveled up to Paris to visit them. Miller saw some other old friends, among them Beauford Delaney, the black artist whom he had met back in the forties. The couple also visited Georges Belmont and his wife. That night, after dinner, Miller and Belmont's wife and daughter retired, but Hoki stayed up drinking with Belmont. According to Belmont, she confided to him that she had married Henry in order to become an American citizen, and that he knew it. "He's very merry," she said, adding cryptically, "when we go to bed he's my grandfather."

The marriage was a failure almost from the start. Before long, Miller privately referred to Hoki as "l'Impératrice," or, when particularly annoyed, "Lady Precious Stream." The couple returned to the United States at the end of the month, barely speaking to each other. Hoki made it quite clear that she was not to be taken for granted sexually. Night after night she disappeared in her Jaguar convertible, a gift from Miller. He had forbidden her to sing at piano bars ("the piano bar is the gateway to the hall of masturbation," he had written ruefully in *Insomnia*) so she had to invent reasons to leave the house. She installed two friends from Japan at Ocampo Drive, Michiko Watanabe and a woman named Puko, whom Miller called his "massage wife." All he was missing, he told Hoki, was a "fucking wife."

In 1968 Hoki made three trips to Japan—once to visit her ailing father, once to promote Miller's watercolors, and once to promote her own career. The Japanese public was avid for any crumb of news about their marriage, every detail of which—accurate or not—appeared in the Japanese press. Miller was immersing himself in things Japanese, taking Japanese-language lessons and reading up on Zen Buddhism. To Hoki's amusement—she claimed the words meant no more than "Have a nice day"—he began chanting daily *"nam myo renge kho."* It was his good luck charm, he told her.

But Hoki seldom wrote Henry during her absences in Japan, and he was tortured by her silences. He pleaded for her to send naked photographs of herself, to give him some token of love. He began to speak of men menstruating again, always a sure sign that he was unhappy in love, concerned about his manhood. He complained to her about his loneliness, about money problems, about his health.

The truth was that matters were not much better when Hoki was in residence. Miller complained that she was out on the town night after night, playing Mah-Jongg with her girlfriends or visiting nightclubs with mysterious escorts. In his letters to Hoki, Miller complained about her withholding sex and refusing to accompany him on social calls (she complained that his friends were boring). She and her Japanese houseguests, Miller said, alternately teased and ridiculed him, often disappearing upstairs in fits of giggling. Masochistically, he scolded her and, time and again, forgave her.

Meanwhile, negotiations had started up again for the film version of *Tropic of Cancer*. Joseph Strick, who had directed the films *Ulysses* and Jean Genet's *The Balcony*, was writing, directing, and producing. He had lined up Rip Torn to play the Miller figure, and the then unknown Ellen Burstyn to play the part of June/Mona (after Shirley MacLaine backed out). Shooting was scheduled for the summer of 1969 in Paris, and Miller was paid to be there to consult for six weeks.

Hoki was in Europe at the time and intended to join Henry in Paris, where she hoped for a bit part in the film. When he flew over at the end of June, he stopped first in London to see John Calder, who published his books in Britain from the house of Calders and Boyars. Hoki had passed through London only two weeks before—Calder remembered chauffeuring a bored Hoki, with what he said looked to him like "beard burn," around the city—and Miller questioned him closely about her visit. He asked to be driven to the Dorchester, where Hoki had stayed; once there, he asked Calder to stop the car. He spent five minutes gazing pensively at the hotel, then told Calder to drive on.

Matters didn't improve in Paris, where Hoki insulted him in public, calling him "rich, stupid Henry." Miller rented an apartment in Passy, but Hoki soon departed for St. Tropez with Puko and other Japanese friends. While Miller took some interest in the shooting of the movie—he was cast as an old man in a church wedding scene—he was besieged by the press and very tired. Tony, who had enlisted in the Army and quickly deserted, had joined him in Paris and was working on the film; Miller felt that he and Tony were at last becoming good friends. He had hopes that Tony might become a writer himself one day.

As it turned out, the film was not a success. Miller's masterpiece translated very badly to the screen. John Simon wrote a not unfavorable review of *Tropic of Cancer* for the *New York Times*, but he pointed out that the movie's extensive use of narration to accompany drastically shortened scenes was symptomatic of a larger weakness in the script. Miller was aware that many scenes were cut or foreshortened, but he could not have predicted the effect, which was to make people laugh at Rip Torn, the actor who played him. Miller thought that the narration, taken verbatim from the novel, preserved its original qualities, but the juxtaposition of lengthy narration and short, slapstick scenes—especially sexual scenes—was unintentionally comic. "The narration wallow[s] in mendacious accounts of gigantic sexual feats while the camera tells the sober and pitiful truth," Simon wrote, adding that the effect was humorous but the joke overused. Whatever the effect, Miller's novel had been badly used and Miller indirectly humiliated.

Joe Strick himself acknowledged that his film didn't work. The narration, he felt, stopped the action cold. Reviewers also felt that updating the action to sixties Paris was a mistake, and some raised a new charge—which would soon be heard more and more in connection with Miller's work—that the movie was grossly sexist. Worst of all, though Joe Strick had elicited a guarantee against censorship, the movie was effectually censored in the United States when it received an "X" rating under the newly instituted rating system. The movie was a complete flop; in Paris on opening day there were eleven people in the theater. Aside from his warm friendship with Strick, Miller had no good memories of what would be his last visit to Paris.

He had somewhat higher hopes for the film version of *Quiet Days in Clichy*, which was being made at the same time by the Danish director Jens Jorgen Thorsen. It had an undistinguished cast and was decidedly explicit in sexual content, but Grove Press was distributing it and Miller thought Rosset knew what he was doing. Nevertheless, like the *Tropic of Cancer*, *Quiet Days in Clichy* was poorly received and met a dreadful fate at the box office. It, too, is grossly misogynistic and dated, with none of the humor and energy of Miller's book. A representative lyric from the score performed by Country Joe McDonald is "She spoils the coffee, burns the eggs/Her brains are all between her legs."

Nor was the Robert Snyder documentary faring well. Snyder was still plagued by money troubles, and Miller tried to help him out. He told Barney Rosset that he intended to approach the Beatles who, he understood, were fans of his, to see if they would like to invest in the film.

Miller's sister, Lauretta, died in December 1969 after a short bout with cancer, and Miller had Val, who had divorced Ralph Day and was now living at Big Sur with a man named Geoffrey Palmer, pick up her ashes. The only memento Lauretta left was a photograph of her kindergarten class on Fillmore Place—the same kindergarten Miller had attended. Christmas of 1969—and Miller's seventy-eighth birthday—was bleak. Over the holidays he wrote to Durrell complaining again of insomnia. He commonly took a sleeping pill at four in the morning, he said, and it knocked him out until noon. He warned Durrell that the new year might see him doing "new, strange things"; he had been acting foolishly, and he knew it. He vowed that the seventies would be different.

At seventy-eight, Miller met new and unpleasant notoriety when the feminist movement took note of him. Kate Millett's *Sexual Politics* appeared in 1969, a scathing indictment of contemporary sex roles, which also explored male tyranny and misogyny in modern literature, most specifically in the work of Lawrence, Genet, Mailer, and Miller. In Miller she found a rich supply indeed; while allowing that his works had many good qualities, she found him to be a "compendium of American sexual neuroses," incapable of writing about women except as "cunts." Miller's ideal woman, Millett concluded, was a whore.

Norman Mailer leaped to Miller's defense in *The Prisoner of Sex*, published in 1971. Millett had misread Miller, he argued; she had quoted him out of context and drawn mistaken conclusions. He saw Miller as a sexual conservative, relegating women to what he considered to be their proper roles, and at the same time as a sexual revolutionary, celebrating the difference between the sexes.

Miller professed not to understand what the argument was about. Whenever the topic came up, he asserted that he loved women, that the problem was rather that too many people were having sex without love. He took a dim view of the sexual revolution, he claimed.

Yet Miller, an octogenarian now, was as obsessed as ever with sexual difference between women and men, and his preoccupation continued to compel him to equate sexual performance with virility. His letters to Hoki show not only considerable anxiety about his own potency, but also an almost adolescent interest in matters sexual: as he put it, he preferred Swedish "split beaver" pornography to *Playboy* any day. In any case, the public saw Miller as the apotheosis of the *Playboy* man, and it is no coincidence that he appeared frequently in the magazine's pages during the 1960s and 1970s. He was encouraged in this continued—if not intensified—preoccupation with the sexual by his fans, who sent him a steady stream of dirty cartoons and jokes, sexual aids like aphrodisiacs, photographs of naked men and women, and rubber stamps with four-letter words on them.

All of this made it extremely difficult for him to evade charges of sexism—particularly once Anaïs Nin's diaries began appearing in 1966, just five years after *Tropic of Cancer*'s official publication in America. As the *Tropics* had for Miller, the *Diary* brought Nin fame, critical acclaim, and financial security. She attracted a huge following among young women who regarded her, with her belief in sexual liberation and her intense absorption in the details of female life, as a model of modern womanhood. Many of them were perplexed by her relationship with Miller, whom they saw as unfeeling, sexist, and a consummate degrader of women. But Nin herself made careful distinctions between Miller the man and Miller the writer, insisting that he himself was much gentler and more loving than his books suggested. Some women readers were convinced by Nin's portrayal of him to read Miller's work, and some of them came to admire him.

Thoroughly misunderstanding the central issue of the feminist debate, Miller insisted, repeatedly, that he loved women, wrongly taking that to be the central issue. He spoke, for example, of his admiration for Germaine Greer—although what he admired, it turned out, was a statement she had made to the effect that love was painful. He believed that women were the superior sex, he told the novelist Erica Jong, who had just written *Fear of Flying*, a book many reviewers compared to *Tropic of Cancer*. Miller was simply too old-fashioned to embrace or even understand the goals of the women's movement. As with some of his literary predecessors—Hamsun, most notably—his surrealist prose and modernist pose masked a chivalric nature. Miller was a true romantic. Waverley Root, who knew him in Paris, once called his work the "literature of disgust," noting that modern sexuality was clearly one of the things that disgusted him. A crude analysis, perhaps, but some of the sheer nastiness of Miller's descriptions of sex must certainly be related to his feeling that he had been cheated by being born in a world where true chivalry and romanticism were no longer possible. Surely his support of individual women was sincere and generous, as, for example, when he encouraged the artistic careers of Anaïs Nin and his fourth wife, Eve. But he could not grasp the idea of equality between the sexes. His own sexual anxieties bound him irrevocably to the distinctions between the sexes, and he could be truly comfortable only when his female partner conformed to his old and now outdated stereotypes of the feminine.

These stereotypes were partly what drew him to Hoki, of course, for Miller shared a common Western fantasy about the gentle subservience of Asian women. Hoki conformed to none of his expectations, however; rather than being the geisha he had fantasized, she was the exact opposite: an independent, hard-as-nails woman with little interest in romance. In time, the only element in her character that Henry would perceive as "feminine" was a quality he believed all women shared: duplicity. She was like June in her constant deceptions, he said, and he was helpless to free himself from her, always jealous and always suspicious, feeling himself used and abused. Time and again, in the face of her humiliations, Miller made up with Hoki, often showering her with expensive gifts. His innate masochism battled with common sense.

As time passed, Hoki continued to withhold sex, and without sex the marriage faltered. Miller had liked the illusion that he was surrounded by a bevy of Oriental beauties, but in reality most of the Asian women he surrounded himself with were simply freeloaders. (One visitor remembered someone in the house making frequent telephone calls to the local liquor store for cases of liquor to be charged to Miller's account.) None of these women paid particular attention to him, except to give him an occasional massage. Hoki herself was frequently out all night, night after night; in his letters Miller referred to her coming home drunk. Miller tortured himself with the memory of a conversation they had before their marriage in which he had suggested that Hoki marry a Chinese-American friend in order to solve her visa problems and then refuse to sleep with him. Hoki's response was "Oh no, I could never do that. I would have to sleep with him." In other words, Miller wrote her, "you were ready to do for him what you would not do for me." The humiliation was finally too much and in May 1970 Hoki moved out—though not before she convinced Miller to buy her a boutique in Beverly Hills. She remained in his life for a few years and then disappeared altogether; they were divorced in 1977.

With Hoki gone, the early seventies were Miller's last happy, even relatively productive years. He had given up work on the second volume of *Nexus* and could no longer summon the energy for a new extended work, but he continued to write, and also was pleased to see many volumes appear that discussed his work. *Insomnia* was reissued in 1974 by Doubleday. Noel Young's Capra Press, in Santa Barbara, issued a series of chapbooks of his writing, eventually collected as *Sextet* in 1977. These included an essay on the suicide of the Japanese writer Yukio Mishima, which interested Miller extraordinarily; a remarkably honest essay called "On Turning Eighty"; and an essay on Greece. Miller's correspondence with the critic and translator Wallace Fowlie appeared in 1975. In the same year, Playboy Press and Bradley Smith brought out a coffee table volume by Miller entitled *My Life and Times*, replete with photographs (appropriately enough, a mixture of fascinating early photos of the young Miller and his family along with some less distinguished shots of the old man surrounded by naked women), reproductions of manuscript pages, watercolors, and a few of the wall charts on which Miller diagrammed his books.

My Life and Times is sadly representative of Miller's late years. In it he recycles familiar stories that his followers had already heard: the old account of his meeting with Emma Goldman, his relations with the Jewish cutters at his father's tailor shop, wild nights in Clichy, his first attempts at painting. He had written so extensively about his literary tastes that even the books he recommended sounded familiar rather than idiosyncratic: Hamsun's *Hunger*, Dostoevsky's *The Eternal Husband* and *The Idiot*, anything by Marie Corelli, Blaise Cendrars's *Moravagine*. He had some new enthusiasms, most notably Isaac B. Singer and Saul Bellow; he also rediscovered a book he had loved as a child, Edmondo De Amicis's *The Heart of a Boy*. But for the most part he worked on repairing his own image, presenting himself as at once a sage and a naif, a man who believed in artistic and sexual freedom, and a proponent of acceptance. Fans *wanted* to hear the same old stories, it seemed. But when he told one fan a remarkable—and unverifiable—story about appearing before a French court in the early fifties and becoming so agitated on the witness stand that he lost bladder control, the fan didn't know what to make of it; it did not fit the Miller legend.

His politics were misunderstood as well. His readers expected that he would show sympathy with the aims of the youth movement, but Miller purported not to understand their goals. He didn't like rock music, and he was vehemently against drugs. He sympathized with rebels, of course—he always had. But he never made the political pronouncements or gestures his admirers expected of him. When his Big Sur friend Bill Webb stopped paying his taxes to protest the Vietnam War, Miller expressed his admiration. When Webb asked Miller why he didn't do the same, Henry said that he wouldn't dare to, that he just didn't have it in him. He was temperamentally suspicious of organized politics, and he distrusted causes. Tasha Doner, the daughter of another Big Sur friend, asked him for $1,000 for Cesar Chavez's farmworkers movement, but he declined; he would give the young woman the money, he said, but would not make a check out to Chavez.

His health continued to decline steadily, and in the early seventies he was spending more and more time in bed. His hip bothered him; there was a problem with the cartilage at the socket. He had to undergo an operation to insert an artificial artery from his neck to his groin in order to get blood to circulate in his right leg. When the first operation failed, he had to go through a second. His doctors told him that, after nearly sixty years of smoking non-filter cigarettes, he had to quit smoking. But he managed to do so with far more ease than he had anticipated, and later became something of a fanatic about others smoking in his presence.

Another operation in the fall of 1973, scheduled to remove the faulty artificial artery, was far more serious; Miller was on the operating table for more than ten hours, and in the process went into shock. A blood clot formed near his optic nerve and he found himself unable to see out of his right eye. He told Perlès that his Swiss astrologer, Jacqueline Langmann, predicted that his sight would return within the year. When it did not, Miller found he had to curtail sharply his reading and letter writing.

The early seventies also saw Miller's years of casual benevolence finally backfire on him, as he suffered an inordinate number of betrayals at the hands of those he had considered friends. The departure of Gerald Robitaille was perhaps the most painful loss. Robitaille claimed that Miller had reneged on a promise to pay him during his lifetime $10,000 that he had been planning to will to Robitaille. Whether Miller had written Robitaille into his will or not, he perceived Robitaille's quitting as a betrayal, and he was doubly stung when Robitaille wrote a diatribe against him, published as *Le Père Miller* in 1971. It revealed less about Miller's failings than it did about the toadying and exploitation going on around him in those years—in which Robitaille appears to have participated fully.

Another he perceived as a traitor was his old friend Robert Fink, who Miller felt had turned on him in 1972, when Fink proposed to put together a book of his letters; he told Emil White he feared it would be a duplicate of the Robitaille affair. The book was never published, but another, which appeared in France in 1975, enraged him. Written by his old friend the photographer Brassaï, *Henry Miller: Grandeur Nature* purported to be a biography. But Miller found numerous inaccuracies and distortions in the manuscript and wrote Brassaï a bitter letter maintaining that Brassaï obviously had never understood him. Another disappointment came from a more familiar quarter: Anaïs Nin broke off contact with both Miller and Durrell because they continued, in their letters to her, to refer to Hugo as her husband, without acknowledging that she was now known on the West Coast as Rupert Pole's wife. Miller found himself speaking far less positively about Nin, and he would criticize her openly after her death in 1977, writing darkly of her "chicanery" and "duplicity."

The children, now grown, were a comfort to him, if sometimes a cause for worry. Valentin and Tony lived alternately at the Ocampo Drive house and at the shack on Partington Ridge, which was still jointly owned by Henry and Lepska. Val had spent part of the sixties in Aspen; Tony, an expert surfer, had finally turned himself in to the Army as a deserter and been given a discharge. In 1971 he took over Gerald Robitaille's job as Miller's secretary, answering his father's non-essential mail and sometimes, according to a letter from Miller to Durrell, writing reviews that came out under his father's name. He also inherited some of Miller's cast-off women, and his father tried to arrange liaisons for him with Hoki's friends. Miller worried terribly that his fame had injured his children; referring to Picasso's son Paulo he exclaimed, "What a tragedy for a son to have a father so famous!"

After Hoki's departure, Miller fell in love yet again, this time with a Chinese actress in her thirties, Lisa Lu, whom he had known for many years. Describing her in a letter to Valentin, he praised her for having played a leading role in the Chinese film *The Arch*, performing with Marlon Brando in *One-Eyed Jacks*, and participating in a Chinese opera company as a singer and a dancer. Judging from Miller's references to her in his letters, it seems that Lisa Lu treated him far more decently than Hoki had. But she had little success in breaking into Hollywood films and worked on location for long periods of each year in Taiwan and Hong Kong, so the romance was largely an epistolary one. (In one nine-month period Miller wrote her 224 letters.)

He had just about written himself out. In 1975 he began a trilogy of short chapbooks for Capra about the friends in his life. The first book contained portraits of Brooklyn friends like Stanley Borowski and Bill Dewar. The second was about his California friends and also about his bike, which he called his best friend. The third volume, about Perlès and some of the women in his life, contained some particularly bitter remarks about Nin. Though Miller rambles, repeats himself, and digresses maddeningly, the trilogy *Book of Friends* is remarkable for its candor. Here Miller revealed many things about his past that he had previously suppressed: his homosexual experiences as a boy, his unsatisfactory relationships with Melpo Niarchos and Sevasty Koutsaftis, and some sad facts about his exploitation by some of the companions of his later years. Perhaps most interestingly, Miller made no mention of his wives, or of Lawrence Durrell, Emil Schnellock, or Anaïs Nin. His publishers were left out of the book as well, for reasons that can only be guessed at, since all were good friends—Girodias, Laughlin, Porter, Rosset, and Noel Young. Miller seems to have deliberately chosen as subjects those friends with whom his relations were relatively uncomplicated, and whose friendship thus gave him the occasion to reflect on his own life—which was still, of course, his favorite subject.

A chapbook he wrote at roughly the same time, *Mother, China, and the World Beyond*, makes it clear that Miller was preparing for death. In it he describes a dream in which he meets his mother in Limbo. To his amazement, she is tolerant and wise; he has no desire to search out his father (who he imagines is off drinking, perhaps with John Barrymore), but stays by his mother's side, listening while she explains how Limbo works. He asks his mother why she never liked Cora Seward or Pauline, his boyhood loves, and is astonished when she answers simply that she thought they weren't good enough for him. He is surprised as well to hear that he had had a brother, or, more precisely, that his mother had a stillborn boy before his birth. And he is all but bowled over to learn that his mother has read his beloved Marie Corelli and that she intends to return to life as a black man. Although the piece seems to have been written out of a desire to come to terms with his mother, the dream mother is highly idealized (and, significantly, very male); she has committed none of the crimes for which Henry held Louise Miller guilty, and the resolution is artificial and forced. Even in old age his anger at his mother had stayed with him, and he would nurse his grievances on his deathbed.

By 1976 Miller was an invalid. Now eighty-four, he shuffled about the house leaning on a walker, usually clad in a blue terrycloth bathrobe and pajamas. He wore slippers even on his infrequent trips out of the house—when, for instance, he gave a series of talks at Jack Garfein's Artists and Writers Laboratory, or when he entertained a female friend at the Imperial Gardens, still his favorite restaurant. He was cared for during these months by an able secretary and companion, Twinka Thiebaud, who would later collect his last reminiscences in book form as *Reflections*. Charles Robinson, a nurse, came regularly to exercise his limbs and give him necessary medications. A succession of women cooked his meals for him. (An injunction on a list taped to a kitchen cupboard stated "No health foods!") On his front door was posted a quotation from Meng-tse that Hermann Hesse—another Miller enthusiasm—had posted on his own door:

> When a man has reached old age and has fulfilled his mission, he has a right to confront the idea of death in peace. He has no need of other men, he knows them already and has seen enough of them. What he needs is peace. It is not seemly to seek out such a man, plague him with chatter, and make him suffer banalities. One should pass by the door of his house as if no one lived there.

But very few of Miller's visitors paid any attention to the notice. His fans were persistent. Other writers sought him out, including Erica Jong, whom he promoted vigorously, and Norman Mailer, who in 1976 put together *Genius and Lust*, an anthology of Miller's writings intermingled with a perceptive commentary. Durrell paid a number of visits when he held a visiting lecturer's post at nearby CalTech. Other old friends surfaced as well, most notably Irving Stettner, whom he had not seen since the forties. Stettner, a poet and painter, was just starting a literary magazine called *Stroker*, to which Miller became an enthusiastic contributor. He introduced Miller to the work of Tommy Trantino, an artist and poet who was serving a life sentence for murder in a New Jersey jail; Trantino became another of Miller's causes.

During this period, Miller began to talk of winning the Nobel Prize —something he had dreamed of as far back as 1946. He had received very few awards for his work: he was awarded France's Légion d'Honneur in 1976 (outraged prostitutes, who felt Miller portrayed them negatively, picketed outside the Elysée in protest), and in Italy he had won the Book of the Year award for *Stand Still Like the Hummingbird* in 1970. Since 1957, when he had been sponsored by Van Wyck Brooks, he had been a member of the National Institute of Arts and Letters, and he proudly wore its rosette on the rare occasions that he wore a sports jacket. But the Nobel was the prize he wanted. He told Rosset and Durrell that it was simply because he needed the money—that his assets would just pay the estate taxes at his death. He professed not to be disappointed when Isaac B. Singer was awarded the Nobel Prize in 1978: he admired Singer, he said, and at any rate he was "applying" for the 1979 prize. Durrell told him he had met a man on the prize committee a few years back who had said, "We are waiting for Mister Miller to become *respectable.*" Privately, Miller thought he had botched his chance years before, in Europe, when he had snubbed the Swedish critic Arthur Lundkvist.

But he had some consolation in these final years. In June 1976 he began corresponding with a young Mississippi woman who had come to Los Angeles to further her acting career. Brenda Venus—not a pseudonym, she claimed—sent him photographs of herself that captivated him. He liked her exotic looks: she was a tall, athletic woman, part American-Indian, with long brown hair and almond-shaped eyes. She had appeared in the film *The Eiger Sanction* with Clint Eastwood and in some B movies, but was having a hard time landing major roles; she taught ballet in the mornings to make ends meet.

Miller wrote Brenda that he couldn't imagine why she wanted to see an eighty-four-year-old man, but he almost immediately pledged his love. When he met her a month later he was won. Upon hearing of her Indian blood, he insisted they become blood brothers. Before long he was writing her long, erotic letters, which she accepted without complaint. Tactfully, she did not tell him she had a steady boyfriend, and when he asked what she did for sexual release, she replied that she exercised. He told her that he wanted to initiate her into esoteric sexual secrets, and gave her erotic Oriental prints, books about Tantric yoga, and a book on the Konarak Temple in India, known for its erotic images.

Miller wrote her that actual sex was out of the question: he worried that his heart would give out if he tried intercourse, he said, and he seldom got erections. But he was haunted by erotic dreams about Brenda, who he believed was highly sexed, and in November 1978 he asked her to give him the privilege of fondling her. He understood, he wrote, "how repugnant it must be for a young beautiful creature like you to be asked to make love to a man almost ninety years old," but perhaps she could reciprocate, he said. Brenda answered by appearing in his bedroom clad only in a white robe, which she let fall to her feet for a minute before drawing it around her again. Nothing further happened, according to Brenda.

Miller provided Brenda with lists of books to read, words to learn, music to listen to, and plays to see, and he tried to help her in her career; he wrote scenes for her to act and steered her to his influential Hollywood friends. When Warren Beatty asked him to appear as a "witness" in his film *Reds*, Miller accepted—though he had never known John Reed or Louise Bryant, the subjects of the film—on the condition that Brenda appear in Beatty's next movie. (Brenda never appeared in a Beatty film, but Miller's segment in *Reds* is an entertaining commentary on love and sex among the bohemians of the century's early decades.) Miller also gave Brenda permission to try to sell some of his books as film vehicles for herself. She planned a trip to Paris in late 1979, hoping to interest either Fellini or Truffaut in *The Smile at the Foot of the Ladder* or, failing that, another Miller title. Truffaut expressed some interest in making a film of the Conrad Moricand story, *The Devil in Paradise*, but otherwise the trip was not a success.

Some of Miller's friends, Lawrence Durrell among them, believed that Brenda kept Miller alive for a couple of years longer than would otherwise have been the case. Whether or not this is true, it is clear that Miller was convinced she loved him, and the love of a beautiful woman might very well have sustained a man as romantic as he. If Brenda hoped to gain anything tangible from her relationship with him, she never showed it, and she did what she could to make his last days happy ones.

But others maintain that Brenda was yet another bystander who hoped to cash in on her acquaintance with Miller. Virtually a prisoner in the Ocampo Drive house, and without a car, he was almost entirely dependent on those around him. Twinka had been replaced by a girl-friend of Tony's named Sandi Stahl, who served him competently enough for a time. Stahl had considerable power in the household, and in this position she aroused resentment in many of Miller's fans, who grew suspicious about her attentions; after about six months she left. Matters stabilized somewhat when one of Miller's friends, Barbara Kraft, found a young artist named Bill Pickerill to attend Miller. Pick-erill devoted himself to his charge.

By March 1980 Miller was failing rapidly. He was nearly blind and quite deaf, confined to a wheelchair. In May Georges Hoffman, who had taken over as Miller's agent following his father's death, arrived to film him for yet another documentary, despite the fact, Miller wrote Durrell, that he was "half gaga." He wrote his friends—Perlès, Dur-rell, Irving Stettner, Brenda Venus—that he was dying, or, as he wrote Perlès, "definitely leaving the planet." They were strong, confident letters; he had few regrets. In May his mind went completely—he appeared to believe he was in Paris—and, attended by Bill Pickerill, he died of cardiovascular failure on June 7.

"Henry Miller is not dead," reads a graffito in southern California, a photograph of which appears on a recent book collector's catalogue dedicated to Miller's work. A man who surrounded himself with activ-ity, Miller had become a small cottage industry in the forties and fifties. With the publication of the banned books in the early sixties, he be-came a full-scale, diversified business. It did not shut its doors after his death.

The seeming deluge began on July 17, 1980, just a little more than a month after he died, when his last book appeared; ironically, it was "the Brochure" about D. H. Lawrence that had so preoccupied him in his Paris years. The editors, Evelyn Hinz and John Teunissen, labored mightily to pare down Miller's bulky manuscript, but the result is still virtually unreadable. In 1984, Irving Stettner brought out *From Your Capricorn Friend,* a collection of Miller's letters to him and pieces he wrote for *Stroker;* to this day Stettner reprints items from the book in *Stroker.* Twinka Thiebaud's collection, *Reflections,* appeared in 1985. In 1986 the collections of his letters to Brenda Venus and to Hoki Tokuda were published. His *Hamlet Letters,* an abridged edition of his

1930s correspondence with Michael Fraenkel, was published in 1988, as was his correspondence with Lawrence Durrell. And 1989 saw New Directions publish the most revealing batch of correspondence yet, his letters to Emil Schnellock; the letters were edited by George Wickes, whose most notable deletions were several lengthy anti-Semitic passages.

Nineteen eighty-seven saw the birth of a thriving subindustry, with the appearance of two books relating to Miller's affair with Nin: one a selection from her unedited diaries called *Henry and June*, and the other a volume of correspondence. A year before the centennial of his birth, the director Philip Kaufman finished a movie of the diary entries. This movie, *Henry and June*, was initially given an X rating, but on its American release in October 1990, the rating was changed to the NC 17, a new category altogether. And a new film version of *Quiet Days in Clichy*, directed by Claude Chabrol and with the decidedly not-bald and not-middle-aged Andrew McCarthy playing Miller, was recently released in Europe.

Miller is still collected widely. A young California writer, Michael Hargraves, published a bibliography immediately after his death, citing the need of a "quick, handy guide" to help collectors "in the coming crazy days." They were crazy days indeed. In 1986 Valentin Miller removed the manuscript of *Tropic of Cancer* from the archives at UCLA and took it to Sotheby's, where it was auctioned for $165,000, a price higher than any before paid for a twentieth-century literary manuscript. First editions of *Tropic of Cancer* sell for as much as $9,000; a manuscript notebook from the Paris years was recently offered for sale for $5,000.

There have been several attempts to write Miller's biography. In 1978, over Miller's strenuous objections, Jay Martin published *Always Merry and Bright* Capra Press, the small California publisher who issued some of Miller's final works. In 1986 Kathryn Winslow's *Henry Miller: Full of Life* appeared; it is a memoir by the woman who ran "M: The Gallery for Henry Miller" in Chicago in the forties. As their titles suggest, both works are fairly uncritical.

The Henry Miller Literary Society is long defunct, but Miller still has hundreds of loyal and devoted fans. They have contributed to two volumes of homage to him, and many also subscribe to the international journal *Anaïs*. Miller is seldom read in schools or colleges, and there is little good academic criticism on him (or, for that matter, on Nin). His books do not sell well in this country, but they sell steadily.

They are more successful abroad, most notably in France, Germany, and Japan.

Emil White, Miller's boon companion—as a recent story in *Life* magazine called him—died in August 1989, leaving his land and the Henry Miller Memorial Library he had established to the Big Sur Land Trust. The Library, which was Emil's cabin, has meager holdings indeed—barely a complete set of Miller's work. A little further down the coast, the Coast Gallery does a brisk business in postcards of Henry Miller watercolors. At Nepenthe, Miller's books are for sale. Val and Tony still live in the small community. Barbara, now retired, lives in Pasadena; Beatrice died in 1984. Hoki runs a nightclub in Tokyo called "Tropic of Cancer." The house on Ocampo Drive was sold shortly after Miller's death, but before the sale the remarkable bathroom was dismantled and sold to a collector.

Miller remains very much with us as a cultural icon, as two recent Hollywood films demonstrate. In Martin Scorsese's 1985 *After Hours,* the main character, who will be taken on a hairraising tour of the city's nether regions, is first spotted in a café reading *Tropic of Cancer;* appropriately enough, it is a world of sex and danger that awaits him. In the 1989 *sex, lies, and videotape* the hero, a sexual misfit whose fetish is videotaping women talking about sex, has a photo of Miller on his wall, his tribute to a heroic voyeur. In both films the specter of Henry Miller calls forth a remarkably diverse range of meanings, from sexual freedom to alienation to anarchism.

All this activity notwithstanding, Miller occupies a curious place in the American cultural canon. Many writers acknowledge their indebtedness to Miller, but largely because he was a pioneer in the cause of free speech. Without *Tropic of Cancer,* it is possible that such major American works as Philip Roth's *Portnoy's Complaint* and William S. Burroughs's *Naked Lunch* could not have been published in America. Writers as diverse as Durrell, Patchen, Mailer, and Ginsberg acknowledge their debt to him. Others, such as the "new journalists"—Hunter Thompson among them—who deliberately turned their reportage into highly personal accounts about their reactions to what they saw around them, clearly were influenced by Miller. Yet there are few writers who consciously emulate Miller in their prose. His work is too difficult to classify, his verbal flights too idiosyncratic to imitate. Still, few would deny the greatness of the Paris books, and the small successes he achieved with *The Rosy Crucifixion, Big Sur and the Oranges of Hieronymus Bosch,* and *The Colossus of Maroussi.*

But Miller was equally important as a twentieth-century personality. His life was, finally, as much of an achievement as his work, as he often acknowledged in his later years. In spite of his faults—the worst of which was, in the balance, an egotism so massive that one can almost forgive him for it, as one does a child—and in spite of the great obstacles that confronted him, he carved out a life for himself and found a way to survive and even flourish in a society that was at best indifferent to artists. His rejection of his bourgeois family and everything they stood for was heroic and hard won; his ensuing years with June were a kind of crucible from which he emerged, at thirty-nine, in Paris and penniless but somehow reborn. There, living on the streets, he learned finally how to write: by making his own suffering and rebirth the subject of his art.

In *Tropic of Capricorn*, Miller described how June was at once his damnation and his salvation.

> I thought, when I came upon her, that I was seizing hold of life. . . . Instead I lost hold of life completely. I reached out for something to attach myself to—and I found nothing. But in reaching out, in the effort to grasp, to attach myself, left high and dry as I was, I nevertheless found something I had not looked for—*myself.*

And he learned, as well, that what he wanted was "not to live—if what others are doing is called living—but to express myself."

Writing was what saved Miller—saved him from the tailor shop, saved him from the horrors of the home his parents had made, saved him from the madness that threatened him in his marriage to June. For Miller, the line between literature and life barely existed; everything he wrote, from *Tropic of Cancer* to his occasional literary criticism, was autobiographical. His favorite subject was his own mind and his memories. Sex was an element in the mix that, through censorship, became a red herring that misled his readers for years. The theme of his greatest books is survival, for Miller was first of all a survivor. It was the quality he admired most in June and in friends like Perlès: people like "Max" and Moricand engaged both his pity and his wrath because they were potential survivors who undermined their own efforts with their perverse and stubborn fatalism. Himself perverse and stubborn, Miller knew well the seductiveness of fatalism. His compassion for misfits came from the most honest and honorable source—his recognition that their struggle against the forces that threatened to engulf them (and often did) was his struggle as well.

Miller's autobiographical heroes walk a narrow line—as did their creator—between acceptance and rebellion, rejoicing and disgust. It was inevitable that Miller would attempt to derive a truly positive philosophy in his later years, and it was just as inevitable that he should fail; he was much more convincing as the literary *clochard,* the "evil product of an evil soil" he describes in *Tropic of Capricorn.* Thus he chose as the subject for his mighty autobiographical trilogy his early years with Beatrice and then with June; his subject was how his soul was forged in suffering. Whenever he attempted another tack, he drifted. But he knew there were other, loftier subjects, and couldn't help admiring and attempting to emulate the sages and seers of earlier times.

Another aspect of Miller's life, his almost uncanny knack for staying out of step with his own times, needs to be acknowledged. Almost every move he made went against the grain of the age. He often said that Americans mature later than people of other nationalities, but his seems rather an extraordinary case. In Paris, he lamented being forty, wearing glasses, and being bald; he was there a decade too late, after most of the famous expatriates, the Hemingways and Fitzgeralds, had gone home. Similarly, his blistering attack on America was written during World War II—hardly good marketing judgment. He lived out the forties and fifties in isolation in Big Sur, and then, in the sixties, when the counterculture took up some of the ideas he espoused, he perversely moved to the affluent, bourgeois setting of Pacific Palisades. But the single most harmful piece of mistiming in Miller's life was one over which he had no control: the twenty-five-year ban on the Paris books in the United States. For most of his adult life his greatest works remained unavailable in his own country, and largely unread. He enjoyed notoriety but not fame; he subsisted on handouts. Critical acclaim came only when he was an old man, when his life work was finished, when he hardly cared about writing any more. These years of his life stand as a scathing indictment of the way American society treats its iconoclastic artists. Unheralded, unreviewed, unappreciated, virtually unknown, he insisted on being heard. What he had to say may have been unpalatable. But as Miller wrote in defense of *The Rosy Crucifixion*—and the statement might apply to all of his best work— "If it was not good, it was true; if it was not artistic, it was sincere; if it was in bad taste, it was on the side of life."

Notes

Abbreviations

I have used the following abbreviations for published works by Henry Miller (who is designated as HM below).

TCan	*Tropic of Cancer.* 1934; rpt. NY: Grove Press, 1961.
BS	*Black Spring.* 1936; rpt. NY: Grove Press, 1963.
TCap	*Tropic of Capricorn.* 1938; rpt. NY: Grove Press, 1961.
WOS	*The World of Sex.* 1941; rpt. NY: Grove Press, 1965.
COM	*The Colossus of Maroussi.* 1941; rpt. NY: New Directions, 1958.
ACN	*The Air-Conditioned Nightmare.* NY: New Directions, 1945.
TOA	*The Time of the Assassins: A Study of Rimbaud.* NY: New Directions, 1946.
BIML	*The Books in My Life.* NY: New Directions, 1952.
BSOHB	*Big Sur and the Oranges of Hieronymus Bosch.* NY: New Directions, [1957].
Sexus	Volume 1 of *The Rosy Crucifixion.* 1962; rpt. NY: Grove Press, 1965.
Plexus	Volume 2 of *The Rosy Crucifixion.* 1963; rpt. NY: Grove Press, 1965.

Nexus   Volume 3 of *The Rosy Crucifixion*. 1960; rpt. NY: Grove Press, 1965.

BOF   *Henry Miller's Book of Friends: A Tribute to the Friends of Long Ago*. Santa Barbara, Calif.: Capra Press, 1976.

Volumes of correspondence, interviews, memoirs, etc., are abbreviated as follows:

LAN   *Letters to Anaïs Nin*, ed. Gunther Stuhlmann. 1965; rpt. NY: Paragon Books, 1988.

MLT   HM, *My Life and Times*. NY: Playboy Press, 1971.

Belmont   *Henry Miller in Conversation with Georges Belmont*, trans. Anthony Macnabb and Harry Scott. Chicago: Quadrangle Books, 1972.

Gertz   *Henry Miller: Years of Trial and Triumph, 1962–1964*, ed. Elmer Gertz and Felice Flannery Lewis. Carbondale, Ill.: Southern Illinois University Press, 1978.

LCF   *Letters from Your Capricorn Friend: Henry Miller and the Stroker, 1978–1980*. NY: New Directions, 1984.

HTM   *Letters from Henry Miller to Hoki Tokuda Miller*, ed. Joyce Howard. NY: Freundlich, 1986.

Venus   *Dear, Dear Brenda: The Love Letters of Henry Miller to Brenda Venus*, ed. Gerald Seth Sindell. NY: Henry Holt, 1986.

ALP   *A Literate Passion: Letters of Anaïs Nin and Henry Miller, 1932–1953*, ed. Gunther Stuhlmann. NY: Harcourt Brace Jovanovich, 1987.

DML   *The Durrell-Miller Letters, 1935–1980*, ed. Ian MacNiven. NY: New Directions, 1988.

LE   *Letters to Emil*. NY: New Directions, 1989.

Miller's unpublished writings include the novels *Crazy Cock* and *Moloch*, which are in the Henry Miller Collection in the Department of Special Collections at the University Research Library, UCLA.

HM's "Notes for Tropic of Capricorn," deposited in the Herbert West Collection at the Baker Library, Dartmouth College, are abbreviated as "TCap Notes." This collection is referred to as "Dartmouth."

The papers of Frances Steloff and Francis X. Dobo at the Berg Collection at the New York Public Library are referred to as "NYPL."

The Miller Collection at the Harry Ransom Humanities Research Library at the University of Texas, Austin, is referred to as "Univ. of Texas."

Letters to Ned Calmer are in the private collection of Gloria Calmer; letters to Georges Belmont (Roger Pelorson) and Huntington Cairns are in the private collection of Georges Belmont. Letters to Emil Conason and Abe Elkus are in the collection of Celia Conason, and letters to James Laughlin are in his New Directions archive. Other references to archives are given in full.

Part 1. New York City

Chapter 1. The Skater: 1891–1900

p. 19 "Henry Miller, thoroughly German-American": *LCF*, pp. 80–1.

p. 19 " 'I never realized' ": *TCap*, p. 11.

p. 20 "So Nieting": *Moloch*, p. 156.

p. 20 "He soon met": HM to Emil White, 2/19/43.

p. 20 "The same year": For Nieting's naturalization certificates, see National Archives—NY Branch, Common Pleas, bundle 418.

p. 21 "Miller's Aunt Mary": Mary Smith to HM, 2/15/61, Box 20B, UCLA.

p. 21 " 'she *had* to be' ": HM, *Reflections*, ed. Twinka Thiebaud (Santa Barbara, Calif.: Capra Press, 1984), p. 68.

p. 21 "His grandfather": HM to F.-J. Temple, [n.d.], Box 41, UCLA.

p. 21 " 'too kind-hearted' ": HM to Heinrich Miller, 6/15/36, Box 20B, UCLA.

p. 22 " 'a decade in which' ": *TOA*, p. 162.

p. 22 "He had been born": *Sexus*, p. 15.

p. 22 " 'clutching womb' ": *TCap*, p. 10.

p. 23 " 'It's as though' ": *TCap*, p. 10.

p. 23 " 'ringing slap' ": *BOF*, p. 30.

p. 23 "He remembered": Venus, p. 158.

p. 23 "Its first mayor": David McCullough, *Brooklyn and How It Got That Way* (NY: Dial, 1983), p. 130.

p. 24 " 'Every other city' ": Julian Ralph quoted in McCullough, p. 53.

p. 24 "The same commentator": Quoted in McCullough, p. 54.

p. 24 "As a very young boy": *TCap*, p. 132.

p. 24 " 'frightening, odious' ": *TCap*, p. 134.

p. 24 "The Nieting sisters": *Nexus*, p. 65.

p. 24 "he was outfitted": *Moloch*, p. 160.

p. 24 "Only then": *BOF*, p. 11.

p. 24 "Henry Ward Beecher": McCullough, p. 135.

p. 25 " 'a fink' ": HM, "Manuscript notebook," [n.d., 1930s]; see Joseph the Provider, Catalogue 22, item G1, [n.d., n.p.].

p. 25 "Nieting passed": *Plexus*, p. 75.

p. 25 "Henry read of": *BIML*, p. 42.

p. 26 "a Miller uncle": HM, "An Anecdotal Remembrance for the Franz Schneider Verlag," p. 1, Grauer Collection, Columbia Univ.

p. 26 "But his earliest": *BIML*, p. 165.

p. 26 "When he gave": *BOF*, p. 20.

p. 26 "Louise's behavior": *MLT*, p. 202.

p. 27 "Her head would not": *MLT*, p. 202; see also *Moloch*, in which Lauretta appears as Babette.

p. 27 " 'a sort of harmless' ": *TCap*, p. 326.

p. 27 " 'they have found' ": Stanley Borowski to HM, 11/22/55, Box 10, UCLA.

p. 28 " 'Because [my sister]' ": *TCap*, p. 326.

p. 29 " 'That little stain' ": *TCap*, p. 350.

p. 29 " 'lived the life' ": HM to Henri Fluchère, [n.d.], Box 14A, UCLA.

p. 29 "An ongoing turf war": *BOF*, p. 23.

p. 29 "Henry had at least": *Nexus*, p. 79.

p. 30 " 'demigod' ": *BSOHB*, p. 115.

p. 30 " 'Were they to give us' ": *LCF*, p. 78.

p. 30 "Stanley might have": *TCap*, pp. 125–8.

p. 30 "And Henry's friend Jack": *MLT*, p. 202.

p. 31 " 'Don't make too much' ": *BOF*, p. 12.

p. 31 "In Glendale": See, for example, *Plexus*, pp. 72–3.

p. 31 " 'had acquired the habit' ": *BOF*, p. 43.

p. 32 "Henry, deeply disturbed": Belmont, p. 29.

p. 32 "The boys' writer": *BIML*, p. 205.

p. 32 "Turn-of-the-century American culture": Peter Gabriel Filene, *Him/Her/Self: Sex Roles in Modern America* (1974; rpt. NY: NAL, 1975), pp. 70–1; see also Gail Bederman, " 'The Women Have Had Charge of the Work Long Enough': The Men and Religion Forward Movement of 1912 and the Masculinization of Middle-Class Protestantism," *American Quarterly*, 41 (September 1989), 432–65.

p. 32 "The ideology": See, for example, Joe L. Dubbert, *A Man's Place: Masculinity in Tradition* (Englewood Cliffs, NJ: Prentice-Hall, 1979), and Benjamin G. Rader, "The Recapitulation Theory of

Play: Motor Behavior, Moral Reflexes and Manly Attitudes in Urban America, 1880–1920," in J. A. Mangan and James Walvin, eds., *Manliness and Morality: Middle-Class Masculinity in Britain and America, 1800–1940* (Manchester: Manchester Univ. Press, 1987), pp. 123–33.

p. 33 " 'a soldier needs' ": Quoted in Donald J. Mrozek, *Sport in American Mentality, 1880–1910* (Knoxville, Tenn.: Univ. of Tennessee Press, 1983), p. 35.

p. 34 "The group was run": *BOF*, p. 65.

p. 34 " 'almost of nausea' ": *Plexus*, p. 278.

p. 34 " 'the stupid nonsense' ": *Plexus*, pp. 82–3.

Chapter 2. The Tailor's Son: 1900–1915

p. 36 "One of his most cherished": *TCap*, p. 144.

p. 37 " 'The conversation, when it got round' ": *WOS*, p. 33.

p. 37 "He felt intolerable excitement": "Paris Notebook," pp. 188, 190, UCLA.

p. 38 " 'a small Greek world' ": *Plexus*, p. 146.

p. 38 "The Millers had moved": HM and Michael Fraenkel, *Hamlet* (NY: Carrefour, 1941), vol. 1, p. 162.

p. 39 "To Henry's mind, an angel": See, for instance, Belmont, p. 8.

p. 39 " 'Strange that I never thought' ": BOF, p. 98.

p. 39 "He used to dream": *Sexus*, p. 296.

p. 40 "In his senior year": *MLT*, p. 185.

p. 40 "Seeking treatment": *TCap*, pp. 157–8.

p. 40 "Every two weeks they would meet": *MLT*, p. 184.

p. 40 "Members exchanged": *Plexus*, p. 256.

p. 40 "Henry later commented": *BOF*, p. 98.

p. 41 " 'Stand up, O ancient members' ": *BIML*, p. 315.

p. 42 "But as the summer of 1909": *BOF*, p. 274.

p. 42 " 'intolerably Jewish' ": HM to Henri Fluchère, [n.d.], Box 14A, UCLA.

p. 42 " 'I went regularly for my "dose" ' ": *BIML*, p. 51.

p. 42 ' 'The tables themselves' ": *Plexus*, pp. 61–2.

p. 43 " 'The natural thing to do' ": Quoted in Roderick Nash, *The Call of the Wild (1900–1916)* (NY: George Braziller, 1970), pp. 303 and 309.

p. 43 "But for all his scathing": "TCap Notes," Dartmouth.

p. 43 "He never saw a sack": *ACN*, pp. 142–3.

p. 44 "Too poor to go out to lunch": *BSOHB*, p. 83.

p. 44 "During one of these flirtations": *BOF*, p. 95.

p. 45 " 'Pauline was delicate' ": *BOF*, p. 275.

p. 45 " 'platinum moonlight' ": *Sexus*, p. 301.

p. 45 " 'The moment I entered' ": *WOS*, p. 50.

p. 45 "366 Decatur Street": *MLT*, p. 176.

p. 45 "From 1905 to 1908": Robert Snyder, *This Is Henry, Henry*

Miller from Brooklyn (Los Angeles: Nash Publishing, 1974), p. 26.

p. 46 "Physical culturists were given to such habits": On Macfadden, see Mary Macfadden and Emile Gaurveau, *Dumbbells and Carrot Sticks: The Story of Bernarr Macfadden* (NY: Henry Holt, 1953), and Clement Wood, *Bernarr Macfadden: A Study in Success* (NY: Lewis Copeland, 1929).

p. 47 " 'The great importance of strong sexual powers' ": James G. Whorton, *Crusaders for Fitness: The History of American Health Reformers* (Princeton, NJ: Princeton Univ. Press, 1982), pp. 299–300.

p. 47 "He bought his own favorite": *BOF*, p. 221; HM to Emil White, 1/20/78, Univ. of Texas.

p. 48 " 'There they were again' ": *Plexus*, pp. 123–35.

p. 48 "He would later invent": Richard Elman to author.

p. 48 " 'seven-month toothache' ": *Sexus*, p. 296.

p. 49 " 'an apparently insoluble' ": "Benjamin Fay Mills, Evangelist," p. 7 (an unpublished MS in the collection of Celia Conason). HM writes, in reference to Pauline, "I am wholly unaware of any Oedipus complex, but it is there" (p. 7).

p. 49 " 'fatal infatuation' ": HM, *Stand Still Like the Hummingbird* (NY: New Directions, 1962), p. 48.

p. 49 " 'No more books!' ": *BIML*, p. 208.

p. 49 "The other hands called him": HM, *Reflections*, p. 24.

p. 49 " 'I am alone and working' ": *TCap*, p. 151.

p. 50 " 'it sounded good to me' ": Snyder, p. 118.

p. 51 "He borrowed Bill Parr's copy": HM to Frances Steloff, 4/30/39, Folder 5, NYPL.

p. 51 "One speaker who deeply moved him": "Mills, Benjamin Fay," *The National Cyclopedia* (Oregon, 1907), p. 178.

p. 51 "In 1912, Valentin Nieting": HM to F.-J. Temple, [n.d.], Box 41, UCLA.

p. 51 " 'a joint corporation' ": *BS*, p. 79.

p. 52 "After Dexter left": *BS*, p. 94.

p. 52 " 'The men who passed through' ": *BS*, p. 128.

p. 53 " 'feel sorry for him' ": *BS*, p. 80.

p. 53 " 'The men my father loved' ": *BS*, p. 115.

Chapter 3. "An Obsessional Plant": 1915–1923

p. 55 " 'like a tick' ": *Moloch*, p. 103.

p. 55 " '*be* a writer' ": *DML*, p. 311.

p. 56 "Guido Bruno": See Albert Parry, *Garrets and Pretenders: A History of Bohemianism in America* (1933; rpt. NY: Dover, 1960), pp. 307–10.

p. 56 "Miller wrote a friend": HM to Charles Keeler, 12/9/16, The Huntington Library.

p. 56 " 'unpatriotic habit' ": *Moloch*, p. 4.

p. 56 "He commonly carried": *Plexus*, p. 402.

p. 56 "For a time": *Moloch*, p. 4.

p. 57 "(Henry believed": *Sexus*, pp. 220–1.

p. 57 "On one typical": *WOS*, p. 54.

p. 57 "Miller grimly wrote": HM to Charles Keeler, 12/9/16, The Huntington Library.

p. 57 "Often she would stop": *WOS*, p. 53.

p. 58 "One morning in the summer": *Moloch*, p. 3.

p. 58 "He was frightened": Interview with Georges Belmont, 11/2/88.

p. 58 "(He later wrote": HM to Henri Fluchère, [n.d.], Box 14A, UCLA.

p. 58 "There they devoted": *Moloch*, pp. 346–7.

p. 59 "although Henry had to borrow": *Moloch*, p. 4.

p. 59 "The couple managed": HM and Michael Fraenkel, *Hamlet*, Vol. 1, p. 159.

p. 59 "He even came to hate": *Moloch*, p. 142.

p. 59 "One night he decided": *Moloch*, p. 174.

p. 60 " 'How much do you know?' ": *Moloch*, p. 542.

p. 61 "Something about Beatrice": *COM*, p. 120.

p. 62 " 'running battle' ": HM to Huntington Cairns, 4/30/39.

p. 62 " 'all great men' ": *LE*, p. 6.

p. 62 " 'The eye cannot take in' ": *LE*, p. 8.

p. 62 "A five-cent 'pulp' ": *The Black Cat* (January 1919), p. 45.

p. 62 " 'there is a pleasant feeling' ": *The Black Cat* (May 1919), p. 43.

p. 63 "he was a working author": A letter to Charles Keeler, 12/9/16, contains a reference to Guido Bruno that suggests HM may have been published in one of Bruno's numerous little magazines circulated around Greenwich Village; the reference, however, is to being cheated of $200 by Bruno, so in all likelihood *The Black Cat* was the first organ in which his writing appeared.

p. 63 "In his critique": *The Black Cat* (August 1919), pp. 44–5.

p. 63 "In another critique": *The Black Cat* (June 1919), p. 43.

p. 63 "His heroes remained": *LE*, p. 5.

p. 64 "His contempt was evident": *TCap*, p. 17.

p. 66 " 'hiring and firing' ": *TCap*, p. 19.

p. 66 "He decided he needed a secretary": Interview with Muriel Cowley, 10/9/88.

p. 66 "In reality, Miller's empire": *Moloch*, p. 21.

p. 67 "When Miller first began": *Moloch*, p. 47.

p. 67 " 'Being desirous of becoming connected' ": Nathan Stillman to HM, 9/13/21, Box 8, UCLA.

p. 67 "Grimmond accused": William J. Grimmond to HM, 4/8/22, Box 8, UCLA.

p. 67 "As he later told": *DML*, p. 310.

p. 68 "Every day he was given": *Moloch*, p. 21.

p. 68 "Miller continued his active": HM to Richard Osborn, 7/20[34], Box 25, UCLA.

p. 68 "Miller was in the habit": See M. J. (Mike) Rivise, *Inside Western Union* (NY: Sterling, 1950), p. 128.

p. 68 "Describing one such evening": *Moloch*, p. 75.

p. 69 " 'the whole American tribe' ": *LE*, p. 123.

p. 70 "He was delighted to find": *Moloch*, p. 374.

p. 70 " 'I must run free' ": *Moloch*, p. 376.

p. 70 "The book Miller had written": *Sexus*, p. 24.

p. 71 "He began the work in response": *TCap*, p. 34.

p. 71 "As he wrote Schnellock": *LE*, p. 4.

p. 71 "He began by writing about": *LE*, pp. 4–5.

p. 72 " 'there grew up inside me' ": *TCap*, p. 53.

Chapter 4. Mona: 1923–1924

p. 73 " 'so that the American people' ": *TCap*, p. 72.

p. 73 "In every branch office": Rivise, p. 124.

p. 74 "(Miller himself had once": HM to Huntington Cairns, 4/30/39.

p. 74 " 'Chaos!' ": *TCap*, p. 80.

p. 74 " 'I was saturated' ": *TCap*, p. 30.

p. 74 " 'bosom friend' ": HM to Donahue, 12/12/42, Dudley Nichols Folder, Beinecke Library, Yale Univ.

p. 74 "Miller, overwhelmed": *TCap*, pp. 66–7.

p. 74 "With his fellow": "TCap Notes," Dartmouth; *Plexus*, pp. 101–2.

p. 75 "Just as he had loved": HM to Henri Fluchère, [n.d.], Box 14A, UCLA.

p. 75 "(he had seen it": *TCap*, p. 217.

p. 75 "A waitress in a Greek": See *TCap*, p. 80 and the Mezzotint "The Awakening."

p. 75 'He was *different*": *TCap*, pp. 102–3.

p. 75 " 'I could never get myself' ": *TCap*, p. 55.

p. 76 " 'they seemed to spring up' ": *TCap*, p. 47.

p. 76 "In fact, few": *TCap*, p. 47.

p. 76 "Miller's life was": "TCap Notes," p. 4.

p. 76 "He found the streets dirty": *Moloch*, pp. 147–8.

p. 77 " 'renegade Jew' ": HM to Maurice Girodias, 5/10/46, NYPL; see also HM to James Laughlin, 1/9/71.

p. 77 " 'How do I know' ": HM to Hilaire Hiler, 11/29/34, Box 14A, UCLA.

p. 78 "Miller's favorite haunts": See, for example, Paul G. Cressey, *The Taxi-Dance Hall* (1932; rpt. NY: Greenwood, 1968).

p. 78 "After climbing": *Nexus*, p. 169.

p. 79 " 'knowing, mysterious' ": *TCap*, p. 340.

p. 79 "She thought he looked": Kenneth C. Dick, *Henry Miller: Colossus of One* (The Netherlands: Albert Sittard, 1967), p. 165.

p. 79 "This man was full": "TCap Notes," p. 1.

p. 79 "The Gypsy blood was": HM to Frank Dobo, 10/22/58, NYPL.

p. 80 "Her father was": See Naturalization Service, Petition and Record, Vol. 267, p. 181, Supreme Court of Kings County Records.

p. 80 "The 'Smerth' ": The word *smerdt* means "death" in Russian, and June told Kenneth C. Dick she chose "Mansfield" because as "man's field" it meant "cemetery"; see Dick, pp. 163–4.

p. 80 "She insisted to Miller": Dick, p. 169.

p. 80 "June later claimed": Dick, p. 166.

p. 80 "Early in their relationship": "TCap Notes," p. 1.

p. 80 "One night, encouraged": "TCap Notes," p. 1.

p. 81 " 'Great despair' ": "TCap Notes," p. 2.

p. 81 "Her talk": Anaïs Nin, *Henry and June*, ed. Gunther Stuhlmann (NY: Harcourt Brace Jovanovich, 1986), p. 21.

p. 81 "On another occasion": "TCap Notes," p. 2.

p. 82 " 'Fine, is that all' ": *Sexus*, p. 102.

p. 82 "Finally, weeks after": "TCap Notes," p. 2.

p. 82 "On the heels": "TCap Notes," pp. 2–3.

p. 82 " 'marvelous night' ": "TCap Notes," p. 3.

p. 83 "Miller said later": Dick, pp. 82–3.

p. 83 "They lived at a succession": Interview with Celia Conason, 2/14/90.

p. 83 "June expected Henry": *Sexus*, pp. 168–9.

p. 84 " 'if that had been my child' ": HM to Emil Conason, [n.d.].

p. 84 "She telephoned Beatrice": "TCap Notes," p. 3.

p. 84 "At Cockroach Hall": "TCap Notes," p. 4.

p. 85 "She began taking classes": Interview with Celia Conason, 2/14/90.

p. 85 "Miller, the Hickersons, and the Conasons": "TCap Notes," p. 4.

p. 85 "The divorce, which was": See Index to Divorce and Separation Proceedings, Vol. M-1, Kings County Records.

p. 85 "The judge was severe": "TCap Notes," p. 4.

p. 85 " 'stabbed to the heart' ": "TCap Notes," p. 4.

p. 86 " 'typical touch' ": "TCap Notes," p. 5.

p. 86 " 'And now for the dirt' ": *Sexus*, p. 59.

p. 86 " 'I was quite willing' ": *Sexus*, p. 259.

p. 87 "Their wedding day": See Dick, p. 167, and "TCap Notes," p. 5.

p. 87 "June threw": *Sexus*, pp. 458–9.

Chapter 5. At June's Side: 1924–1926

p. 88 " 'at her very best' ": "TCap Notes," p. 5.

p. 88 "The place was sumptuous": *Plexus*, p. 10.

p. 88 "(She actually asked for $500": Dick, p. 168.

p. 88 " 'Japanese love nest' ": *Plexus*, p. 30.

p. 89 "For June decided": Dick, p. 171.

p. 89 "Once, on an occasion when June": "TCap Notes," p. 6.

p. 89 " 'Closed for the day' ": Dick, p. 54.

p. 89 "He had Sam": Dick, p. 54.

p. 89 "He sent June around": "TCap Notes," p. 6.

p. 90 "Soon Miller abandoned": "TCap Notes," p. 6.

p. 90 " 'It was morning' ": *Plexus*, p. 53.

p. 90 "Financially, she and Henry": "TCap Notes," p. 7.

p. 90 " 'It is easier' ": *Sexus*, p. 51.

p. 91 "Once Angus Bolton": HM to Emil Schnellock, [n.d., 1935?], Box 30B, UCLA; see also "TCap Notes," p. 7.

p. 91 In a recent dramatic scene": "TCap Notes," p. 5.

p. 91 " *'Acte gratuit'* ": "TCap Notes," p. 7; see also *Plexus*, pp. 160–1.

p. 92 " 'long, fatuous' ": *Plexus*, p. 55.

p. 92 "Encouraged, he began": *Plexus*, p. 284.

p. 92 "Henry found that": *Plexus*, p. 59.

p. 92 "For an article": *Plexus*, p. 63.

p. 93 "At first Miller": *LE*, p. 10.

p. 93 "Masochistically": HM, *Semblance of a Devoted Past* (Berkeley, Calif.: Bern Porter Books, 1944), p. 22.

p. 93 "Crestfallen, Henry retaliated": "TCap Notes," p. 8.

p. 93 "Another avenue proved": *Plexus*, p. 131.

p. 93 "His friends were forced": *Plexus*, pp. 152–4.

p. 94 "Henry and June worked out a plan": *Plexus*, pp. 98–9.

p. 95 " 'Failure' ": "TCap Notes," p. 10.

p. 95 "He always maintained": HM to Richard Osborn, [n.d.], Box 25, UCLA.

p. 95 "Henry drafted the first": See Bern Porter, *Henry Miller: A Chronology and Bibliography* (Berkeley, Calif.: Bern Porter Books, 1945), p. 35.

p. 96 "The response was a letter": "TCap Notes," p. 10.

p. 96 " 'God knows I'd like' ": *LE*, pp. 13–14.

p. 97 "From there the couple went": "TCap Notes," p. 11.

p. 97 "a Broadway speculator": *Nexus*, p. 159.

p. 98 "The trip was a failure": See HM, *Gliding into the Everglades* (Lake Oswego, Ore.: Lost Pleiade Press, 1977), p. 22.

p. 99 " 'No more hopes' ": "TCap Notes," p. 13.

p. 99 " 'too bad, he's no good' ": Dick, p. 72.

p. 99 "She had tried to adjust": *Plexus*, p. 180.

p. 99 "He was happy with the church": See *TCap*, pp. 163–7.

p. 100 "He sat at the typewriter": *Plexus*, p. 505.

p. 100 *"Pearson's* accepted": June E. Mansfield, "A Bowery Phoenix," *Pearson's* (February 1925), p. 58.

p. 100 "Miller submitted": HM, "Dreiser's Style," *New Republic*, 46 (4/38/26).

p. 100 "One evening June telephoned": "TCap Notes," p. 14.

p. 101 "June had a new scheme": "TCap Notes," p. 14.

p. 101 " 'shock of blanched faces' ": "TCap Notes," p. 15.

Chapter 6. Henry Street and Love Lane: 1926–1930

p. 102 " 'determined to extricate' ": "TCap Notes," p. 15.

p. 102 "Her looks changed": "TCap Notes," p. 15.

p. 103 "A new set of admirers": *Plexus*, p. 555.

p. 103 "Miller felt almost": *Plexus*, p. 279.

p. 103 " 'There were nothing' ": *Plexus*, p. 197.

p. 103 " 'Jean a typical' ": "TCap Notes," p. 16.

p. 104 "Born in the West": Dick, pp. 181–2.

p. 104 "The record is sketchy": "TCap Notes," p. 16.

p. 104 " 'Because there must be' ": *Nexus*, p. 17.

p. 104 " 'Is this another' ": "TCap Notes," p. 16.

p. 104 " 'Commence to go' ": "TCap Notes," p. 16.

p. 105 " 'Lesbianship' ": Dick, p. 181.

p. 105 "With Conason's help": "TCap Notes," p. 18.

p. 105 "Miller took the pills": "TCap Notes," p. 19.

p. 106 "Jean decorated the walls": *Crazy Cock*, p. 76.

p. 106 "They took possession": *Nexus*, p. 93.

p. 106 " 'Bed unmade all day' ": Nin, *Henry and June*, p. 46.

p. 106 "Miller hung about": "TCap Notes," p. 18.

p. 107 "The new apartment": "TCap Notes," p. 19.

p. 107 "He was getting professional": "TCap Notes," p. 20.

p. 107 "Twice he set out": "TCap Notes," p. 21.

p. 107 "He gave in to June's pleas": See *Nexus*, pp. 80–7.

p. 108 "Most of the time": *Nexus*, p. 75.

p. 108 "June, who called everyone": *Nexus*, p. 12.

p. 108 "He claimed to be writing": "TCap Notes," p. 21.

p. 108 " 'More golddigging' ": "TCap Notes," p. 22.

p. 109 "This last admission": "TCap Notes," p. 22.

p. 109 "Mrs. Smerth even produced": Naturalization Service, Petition and Record, Vol. 267, p. 181.

p. 109 "The detail that really struck": *Nexus*, pp. 146–7.

p. 110 "Whatever June wanted": *Nexus*, p. 159.

p. 110 "On May 21, 1927": *Nexus*, p. 164.

p. 110 "That same day": "TCap Notes," [p. 1]; HM writes: "Originally compiled in space of 24 hours handrunning at the office of the Park Commissioner, Queen's County in 1927 while June was in Europe with her friend Jean Kronski. . . ."

p. 111 " 'the most civilized' ": *Nexus*, p. 204.

p. 111 "Miller's parents hoped that": *Nexus*, p. 182.

p. 112 "From his writing table": *Nexus*, p. 186.

p. 112 " 'pestilential cronies' ": *Nexus*, p. 238.

p. 112 "June scraped enough": HM to Witter Bynner, 3/4/54, Witter Bynner Collection, Houghton Library, Harvard Univ.

p. 112 " 'The chances were' ": *Nexus*, p. 186.

p. 112 "Its real subject": *Moloch*, p. 1.

p. 113 " 'Every time I sat down' ": *Nexus*, p. 249.

p. 113 "On sunny days": *Plexus*, p. 224.

p. 113 " 'But I have pushed' ": *Nexus*, p. 194.

p. 113 " 'Sometimes I sailed' ": *Nexus*, p. 196.

p. 113 " 'Dion Moloch walks' ": *Moloch*, p. 1.

p. 114 " 'I was running around' ": HM to Richard Osborn, 6/10[34], Box 24, UCLA.

p. 114 "Pop liked it": *Nexus*, p. 216.

p. 114 "In May 1928": HM to Emil Conason, 5/4/28.

p. 114 "In the Village": *Nexus*, p. 268.

p. 114 "In June they began": *Crazy Cock*, p. 151.

p. 115 "You only had to get on": HM to Emil Schnellock, [November 1931], Box 30B, UCLA.

p. 115 "It was a warm day": Alfred Perlès, *My Friend Henry Miller* (1956; rpt. NY: Belmont Books, 1962), p. 14.

p. 115 "Just after this meeting": HM to Ned Calmer, Saturday [1930].

p. 116 "But June was less confident": HM to Frank Dobo, 10/22/58, NYPL.

p. 118 "Later he would blame": HM to F.-J. Temple, 6/30/65, Box 41, UCLA.

p. 118 "With *Lovely Lesbians*": HM to Richard Osborn, [n.d.], Box 24, UCLA.

p. 118 " 'wonderful how she could vary' ": *Nexus*, p. 183

Part 2. Paris

Chapter 7. An American in Paris: 1930–1931

p. 123 "He passed the voyage": *ALP*, p. 41.

p. 123 "The gloom was so thick": *LE*, p. 17.

p. 124 "The first sights": *LE*, p. 17.

p. 124 "To his dismay": HM, *Remember to Remember* (NY: New Directions, 1947), p. 341.

p. 124 "And a waiter": HM, *Remember to Remember*, p. 342.

p. 124 " ' I'm an American' ": *LE*, p. 18.

p. 124 " 'insufferable idiots' ": *LE*, p. 22.

p. 124 "Very few jobs": HM to Ned Calmer, 3/10/[31].

p. 124 "An American named Fred Kann": *LE*, p. 51.

p. 125 "He gave English lessons": HM to Ned Calmer, 3/10[31].

p. 125 "But he succeeded": HM, "Preface to 'Chair and Metal,' " *International Henry Miller Letter*, 6 (April 1964), p. 4.

p. 125 "Broke, he found a tailor": HM, "Preface to 'Chair and Metal,' " p. 3.

p. 125 " 'bummy condition' ": HM, *Semblance of a Devoted Past*, p. 5.

p. 125 "He took to wearing": Hilaire Hiler, "What I Remember About HM," typed MS, Hilaire Hiler Collection, reel D302, Archives of American Art.

p. 126 " 'a French telephone operator' ": HM to Frank Dobo, [7/27/33], NYPL.

p. 126 "His acquaintances": HM to William Gordon, 9/3/66, Univ. of Texas.

p. 126 "Even this was too steep": HM to Emil Conason, 5/15/[30].

p. 127 "Perlès also solved": Perlès, p. 20.

p. 127 " 'Hearing another language' ": George Wickes, "HM," in George Plimpton, ed., *Writers at Work: The Paris Review Interviews*, 2nd series (NY: Viking, 1963), pp. 179–80.

p. 127 " 'In a letter I can' ": *LE*, p. 47.

p. 127 "For the time being": *LAN*, p. 65.

p. 127 "He also showed it to": HM to John Weston, [10/20/36], Box 15, UCLA.

p. 128 "He showed it to Ned Calmer": HM to Ned Calmer, [n.d. 1931?].

p. 128 "In May he wrote Emil": *LE*, p. 54.

p. 128 " 'Hereafter, in referring' ": MS of *TCan*, Box 1, UCLA.

p. 128 "He wrote in his notebook": MS of *TCan*, Box 1, UCLA.

p. 128 "Mlle Claude": *LE*, p. 69.

p. 128 "When he told her this": HM to Ned Calmer, [n.d. 1931?].

p. 128 "After he finally summoned": HM to George Leite, 12/31[31?], Univ. of Texas.

p. 129 " 'When she cuddles up' ": HM, "Mlle Claude," *The Wisdom of the Heart* (NY: New Directions, 1941), pp. 149–50.

p. 129 "Her departure left": *LE*, p. 63.

p. 130 "Temporarily thrown": *LE*, p. 66.

p. 130 " 'The sap is running' ": *LE*, p. 67.

p. 130 "Fortuitously, Richard Osborn": See Richard G. Osborn, "No. 2 Rue Auguste Bartholdi," in Bern Porter, ed., *The Happy Rock* (Berkeley, Calif.: Bern Porter, 1945).

p. 131 "On New Year's Eve": *LE*, p. 75.

p. 131 " 'a broken vomit' ": *LE*, p. 74.

p. 131 " 'I will explode' ": HM to Emil Schnellock, 10/14/[34], Box 30B, UCLA.

p. 131 "Nichols came from": HM to Emil Schnellock, 10/14/[34], Box 30B, UCLA.

p. 131 " 'a sort of mutual' ": Osborn, p. 31.

p. 132 "Miller himself had tried": Lawrence Durrell, Foreword, in Noel Young, ed., *The Paintings of Henry Miller: Paint as You Like and Die Happy* (San Francisco: Chronicle Books, 1982), p. 18.

p. 132 "He found he had": See HM, *Semblance of a Devoted Past*, p. 10.

p. 132 " 'a fine Seurat night' ": HM, *Semblance of a Devoted Past*, p. 7.

p. 132 "English-language pupils": HM to Ned Calmer, 3/10/[31].

p. 132 " 'like being grabbed' ": HM to Ned Calmer, [n.d. 1931?].

p. 132 "Even if it was dishonest": HM, "Preface to 'Chair and Metal,' " p. 5.

p. 133 The 'death school' ": Michael Fraenkel, "The Genesis of *Tropic of Cancer*," in Porter, ed., *The Happy Rock*, p. 40.

p. 133 " 'Not alive, exactly' ": Fraenkel, "The Genesis of *Tropic of Cancer*," p. 45.

p. 133 "Miller reported proudly": *The Diary of Anaïs Nin: Volume 1*, ed. Gunther Stuhlmann (NY: Harcourt, Brace & World, 1966), p. 359. See Patrick Freiherr von Richthofen, "The Booster/Delta Nexus," unpub. Ph.D. diss., Univ. of Durham (England), 1987, vol. 1, p. 129. HM would later spend close to four years at 18 rue Villa Seurat, and most of his memories and those of his friends date to that later stay rather than to this stay of four months.

p. 134 " 'A writer's first duty' ": Fraenkel, "The Genesis of *Tropic of Cancer*," p. 45.

p. 134 " 'This then?' ": *TCan*, p. 2.

p. 134 " 'They talked a sort' ": *TCan*, p. 168.

p. 134 " 'being a Gentile' ": *TCan*, p. 168.

p. 134 "(In the same letter": HM to Michael Fraenkel, 6/25/33, Box 10, UCLA.

p. 135 "(It gave him a secret thrill": HM to Ned Calmer, [n.d. 4/31?].

p. 135 "After their shift": Perlès, p. 36; see also Waverley Root, *The Paris Edition, 1927–1934* (San Francisco: North Point Books, 1989).

p. 135 "In the *Tribune* production room": *LE*, pp. 83–4.

p. 135 "A series of columns": See clippings in Alfred Perlès's Scrapbook, Univ. of Texas.

p. 135 " 'a fine sadistic pleasure' ": HM to Ned Calmer, [7/31].

p. 136 " 'We are against admirals' ": HM and Perlès, "The New Instinctivism," p. 8, Univ. of Texas.

p. 136 "and Putnam wrote back": Samuel Putnam to Alfred Perlès and HM, 8/21/31, Perlès's Scrapbook, Univ. of Texas.

p. 136 "Wambly Bald singled it out": Wambly Bald, *On the Left Bank, 1929–1933*, ed. Benjamin Franklin V. (Athens: Ohio Univ. Press, 1987), pp. 73–4.

p. 136 "and Peter Neagoe asked Miller": George Wickes, Preface, in Wickes, ed., *Henry Miller and the Critics* (Carbondale, Ill.: Southern Illinois Univ. Press, 1963), pp. v–vi.

p. 137 " 'the orphic myth' ": *LE*, p. 101.

p. 137 " 'fuck the boys' ": HM to Ned Calmer, [n.d.].

p. 137 "In this way he lined up": See HM to Richard Osborn, [n.d. 1931?], Box 24, UCLA, and HM to Ned Calmer, Tuesday [n.d.].

p. 137 "(which Miller thought strange": HM to Ned Calmer, 1/12/[31].

p. 138 "She even admired": *ALP*, p. 60.

Chapter 8. "The Phallic Significance of Things": 1931–1933

p. 139 "Bertha Schrank": HM to Ned Calmer, [n.d. 7/32?].

p. 139 " 'mortally afraid' ": *ALP*, p. 198.

p. 140 " 'incapable of friendship' ": HM to Richard Osborn, 7/4/[34], Box 24, UCLA.

p. 141 " 'That her husband' ": *LE*, p. 96.

p. 142 "The house at Louveciennes": HM to Emil Schnellock, [n.d.], Box 30B, UCLA. See also Nin, "A House and a Garden: The Rise and Fall of 2 bis rue Monbuisson," *Anaïs: An International Journal*, 7 (1989), pp. 32–46.

p. 143 "Anaïs showed him about": Nin, "With Antonin Artaud," *Anaïs: An International Journal*, 6 (1988), pp. 14–15.

p. 143 " 'this should interest' ": Bald, pp. 75–6.

p. 143 " 'a fairy address' ": HM to Ned Calmer, [n.d.].

p. 143 "Almost immediately": *LAN*, p. 3.

p. 144 " 'would only prejudice you' ": *LAN*, p. 3.

p. 144 " 'As she came towards me' ": Nin, *Henry and June*, p. 14.

p. 144 "Henry dispatched": For June's departure, see *LE*, pp. 88–9.

p. 145 " 'Almost every word' ": Nin, *Henry and June*, p. 11.

p. 145 "Very early on": Nin, *Henry and June*, p. 14.

p. 145 "Miller was encouraged enough": HM to Emil Schnellock, [?]/16/[34?], Box 30B, UCLA.

p. 145 "Bald portrayed him": Bald, p. 77.

p. 146 "She had changed": Bald, pp. 87–9.

p. 146 " 'living moment' ": Nin, *Henry and June*, p. 16.

p. 146 "To Henry June explained": Nin, *Henry and June*, p. 27.

p. 147 "indeed, he later wrote": *LE*, p. 122.

p. 147 "Anaïs would always intimate": Evelyn Hinz, ed., *A Woman Speaks: The Lectures, Seminars and Interviews of Anaïs Nin* (Chicago: Swallow Press, 1975), p. 63.

p. 147 "The cross-examinations built up": *ALP*, p. 120.

p. 147 " 'One cold, solid smack' ": *LAN*, p. 9.

p. 147 "Miller disliked Krans": *ALP*, p. 60.

p. 147 "The terms were": HM to Joe O'Regan, 1/25/32, Box 24, UCLA.

p. 147 "He had a feeling": *LAN*, p. 8.

p. 147 " 'fatal mistake' ": *TCan*, p. 267.

p. 148 "The Lycée itself reminded": *LAN*, p. 7.

p. 148 "As he did in Paris": HM to Richard Osborn, [n.d. 2/32], Box 25, UCLA.

p. 148 " 'I deliberately tortured' ": *LAN*, p. 19.

p. 148 "He wrote Nin that he was reading": *LAN*, p. 13.

p. 148 " 'I am where Proust was' ": *ALP*, p. 7.

p. 148 "In the same letter he wrote": *ALP*, p. 21.

p. 149 "But when Waverley Root's": Snyder, *Anaïs Nin Observed*, [n.p.].

p. 149 " 'I know one Anaïs' ": *ALP*, p. 43.

p. 150 "She wrote in her diary": Nin, *Henry and June*, p. 53.

p. 150 " 'dried Andalusian blood' ": See *ALP*, pp. 16–18, and Nin, *Henry and June*, p. 54.

p. 150 " 'Here is the first woman' ": *ALP*, p. 33.

p. 150 " 'clamored for Henry' ": Nin, *Henry and June*, p. 79.

p. 150 " 'Can't you picture' ": *LE*, p. 107.

p. 150 " 'Anaïs, you've started' ": *ALP*, p. 18.

p. 151 " 'Henry, save me' ": Nin, *Henry and June*, p. 104.

p. 151 "With Perlès, he moved": Perlès, p. 68.

p. 151 "devote [him]self": HM to Richard Osborn, 6/10/[34], Box 24, UCLA.

p. 152 " 'My life in Paris' ": *LE*, p. 107.

p. 152 " 'beautiful big valise' ": *LE*, p. 93.

p. 152 "This practice": Jack P. Dalton, "A More Modern Instance," *The Wake Newslitter* (January 1963), pp. 8–10.

p. 152 "Following a conversation": MS of *TCan*, Box 1, UCLA.

p. 153 "Instead, he worried": *LAN*, p. 59.

p. 153 "The last volume": *ALP*, p. 80.

p. 153 " 'I am living' ": *TCan*, p. 2.

p. 154 " 'it is written' ": *TCan*, p. 185.

p. 154 " 'always there, quiet' ": *TCan*, p. 318.

p. 154 "But Fraenkel didn't like": *ALP*, p. 58.

p. 154 "Bradley, who with his French wife": Samuel Putnam, *Paris Was Our Mistress: Memoirs of a Lost-and-Found Generation* (1947; rpt. Carbondale, Ill.: Southern Illinois Univ. Press, 1970), p. 17.

p. 154 "Like his hero Dostoevsky": *LE*, p. 116.

p. 154 " 'After writing a book' ": HM to Hilaire Hiler, 11/29/34, Box 14A, UCLA.

p. 155 "At the height": *ALP*, p. 67.

p. 155 "(he once owned": Hugh Ford, *Published in Paris* (NY: Macmillan, 1975), p. 347.

p. 155 "Kahane stayed in business": Maurice Girodias, *The Frog-Prince: An Autobiography* (NY: Crown, 1980), p. 114.

p. 155 " 'At last!' he murmured": Jack Kahane, *Memoirs of a Booklegger* (London: Michael Joseph, 1939), p. 260.

p. 156 "He wouldn't have Kahane": *ALP*, p. 109.

p. 156 " 'splendid chance to reap' ": HM to Richard Osborn, [1932], Box 25, UCLA.

p. 156 "Kahane, however, was having": Kahane, pp. 261–2.

p. 156 " 'magnificent, overwhelming' ": *LAN*, p. 65.

p. 157 " 'influences, gods, books' ": *LAN*, p. 67.

p. 157 "He was as fired up": *LE*, p. 110.

p. 157 "In early October, Kahane": HM to Richard Osborn, [n.d.], Box 25, UCLA.

p. 157 " 'some crummy Jew' ": HM to Richard Osborn, 9/3/[34?], Box 25, UCLA.

p. 157 " 'a bunch of kikes' ": HM to Huntington Cairns, 3/2/41, Cairns Collection, Library of Congress.

p. 157 "(Covici was about the only": Putnam, p. 114.

p. 157 " 'America will call me' ": HM to Richard Osborn, 7/20/[33?], Box 25, UCLA.

p. 157 " 'Fuck my god-damned' ": HM to Hilaire Hiler, [n.d. 1935?], Box 14A, UCLA.

p. 158 " 'This time I am not' ": HM to Emil Schnellock, 10/23/[32], Box 30B, UCLA.

p. 158 "She hadn't brought the manuscripts": *LE*, p. 110.

p. 158 "Almost immediately": *LE*, p. 109.

p. 158 "Henry thought the best course": *ALP*, p. 121.

p. 158 "Anaïs revealed": Nin, "With Henry and June—From the Original, Unedited Diary, November, 1932," *Anaïs: An International Journal*, 5 (1987), pp. 3–14.

p. 158 "He wrote Anaïs that June": *ALP*, p. 120.

p. 159 "After a bitter quarrel": HM to Richard Osborn, 12/6/32, Box 25, UCLA.

p. 159 "At the grocer's": HM, "Via Dieppe Newhaven," *The Cosmological Eye* (NY: New Directions, 1939), pp. 198–9.

p. 159 " 'I listened to the worst' ": *LE*, p. 123.

p. 160 " 'Please get a divorce' ": *LE*, p. 112.

p. 160 "The day she sailed": HM to Ned Calmer, [n.d. 1933]; see also HM to Emil Schnellock, [November 1933], Box 30B, UCLA.

p. 160 " 'June Smith-Smerth' ": *LE*, p. 123.

p. 160 " 'because I don't give a fuck' ": *LE*, p. 126.

p. 161 " 'a tomb of June' ": HM to Richard Osborn, [n.d.], UCLA, Box 24.

Chapter 9. Tropical Storms: 1933–1935

p. 162 " 'I'm covering' ": HM to Richard Osborn, 2/2/33, Box 25, UCLA.

p. 162 " 'Big Macrocosmic Connections' ": *LAN*, p. 69.

p. 162 "Everything was going into": HM, "The Brochure," pp. 80 ff., Box 10, UCLA.

p. 162 "He quoted at length": *ALP*, p. 126.

p. 162 "A fourth book": HM to Richard Osborn, [n.d.], Box 25, UCLA.

p. 163 " 'I am not ashamed' ": HM, manuscript fragment, p. 15, Northwestern Univ. Library.

p. 163 " 'If I am to be' ": manuscript fragment, p. 4, Northwestern Univ. Library.

p. 163 " 'obliged' ": HM to Richard Osborn [n.d.], Box 25, UCLA.

p. 163 " 'You do not have' ": *ALP*, p. 194.

p. 163 " ('Either the world' ": *BS*, p. 26.

p. 163 " ('our triune god' ": *BS*, p. 24.

p. 163 " ('For all your ills' ": *BS*, p. 26.

p. 164 " 'hallucinating stuff' ": *LE*, p. 119.

p. 164 "He and Nin had avidly": *LAN*, p. 77.

p. 164 "(He had been disappointed": HM to Drake, 5/29/32, Univ. of Texas.

p. 164 " 'My head's bursting' ": *LAN*, p. 116.

p. 164 "Kahane's son Maurice": Girodias, p. 116.

p. 164 " 'worst enemy' ": HM to Richard Osborn, [n.d.], Box 25, UCLA.

p. 165 "Bradley and Kahane both": The letter is reprinted in HM's *The Wisdom of the Heart*.

p. 165 "She also immediately": HM to George Leite, [n.d.], Univ. of Texas.

p. 165 " 'slightly ridiculous' ": *ALP*, p. 218.

p. 165 "She fired back": *ALP*, pp. 219–23.

p. 165 "But in her diary": *The Diary of Anaïs Nin: Volume 1*, p. 170.

p. 165 "She found his ignorance": *The Diary of Anaïs Nin: Volume 1*, p. 311.

p. 166 "Miller began taking": *ALP*, p. 226.

p. 166 "Brassaï was in touch": See Brassaï, *Picasso and Company*, trans. Francis Price (Garden City, NY: Doubleday, 1966).

p. 166 "He inserted Brassaï": *TCan*, p. 189

p. 166 "(One story has it": Jules Frantz, "I Did Not Fire HM," *Lost Generation Journal*, 1 (May 1973), p. 7.

p. 166 "He had met Rank": *LAN*, p. 82.

p. 167 "What excited Miller about Rank": For HM's description of his meeting with Rank, see *LAN*, pp. 80–6; on Rank, see E. James Lieberman, *Acts of Will: The Life and Work of Otto Rank* (NY: Free Press, 1985).

p. 167 " 'tediously stupid' ": *ALP*, p. 179.

p. 167 " 'vindictiveness' ": *ALP*, p. 197.

p. 168 "Recording in his diary": David Gascoyne, *Paris Journal 1937–1939* (London: Enitharmon, 1978), p. 49.

p. 168 " 'You detest' ": HM, "Max," *The Cosmological Eye*, p. 8.

p. 169 " 'Millions must go' ": *LAN*, p. 100.

p. 169 " 'universal truth' ": HM, "The All-Intelligent Explosive Rocket," Univ. of Texas.

p. 170 " 'The individual as against' ": *Henry Miller on Writing*, selected, Thomas H. Moore (NY: New Directions, 1964), p. 163.

p. 170 " 'work with pleasure only' ": *Henry Miller on Writing*, p. 161.

p. 170 "He wrote Hilaire": HM to Hilaire Hiler, [fall 1933], Box 14A, UCLA.

p. 170 " 'I am seeing' ": HM to Emil Schnellock, 12/4/[33], Box 30B, UCLA.

p. 170 "He asked Nin to see": *ALP*, pp. 228–9.

p. 170 "At forty-two": HM, *Semblance of a Devoted Past*, p. 22.

p. 171 "He found it not as good": *LAN*, p. 129.

p. 171 "Taking advantage": *ALP*, p. 230.

p. 171 " 'just a stone's throw' ": HM, *Semblance of a Devoted Past*, pp. 40–1.

p. 171 " '*the* book' ": *LAN*, p. 129.

p. 171 "It gave the impression": *ALP*, p. 231.

p. 171 "Kahane was claiming": HM to Richard Osborn, 7/20/[34], Box 25, UCLA.

p. 171 "Then, in June": *ALP*, p. 231.

p. 171 "Instead, he wrote": HM to Richard Osborn, 4/20/[34], Box 25, UCLA.

p. 172 "(who were apparently": HM to Emil Schnellock, [n.d. 1934], Box 30B, UCLA; see also *ALP*, p. 247, fn.

p. 172 "He acknowledged": HM to Richard Osborn, 11/1/34, Box 25, UCLA.

p. 172 " 'From a distance' ": HM to Richard Osborn, 11/7/34, Box 25, UCLA.

p. 172 "Though he wrote Schnellock": *LE*, p. 149.

p. 173 "Kahane, in his memoirs": Kahane, p. 263.

p. 173 "Miller consigned": Perlès, p. 102.

p. 173 " 'What is money?' ": *LAN*, p. 136.

p. 173 " 'Here's a dirty book' ": Karl Shapiro, Introduction, *TCan*, p. x.

p. 173 "though Eliot became": T. S. Eliot to HM, 6/13/35, Box 8, UCLA.

p. 173 " 'very slight suggestion' ": Quoted in Waverley Root, "Montparnasse Memories," *International Herald Tribune*, 11/8/82, p. 7W; interview with Frank Dobo, 1/12/89.

p. 174 "Miller complained in a letter": HM to Hilaire Hiler, 11/29/34, Box 14A, UCLA.

p. 174 " 'ordinary wench's reaction' ": HM to Emil Schnellock, 10/14/[34], Box 30B, UCLA.

p. 174 " 'You see, much as I like him' ": HM to Meyer Hiler, [n.d.], Box 14A, UCLA.

p. 174 "Kahane pointed out": *ALP*, p. 248.

p. 174 " 'a little shit' ": HM to Hilaire Hiler, 11/29/34, Box 14A, UCLA.

p. 174 " 'Now my whole life' ": HM to Emil Schnellock, 10/14/[34], Box 30B, UCLA.

p. 175 " 'old treadmill' ": *ALP*, p. 263.

p. 175 " 'truthful lies' ": *ALP*, p. 245.

p. 175 " 'there are some' ": HM and Fraenkel, *Hamlet*, Vol. 2, p. 161.

p. 176 " 'New York is malign' ": HM to Hilaire Hiler, [January 1935], Box 14A, UCLA.

p. 176 " '[It's] not that I give' ": HM to Hilaire Hiler, [January 1935], Box 14A, UCLA.

p. 176 "He fed his patients": HM and Fraenkel, *Hamlet*, Vol. 2, pp. 272–3.

p. 177 " *'Jews mostly'* ": HM to Osborn, 2/4/[34?], Box 25, UCLA, emphasis HM's.

p. 177 "He found the Jewish New Yorker": HM to Joe O'Regan, 10/11/37, Box 24, UCLA.

p. 177 "In a long letter to Hiler": HM to Hilaire Hiler, 11/29/34, Box 14A, UCLA.

p. 178 "(Not long after": HM to John Weston, [10/20/36], Box 115, UCLA.

p. 178 "Miller's other significant": *The Diary of Anaïs Nin: Volume 2*, ed. Gunther Stuhlmann (NY: Harcourt, Brace & World, 1967), p. 17.

p. 179 "Significantly, the story": HM, "Murder in the Suburbs," in John Singer, ed., *New Short Stories 1945–1946* (Glasgow: William Maclellan, 1946), pp. 176–83.

p. 179 "Rumors circulated": HM to Walter Lowenfels, Sunday [1935], Univ. of Virginia.

p. 179 "He believed the atmosphere": HM to Emil Conason, [n.d.].

p. 179 "He was disappointed to hear": HM to John Weston, [10/20/36], Box 15, UCLA.

p. 179 "(He told a friend)": HM to Ned Calmer, [n.d.].

p. 179 "West he liked": HM to Hilaire Hiler, [1935], Box 14A, UCLA.

p. 179 "He thought he might do better": HM to Hilaire Hiler, 11/20/[35], Box 14A, UCLA.

p. 179 " 'I don't like that hard-boiled' ": HM to Alfred Perlès, 4/5/35, Box 30B, UCLA.

p. 180 "In her diary entry": *The Diary of Anaïs Nin: Volume 2*, p. 28.

p. 180 " 'When I think of New York' ": HM, *Aller Retour New York* (Paris: Obelisk [1935]), p. 80.

p. 180 "When Nin and Guiler returned": In a letter to Richard Osborn dated 12/18/[35], HM mentions having returned to Paris six months before.

p. 180 "In a letter to Michael": HM and Fraenkel, *Hamlet*, Vol. 2, p. 250.

Chapter 10. The Villa Seurat: 1935–1939

p. 182 " 'The activity Henry has created' ": *The Diary of Anaïs Nin: Volume 2*, p. 267.

p. 182 "The entire building": *DML*, p. 30.

p. 182 "Perlès moved": Lawrence Durrell, Introduction, in HM, *Order and Chaos Chez Hans Reichel* (Tucson, Ariz.: Loujon Press, 1966), p. 10.

p. 182 "Describing life at the Villa Seurat": HM, *Order and Chaos Chez Hans Reichel*, p. 72.

p. 183 "As Miller described it": HM, *A Devil in Paradise* (NY: Signet, 1956), p. 21.

p. 183 "The one saving thing": HM, *Order and Chaos chez Hans Reichel*, p. 72.

p. 183 " 'our happy life of shame' ": HM, *What Are You Going to Do About Alf?* (1935; rpt. Berkeley, Calif.: Bern Porter, 1944), p. 10.

p. 183 " 'We made him blow us' ": HM to Emil Schnellock, [October 1935], Box 30B, UCLA.

p. 184 " 'We treated him abominably' ": Perlès, p. 47.

p. 184 "Miller worried that": HM to Emil Schnellock, 12/4/[33], Box 30B, UCLA.

p. 184 "(In response": *The Diary of Anaïs Nin: Volume 2*, p. 44.

p. 184 "Not only had he put Miller up": HM to Michael Fraenkel, 4/7/40, Box 10, UCLA.

p. 185 "Miller later called": *MLT*, p. 165.

p. 185 "Over the summer": Joseph the Provider, Catalogue 22, Item A18, [n.p.].

p. 185 "What money did come in": *BOF*, p. 239.

p. 185 "In 'The Fourteenth Ward' ": *BS*, p. 3.

p. 185 " 'For me the book' ": *BS*, p. 23.

p. 186 "Other Siana books": HM to Richard Osborn, [9/12/35], Box 24, UCLA.

p. 186 "It is impossible": HM to Richard Osborn, [9/12/35], Box 24, UCLA. Herbert West in *The Mind on the Wing* asserts that the first edition was of 1,000 copies: Anaïs Nin reports in her *Diary* in June 1935 that 130 copies have been sold. As Joseph the Provider, Catalogue 22, Item A1, points out, a tremendous number of first editions may have been seized and/or destroyed by postal and Customs officials.

p. 186 "(From Mary Reynolds)": *BOF*, p. 186.

p. 186 "Miller wasn't satisfied": *DML*, p. 7. See also HM to Richard Osborn, [12/18/35?], Box 25, UCLA.

p. 186 "James Laughlin": HM to Frances Steloff, [1935], Folder 59, NYPL.

p. 187 " 'God (!) will take care' ": HM to Frank Dobo, [1936], Folder 2, NYPL.

p. 188 "In July 1935 she had called": Nin, "A House and a Garden," *Anaïs: An International Journal*, 7 (1989), p. 44.

p. 188 "But the next month": *The Diary of Anaïs Nin: Volume 2*, pp. 51, 65.

p. 188 " 'absolutely sterile' ": Nin to Emil White, [n.d.], Univ. of Texas.

p. 188 "The climate of the Villa Seurat": Perlès, p. 117.

p. 188 "His writing was bringing in": Brassaï, *Henry Miller: Grandeur Nature* (Paris: Gallimard, 1975), pp. 18–19.

p. 189 "He was also planning": HM to Richard Osborn, 12/18/[35], Box 25, UCLA.

p. 189 "And he projected ten or twelve": von Richthofen, p. 145. See press release from Obelisk Press, [n.d.], Univ. of Texas.

p. 189 "He also assembled": HM to Richard Osborn, 11/25/38, Box 25, UCLA.

p. 189 "He was working on 'the June book' ": HM to Emil Schnellock, 7/6/36, Box 30B, UCLA.

p. 189 "In August he wrote Durrell": *DML*, p. 15.

p. 189 " 'and mad' ": HM to Hilaire Hiler, [April 1936], Box 14A, UCLA.

p. 189 "Maurice Girodias describes": Girodias, pp. 202–3.

p. 189 "On another evening": Interview with Eric Kahane, 10/31/88.

p. 190 "One evening at the Villa Seurat": Interview with Georges Belmont, 11/2/88.

p. 190 " 'The inverse law' ": HM to Roger Pelorson, [1938].

p. 190 "In early 1937": HM to Lawrence Durrell, Sunday [1937?], Box 1, UCLA.

p. 190 " 'I *like* that last speech' ": HM to Lawrence Durrell. 1/15/[38?], Box 1, UCLA.

p. 190 " 'cheap, butter-and-egg mysticism' ": HM to Richard Osborn, 7/20/[34], Box 24, UCLA.

p. 190 " 'Jew-baiter' ": HM to Frank Dobo, 9/15/36, Folder 3, NYPL.

p. 191 "that a world war": HM, "In the Future Is Contained All," typescript, p. 5, Dartmouth.

p. 191 "that war between the West": "In the Future Is Contained All," p. 6.

p. 191 "and that Germany would be divided": HM to Richard Osborn, 7/20/[34], Box 25, UCLA.

p. 191 "Perhaps his most": *DML*, p. 101.

p. 191 " 'Man is not a Yahoo' ": George Orwell, *Collected Essays* (NY: Harcourt, Brace & World, 1968), Vol. 1, p. 279.

p. 191 "He was less enthusiastic": Orwell, "Black Spring," *The New English Weekly*, 9/24/36.

p. 191 "The two men parted": Perlès, p. 131; see also Bernard Crick, *George Orwell: A Life* (Boston: Little, Brown, 1980), pp. 208–9.

p. 192 "But is it right": George Orwell, "Inside the Whale," in Wickes, ed., *Henry Miller and the Critics*, pp. 31–43.

p. 192 "Miller dismissed": *LAN*, p. 324.

p. 192 "He considered himself": *DML*, p. 315.

p. 192 " 'only about heroic Englishmen' ": *DML*, p. 52.

p. 193 " 'Big Bertha' ": *DML*, p. 97.

p. 193 "Durrell, Miller, and Perlès": HM to Herbert West, [summer 1938], Dartmouth.

p. 194 "Most of the editors": von Richthofen, pp. 320–1.

p. 194 "The magazine inherited": von Richthofen, p. 384.

p. 195 "Although he wore": Interview with Georges Belmont, 11/2/88.

p. 195 " 'taken care of' ": *DML*, p. 69.

p. 196 " 'And finally I don't give' ": HM to Huntington Cairns, [n.d.], Library of Congress.

p. 196 "(he was holding out": HM to Joe O'Regan, 10/11/37, Box 24, UCLA.

p. 196 "While he had a regular buyer": *BIML*, p. 31.

p. 196 "He reprinted": Betty Ryan to Frances Steloff, 2/15/38, NYPL.

p. 196 "(Each of *Volontés*' ": Interview with Georges Belmont, 11/2/88.

p. 196 "In October 1937": HM to Joe O'Regan, 10/11/37, Box 24, UCLA.

p. 196 "They mounted an effort": HM to Huntington Cairns, 6/24/37 and 7/27/37, Cairns Collection, Library of Congress.

p. 196 "Blanche Knopf continued": HM to Frank Dobo, 5/10/37, Folder 4, NYPL.

p. 196 "In the same month": HM to Huntington Cairns, 10/31/37, Cairns Collection, Library of Congress.

p. 197 "He had a feeling": HM to Frank Dobo, 12/5/[38], Folder 5, NYPL.

p. 197 "He announces himself at the outset": *TCap*, p. 13.

p. 198 "As he wrote Frances Steloff": HM to Frances Steloff, 2/22/39, Folder 4, NYPL.

p. 198 "He fantasized": *LAN*, pp. 149–50.

p. 199 "If he made it back": *LAN*, p. 152.

p. 199 "Miller wrote Durrell that he had": *DML*, p. 103.

p. 199 " 'sitting on the edge' ": HM, *Hamlet Letters*, ed. Michael Hargraves (Santa Barbara, Calif.: Capra Press, 1988), p. 154.

p. 199 " 'I am struck' ": *DML*, p. 112.

p. 200 "Miller was so taken": HM to Frederick Carter, 4/22/38, Univ. of Texas.

p. 200 "Miller sent several": "Four Letters of HM to Count Keyserling," *International Henry Miller Letter*, 5 (August 1963), p. 17.

p. 200 " 'I am seeking' ": HM to Frederick Carter, 4/22/38, Univ. of Texas.

p. 200 " 'I have ceased warring' ": HM to Frances Steloff, 4/30/39, Folder 5, NYPL.

p. 201 "In 1937, a bookshop": HM to Frances Steloff, 4/30/39, Folder 5, NYPL.

p. 201 "was priced at $10": HM to Frances Steloff, 3/25/39, Folder 5, NYPL.

p. 202 "Plans for an underground edition": Gershon Legman to author, 2/21/89.

p. 202 "He also began making": HM to Frank Dobo, 3/16/39, Folder 7, NYPL. See also Gershon Legman, "Henry Miller," forthcoming in *The Adventures of Peregrine Penis* (Valbonne, France: Samizdat Press).

p. 202 " 'If I can steal it' ": HM to Frank Dobo, 4/15/39, Folder 7, NYPL.

Part 3. AMERICA

Chapter 11. The Air-Conditioned Nightmare: 1939–1944

p. 205 "Then he would continue": HM to Herbert West, 8/20/[40?], Dartmouth.

p. 205 "in the village": *COM*, p. 41.

p. 206 "He visited an Armenian soothsayer": *COM*, p. 202–203.

p. 206 "Very soon after he arrived": HM to Huntington Cairns, 7/24/[39], Cairns Collection, Library of Congress.

p. 206 " 'spiritually . . . still the mother' ": *COM*, pp. 210–11.

p. 207 "not least the 500 francs": HM to Huntington Cairns, [n.d.].

p. 207 "and he informed Steloff": HM to Frances Steloff, 10/31/39, Folder 6, NYPL.

p. 208 "When the ship docked": Lawrence Clark Powell, "Remembering Henry Miller," *Southwest Review* (Spring 1981), p. 122.

p. 209 " 'his I-am-God attitudes' ": *The New Yorker*, 15 (11/18/39), p. 105.

p. 209 "He asked Steloff not": HM to Frances Steloff, 3/1/[40], Folder 7, NYPL.

p. 210 "He had learned how to cast": Legman, pp. 4–7, 19.

p. 210 "A veritable combine of writers": *The Diary of Anaïs Nin: Volume 3*, ed. Gunther Stuhlmann (NY: Harcourt Brace Jovanovich, 1969), p. 157.

p. 210 " 'something splendid' ": HM to Frances Steloff, 3/1/[40], Folder 7, NYPL.

p. 211 "He did acknowledge": HM to James Laughlin, 4/16/45.

p. 211 "The manuscript made the rounds": HM to James Laughlin, 5/2/41.

p. 212 "He half-imagined": HM to Huntington Cairns, [1941?], Cairns Collection, Library of Congress.

p. 213 " 'I don't understand' ": HM to Frances Steloff, 8/8/[41?], Folder 15, NYPL.

p. 214 "(The list included": HM, *The Red Notebook* (privately published), [n.p.].

p. 215 'I had to travel' ": *ACN*, p. 19.

p. 215 "If he were Czar": *LAN*, p. 219.

p. 215 "in his friend's absence": HM, *Remember to Remember*, p. 79.

p. 215 "He later told a friend": HM to Knud Merrild, 7/4/[n.d.], Box 20A, UCLA.

p. 215 " 'Your father was a man' ": *Reflections*, ed. Thiebaud, p. 55.

p. 216 "He told Slocum to give it": HM to Ben Abramson, [n.d.], Beinecke Library, Yale Univ.

p. 216 "Welty showed him the gate": HM to James Laughlin, 4/16/45.

p. 216 "There he wrote a long letter": *LAN*, pp. 252–4.

p. 217 " 'Nowhere have I encountered' ": *ACN*, p. 20.

p. 217 " 'What have we to offer' ": *ACN*, p. 20.

p. 217 "He intended to stay a while": HM to Frances Steloff, 5/5/[41], Folder 14, NYPL.

p. 217 "The director Josef von Sternberg": *LAN*, p. 265.

p. 218 "He hoped to make side trips": *The Diary of Anaïs Nin: Volume 3*, p. 119.

p. 218 "Steinbeck and his friend": Clay McDaniel to author, 1/28/88.

p. 219 "He was becoming interested": HM to James Laughlin, [spring], 1944; *DML*, p. 162.

p. 220 "He confided to Abe Rattner": Abe Rattner, journal entry, 12/14/41, Archives of American Art, reel D204.

p. 220 "He passed Christmas": HM to Huntington Cairns, 12/26/41, Cairns Collection, Library of Congress.

p. 220 "Miller first referred to": *TCap*, p. 325.

p. 221 "One of the things he would remember": HM, *The Red Notebook*, [n.p.].

p. 222 " 'the money question' ": HM to Cyril Connolly, 1/9/43, Univ. of Texas.

p. 222 " 'just plain shit' ": *LAN*, pp. 315–16.

p. 222 "Gilbert Nieman had gone North": *LAN*, p. 314.

p. 222 "In December Miller appealed": HM to Bernard Levinson, 12/8/42, collection of Ken Du Main.

p. 223 "He literally wore out": *LAN*, p. 317.

p. 223 " 'It goes without saying' ": "Layout for Printed Notice," Dartmouth.

p. 224 "Man Ray and Miller": Neil Baldwin, *Man Ray, American Artist* (NY: Clarkson Potter, 1988), pp. 239–40.

p. 224 "Man Ray photographed Miller": Interview with Juliette Man Ray, 11/5/88.

p. 224 "He particularly admired": HM to Claude Houghton Oldfield, 5/10/42, Box 23, UCLA.

p. 225 " 'apotheosis of all Greek womanhood' ": *DML*, p. 157.

p. 225 "Melpo was quickly replaced": See Sevasty Koutsaftis to HM, 6/11/[43], Box 17B, UCLA, and HM to Herbert West, [n.d.], Dartmouth.

p. 226 "The fragment contained": "Open Letter to All and Sundry," copies in Dartmouth; Univ. of Texas.

p. 226 "one man suggested": Henry M. Robinson to HM, 7/16/43, Columbia Univ.

p. 226 "He wrote a New York friend": HM to Harvey Breit, 3/12/43, Northwestern Univ.

p. 226 " 'when I hear the word Culture' ": HM, *RIR*, p. 93.

p. 226 "What he missed most": HM to Abe Rattner, 11/8/43, Box 28, UCLA.

Chapter 12. "Little Henry, Big Sur": 1944–1949

p. 227 "James Laughlin bought": HM to Herbert West, 1/11/44, Dartmouth.

p. 227 "(In recent years": See Joseph the Provider, Catalogue 22, Item A100.

p. 229 " 'I have much work' ": *The Diary of Anaïs Nin: Volume 3*, p. 310.

p. 229 " 'little Henry, Big Sur' ": HM to Geraldine Fitzgerald, [n.d.], Box 14A, UCLA.

p. 229 "Soon Miller found that": HM to Frances Steloff, 9/26/44, Folder 27, NYPL.

p. 230 "He described for Durrell": *DML*, p. 179.

p. 230 " 'Yes, there we are' ": *DML*, p. 162.

p. 230 "On many evenings": Interview with Bern Porter, 10/8/88.

p. 231 "In April, Miller wrote": HM to Emil White, 4/24/44, Univ. of Texas.

p. 231 "Miller dissuaded Hershkowitz": HM to Harry Hershkowitz, 4/[44], Box 14, UCLA.

p. 232 "Winters were especially difficult": HM to Emil White, [n.d., 1944], Univ. of Texas.

p. 232 "She told Hershkowitz she feared": Harry Hershkowitz to HM, [n.d.], Box 14, UCLA.

p. 232 "But Miller wrote Harry": Harry Hershkowitz to HM, [n.d.], Univ. of Texas.

p. 232 "In a flourish of ceremony": Kathryn Winslow, *Henry Miller: Full of Life* (Los Angeles: Jeremy P. Tarcher, 1986), p. 123.

p. 234 "Nin was angry at him": See *ALP*, pp. 363–4.

p. 234 "The letter was a bitter one": HM to Huntington Cairns, 5/19/44, Dartmouth.

p. 235 "To the latter, he wrote a long letter": HM to Judson Crews, 5/19/[44], Dartmouth.

p. 235 " 'so many sloppy-eyed nobodies' ": Porter, ed., *The Happy Rock*, p. 124.

p. 237 "He was determined, he wrote Emil": HM to Emil White, [10/44], Univ. of Texas.

p. 238 "and on the train ride West": Interview with Noel Young, 12/3/88.

p. 239 "Looking back at his past": *TOA*, p. 50.

p. 239 " 'To begin with, accept any loaf' ": *RTR*, p. 53.

p. 240 "Often the results of his begging": Interview with Bern Porter, 11/9/88.

p. 241 "In the fall of 1945 Girodias": See *ALP*, p. 371.

p. 241 "Durrell and Perlès urged Miller": *DML*, p. 210.

p. 241 "Sales received a further boost": See "HM Affair [Pucciani]," Box 20B, UCLA.

p. 242 "Miller devised all sorts": *DML*, p. 210.

p. 242 "He even enlisted Nin's husband": See HM to Leon Shamroy, 7/14/[47], Lilly Library, Indiana Univ.

p. 242 "Around the same time, he wrote": HM to Leon Shamroy, [1947], Lilly Library, Indiana Univ.

p. 242 "She's 'a real back-to-the-womber' ": *DML*, p. 189.

p. 243 "Matters only got worse": Interview with Lynn Bloom, 12/12/88.

p. 243 "Much later, Miller's old Paris friend": Walter Lowenfels to HM, 9/10/60, Box 14B, UCLA.

p. 244 "He devised a system": Harry Kiakis, "At Henry Miller's: Notes for a Casual Portrait," *Anaïs: An International Journal*, 7 (1989), p. 76.

p. 244 "June Mansfield wrote": June Mansfield to Lepska Miller, [9/5/47], Box 4A, UCLA.

p. 246 "In October Miller wrote Durrell": *DML*, p. 225.

p. 247 "Miller had not taken the criticisms": *DML*, pp. 228–31.

p. 247 " 'a reversion to pre-*Tropic* writing' ": *DML*, p. 230.

p. 247 "SEXUS DISGRACEFULLY BAD": *DML*, p. 233.

p. 248 " 'If it was not good' ": *DML*, p. 235.

p. 248 " 'Suffering *is* unnecessary' ": *Plexus*, p. 640.

p. 248 " 'To be yourself' ": HM, *The Smile at the Foot of the Ladder* (1948; rpt. NY: New Directions, 1966), p. 22.

Chapter 13. The Family Man: 1949–1959

p. 250 "He put a great deal": HM to Audrey Shamroy, 3/10/49, Lilly Library, Indiana Univ.

p. 250 "As before, he offered": HM to Audrey Shamroy, 2/27/49, and HM to Oscar Baradinsky, 3/18/49, Univ. of Texas, and HM to Kathryn Winslow, 5/18/49, reprinted in her *Henry Miller: Full of Life*, pp. 213–16.

p. 251 "In response, Miller admitted": Winslow, p. 262.

p. 252 " 'On the one hand' ": *ALP*, p. 391.

p. 254 " 'I leave it to the gods' ": *DML*, p. 256.

p. 255 "Miller wrote a friend": HM to Leon Shamroy, 7/4/51, Lilly Library, Indiana Univ.

p. 256 " 'Wherever I strayed' ": *BSOHB*, p. 191.

p. 257 "When he returned to Big Sur": HM to F.-J. Temple, 4/1/52, Box 41, UCLA.

p. 257 "(They would not marry": Robert Fink, "A Profile of Henry Miller," unpublished MS, Univ. of Minnesota.

p. 257 "He approved of the description": HM to Eve Miller, 4/27/[60], Univ. of Texas.

p. 257 " 'living on velour' ": *DML*, p. 261.

p. 257 " 'Darling Evie-O' ": Val Miller to Eve Miller, 4/27/[60], Univ. of Texas.

p. 258 "In New York, they had planned": HM to Frank Dobo, 12/15/52, Folder 16, NYPL.

p. 258 "There they received an offer": Eve Miller to Emil White, 3/2/53, Univ. of Texas.

p. 258 "Miller still regarded": HM to Georges Belmont, 2/10/53.

p. 260 "Nostradamus's prophecy was": HM to Emil White, 2/18/53, Univ. of Texas.

p. 260 "In the forties, he had written": HM to Kenneth Rexroth, 3/18/45; Rexroth to HM, [n.d.], Box 28, UCLA.

p. 260 "Miller was also a passionate": See HM to Robert Fink, 8/6/50, 8/18/50, Univ. of Texas.

p. 260 " 'even emptier and more poisonous' ": *DML*, p. 271.

p. 260 "He told Georges Belmont": HM to Georges Belmont, 8/1/53.

p. 261 " 'circularizing and begging' ": HM to Emil White, 1/29/53, Univ. of Texas.

p. 261 "She was, however, good at sports": HM to Paul Geheeb, 6/6/58, Box 17, UCLA.

p. 261 "He played games": HM to Georges Belmont, 8/28/53.

p. 261 "In February 1954 Miller heard": HM to Frances Steloff, 1/20/44, Folder 24, NYPL.

p. 262 "Perlès refused to compromise": Alfred Perlès to Frank Dobo, [3/30/55], Folder 16, NYPL.

p. 262 "Emil White had tried briefly": See undated letters of Nin to Emil White, Univ. of Texas.

p. 262 " 'She was like a *duchesse*' ": *BOF*, p. 233.

p. 264 "Harry Hershkowitz, for example": Harry Hershkowitz to HM, [n.d., 1944?], Box 14, UCLA.

p. 264 "Miller toyed with the idea": HM to Huntington Cairns, 7/23/44.

p. 264 "More practically, Frank Dobo": Frank Dobo to HM, 2/4/55, Folder 16, NYPL.

p. 265 " 'Henry was always' ": Alfred Perlès to HM, [Nov. 1954], Box 26B, UCLA.

p. 265 " 'With it, a great wave of emotion' ": HM. See Mabel Farrell to HM, 2/6/55, Box 14, UCLA.

p. 265 "Lauretta slept on a broken-down": HM to Robert Fink, [2/8/56], Univ. of Texas.

p. 266 "Before long it became clear": HM to Emil White, 3/14/56, Univ. of Texas.

p. 266 "There was nothing organically wrong": HM to Robert Fink, [2/8/56], Univ. of Texas.

p. 266 "Miller struggled with her": *MLT*, p. 204.

p. 267 "After a few painful days": HM to Tullah and Ed Hanley, 7/9/56, Univ. of Texas.

p. 267 "He and Eve looked frantically": HM to Robert Fink, 6/11/56, Univ. of Texas.

p. 267 "Conason visited her there": HM to Emil White, 2/7/56, Univ. of Texas.

p. 267 "She was released": June Mansfield to HM, [6/11/56] and 9/26/56, Box 4A, UCLA.

p. 267 "She was still severely underweight": James and Annette Baxter to HM, 11/3/56, Box 4A, UCLA.

p. 267 "Lepska still owned": HM to Robert Fink, 1/3/59, Univ. of Texas.

p. 267 "On his sixty-fifth birthday": HM to Robert Fink, 12/31/56, Univ. of Texas.

p. 268 "Big Sur had finally been wired": Fink, p. 22.

p. 268 "Although Eve confided": Fink, p. 53.

p. 269 "*Cancer* would be twenty-five": HM to Barney Rosset, 4/4/59, Grove Press Collection, George Arents Research Library, Syracuse Univ.

p. 269 "Naturally rebellious, Rosset": See Barney Rosset, "Henry Miller v. 'Our Way of Life,' " 5/9/41, Grove Press Collection, George Arents Research Library, Syracuse Univ.; his teacher's comment was "Perhaps the jaundice is in the cosmological eye itself, not in the world it sees."

p. 269 "He flew to San Francisco": Interview with Barney Rosset, 10/10/88.

p. 270 "Evidently Miller believed": Maurice Girodias to Barney Rosset, 5/7/59, Grove Press Collection, George Arents Research Library, Syracuse Univ.

p. 270 "By the publishing standards": Barney Rosset to Michel Hoffman, 1/18/60, Grove Press Collection, George Arents Research Library, Syracuse Univ.

p. 270 "There were major upheavals": HM to Barney Rosset, 1/20/60, Grove Press Collection, George Arents Research Library, Syracuse Univ.

Chapter 14. Fame: 1959–1965

p. 271 "Miller complained": HM to Emil White, 7/30/59, Box 30B, UCLA.

p. 271 " 'In this house' ": *DML*, p. 358.

p. 272 " 'It makes her a woman' ": *DML*, p. 356.

p. 272 "In September Eve wrote": Eve Miller to Lawrence Durrell, 9/7/[59], Box 7, UCLA.

p. 272 "Eve took action": Eve Miller to Lawrence Durrell, 12/6/[59], Box 7, UCLA.

p. 272 "His spirits lifted": *DML*, p. 371.

p. 273 "One evening in Paris": Interview with Georges Belmont, 11/2/88.

p. 273 "She reminded him": HM to Eve Miller, 11/29/60, Box 20C, UCLA.

p. 273 "In May, when Miller was in Cannes": Eve Miller to HM, 5/27/60, Box 20C, UCLA.

p. 274 "He thought about writing": *DML*, p. 375.

p. 275 " 'Can't understand how my grandfathers' ": HM to Alfred Perlès, 10/23/60, HM Literary Society *Newsletter* (Nov. 1960), [n.p.].

p. 275 "(Simenon was relieved": Georges Simenon, *When I Was Old* (NY: Harcourt Brace Jovanovich, 1971), p. 127.

p. 275 "Henry and Chaplin laughed": HM to Eve Miller, 11/18/60, Box 20C, UCLA.

p. 275 "By January 13, 1961": Renate Gerhardt to HM, [n.d.], Box UM1, UCLA.

p. 276 "He now said that he thought": HM to Eve Miller, 11/29/60, Box 20C, UCLA.

p. 276 "Some of the books Rosset": HM to Eve Miller, 12/25/60, Box 20C, UCLA.

p. 276 "Unaware that their temperaments": Interview with Barney Rosset, 10/10/88.

p. 277 "Astrologically speaking": HM to Eve Miller, 2/5/61 and 2/20/61, Box 20C, UCLA.

p. 277 "He worried, for instance": HM to Barney Rosset, 6/3/61, Grove Press Collection, George Arents Research Library, Syracuse Univ.

p. 277 " '*Tropic* will be defended' ": Quoted in E. R. Hutchison, *Tropic of Cancer on Trial: A Case Study of Censorship* (NY: Grove Press, 1968), p. 64.

p. 278 " 'on a level reached' ": *San Francisco Chronicle*, 6/11/61, p. 26.

p. 278 "Miller blamed it": HM to Eve Miller, 4/12/61, Box 20C, UCLA.

p. 279 "He remembered a poster": HM to Emil White, 7/6/61, Box 30B, UCLA.

p. 279 "In a long letter to Barney Rosset": Quoted in Martin, pp. 462–3.

p. 280 "June looked terrible": HM to Eve Miller, 9/20/61 and 10/27/61, Box 20C, UCLA.

p. 281 " 'handsomely homely' ": June Mansfield to HM, [n.d.], Box 4A, UCLA.

p. 281 " 'one of the silliest' ": *The New Yorker*, 41 (11/27/65), p. 245.

p. 281 "It had been sixteen years": HM to Eve Miller, 7/31/62, Box 20C, UCLA.

p. 282 "Meanwhile, Renate Gerhardt was writing": Renate Gerhardt to HM, 9/11/61, Box UM1, UCLA.

p. 282 "The furor surrounding *Tropic of Cancer*": See Charles Rembar, *The End of Obscenity: The Trials of Lady Chatterley, Tropic of Cancer, and Fanny Hill* (NY: Random House, 1968).

p. 283 " 'Even on the tarmac' ": Interview with Georges Belmont, 11/2/88.

p. 283 " 'This is a book' ": Lionel Trilling to Barney Rosset, 2/23/63, Grove Press Collection, George Arents Research Library, Syracuse Univ.

p. 283 "Leon Edel complained": *New York Herald Tribune*, 4/14/53.

p. 283 "*Time* rightly thought": *Time*, 79 (6/29/62), p. 78.

p. 283 "*The New Yorker* found": *The New Yorker*, 39 (4/27/63), p. 180.

p. 284 "At the Nepenthe restaurant": Interview with Ephraim Doner, 6/18/89.

p. 284 "He could get along fine": HM to Eve Miller, 10/14/62, Box 20C, UCLA.

p. 284 "Soon he was writing enthusiastically": *DML*, p. 387.

p. 285 " 'I am not only trying' ": Gertz, p. 184.

p. 286 "He found Allen Ginsberg's": Interview with Irving Stettner, 9/25/88.

p. 286 "he championed Burroughs": Ted Morgan, *Literary Outlaw: The Life and Times of William S. Burroughs* (NY: Henry Holt, 1988), pp. 328–9.

p. 286 "He was impatient": See Ferlinghetti correspondence, Bancroft Library, San Francisco.

p. 287 "The one time Kerouac": Interview with Allen Ginsberg, 11/7/88; Gerald Nicosia, *Memory Babe: A Critical Biography of Jack Kerouac* (1983; rpt. NY: Penguin Books, 1986), p. 613.

p. 287 "Late in 1963 he surveyed": Gertz, p. 246.

p. 287 "His hip bothered him": *DML*, p. 421.

p. 287 "In a letter to Eve": HM to Eve Miller, 11/12/63, Box 20C, UCLA.

p. 287 "He resisted Rosset's pleas": HM to Barney Rosset, 1/22/64, Grove Press Collection, George Arents Research Library, Syracuse Univ.

Chapter 15. Pacific Palisades: 1965–1980

p. 291 "The telephone rang all day": HM to Georges Belmont, 10/7/65, Box 4A, UCLA.

p. 291 "Ava Gardner was a devoted": HM to Robert Fink, 1/30/64, Univ. of Texas.

p. 292 "She still had the capacity": Interview with Barbara Sylvas Miller, 11/5/89.

p. 292 "He finally met Hoki": Josei Jishin, "Henry Miller Proposed to Hoki Tokuda," press release, Grove Press Collection, George Arents Research Library, Syracuse Univ.

p. 293 "He felt young": See, for example, the letters of Tullah Hanley to HM, Univ. of Texas.

p. 293 "In December he wrote Emil": HM to Emil White, 12/12/66, Univ. of Texas.

p. 293 "In the summer of 1967": HM to S. Kubo, 8/26/67, Box 17B, UCLA.

p. 294 "His crew had virtually": Snyder, *This Is Henry, Henry Miller from Brooklyn*, p. 53.

p. 294 "That night, after dinner": Interview with Georges Belmont, 11/2/88.

p. 294 " ('the piano bar' ": HM, *Insomnia Or The Devil at Large* (Garden City, NY: Doubleday, 1974), p. 24.

p. 294 "She installed two friends": *Letters from Henry Miller to Hoki Tokuda Miller*, ed. Joyce Howard (NY: Freundlich Books, 1986), p. 76. Hoki declined all requests to be interviewed for this book.

p. 295 "He began to speak of men": *Letters from Henry Miller to Hoki Tokuda Miller*, p. 40.

p. 295 "Hoki had passed through London": Interview with John Calder, 11/9/88.

p. 296 "Matters didn't improve in Paris": Interview with Joe Strick, 10/14/88; interview with Georges Belmont, 11/2/88.

p. 296 "Miller rented an apartment": HM to Alfred Perlès, 7/18/69, Box 26B, UCLA.

p. 296 "He had hopes": HM to Alfred Perlès, 12/25/71, Box 26B, UCLA.

p. 296 " 'The narration wallow[s]' ": Simon quoted in Leonard Maltin, "American Film Comedy," press release #276, The Museum of Modern Art, Department of Film, p. 2.

p. 296 "Joe Strick himself acknowledged": Interview with Joe Strick, 10/14/88.

p. 296 "Reviewers also felt": *New Republic* (3/7/70), p. 39.

p. 296 "in Paris on opening day": Interview with Joe Strick, 10/14/88.

p. 297 "He told Barney Rosset": HM to Barney Rosset, 4/15/68, Grove Press Collection, George Arents Research Library, Syracuse Univ.

p. 297 "and Miller had Val": HM to Valentine Miller, 1/8/70.

p. 297 "He warned Durrell": *DML*, p. 437.

p. 297 " 'compendium of American' ": Kate Millett, *Sexual Politics* (1969; rpt. NY: Ballantine Books, 1978), p. 413.

p. 298 "he preferred Swedish": Harry Kiakos, "At Henry Miller's— Notes for a Casual Portrait," *Anaïs: An International Journal*, 7 (1989), p. 71.

p. 299 "Waverley Root, who knew him": Waverley Root, "Montparnasse

Memories: Henry Miller and Anaïs Nin," *International Herald Tribune*, 11/19/82, p. 7W.

p. 299 "(One visitor remembered": Kiakos, p. 72.

p. 300 "Hoki's response was": *Letters from Henry Miller to Hoki Tokuda Miller*, p. 161.

p. 301 "But when he told one fan": Brian T. Maeda, "Dinner with the 'Grand Old Man,' " in Jim Haynes, ed., *Homage to Henry* (Paris: Handshake Editions, [n.d., 1978]), [n.p.].

p. 301 "When his Big Sur friend": Interview with Bill Webb, 6/24/89.

p. 301 "Tasha Doner, the daughter of": Interview with Ephraim Doner, 6/23/89.

p. 301 "He told Perlès": HM to Alfred Perlès, 4/28/74, Box 26B, UCLA.

p. 302 "he told Emil White": HM to Emil White, 11/9/72, Univ. of Texas.

p. 302 "Miller found himself speaking": *BOF*, p. 265.

p. 302 "In 1971 he took over": *DML*, p. 479.

p. 302 " 'What a tragedy for a son' ": Brassaï, p. 37.

p. 303 "(In one nine-month period": *DML*, p. 479.

p. 304 " 'When a man has reached old age' ": Quoted in *LCF*, p. 24.

p. 305 "During this period, Miller began": See *Letters of Wallace Fowlie and Henry Miller (1943–1972)* (NY: Grove Press, 1975), p. 107.

p. 305 "and he proudly wore": Georges Simenon, *When I Was Old* (NY: Harcourt Brace Jovanovich, 1971), p. 285.

p. 305 "Durrell told him": *DML*, p. 497.

p. 305 "Privately, Miller thought": See *Venus*, pp. 74–5.

p. 306 " 'how repugnant it must be' ": *Venus*, p. 150.

p. 306 "When Warren Beatty asked": *LCF*, p. 52.

p. 307 "Virtually a prisoner": Interview with Barbara Kraft, 1/25/89; interview with Sandi Stahl, 11/7/89.

p. 307 " 'half gaga' ": *DML*, p. 511.

p. 307 " 'definitely leaving' ": Reproduced in Alfred Perlès, "Henry Miller—Dead?" *Black Messiah: A Tribute to Henry Miller* (Ellensburg, Wash.: Vagabond Press, [n.d.]), p. 16.

p. 307 "he appeared to believe": Interview with Sandi Stahl, 11/7/89.

p. 307 " 'Henry Miller is not dead' ": Joseph the Provider, Catalogue 22, back cover.

p. 308 "A young California writer": Michael Hargraves, ed. and comp., *Henry Miller Bibliography with Discography* (San Francisco: Michael Hargraves, 1980), [n.p.].

p. 308 "First editions of": Joseph the Provider, Catalogue 22, Items A1 and G1.

p. 310 " 'I thought, when I came upon her' ": *TCap*, p. 13.

p. 311 " 'If it was not good' ": *DML*, p. 235.

Sources

Because of his erratic publications history, Henry Miller presents a challenge for the bibliographer. The following selected bibliography is intended as a guide for further reading rather than as a comprehensive source list. Miller scholars and collectors should refer to such bibliographic guides as Michael Hargraves, *Henry Miller Bibliography with Discography* (San Francisco: Michael Hargraves, 1980); Joseph the Provider, Catalogue #22, *A Descriptive Catalogue of the Dr. James O'Roark Collection of the Works of Henry Miller* (Santa Barbara, Calif., [n.d.]); and Lawrence J. Shifreen, *Henry Miller: A Bibliography of Secondary Sources* (Metuchen, N.J.: Scarecrow Press, 1979). The following list does not include collections of correspondence, sound recordings, magazine appearances, or prefaces written by Miller; references to some of these items can be found in the Notes.

Selected Bibliography

Books

The Air-Conditioned Nightmare. New York: New Directions, 1945.

Aller Retour New York. Paris: Obelisk Press (Siana Series No. 1), 1935.

The Angel Is My Watermark. Fullerton, Calif.: Holve-Barrows, 1944. Reprint, New York: Harry N. Abrams, 1962.

Big Sur and the Oranges of Hieronymus Bosch. New York: New Directions [1957].

Black Spring. Paris: Obelisk Press, 1936. Reprint, New York: Grove Press, 1963.

The Books in My Life. New York: New Directions, 1952.

The Colossus of Maroussi. San Francisco: The Colt Press, 1941. Reprint, New York: New Directions, 1958.

The Cosmological Eye. New York: New Directions, 1939.

A Devil in Paradise. New York: New American Library, 1956.

Hamlet (with Michael Fraenkel). Volume 1: New York: Carrefours, 1939. Volume 2: New York: Carrefours, 1941. Reprint, *Henry Miller's Hamlet Letters*, ed. Michael Hargraves. Santa Barbara, Calif.: Capra Press, 1988.

Henry Miller's Book of Friends: A Tribute to the Friends of Long Ago. Santa Barbara, Calif.: Capra Press, 1976.

Insomnia Or The Devil at Large. Albuquerque, N.M.: Loujon Press, 1966. Reprint, New York: Doubleday, 1974.

Just Wild About Harry. New York: New Directions, 1963.

My Life and Times. New York: Playboy Press, 1972.

Nexus (volume 3 of *The Rosy Crucifixion*). Paris: Corrêa, 1960. Reprint, New York: Grove Press, 1965.

On Turning Eighty. Santa Barbara, Calif.: Capra Press, 1972.

Plexus (volume 2 of *The Rosy Crucifixion*). Paris: Olympia Press, 1963. Reprint, New York: Grove Press, 1965.

Quiet Days in Clichy. Paris: Olympia Press, 1956. Reprint (with *The World of Sex*), New York: Grove Press, 1978.

Remember to Remember. New York: New Directions, 1947.

Semblance of a Devoted Past. Berkeley, Calif.: Bern Porter Books, 1945.

Sexus (volume 1 of *The Rosy Crucifixion*). Paris: Obelisk Press, 1949. Reprint, New York: Grove Press, 1965.

The Smile at the Foot of the Ladder. New York: Duell, Sloane and Pearce, 1948.

Stand Still Like the Hummingbird. New York: New Directions, 1962.

Sunday After the War. New York: New Directions, 1944.

The Time of the Assassins. New York: New Directions, 1956.

Tropic of Cancer. Paris: Obelisk Press, 1934. Reprint, New York: Grove Press, 1961.

Tropic of Capricorn. Paris: Obelisk Press, 1939. Reprint, New York: Grove Press, 1962.

The Wisdom of the Heart. New York: New Directions, 1941.

The World of Lawrence (compiled by Evelyn J. Hinz and John J. Teunissen). Santa Barbara, Calif.: Capra Press, 1980.

The World of Sex. Chicago: privately published, 1940. Reprint (with *Quiet Days in Clichy*), New York: Grove Press, 1978.

Brochures, Pamphlets, and Other Items

The Amazing and Invariable Beauford Delaney. Yonkers, NY: Alicat Bookshop, 1945.

Money and How It Gets That Way. Paris: *Booster Broadside* no. 1, 1938. Reprint, Berkeley, Calif.: Bern Porter Books, 1946.

Murder the Murderer. Berkeley, Calif.: Bern Porter Books, 1944.

The Plight of the Creative Artist in the United States of America. Berkeley, Calif.: Bern Porter Books, 1944.

Scenario (A Film with Sound). Paris: Obelisk Press, 1937.

Varda, The Master Builder. Berkeley, Calif.: Circle Editions, 1947.

What Are You Going to Do About Alf? Paris; privately published, 1935. Reprint, Berkeley, Calif.: Bern Porter Books, 1943.

Acknowledgments

Although this is in no way an authorized biography, I am grateful to Henry Tony Miller, Valentin Lepska Miller, and Barbara Sylvas Miller for answering routine requests, allowing me to examine their father's letters and manuscripts at UCLA, and granting me permission to quote from Henry Miller's unpublished letters.

The Society of Fellows in the Humanities at Columbia University kindly provided me not only with workspace but with a collegial and supportive atmosphere; I am grateful to the Society's former Chairpersons, Barbara Miller and Richard Kuhns, and especially to the Society's former Director, Loretta Nassar. Also at Columbia, Jack Salzman at the Center for American Culture Studies and the staff of the Department of English and Comparative Literature were the source of much encouragement. Other support came from the National Endowment for the Humanities, in the form of a Travel to Collections Grant.

The list of people who consented to interviews, corresponded with me in substantive fashion, granted me hospitality in strange cities, and otherwise lent critical support, is long indeed. It is fair to say that without the assistance of the following people this book could not have been written; it is also only fair to say that they do not all necessarily concur with my interpretations or conclusions. Those who provided such help include, along with others I may have inadvertently omitted: Georges Belmont, Lynne Bloom, Andreas Browne, Karen Burke-LeFevre, John Calder, Richard Centing, Gloria Calmer, Celia Conason, Muriel Cowley, Francis Dobo, Ephraim Doner, Peter Dreyer, Ken Du Main, Richard Elman, Lawrence Ferlinghetti, Harry Finestone, Noël Riley Fitch, Hugh Ford, Benjamin Franklin V, Allen Ginsberg, the late Maurice Girodias, Michael Hargraves, John Hayes, Joyce Howard, Roger Jackson, Erica Jong, Eric Kahane, Michal Kane, Brian Kilner, Barbara Kraft, James Laughlin, Gershon Legman, Manfred Linus, Milt Luboviski, Juliette Man Ray, John Manola, John Martin, Bertrand Mathieu, Clay McDaniel, Sidney P. Moss, Mario Muchnik, Michael Neal, Sava Nepus, Margaret Nieman, James O'Roark, Rupert Pole, Esther Gentle Rattner, Ernst Richter, Barney Rosset, Barnet Ruder, Mark SaFranko, Robert Sharrad, Mahmud Shurayh, Bradley Smith, Robert Snyder, Sandi Stahl, Irving Stettner, Joe Strick, John Tytell, Brenda Venus, Patrick Freiherr von Richthofen, Lepska Warren, Howard Welch, Edmund White, and the late Emil White. I am especially grateful to Elmer Gertz, Fred Jordan, Phil Nurenberg, Bern Porter, Gunther Stuhlmann, Bill Webb, and Noel Young.

Several curators and librarians have been instrumental in facilitating my research, among them J. Rossi at the Alderman Library, University of Virginia; Jennie Rathbun at the Houghton Library, Harvard University; Sigrid P. Perry at Northwestern University Library; Patricia C. Willis at the Bienecke Rare Book and Manuscript Library, Yale University; Sara S. Hodson at The Huntington Library; Philip N. Cronenwett at the Dartmouth College Library; Cynthia Wall at The Newberry Library; Stanley A. Carroll at the San Francisco Public Library; Saundra Taylor at the Lilly Library, Indiana University; Vivian K. Newbold at the University Libraries, University of Minnesota; and, especially, the following: Cathy Henderson at the Harry Ransom Humanities Research Center, University of Texas at Austin; Wayne Furman and the late Lola Szladits at the New York Public Library; Monte Olenick at the Brooklyn Public Library; the staff at the George Arents Research Library, Syracuse University; and Anne Caiger, Simon Eliot, and Lilace Hatayama (among others) at the Department of Special Collections, University Research Library, UCLA.

I was extremely fortunate in my research assistants, whose perseverance, ingenuity, and good humor improved this work immeasurably: David Gratt, Jill Wacker, Deborah Brudno, Marianna Cherry, Jean King, Brendan Mernin, and Jason McLachlan.

At Simon & Schuster, Nancy Nicholas and, subsequently, Bob Bender have been able and enthusiastic editors, and Johanna Li provided critical assistance. Debbie Goodsite and Toby Greenberg helped locate some important photographs. I am also grateful to Carol O'Brien at HarperCollins and my peerless agent, Maxine Groffsky.

Finally, for contributions at once momentous and impossible to define: Meryl Altman, Nat Austern, Roger Blumberg, Mary Campbell, John T. G. Dearborn, Richard and the late Margery Dearborn, Miriam Gurniak, Martin Hurwitz, Warren Johnson, Joe Markulin, and, most of all and once again, Eric Laursen.

Index